Modern Real Estate Practice IN New York FOR
BROKERS
BY EDITH LANK

TENTH EDITION

Dearborn™
Real Estate Education

This publication is designed to provide accurate and authoritative information in regard to the subject matter covered. It is sold with the understanding that the publisher is not engaged in rendering legal, accounting, or other professional service. If legal advice or other expert assistance is required, the services of a competent professional should be sought.

President: Mehul Patel
Executive Director of Product Development & Publishing: Kate DeVivo
Managing Editor: Anne Huston
Managing Editor: Tony Peregrin
Development Editor: Megan Bacalao Virkler
Director of Production: Daniel Frey
Production Editor: Samantha Raue
Senior Production Artist: Virginia Byrne
Creative Director: Lucy Jenkins
Vice President of Product Management: Dave Dufresne
Director of Product Management: Melissa Kleeman

Published by Dearborn™ Real Estate Education
30 South Wacker Drive
Chicago, Illinois 60606-7481
(312) 836-4400
www.dearbornRE.com

Printed in the United States of America

08 09 10   10 9 8 7 6 5 4 3 2 1

Library of Congress Cataloging-in-Publication Data
Lank, Edith.
    Modern real estate practice in New York for brokers / Edith Lank. -- 10th ed.
        p. cm.
    This is the broker portion of the ninth edition book. The tenth edition is now two books: Modern real estate practice in New York for salespersons and Modern real estate practice in New York for brokers.
    Rev. ed. of: Modern real estate practice in New York / Edith Lank. 9th ed. c2006.
    Includes index.
    ISBN-13: 978-1-4277-6818-6
    ISBN-10: 1-4277-6818-8
    1. Vendors and purchasers--New York (State) 2. Real estate business--Law and legislation--New York (State) 3. Real property--New York (State) I. Lank, Edith. Modern real estate practice in New York. II. Irlander, Sam. Modern real estate practice in New York for salespersons. 10th ed. III. Title.
    KFN5166.L363 2008
        346.74704'37--dc22
                                                            2008006635

Contents

Preface   vii

About the Author   xi

Note to the Student   xiii

CHAPTER 1

License Law   1

Key Terms   1

Purpose of Real Estate License Laws   1

Qualifications for Licensure   5

License Examinations   7

Licensing Procedure   9

Maintaining a License   13

Termination or Changes In Association   14

Renewal and Continuing Education   15

Brokerage Management In Accordance with License Laws   16

Other Licenses or Registrations Involving Real Estate   18

Advertisements   20

Suspension and Revocation of Licenses   21

Unlicensed Real Estate Assistants   23

DOS Determinations   25

Summary   25

Questions   27

CHAPTER 2

The Law of Agency   30

Key Terms   30

Overview of Agency Discussion   31

What Is an Agent?   31

Creation of Agency   33

Agency and Brokerage   35

Fiduciary Responsibilities   39

The Broker's Compensation   47

Termination of Agency   49

Antitrust   49

Antitrust Laws   50

Summary   52

Questions   54

CHAPTER 3

Agency and Real Estate Brokerage   56

Key Terms   56

New York Agency Disclosure Requirements   56

Agency Alternatives   63

Subagency   64

Dual Agency   65

Single Agency   69

Agency Forms   70

Buyer Agency   87

Summary   92

Questions   96

CHAPTER 4

The Broker's Office   98

Key Terms   98

Who Needs a License   98

Other Related Licenses   98

Who Does Not Need a License   99

Obtaining a License   99

Renewal of License   103

Review of Chapter One   103

Antitrust Laws   107

Multiple Listing Services   110

Salesperson Employment Status   111

Antitrust Laws   114

The Broker's Responsibility To Manage and Supervise   117

Audits for Compliance   123

Professional Organizations   124

Designations   125

Law of Agency   126

Summary   129

Questions   130

CHAPTER 5
Real Estate Finance   132

Key Terms   132

The Use of the Mortgage   132

Home Mortgages   133

Types of Mortgages   133

Brokers' Issues In Real Estate Finance   134

Ground Leases   137

FHA Financing   137

The Economy and Real Estate Cycles   138

Summary   141

Questions   142

CHAPTER 6
Real Estate Investments   143

Key Terms   143

The Nature of Real Estate Investment   143

Preparing to Be an Investor   144

Analyzing Property Income   145

Investment Ownership Structure   148

Holding Period and Disposition   149

Types of Investment Properties   150

Investment Analysis Techniques   151

Income Tax Considerations   151

Summary   154

Questions   156

CHAPTER 7
General Business Law   159

Key Terms   159

Sources of Law   159

Uniform Commercial Code   160

Negotiable Instruments   161

Business Organizations   163

The Federal Court System   166

New York Court System   166

Substantive and Procedural Law   167

Civil Law   167

Statute of Limitations   173

Summary   173

Questions   176

CHAPTER 8
Construction and Development   178

Key Terms   178

Construction Standards   178

The Role of the Real Estate Agent   181

Building Inspections   181

Subdivision   183

The Process of Subdivision   185

Costs and Financing   185

Restrictive Covenants   186

Land-Use Regulations   187

Condominiums   189

Cooperative Ownership   191

Condominium/Cooperative Construction and
  Conversion   192

Town Houses, PUDs, and Time-Sharing   193

Summary   194

Questions   196

CHAPTER 9
Conveyance of Real Property   198

Key Terms   198

Title   198

Voluntary Alienation   199

Involuntary Alienation   199

Transfer of a Deceased Person's Property   200

Summary   203

Questions   204

CHAPTER 10
Property Management   205

Key Terms   205

Property Management   205

The Property Manager   206

Types of Property That Are Managed   206

The Management Agreement   207

Functions of the Property Manager   208

Planning and Budgeting   208

Marketing   211

Managing Leases and Tenant Relations   213

Maintaining the Property   217

Owner Relations, Reports, and Insurance   217

Skills Required of a Property Manager   219

The Management Field   220

Rent Regulations   221

Summary   222

Questions   223

CHAPTER **11**

Taxes and Assessments   225

Key Terms   225

Tax Liens   225

The Taxation Process   226

Summary   231

Questions   232

Broker's Practice Examination   233

Glossary   242

Answer Key   272

Index   275

Preface

This tenth edition of *Modern Real Estate Practice in New York for Brokers* has been completely updated to reflect changes in the real estate industry as well as requirements for prelicensing courses set forth in the Department of State's syllabus. Each topic closely follows the state outlines for the broker's course.

With this new edition, we are launching a Web site dedicated exclusively to *Modern Real Estate Practice in New York for Salespersons* and *Modern Real Estate Practice in New York for Brokers*, as well as all of their ancillary products. At *www.mrepny.com*, both students and instructors will have access to a robust assortment of study and teaching tools, including the instructor's manual.

> To access learning objectives, key terms, chapter outlines, and other instructor materials created for students, please go to *www.mrepny.com* and enter the following Student Access Code: 97258.

Like previous editions, this one is dedicated to the hundreds of thousands of real estate students and instructors whose enthusiastic acceptance has made this the best-selling real estate textbook in the Empire State. Once again, many valuable suggestions for the new edition have come from those who use the book.

Those suggestions have always played a great part in the evolution of the text. For this tenth edition, we paid particular attention to your classroom needs and the state's revised syllabus. We also made every effort to make this textbook learning-friendly, using classroom-tested features such as highlighted key terms and concepts and margin notes. Web addresses also have been included.

The author wishes to thank those who participated in the preparation of the tenth edition of *Modern Real Estate Practice in New York for Brokers*, including the following:

- Roberta Bangs, Associate Broker, Director of Training & Compliance, Prudential Rand Realty, New City, New York
- Neil Garfinkel, Esquire, Abrams Garfinkel Margolis Bergson LLP
- Barry Hersh, Associate Director, Education, Steven L. Newman Real Estate Institute, Baruch College
- Diane Levine, Esquire, Office Brokerage Manager, Sotheby's International Realty, Inc.

The publisher also wishes to acknowledge the contributions of Frank P. Langone of the Real Estate Training Center, who has offered his insight and knowledge on the development of this text.

Their combined criticisms and comments have made this the best edition yet.

Special thanks must go to Joseph Amello and Jodi DeLollo of the DOS, as well as to Steven Spinola, Education Chair of New York State Board of Real Estate and president of the Real Estate Board of New York.

Previous editions over the years owe a great debt of thanks to the following: Anthony Aguelire, RETC of Greater New York; John Alberts; Newt Alderman; David M. Alexander, Greater Rochester Association of REALTORS®; Joseph Amello, New York Department of State; Georgianne Bailey, New York State Association of REALTORS®; Ronald Baroody; Gail Bates, New York Department of State; Professor Kenneth Beckerink; Abraham Berkowitz; Rose Bernstein; Michael K. Brady, IFA, RAM, State University of New York; Antonio F. Brown; Rhonda Brown, Esq.; Robin Carlson, MS Ed, Manfred Real Estate Learning Center, Inc.; Thomas Carozza; John Cyr; Demetrios Cortisides; Charles E. Davis; Beverly L. Deikler, Esq.; Barry Deickler; Judith J. Deickler, GRI; William R. Deickler, William R. Deickler Contracting, Inc.; Ruth De Roo; Paul Desseault; Thomas E. DeCelle; Anthony J. DiChiara, GRI, ME, MS, Niagara University; Joseph DiIanni; Liz Duncan, National Association of REALTORS®; Jonathon Easterling; Arthur Elfenbein, New York University Real Estate Institute; Marie Esposito; Cindy Faire; Professor Patrick J. Falci, St. John's University; Jim Foley; Alexander M. Frame, Real Estate Education Center; Donald Friedman; Richard Fuchs; Thomas Galvin; Harold Geringer; Harry Goldberg; Christine di Grande Jones; Gaye Green; Paul Henderson; David Henehan; Benjamin Henszey; Gerry Hoffman; Michael J. Jesmer, Syracuse Real Estate, Inc.; Harold Kahn; Peter A. Karl III, SUNY Institute of Technology; Leon Katzen, Esq.; Ezra Katzen; John Keaton; Walter Kerut; Eli Kimels; Eileen Klempner, Orange County Association of REALTORS®; Sandra Kleps, Greater Rochester Association of REALTORS®; Garrett Lacara; William Lang, Jr.; Norman Lank; George Lasch; William Lester; Richard Levin, Greater Rochester Association of REALTORS®; Irving Levine; Richard Levine, New York Real Estate Institute; William Lippman, Esq.; James Loeb; Jeff Lubar, National Association of REALTORS®; Mary Manfred, Real Estate Learning Center, Inc.; John Mataraza; Bill Mattle; Robert Mendohlson; Stephen Mendolla; P. Gilbert Mercurio, Westchester County Board of REALTORS®; Robert Michaels; Don Milton, Greater Rochester Association of REALTORS®; Mary Ann Monteleone, Long Island Board of REALTORS®; Mary Anne Moore, New York Department of State; Nicholas Morabito; Mark Morano, New York State Association of REALTORS®; Professor Karen Morris, Esq.; James Myers, Esq.; Joseph M. O'Donnell; Amy Penzabene, New York Department of State; Hung Pham; John Piper, Greater Rochester Association of REALTORS®; William Plunkett, New York Real Estate Institute; Barbara Portman; Selwyn Price; James V. Pugliese, CRB, GRI, Coldwell Banker Prime Properties; Edween Reagh; Larry Rockefeller; Willard Roff, New York Department of State; Louis Ryen; Rolando Santiago; Ernest Schade; Karen Schafer; Rita Scharg; Alvin Schwartz; Norman Schwartz; Professor Uri Shamir, Queens College; Sally Smith; John Sobeck; Richard J. Sobelsohn, The Sobelsohn School; Marcia Spada; D.J. Sperano, Fingerlakes Community College/Corning Community College; Robert Stack, American Real Estate School; Charles M. Staro, New York State Association of REALTORS®; William Stavola, New York Department of State; Micheal Stucchio; Anna Y. Tam, American Real Estate School; Eileen Taus, Westchester Board of REALTORS®; Dominic Telesco; Thomas Thomassian; Wendy A. Tilton, New York University; James R. Trevitt, Broome County Board of REALTORS®; Dorothy Tymon; John Tyo; Rex Vail; Christine Van Benschoten; Karen Van DeViver, Greater Rochester Association of REALTORS®; George M. Vaughn, GRI, CRB, CRS, LTG; Thomas R. Viola, State Division of Housing and Community

Renewal; John Viterirri; Michael Wallender, counsel to the New York State Association of REALTORS®; Thomas Wills III; Jane A. Willson, Expo Services, Ltd.; Chris W. Wittstruck, Esq.; Jeff Wolk; John A. Yoegel, PhD, DREI, John Yoegel Seminars; and Babette Yuhas, Greater Syracuse Board of REALTORS®.

Instructors are encouraged to contact their sales representative to obtain access to the PIN-protected instructor's manual that accompanies this textbook.

The author would also like to recommend to them the Real Estate Educators Association, which may be contacted at *www.reea.org*. The association offers workshops, publications, and conferences, and has a chapter in New York State.

About the Author

Edith Lank has been a licensed broker in New York for more than 30 years and has taught real estate at St. John Fisher College. Her award-winning weekly column on real estate, distributed by Creators Syndicate, has appeared in newspapers in Buffalo, Rochester, Syracuse, Schenectady, Amsterdam, Elmira, Brooklyn, Binghamton, Kingston, Ithaca, Middletown, Westchester, and Rockland counties, and Long Island, as well as in 100 other newspapers around the country and various Web pages.

She has hosted her own television and radio shows, and is a frequent speaker at Associations of REALTORS® functions. Edith has published eight books on real estate, including *The 201 Questions Every Homebuyer and Homeseller Must Ask*, *The Homebuyer's Kit*, and *I've Heard It All: Confessions of a Real Estate Columnist*, all available from Dearborn Financial Publishing, Inc.® Her work has been honored by the Monroe County Bar Association, Women in Communications, local and national associations of REALTORS®, the National Association of Real Estate Editors, the Real Estate Educators Association, and Governor Mario Cuomo. A graduate of Penn Yan Academy and Syracuse University, she is a member of Phi Beta Kappa and is listed in *Who's Who*.

Note to Student

Chapters 1, 2, and 3 (License Law, Law of Agency, and Real Estate and Broker-age) have been reprinted from *Modern Real Estate in New York for Salespersons* by Sam Irlander as a review of the salesperson material and as an introduction to the broker topics.

CHAPTER 1

License Law

■ KEY TERMS

administrative discipline
agency disclosure forms
apartment information
　vendor
apartment-sharing agent
appraisers
Article 12-A
Article 78 procedure
associate broker
blind ads
change of association
change of broker
commingling

continuing education
denial, suspension, or
　revocation of license
Department of State
　(DOS)
distance learning
escrow
exemption
home inspectors
irrevocable consent
kickbacks
misdemeanor
mortgage bankers

mortgage brokers
net listing
pocket card
real estate broker
real estate salesperson
reciprocity
record of association
revocation
sponsoring broker
suspension
termination of association
　notice
violations

■ PURPOSE OF REAL ESTATE LICENSE LAWS

In 1922, New York State passed laws that regulated the real estate industry. The primary purpose of these laws was to provide consumer protection and to protect the welfare, health, and safety of the general public and prevent economic loss resulting from the dishonest practices of others in expectation of a fee or other valuable consideration.

TABLE 1.1 **Important State Laws to Remember**	**REAL PROPERTY LAW ARTICLE 12A – COVERS BROKER'S LICENSE LAW** **Section:** 440 – Definitions 440-a – License required for real estate brokers and salespersons 441 – Application for license 441-a – License and pocket card 441-b – License fees 441-c – Revocation and suspension of licenses 441-d – Salesperson license suspended by revocation of employer's license 441-e – Denial of license; complaints; notice of hearing 441-f – Certiorari to review action of department 442 – Splitting commissions 442-a – Compensation of salesperson; restrictions 442-b – Discontinuance or change of salesperson's association; report 442-c – Violations by salesperson; broker's responsibility 442-d – Actions for commission; license prerequisite 442-e – Violations 442-f – Saving clause 442-g – Nonresident licensees 442-h – Rules of the Secretary of State 442-i –State Real Estate Board 442-j – Effect of invalid provision 442-k – Power and duties of the State Real Estate Board 442-l – After-the-fact referral fees 443 – Disclosure regarding real estate agency relationships 443-a – Disclosure obligations Sections 175.1–175.27 – Rules for the guidance of real estate brokers and salespersons Section 176.1 – Rules relating to approval of courses of study in real estate Sections 176.2–176.21 – Requirements for qualification of an approved entity to offer real estate courses for initial licensing as broker or salesperson Sections 177.1–177.19 – Continuing education

The New York **Department of State (DOS)**, Division of Licensing Services, has the power to issue licenses and enforce the real estate license law. The law is enforced through fines, reprimands, and the denial, **suspension, or revocation of licenses.** The Department currently licenses more than 155,000 brokers and salespersons.

State Board of Real Estate

The Division of Licensing Services shares regulatory duties with New York's State Board of Real Estate, which has 15 members. At least five are real estate brokers; the remainder are members of the public, and the secretary of state serves as chairperson. The board has the power to promulgate rules and regulations in some legal areas and also examines applicants, approves real estate schools, and helps enforce the real estate laws.

Violation of the license law is a misdemeanor punishable by up to a year in jail and a fine of up to $1,000. A misdemeanor can be defined as a criminal offense or infraction of criminal laws that is punishable by fine and/or imprisonment, but other than in a penitentiary.

The New York Real Property Law, **Article 12-A**, which went into effect in 1922, is the main source of law for real estate licenses in New York. Copies of the law and regulations may be obtained by writing to the following:

New York Department of State
Division of Licensing Services
A.E. Smith Office Building
80 South Swan Street
Albany, NY 12231

The Licensing Division maintains a consumer assistance phone line in Albany at 518-474-4664, and a Web page at *www.dos.state.ny.us/lcns/realest.html*. The e-mail address is *licensing@dos.state.ny.us*. New York State's TTY phone number is 800-662-1220.

Who Must Be Licensed?

Real Estate licensing is required by any person who

1. performs a real estate act;
2. for another; and
3. for or in anticipation of compensation or other valuable consideration (unless otherwise specifically exempt from state license laws).

Broker.   A real estate broker can be defined as any person, firm, partnership, or corporation that for a fee (or the expectation of a fee) performs for another any of the following 11 services:

1. Negotiates any form of real estate transaction
2. Lists or attempts to list real property for sale
3. Negotiates a loan secured by a mortgage (other than a residential mortgage loan (one- to four-family dwelling), as defined in §590 of the Banking Law)
4. Negotiates a lease
5. Collects rents for more than one client
6. Sells a lot or parcel of land by auction
7. Negotiates the sale of a parcel of subdivided land
8. Exchanges real property
9. Relocates commercial or residential tenants
10. Engages in the sale of condominiums and cooperatives
11. Sells a business that has more than half its value in real estate.

In addition to holding a real estate brokerage license, soliciting, processing, placing, and/or negotiating mortgage loans on one- to four-family dwellings for a fee requires registration with the state banking department as a mortgage broker.

Salesperson.   A real estate salesperson is one who assists a broker in the performance of any of the aforementioned 11 services performed by the broker. A broker is authorized to operate his or her own real estate business, but a salesperson may work only in the name of and under the direct supervision of a sponsoring broker. The salesperson may never accept a commission or other compensation of any kind from anyone except his or her supervising/principal broker.

Associate broker. An **associate broker** is an individual who is qualified to be a broker but has chosen to work in the role of a salesperson under the sponsorship and supervision of another broker. The associate broker must meet all the same qualifications for a broker's license and pass the broker's examination, but he or she is licensed to transact business in the name of the **sponsoring broker,** exactly as a salesperson would. In New York, an associate broker may also hold a broker's license in his or her own individual name.

Note: In New York, an individual bearing a broker status may only work within the association of another broker in the following manner:

1. As an officer or director of a real estate brokerage corporation, he or she must be registered and classified as a broker with the Department of State, Division of Licensing Services. (class 31 license)
2. As a general partner of either a general partnership or limited partnership, he or she must be registered and classified as a broker with the Department of State, Division of Licensing Services. (class 33 license)

It should be noted that salespersons and associate brokers may never hold

1. officer positions (or have officer titles in a corporation) or
2. the position of a general partner in either a general partnership or limited partnership.

Licensing of legal entities such as corporations and partnerships will be covered later in this chapter.

Exceptions. The provisions of the license law requiring licensure do not apply to the following:

- Public officers while they are performing their official duties
- Persons acting under order of a court (executors, guardians, referees, receivers, administrators)
- Attorneys licensed in New York (Note: Any attorney who sets up a brokerage business with associated salespersons under his or her sponsorship and supervision must obtain a license but need not take the prelicense courses or state examination.)
- A resident manager employed by only one owner to manage or maintain rental property when the leasing of units or the collection of rents is part of the manager's regular duties
- Certain authorized tenant organizations and not-for-profit corporations enforcing the housing code of the City of New York

REALTOR®. The term REALTOR® has nothing to do with state licensing. It refers to a member of a private trade organization, the National Association of REALTORS®. Use of the logo (which is registered) is reserved only for members of the National Association of REALTORS®.

	Salesperson	Broker
TABLE 1.2	At least 18	At least 20
	No felony or misdemeanor*	No felony or misdemeanor*
Requirements for Licensing in New York	Permanent resident of United States	Permanent resident of United States
	Sponsoring broker	Two full years' experience or three years' equivalent experience*
	75-hour course	120 hours' study
	Pass state exam ($15)	Pass state exam ($15)
	$50 (two years) license fee	$150 (two years) license fee

* Some exceptions possible

■ QUALIFICATIONS FOR LICENSURE

A licensed salesperson must

- be 18 or older;
- be honest and trustworthy;
- never have been convicted of a felony or misdemeanor (some exceptions are made for an executive pardon, a certificate of good conduct from a parole board, or a certificate of relief from disabilities; however, regardless of these exceptions, it is at the sole discretion of the DOS whether or not they will issue a real estate license to a previously convicted felon);
- be either a citizen or a lawful permanent resident of the United States;
- have a fair and basic understanding of the English language;
- successfully complete a 75-hour prelicensing course that has been approved by the Department of State;
- pass the state's licensing examination;
- pay the required license fee; and
- have a sponsoring broker before obtaining the license.

Table 1.2 shows the requirements for salesperson's and broker's licenses.

A licensed broker must meet the same requirements, except that

1. the minimum age is 20,
2. the required courses of study total at least 120 hours of approved real estate courses as mandated by the secretary of state,
3. a sponsoring broker is not needed, and
4. the prospective broker must submit proof of two full years' experience as a licensed salesperson within the employ and supervision of one or more licensed real estate brokers *or* three years' equivalent experience in the general real estate business. The applicant can establish and satisfy the experience requirement by affidavit sworn under the penalty of perjury. The experience requirement is based on a point system, which will be discussed later in this chapter.

An associate broker must meet all the same requirements as that of any other broker; however, he or she must submit an application signed by the sponsoring employing broker.

With respect to brokers, the DOS issues licenses in several different classes:

- *Class 30* is for the applicant planning to work as an associate broker. Although fully qualified as a broker, the associate chooses to work within another broker's firm. As with a salesperson's application, the associate broker's application is signed by a sponsoring broker. Should the associate broker ever wish to operate independently, no further study or examination would be necessary. Application would simply be made to the DOS for a license in the new class.
- *Class 31* is issued to the officer of a corporation who conducts a brokerage business under a corporate name. (Salespersons and associate brokers may not be principals or own voting stock in a licensed brokerage corporation.) For new corporations, the application must include the filing receipt, which indicates that the corporation has been duly formed.
- *Class 33* is for the broker who intends to do business under the name of a partnership. A copy of the county clerk's certificate of partnership must accompany the application.
- *Class 35* is for the individual broker who will do business in his or her name only, such as "John Smith" or "Jane Brown, licensed real estate broker."
- *Class 37* signifies licensure as a trade-name broker, who will own the business as a sole proprietorship. The local county clerk, after ascertaining that no one else uses the requested trade name, will issue a d/b/a (doing business as) certificate that must accompany the license application, for example, "Juan Sanchez, d/b/a House Calls Realty."
- *Class 49*, *limited liability company* or *limited liability partnership broker*, is for the member or manager of a brokerage operating under one of these types of organizations. For a new limited liability company, a copy of the articles of organization or a filing receipt must be filed with the application.

The broker who intends to use anything other than his or her own name for the firm must submit the proposed name for approval to the DOS, which will check, among other things, whether the name is identical with or misleadingly similar to one already in use for a brokerage. *It is prudent to postpone ordering stationery, advertising, business cards, or a Web page domain until the name has been cleared.*

Education Requirements

The DOS certifies certain educational institutions to offer two qualifying education courses. One qualifying course covers the necessary 75 hours' instruction for a salesperson's license; the second 45-hour qualifying course completes the 120-hour prelicensing requirement for a broker. The courses must be taken in order. Topics to be covered and the time devoted to each are set by law. Successful completion of each course requires at least 67½ hours' (or 90 percent of a 75-hour course) attendance and the passing of a final examination. As of July 1, 2008, the education requirement for prelicensing applicants can be satisfied in the following manner:

1. Salesperson:
   a. By attending 75 hours of state-approved classroom instruction; or
   b. By completing 75 clocked hours of state-approved course content via distance learning, which consists of classes completed online.

Note: Paragraphs b and c of Section 441, Subdivision J, have been changed as follows:

- Paragraph b has been changed to permit computer-based and distance learning; prior to the change in law, computer-based and distance learning (as it applies to prelicensing courses) was prohibited.
- Previously, prelicensing courses were recognized by DOS for life. Under the new paragraph c, they will only be good for eight (8) years from date of completion (see paragraph c change following).

Paragraph c change.   Previously, salesperson prelicensing courses were recognized by DOS for life. Under the new law, salesperson prelicensing courses will only be valid for eight years from date of completion. This eight-year course time limit also includes the *30-hour remedial course* for licensees who completed 45 hours of salesperson prelicense education prior to the change in the law but had not taken the broker's prelicense course prior to July 1, 2008. In that event, such a licensee would have to sit for the 30-hour remedial course to otherwise qualify for a broker's license. A student who takes the 30-hour remedial course can receive continuing education credit for the taking the course; however, the course will *not* satisfy the change in law requiring that all nonexempt students take the required three hours of Fair Housing every license cycle. Therefore, the new 75-hour salesperson course and the 30-hour remedial qualifying course can only be used within eight years from the date of completion.

This specifically means as follows:

- In order to receive credit for the course and completion of same, any broker applicant who has otherwise successfully completed the 75-hour salesperson course will have to apply for their broker license within eight years from completion of the salesperson requirements.
- In the event the applicant fails to do so, he or she will have to repeat the 75-hour prelicense course before enrolling in the broker prelicense course.

The only exception to the aforementioned is if the applicant for a broker's license has completed the 45-hour salesperson prelicense course prior to July 1, 2008, and subsequently completed the 30-hour remedial course. The 30-hour remedial course would expire eight years from the completion date.

■ LICENSE EXAMINATIONS

State license examinations are open to any interested person, whether before or after completion of a 75-hour prelicense course. All exam centers require online reservations with prepayment of a $15 fee. This applies to both broker and salesperson licensing exams.

Test Centers

Each test taker must register online for the exam location and date of his or her choice. Applicants should check the Web site listed below for any specific location:

- Albany (Alfred E. Smith Building), 80 South Swan Street
- Binghamton (State Office Building), 44 Hawley Street, 15th Floor
- Buffalo (State Office Building), 65 Court Street, Hearing Room, Part 5
- Franklin Square (VFW Hall), 68 Lincoln Road, Basement
- Hauppauge (Perry B. Duryea Jr. State Office Building), 250 Veterans Memorial Hwy Basement
- New York City (State Office Building), 123 William Street, 19th Floor
- Newburgh (Federal Building, Orange Ulster BOCES), 471 Broadway, 2nd Floor
- Plattsburgh (Clinton Community College), Lake Shore Drive, Route 9 South
- Rochester (Finger Lakes DDSO), 620 Westfall Road, NYS Testing Sign (DDSO is on the left; do not enter through the main lobby.)
- Syracuse (American Postal Workers Union), 407 East Taft Road (Use back door.)
- Utica (State Office Building), 207 Genesee Street, 1st Floor, Room 107
- Watertown (State Office Building), 317 Washington Street, 11th Floor

For specific dates and complete information, visit the DOS Web site at *www.dos.state.ny.us/lcns/realestate/index.html* and click the eAccessNY link.

NOTE: An applicant who made a reservation for or took the salesperson exam prior to the introduction of eAccessNY should submit a paper application by regular mail.

Applicants who require special testing accommodations should not apply online but should contact DOS for assistance instead.

Examinees should arrive 30 to 45 minutes before the scheduled examination time or up to an hour ahead at the New York City exam center. Each should bring a government-issued signature photo ID and two #2 pencils. An identifying thumbprint will be taken. Scrap paper is furnished and must be turned in before the applicant leaves the room. Calculators must be noiseless and handheld, with no printout or alphabetic keyboard. Cell phones, PDAs, and other electronic devices must be turned off.

The examinations consist of multiple-choice questions such as those in this textbook. One hour is allowed for the salesperson's test and two and one-half hours are allowed for the broker's test. A passing grade is 70 percent, and a successful examination is good for a license application any time during the next two years. For those who fail, unlimited retakes are allowed, with a $15 fee for each.

Test results are available online and also are mailed to applicants. The application for the salesperson license should be completed online after passing the exam. A salesperson license will be issued after acceptance by the sponsoring broker, provided all information is completed correctly and all requirements for licensure are satisfied.

■ LICENSING PROCEDURE

The salesperson's license application (see Figure 1.1) is provided by the school where the 75-hour course was successfully completed and is signed by the broker who will supervise the new licensee and be responsible for his or her activities. It is accompanied by a $50 license fee and proof that the applicant has passed the state licensing exam.

The broker's application includes details of all past transactions during the apprenticeship period as a salesperson, with information about transactions during the required two years' full-time activity as a licensed salesperson or during three years' equivalent experience in general real estate.

The applicant for an associate broker's license not only lists past transactions but also includes the signature of the principal broker with whose firm the new associate broker will be working.

Both applications include a child support statement, certifying whether applicants have any obligation to pay child support and, if so, whether they are four months or more in arrears. The child support statement section must be completed by all applicants. This is regardless of the fact that the applicant may not have children. Failure to complete the section will result in the application being returned by DOS.

Fees

The DOS charges the following application fees:

- Broker, original license and renewal: $150
- Associate broker, original license and renewal: $150
- Salesperson, original license and renewal: $50
- Branch office, original and renewal: $150
- License examination: $15

Note: Fees are subject to change; therefore, the applicant is urged to check with the DOS at the time of application.

Issuing the License

Each license is good for two years from the date of issuance. Each licensee is issued a license and a **pocket card** from the Department of Motor Vehicles.

A salesperson's principal broker keeps the salesperson's license; the pocket card must be carried by the salesperson at all times. Broker licenses must be prominently displayed in the place of business; the salesperson's license may be displayed as well, if the broker wishes. Should the broker choose to display salesperson licenses, the broker should take measures to create a distinct separation between brokers' licenses and salespersons' licenses at the area of display.

The provision under Section 441-a, Subsection 6, has been modified, so that as of July 1, 2008, the DOS requires (with the assistance of the Department of Motor Vehicles) that each pocket card contain a photo of the licensee. The pocket card must be shown on demand. In the event the licensee loses his or her

F I G U R E   1.1

Real Estate Salesperson Application

OFFICE USE ONLY	CLASS	KEY	UNIQUE ID NUMBER	CASH NUMBER	FEE
	4				$ 50

E W S ☐☐☐☐☐ / ☐☐   B ☐☐☐☐☐ / ☐☐

Real Estate Salesperson Application

Read the Instruction Sheet for details before completing this application form. You must answer each question and TYPE or PRINT responses in ink.

APPLICANT'S LAST NAME   FIRST NAME   M.I.   SUFFIX

HOME ADDRESS -NUMBER AND STREET (P.O. BOX MAY BE ADDED TO ENSURE DELIVERY)   APT/UNIT

CITY   STATE   ZIP+4   COUNTY

DAYTIME TELEPHONE NUMBER   SOCIAL SECURITY NUMBER OR FEDERAL ID NUMBER (*SEE PRIVACY NOTIFICATION*)

(   )

E-MAIL ADDRESS (IF ANY)

SPONSORING BROKER OR FIRM NAME (EXACTLY AS IT APPEARS ON THE BROKER'S LICENSE)

OFFICE ADDRESS WHERE APPLICANT WILL BE PERMANENTLY STATIONED - NUMBER AND STREET

CITY   STATE   ZIP+4   COUNTY

1 BACKGROUND DATA

1. What is your date of birth? _____

                                                                YES   **NO**

2. Have you ever been convicted in this state or elsewhere of any criminal offense that is a misdemeanor or a felony? . . . .   _____   _____
    ➜ **IF "YES,"** submit a written explanation giving the place, court jurisdiction, nature of the offense, sentence and/or other disposition. You must provide a copy of the accusatory instrument (e.g., indictment, criminal information or complaint) and a Certificate of Disposition. If you possess or have received a Certificate of Relief from Disabilities, Certificate of Good Conduct or Executive Pardon, you must provide a copy of same.

3. Are there any criminal charges (misdemeanors or felonies) pending against you in any court in this state or elsewhere? . . . .   _____   _____
    ➜ **IF "YES,"** you must provide a copy of the accusatory instrument (e.g., indictment, criminal information or complaint).

4. Has any license or permit issued to you or a company in which you are or were a principal in New York State or elsewhere ever been revoked, suspended or denied? . . . .   _____   _____
    ➜ **IF "YES,"** you must provide all relevant documents, including the agency determination, if any.

5. Have you ever applied for or been issued a real estate broker's or salesperson's license in this state?   _____   _____
    ➜ **IF "YES,"** in what year? _____ Under what name? _____
        UID # (if applicable) _____

F I G U R E   1.1 (CONTINUED)

Real Estate Salesperson Application

Real Estate Salesperson Application

2 Certification of Satisfactory Completion

_____
(Name of School)

Real Estate Salesperson Course (Code) #S- _____

This certifies that _____ has satisfactorily completed a 45-hour salesperson
                              (Name of Student)
qualifying course in real estate approved by the Secretary of State in accordance with the provisions of Chapter 868 of
the Laws of 1977; that attendance of the student was in compliance with the law and that a passing grade was achieved
on the final examination. The course was completed on _____.

Authorized Signature

X_____   *Date* _____

(School Seal)

3 Child Support Statement — *You must complete this section. If you do not complete it, your application will be returned.*

"X" A or B, below

I, the undersigned, do hereby certify that (You *must* "X" A or B, below).

A. [   ] **I am not under obligation to pay child support**.   (SKIP "B" and go directly to **Applicant Affirmation**).

B. [   ] I am under obligation to pay child support (You must "X" any of the four statements below that are true and apply to you):

    [   ] I do *not* owe four or more months of child support payments.

    [   ] I am making child support payments by income execution or court approved payment plan or by a plan agreed to by the parties.

    [   ] My child support obligation is the subject of a pending court proceeding.

    [   ] I receive public assistance or supplemental social security income.

4 Applicant Affirmation — I affirm, under the penalties of perjury, that the statements made in this application are true and correct. I further affirm that I have read and understand the provisions of Article 12-A of the Real Property Law and the rules and regulations promulgated thereunder.

Applicant's Signature

X_____   *Date* _____

F I G U R E   1.1 (CONTINUED)

Real Estate Salesperson Application

Real Estate Salesperson Application
_____

5   Association Statement — I am sponsoring this application in accordance with the Real Property Law, §441.1(d).

Broker Name _____   Date _____

Broker Signature _____

Broker Print Name _____

Please remember to include with this application any required explanations and statements along with your application fee (payable to NYS Department of State).

It is important that you notify this division of any changes
to your business address so you can continue to receive renewal
notices and any other notifications pertinent to your license.

pocket card or the card is damaged or destroyed, a duplicate card will be issued upon request, proof, and submission of loss of same. At this time, a fee of $10 must accompany the request.

To receive a license in the state of New York, an individual must do the following:

- Successfully complete the required education
  — Salesperson: 75 hours
  — Broker: 120 hours
- Pass a state exam (salesperson and broker applicants)
- Submit a fully completed application that includes
  — self-employed/legal entity filing (broker only) or
  — broker signature of association (associate broker or salesperson)
- Pay the required licensing fee

Licensing Corporations, Partnerships, and Other Legal Entities

A license issued to a corporation entitles a designated officer to act as a broker, but that person also must secure a license personally. One officer may act as the real estate broker under the corporate or business license. Every other officer or partner who wishes to act as a broker must secure another license, which will expire on the same day as the corporate or business license. An officer or partner of a licensed corporation or other legal entity may not be licensed as a real estate salesperson or associate broker.

■ MAINTAINING A LICENSE

Various license laws and regulations affect a licensee's business practices.

Change of Business Address, Status, or Name

All principal brokers who are changing either the principal office or a branch office address must notify the DOS online within five days of the change. The broker must pay for the address change for all current licensees at the address being changed before the system will accept the change. The charge per affected license is $10. Once the changes and payment are made and accepted by the system, a new license will be mailed to each licensee at the new business address.

Those desiring a license status change (such as from associate broker to broker), change of employment, or name change must submit notice of change and the appropriate fee online.

Commissions

No individual may legally accept a commission or other compensation for performing any of the activities regulated by the license law, unless he or she

- holds a valid New York real estate license at the time the activity is performed and
- maintains the license from the start of a transaction up to the point that all compensation is received.

A salesperson may not accept a commission from anyone other than his or her supervising broker (except from a former broker for fees already earned but not paid when he or she was associated with that broker).

Brokers may not receive compensation from more than one party to a transaction without the full knowledge and consent of all parties involved (dual compensation). Brokers may share commissions only with their own salespersons and associate brokers or with other licensed brokers.

The law against sharing a commission with any unlicensed person effectively prohibits kickbacks (return of a portion of the commission) to either buyers or sellers (with some exceptions). It should be noted that, generally speaking, the difference between a kickback and a referral fee can be best described as follows:

- A kickback occurs when
    - compensation is passed to another without the full disclosure and informed consent of all interested parties to the transaction.
- A referral fee occurs when
    - all interested parties to a transaction and/or the party being referred have agreed to be referred, and
    - the party being referred has been given full disclosure and has granted informed consent to the receipt of a referral fee.

An example of a referral fee would be when a real estate licensee refers a client to another real estate licensee with the intention that the referring party receive a referral fee from the broker who receives the referral.

A kickback is illegal and will subject the licensee to disciplinary action. A referral fee, given the appropriate procedures, falls within the law. It is important to note that for licensees all referral fees are treated as compensation. As such, all compensation must go directly to and through the broker. A licensee within the employ of a broker may never collect compensation of any kind directly from anyone other than his or her sponsoring broker.

Disclosure of Interest

Licensees may neither buy nor acquire an interest in property listed with them for their own account without first making their true position known to the owners involved. Similarly, licensees may not act as brokers or salespersons in the sale of property in which they have an interest without revealing the interest to all parties to the transaction. When self-dealing, the licensee must be on alert for the potential creation of a dual agency. This topic will be covered in greater detail in Chapter 2.

Offers to Purchase

All offers to purchase property must be presented promptly to the owner of the property.

■ TERMINATION OR CHANGES IN ASSOCIATION

When a salesperson or associate broker terminates an association with a broker, the supervising broker must file a termination of association notice with the DOS. License terminations and changes of associations are to be made online. A termination must be filed by the existing broker prior to the new broker's performing a change of association. When a change of association or change of broker occurs, the former broker returns the license to the salesperson and at the same time files a termination of association with the DOS. Each of these functions requires a $10 fee, which must be paid by credit card at the time of termination or change. Each broker will need the unique identification number of the licensee whom they are terminating or changing. Each principal broker must be logged into his or her personal online real estate account in order to perform these transactions.

If a salesperson's license has expired and he or she wishes to affiliate with and renew under a different broker, the salesperson must establish a new **record of association**. The new broker must file the change of association prior to the renewal. A termination by the prior broker is not required in this situation.

After the new broker notifies the DOS and pays the fee, the salesperson then makes the necessary changes on the license by crossing out the former information and in its place adds in the number, name, and address of the new broker. The salesperson makes the same changes on the pocket card. The new broker retains the license, and the salesperson retains the pocket card.

Revocation or suspension of a principal broker's license automatically causes the licenses of those associated with the broker to be suspended, until they associate with a different broker.

A real estate salesperson who terminates his or her association with a broker must turn over to the broker any and all listing information (and buyer representation agreements) obtained during the association. This is required whether the information was originally given to the salesperson by the broker or acquired by the salesperson during the association. Retention of listing information by a licensee following voluntary or involuntary termination of a licensee is a licensing offense. Listings are the property of the broker. In addition, licensees should also be careful to observe any covenant(s) and/or restriction(s) that may be contained in their employment contracts or independent contractor agreements (as the case may be). Generally speaking, it is advised that an amicable "exit agreement" be executed between a licensee and his or her previous employing broker at termination of association. This exit agreement will protect the rights of the parties to that agreement. To coin a phrase: "Good contracts make for good friends."

■ RENEWAL AND CONTINUING EDUCATION

Real estate licenses must be renewed every two years. A licensee who does not renew within two years of expiration must retake the licensing examination. Online renewal is available at the DOS Web site.

Continuing Education

To renew a license, a licensee must complete 22½ hours of continuing education every two years.

As of July 1, 2008, Section 441 of the RPL has been amended to require that the 22½ hours of continuing education contain at least three hours on fair housing and/or discrimination in the sale or rental of real property.

Continuing education can be accomplished (1) by attendance within a classroom environment with no end-of-class exam required or (2) by clocking 22½ hours of prescribed and approved course material via distance learning or (3) by a combination of classroom attendance and distance learning totaling 22½ hours of approved continuing education.

The hours may be accumulated in modules as short as three-hour courses, and distance learning is available through the Internet or on CD-ROM. A list of approved continuing education courses can be obtained by calling 518-486-3803 or by e-mailing *licensing@dos.state.ny.us*. A list of approved schools is available on the DOS Web site.

Previously, active licensed brokers who had been continuously licensed and active as full-time salespersons and/or brokers for the preceding 15 years and attorneys licensed to practice in the state of New York were exempt from the continuing education requirement. This exemption section will not change for any individual who has achieved **exemption status** prior to July 1, 2008.

After July 1, 2008, this continuing education exemption will no longer be granted to brokers who fulfill the 15-year requirement after that date. No exemption will be granted to any licensee who was not already exempt prior to July 1, 2008.

In order to qualify for the exemption from continuing education after July 1, 2008, a licensee must

1. have a broker's license,
2. have been licensed for 15 years continuously *prior to July 1, 2008,* and
3. have held an exemption prior to the change in law.

Those grandfathered with this exemption under the old laws are advised to be timely in renewing their licenses. If the license is allowed to lapse, the licensee will lose his or her exemption forever and will be required to complete continuing education every two years following the lapse.

■ BROKERAGE MANAGEMENT IN ACCORDANCE WITH LICENSE LAWS

Brokers must follow a variety of laws and regulations as they operate their brokerage businesses.

Place of Business

Every New York real estate broker must maintain a principal place of business within the state (with the rare exception of some nonresident brokers).

Business name and sign. Any business name used by a New York real estate broker must first be approved by the DOS.

- If the signage is outdoors, it must be posted conspicuously on the outside of the building and be readable from the sidewalk.

■ When the signage is posted indoors (as in an office building, for instance), the broker's name and the words "Licensed Real Estate Broker" must be posted in the space that lists the names of the building's occupants. The words "Licensed Real Estate Broker" may be abbreviated to read "Lic. R. E. Broker."

Branch offices.   A broker may maintain a branch office or offices, and a separate license must be maintained for each. Section 441-a, Subsection 3, of the real property law has been amended so that as of July 1, 2008, each branch office must be under the direct supervision of the broker to whom the license to operate a branch office was issued. This would also include the following:

■ A representative broker of a corporation (also known as a corporate broker/ class 31 license)
■ A representative broker or manager of a limited liability company (class 49)
■ A representative broker of a general or limited partnership (class 33)

The principal broker must pay expenses for the branch office and supervise it closely. Except as otherwise provided under Part 175.20, Subsection (b), salespersons and associate brokers may never manage and operate branch offices. Part 175.20, Subsection (b) specifically provides that

■ every branch office shall be under the direct supervision of the broker to whom the license is issued (this includes a representative broker of a corporation or partnership holding such license); and
■ a salesperson licensed for a period of not less than two years and who has successfully completed a course of study in real estate approved by the secretary of state may be permitted to operate such a branch office *only under the direct supervision of the broker* (Part 175.21), provided that the names of such salesperson and supervising broker shall have been filed and recorded in the division of licenses of the DOS.

Maintaining Documents

Every real estate broker must maintain a file of all agency disclosure forms, listings, offers, closing statements, and certain other documents for a period of no less than three years. (Most brokers keep all records indefinitely as a matter of good business practice.)

Delivery of Documents

A real estate broker must immediately deliver to all parties signing the document duplicate originals of any document relating to a real estate transaction prepared by the broker or one of his or her salespeople. Failure to do so may subject the licensee to disciplinary action by the DOS.

Care and Handling of Funds

A real estate broker must not commingle money or other properties belonging to others with his or her own funds. A broker who holds money belonging to others in his or her possession must maintain a separate, federally insured New York bank account (the name of the titled account must include the words escrow or trust account) to be used exclusively for the deposit of these monies and must deposit them immediately. Within a reasonable time period, the broker must render an account of the funds to the client and remit any funds collected to the proper party. Interest earned, if any, does not belong to the broker. The broker's responsibility in this role also includes maintaining information on the institution where escrowed funds have been deposited (including the branch name and address holding the account), recording the account number(s) needed to identify which account is housing the funds, and, if the account is to be interest bearing, noting whom the benefit of the interest will inure to. Any cash deposit of $10,000 or more must be reported to the Internal Revenue Service (IRS).

Obligations to Other Parties and Other Brokers

The license law expressly prohibits a broker from interfering with or trying to frustrate other parties' existing contracts. In addition, license law also prohibits the aggravation of another licensee's agency relationship(s).

No broker may accept the services of any other broker's associates without that broker's knowledge, and brokers may not pay another broker's associates directly without that broker's knowledge.

Brokers are prohibited from negotiating the sale, lease, or exchange of any property directly with an owner who has an existing written contract that grants exclusive authority to another broker. This means that brokers may not interfere with another broker's exclusive listing agreement.

■ OTHER LICENSES OR REGISTRATIONS INVOLVING REAL ESTATE

An **apartment information vendor's** license is available to anyone older than 18 who is trustworthy and able to maintain a $5,000 interest-bearing escrow account. The license is renewable annually for a $400 fee. Apartment information vendors engage in the business of furnishing information concerning the location and availability of residential rental property, including apartments. They must provide prospective tenants a contract or receipt with specific information regarding the services they offer. They also must display a sign in all offices bearing the same information, post their license in all offices, and notify the DOS of any changes in name or address. A buyer or renter is not required to engage the services of a real estate broker, so the services of apartment information vendors allow buyers and renters to facilitate a sale or rental without the assistance of a real estate licensee.

An **apartment-sharing agent** finds roommates and arranges for sharing of homes. The one-year license costs $400, and the agent must maintain a trust account of $2,500.

Certification or licensing of **appraisers** is not required for all appraisal work but is necessary for most appraisals related to mortgage loans. New York State licenses and certifies appraisers at different levels, depending on the applicants' experience, education, and examinations.

Mortgage Banking Companies

Mortgage bankers are not thrift institutions (a financial institution designed to hold personal savings accounts while simultaneously promoting home purchasing; the term is currently used to describe savings banks and savings and loan associations) and do not offer either checking or savings accounts. Because they do not use depositors' money, they are subject to considerably less regulation than thrift institutions. They make or extend real estate loans that may later be sold to investors (with the mortgage company receiving a fee if it continues servicing the loans). Mortgage bankers originate a large percentage of all home loans. Mortgage bankers must file a $50,000 surety bond with the superintendent of banks or establish a trust fund in the same amount that can be used to reimburse customers, if it is determined that the mortgage banker has charged improper fees. They are *not* mortgage brokers.

Mortgage Brokers

Mortgage brokers are *registered* with the State Banking Department to bring borrowers and lenders together. They normally charge a fee, often of the borrower, for their services. The superintendent of banks may require a mortgage broker to obtain a surety bond or establish a trust fund in the amount of $25,000.

Any person who negotiates or seeks to negotiate a mortgage loan other than a mortgage loan on residential property in the state of New York is required to be licensed as a real estate broker or as a salesperson associated with a real estate broker. This license is issued by the DOS. However, in any transaction involving a mortgage loan on residential property (defined as four or fewer units contained within a building intended for dwelling purposes), registration with the New York State Banking Department is required.

Home Inspectors

New York State has required licensing for home inspectors since January 2006. License requirements resemble those for real estate salespersons: required hours of study, examinations, and supervised apprenticeship. Real estate salespersons and brokers who refer buyers to home inspectors must make sure that the ones they suggest are licensed. Lists of licensees are available at the DOS Web site.

Home inspectors are required to complete continuing education for every cycle of licensing. The requirements differ from those of real estate licensees in the following ways:

- An applicant whose license expires on/or before December 2008 will be required to complete 6 hours of DOS-prescribed approved continuing education (prior to completion of their application renewing his or her license).
- An applicant whose license expires after December 2008 will be required to complete 24 hours of DOS-prescribed approved continuing education (prior to completion of their application renewing their license).

Disclosure Required for Uncapped Wells

Chapter 163, amended Section 242 of the real property law, requires a seller of real property to disclose to a buyer, prior to entering into a contract for purchase and sale, the existence of any "uncapped natural gas wells" that are known by the seller to exist on the property in question. The law is intended to protect buyers from the significant expenses that may occur after closing when natural gas wells must be capped.

Reciprocity versus Mutual Recognition of Licensure

Reciprocity.   Reciprocal agreements are reached through and between states that are willing to recognize each others' license laws as well as the requirements needed to achieve licensing within their jurisdictions.

All states devise their statutory laws somewhat differently, but a majority of the requirements for achieving licensing are the same throughout the United States. As a result, state A can reach a reciprocity agreement with state B that recognizes licenses attained in either state as valid in the other. When this type of agreement between states exists, in order to achieve a license within another state after having received a license in one, no additional education or testing is required. At this time, New York has reciprocal agreements with ten states (see Table 1.3); however, certain requirements must be fulfilled, as discussed in the section entitled "Licensing Nonresidents."

Mutual recognition.   Mutual recognition applies to states that are not willing to enter into reciprocal agreements with other states but are willing to recognize previous education completed by a licensee from another state and previous experience achieved while licensed in another state.

These states may require an applicant to achieve additional education if his or her home state has reduced hourly requirements for licensing; the applicant will probably have to take the state law portion of the state licensing exam.

Licensing Nonresidents

Nonresidents of New York may be licensed as New York real estate brokers or salespersons by conforming to all the provisions of the license law, except maintaining a place of business within the state. Some New Jersey brokers, for example, hold licenses in both states.

The department will recognize the license issued to a real estate broker or salesperson by another state if the laws of his or her home state permit licenses to be issued to New York licensees without requiring that he or she take that state's licensing examination. (See Table 1.3.) If a particular state's laws do not include these provisions, the nonresident applicant must pass the licensing examination.

Every nonresident applicant must file an **irrevocable consent** form, which makes it easier for the nonresident to be sued in the state of New York. As a nonresident licensee, the irrevocable consent form allows the nonresident to receive service of legal process within the state of New York. It is designed to allow a nonresident to be sued within the state of New York without the claimant having to serve the nonresident in the state where he or she lives.

■ ADVERTISEMENTS

Advertising must not be misleading in any way. All real estate advertisements must contain the name of the broker's firm and must clearly indicate that the party who placed the ad is a real estate broker. Any ad that does not identify that the advertiser is a real estate broker is termed a **blind ad**. Blind ads that contain only a telephone number are prohibited.

On Web sites as well as in print ads, a salesperson's name may not be displayed more prominently than the broker's or firm's name. Any Internet ad must contain a link to the firm's Web site. The broker must supervise a salesperson's Web site.

All advertisements that state that a *property is in the vicinity of a geographic area or territorial subdivision* must include as part of the advertisement the name of the geographic area or territorial subdivision in which the property actually is located.

TABLE 1.3

Real Estate Reciprocity

Arkansas	Broker only—two years' licensure and current (business and residence must be in Arkansas).
Colorado	Broker and associate broker—current licensure (business and residence address must be in Colorado). Colorado associate brokers must submit a salesperson application fee along with their certification and irrevocable consent form.
Connecticut	Broker and salesperson—current licensure only (business and residence must be in Connecticut).
Georgia	Broker and salesperson—current licensure only (business and residence must be in Georgia). Must have obtained their license by passing Georgia exam.
Massachusetts	Broker only—two years' licensure and current (business and residence must be in Massachusetts).
Mississippi	Broker and salesperson—current licensure only (business and residence must be in Mississippi). Must have obtained their license by passing Mississippi exam.
Nebraska	Broker and salesperson—current licensure only (business and residence must be in Nebraska).
Oklahoma	Broker and salesperson—two years' licensure and current (business and residence must be in Oklahoma).
Pennsylvania	Broker and salesperson—current licensure only (business and residence must be in Pennsylvania).
West Virginia	Broker and salesperson—current licensure only (business and residence must be in West Virginia).

All need current certification (dated within six months) from the real estate commission where the license was obtained, completed application, irrevocable consent form, and the appropriate fee.

Applicants seeking a reciprocal real estate salesperson's license must be sponsored by a broker holding a current New York State broker's license.

For Sale Signs

A broker must obtain an owner's prior consent to place a For Sale sign on the owner's property. Neglecting to do so is considered an infraction of license law and will subject the licensee to disciplinary action by the DOS.

■ SUSPENSION AND REVOCATION OF LICENSES

The DOS may hear complaints and/or initiate investigations into any alleged violations of the license law or its rules and regulations. Anyone found guilty of untrustworthiness or incompetence may have his or her license temporarily suspended (**suspension**) or permanently cancelled (**revocation**) or may be fined or reprimanded (**administrative discipline**). Untrustworthiness or incompetence will include any of the following acts:

- Making any substantial misrepresentation (defined as a false statement or the concealment of a material fact, done in order to induce someone to take a certain action, whether done maliciously, ignorantly, or carelessly)
- Making any false promise likely to influence, persuade, or induce
- Making a false statement or misrepresentation through agents, salespersons, advertising, or otherwise
- Accepting, if a salesperson, a commission or valuable consideration for any real estate service from any person except the licensed broker with whom the salesperson is associated

- Acting for or receiving compensation from more than one party in a transaction without the knowledge and consent of all parties involved (it is always recommended that consent be achieved in writing)
- Failing within a reasonable amount of time to account for or remit any monies belonging to others that come into his or her possession
- Failing to immediately deliver duplicate or original documents to an interested party in a transaction
- Failing to make the appropriate property defect disclosure(s) when these defects are known to the licensee
- Being untrustworthy or incompetent to act as a real estate licensee
- Paying a commission or valuable consideration to any person for services performed in violation of the law
- Obtaining a license falsely or fraudulently or making a material misstatement in the license application
- Negotiating with an owner or a landlord with knowledge that the owner or landlord has an exclusive written contract with another broker
- Aggravating the agency relationship of another
- Offering a property for sale or lease without the authorization of the owner
- Accepting the services of any salesperson who is associated with another broker
- Giving legal opinions or performing title examinations
- Entering into a **net listing** contract (when a seller authorizes a broker to procure a specified amount of money for the property and allows the broker to keep any money above the specified amount obtained from the sale)
- Discriminating because of race, creed, color, national origin, age, sex, disability, sexual orientation, or marital status in the sale, rental, or advertisement of housing or commercial space
- Failing to provide definitions of exclusive-right-to-sell and exclusive-agency listings when the listing involves the sale or rental of three or fewer family dwellings (section 175.24). Section 175.24 does not apply to cooperatives and condominiums.
- Engaging in improper, fraudulent, or dishonest dealing
- Committing any other violation of license law

Investigation of Complaint and Hearing

If the DOS feels that a complaint warrants further investigation, it will send an investigator to interview the alleged violator about the charge. In most cases that involve a complaint against a licensee within the employ of a broker, the interview will begin with the sponsoring broker of record. This interview occurs to determine whether or not the broker has been supervising his staff appropriately (as required under part 175.21 of the Real Property Law). In some cases, the investigation is preceded by a formal letter of complaint from the department. If the investigation results in sufficient evidence, the department will conduct a hearing. Individuals accused of violation of the law may defend themselves or be represented by an attorney. The department investigates roughly 2,500 complaints annually, with about 1,000 resulting in disciplinary action.

Penalties

An offender who has received any sum of money as commission, compensation, or profit in connection with a license law violation may be held liable for up to four times that amount in damages in addition to having his or her license suspended or revoked. If a license is revoked, one year must pass before a new license application can be made.

The DOS also may impose a fine not to exceed $1,000 per violation. Violation of the license law also constitutes a **misdemeanor**, and a licensee may be tried in criminal court in addition to the DOS hearing. Criminal actions can be prosecuted by the attorney general of the state of New York. A misdemeanor is punishable by a fine of not more than $1,000 and/or imprisonment for not more than one year. The DOS does not have the power to imprison license law violators.

Appeal

The action of the DOS is subject to review. Any determination in granting or renewing a license, revoking or suspending a license, or imposing a fine or reprimand may be appealed to the secretary of state. Judicial appeal is made through an **Article 78 procedure**, an appeal to the New York State Supreme Court. An Article 78 proceeding is the appeal process available to any private individual when a public body of government renders an adverse decision against him or her. A private individual might decide to institute an Article 78 proceeding to secure relief/grievance from overcharges applicable to real property assessments or when seeking compensation from condemnation of a private party's property.

Revocation of Broker's License

Revocation of a broker's license automatically suspends the licenses of all salespersons and associate brokers affiliated with that broker until they find another supervising broker and their licenses are reissued.

When a salesperson is accused of violating the license law, the supervising broker is also held accountable if the broker knew or should have known of the violation or, having found out about the problem, retained any fees or commissions arising from the transaction. The broker in this situation is said to have "vicarious liability." As depicted above, vicarious liability can be defined as responsibility for the wrongful acts of another. This subject will be covered in Chapter 2.

■ UNLICENSED REAL ESTATE ASSISTANTS

In today's real estate market, many real estate agents find that using unlicensed assistants is very useful. These assistants can do a fair amount of paperwork and legwork, leaving the agents free to use their time finding clients and negotiating transactions. However, unlicensed assistants may not perform any real estate activities for which a license is required. According to the DOS, an unlicensed assistant may safely engage in the following activities:

■ Answer the phone, forward calls, and take messages
■ Arrange appointments, by telephone, for the licensee
■ Follow up on loan commitments after a contract has been negotiated and generally secure status reports on the loan progress
■ Assemble documents for closing
■ Write ads for the approval of the broker and place approved classified advertising
■ Type contract forms for the approval of the broker
■ Compute commission checks
■ Place signs on or remove them from properties
■ Order items of repair as directed by the broker
■ Prepare flyers and promotional information for approval by the broker
■ Schedule appointments for licensees to show listed property

F I G U R E   1.2

Important Albany Legislative Update of Recent Bills Signed into Law by the Governor

■ **Fair Housing Education (Chapter 474):** This bill amends Chapter 183 (laws of 2006) to require that each licensee, unless otherwise exempt under license law, take at least 3 hours of the 22½ hours of required continuing education every two years (discussed earlier in this chapter in the section entitled "Continuing Education").

■ **Real Estate Agency Disclosure Form Amendments (Chapter 549):** This amendment was intended to further clarify for the general public changes that were made to 2006's agency disclosure form. The following definitions were added: *broker's agent* (discussed in Chapter 3), *tenant's agent, landlord,* and *tenant.*

The bill does not change the definition of "residential real property," and as a result, the exclusion from written disclosure requirements for condominiums and cooperatives located in buildings that contain greater than four units stands. New York State law still requires that *all* real estate licensees verbally make known to all interested parties to the transaction the nature of their agency relationship within a transaction. The rights and obligations of same must also be included.

■ **Real Estate Investment Trusts – REITs (Chapter 94):** This bill, while it is merely a technical amendment, covers "combined reporting" that was as a result of the revenue bill. This amendment excludes publicly traded REITs and regulated investment companies from compliance with this requirement.

■ **New York City Property Tax Rebate (Chapter 483):** This bill's primary purpose was to reauthorize New York City to issue property tax rebates in the amount of $400 to any owner (in the five boroughs) of a one- to three-family home, condominium, and/or cooperative. Authorization under this bill is extended through fiscal year 2009–2010.

■ **Private Activity Bond Allocation Act of 2007 (Chapter 593):** This bill deals with development of large 80/20 housing projects. The bill extends the "multiyear funding feature" of private activity bonds. The cap for future allocations in the carryforward provisions remains at three years; however, the amount has been raised from $300 million to $650 million. It must be renewed annually.

■ **421-a Extension (Chapters 618, 619 & 620):** The 421-a tax abatement program has been extended until December 28, 2010 (effective July 1, 2008). In this bill, modifications to the exclusion zones and eligibility requirements have been made.

■ **Lower Manhattan Tax Abatements (Chapter 60):** This bill extended the property tax abatement ($2.50 per square foot) and commercial rent tax abatement for sections of the lower Manhattan incentives. This is contained within part O of the revenue bill in the 2008 budget.

■ Gather information for a comparative market analysis
■ Gather information for an appraisal
■ Monitor licenses and personnel files
■ Perform secretarial and clerical duties such as typing letters and filing

An unlicensed assistant may not list or sell property, prospect for listings, show property, hold open houses alone, or answer buyer's questions about property. In addition, there have been instances in which some brokers utilize an individual referred to in the marketplace as a "shower" to open doors for customer viewing appointments. Generally, the shower is not a licensed individual, and as such, is committing a licensing infraction. To avoid this infraction of license law, brokers are highly advised to properly license any individuals performing this or any other duty requiring a license.

■ DOS DETERMINATIONS

In recent years, the DOS has acted in cases such as the following:

- Associate broker failed to provide the required written disclosure of agency (as explained in Chapter 3); the DOS fined him $500. The principal broker also was fined and penalized.
- Salesperson lied on her license renewal application and said she had completed continuing education requirements. An audit turned up the false statement. The DOS revoked her license.
- Salesperson did not lie on license renewal but frankly stated he had failed to complete the continuing education courses required. The DOS suspended his license until he provided proof he completed the courses.
- Broker's license was suspended because he failed to pay child support, not to be reinstated until family court confirmed he was up-to-date with his payments.
- Broker had misappropriated rental income he was collecting on behalf of a landlord, and when ordered to make restitution, paid with bad checks. The DOS revoked his license and indicated it could not be reinstated until the full sum was repaid to the landlord including interest.

■ SUMMARY

In New York, licensees must be permanent residents of the United States, must never have been convicted of a felony or misdemeanor, and must pass state examinations before licensure. A salesperson must have completed a prescribed 75-hour qualifying course, be at least 18 years old, and be sponsored by a licensed broker. A broker must be at least 20 years old, with an additional 45 hours of approved study (120 hours total) and two full years' experience as a licensed salesperson. Some exceptions to these requirements are possible.

The real estate license, which covers a two-year period, costs $50 for a salesperson and $150 for a broker. An associate broker's license designates a fully qualified broker who chooses to remain in a salesperson capacity under a supervising broker. Those exempt from licensing requirements include New York state attorneys, public officials while performing their public duties, and persons acting under court order. A license is not required of a resident manager employed by only one owner to collect rents. Certain tenant organizations in New York City may also perform real estate services without being licensed.

Every broker must have a principal place of business within the state, post a sign readable from the sidewalk or in the lobby of an office building, obtain a separate license for each branch office, and display the principal broker's license prominently. Brokers who handle other people's money must maintain a separate escrow account for those funds. The broker must immediately deliver duplicate originals of all documents to the persons signing them and must keep a file of all documents relating to real estate transactions for at least three years.

Commissions may be collected only by the supervising broker and may be shared only with other brokers and the broker's own associated salespersons and associate brokers. Advertisements must contain the name of the broker's firm.

Laws, rules, and regulations governing licensees are administered by the New York DOS, which may, after hearings, suspend or revoke licenses. Violations of these laws, rules, and regulations are also misdemeanors.

QUESTIONS

1. Joan, who has no real estate license, canvasses homeowners by phone to see if they are interested in selling their homes. Shanice, who is licensed, gives Joan $25 for every lead she turns up. Does this violate license law?
   a. No, because the gift is not more than $25.
   b. No, because Joan does not actually list or sell property.
   c. Yes, because Shanice is paying compensation for services that require licensure.
   d. Yes, because Joan is using a home telephone with no broker's sign outside her house.

2. Real estate license laws were instituted to
   a. raise revenue through license fees.
   b. limit the number of brokers and salespersons.
   c. match the federal government's requirements.
   d. protect the public and maintain high standards.

3. In New York, real estate licenses are issued by the
   a. Real Estate Commission.
   b. Board of REALTORS®.
   c. Department of State.
   d. Department of Education.

4. Tom Swift, a New York resident, needs a real estate license to
   a. give his cousin advice about pricing her home for the market.
   b. write a lease for a tenant in a building he owns.
   c. accept a TV from a grateful neighbor for whom he arranged a home equity loan.
   d. sell the house of his dead aunt while he is settling her estate.

5. What is the educational course requirement for a real estate salesperson's license?
   a. 45 hours
   b. 60 hours
   c. 75 hours
   d. 90 hours

6. A duly licensed salesperson may accept a bonus from
   a. a grateful seller.
   b. a grateful buyer.
   c. another salesperson.
   d. None of the above

7. A fully qualified broker who chooses to act as a salesperson under another broker's sponsorship is licensed as a(n)
   a. adjunct salesperson.
   b. sales associate.
   c. associate broker.
   d. principal broker.

8. To obtain a broker's license, you must reach the age of
   a. 18. c. 20.
   b. 19. d. 21.

9. A broker must have completed how many hours of prescribed study?
   a. 45 c. 90
   b. 75 d. 120

10. Which meets a requirement for a broker's license in New York State?
    a. Completion of 50 hours in real estate courses
    b. Age of at least 18
    c. two years' experience as a licensed salesperson
    d. Membership in the New York State Association of REALTORS®

11. Generally, real estate licenses are good for a period of
    a. one year. c. three years.
    b. two years. d. four years.

12. A nonresident broker seeking a New York license must
    a. post a bond of $5,000.
    b. be a citizen of the United States.
    c. find a New York attorney or another broker to act as a sponsor.
    d. file a consent form allowing himself or herself to be sued in New York State.

13. In the office a broker must display
    a. all brokers' licenses.
    b. all licenses.
    c. no licenses.
    d. only salespersons' licenses.

14. Salesperson Jackson told the telephone company to print the following ad under Real Estate in the Yellow Pages: Alissia Jackson, Licensed Salesperson, Residential Property a Specialty, 473-4973. She should have included her
    a. area code.
    b. broker's name.
    c. office address.
    d. home phone number.

15. A real estate license is temporarily suspended or permanently cancelled if a licensee is found to be untrustworthy or
    a. incompetent.   c. irresponsible.
    b. malicious.   d. unproductive.

16. The Department of State has revoked Ted Toller's license for fraud. Which is *TRUE?*
    a. Toller may appeal the revocation.
    b. His salespersons may continue in business for 90 days because they were not found guilty.
    c. Toller may continue his business for 90 days if he posts a bond with the DOS.
    d. Toller may have his license reinstated if he signs an irrevocable consent form.

17. If a principal broker loses her license, her associated salespersons must immediately
    a. appoint one of their number to serve as supervisor.
    b. stop listing and selling.
    c. obtain brokers' licenses.
    d. request that the DOS reassign them.

18. A salesperson need *NOT* be
    a. licensed by the state.
    b. at least 18 years old.
    c. already experienced in real estate.
    d. supervised by a broker.

19. Don Houseknecht lists his house with Bob Broker. Don offers a bonus commission of $500 to the agent who brings a good buyer before December. Sally Salesperson, who is associated with the cooperating firm of Orville Otherbroker, effects the sale on November 1. Sally may collect that bonus from
    a. Don.
    b. Orville.
    c. Bob.
    d. no one.

20. Any business name used by a New York real estate broker must
    a. indicate the business's specialization.
    b. contain the surname of the broker.
    c. be significantly different from other businesses.
    d. be approved by the DOS.

21. A real estate broker must keep all documents for the DOS pertaining to a real estate transaction on file for how long?
    a. Two years
    b. Three years
    c. Seven years
    d. Indefinitely

22. The term *commingling* pertains to
    a. mixing the broker's funds with escrow deposits.
    b. soliciting the services of another broker's salespersons.
    c. failing to deliver duplicate originals of contracts.
    d. promoting business at social gatherings.

23. What size cash deposit must a real estate broker report to the IRS?
    a. $5,000   c. $15,000
    b. $10,000   d. $20,000

24. An apartment information vendor's license is available to individuals who are able to

a. pass the licensing exam.
b. file a $10,000 surety bond.
c. obtain a sponsoring broker.
d. maintain a $5,000 interest-bearing escrow account.

25. After December 2008, the continuing education requirement for license renewal of home inspectors in New York will

a. disappear.
b. require fewer hours.
c. require more hours.
d. become identical to the requirement for brokers.

CHAPTER 2

The Law of Agency

■ KEY TERMS

accountability

agency

agency coupled with an
  interest

agency disclosure form

agent

attorney-in-fact

brokerage

buyer's broker

Clayton Act

client

commercial transaction

commission

confidentiality

cooperating agent

customer

disclosure

dual agency

estoppel

express agency

Federal Trade
  Commission

fiduciary

fiduciary duties

fiduciary relationship

first substantive contact

fraud

general agent

group boycott

implied agency

informed consent

latent defects

law of agency

listing agreement

loyalty

market allocation

meeting of the minds

misrepresentation

multiple listing service

obedience

power of attorney

price-fixing

principal

procuring cause of sale

puffing

ratification

ready, willing, and able
  buyer

reasonable care

residential transaction

restraint of trade

seller's agent

self-dealing

Sherman Act

special agent

subagent

tie-in arrangements

undisclosed dual agency

undivided loyalty

universal agent

■ OVERVIEW OF AGENCY DISCUSSION

In this chapter, the basic **law of agency** is covered, with emphasis on the duties of agents to their clients and standards for dealing with their customers. Chapter 3 discusses the various types of possible agency relationships and the need for brokers to develop policies for disclosure of representation.

■ WHAT IS AN AGENT?

Real estate brokers and salespersons are commonly referred to as agents. Legally, however, the term refers to strictly defined legal relationships. In the case of real estate, it is a relationship between licensees and buyers, sellers, landlords, or tenants. In the law of agency (the body of law that governs these relationships), the following terms have specific definitions:

- **Agent**—an individual who is employed or authorized (and consents) to transact business on behalf of another, usually for a fee. In the real estate business, the broker firm acts as the agent of the
    — seller,
    — buyer,
    — landlord, or
    — tenant.
- **Principal**—the individual who hires and delegates to the agent the responsibility of representing his or her interests.
- **Agency**—the fiduciary relationship that is created between the principal and the agent.
- **Fiduciary**—term describing the role that the agent takes on when the agency relationship is created, a relationship based on the highest form of trust and confidence. The agent is empowered (within the limitations of the agency appointment) to transact business on behalf of the principal.
- **Client**—a term that may be used to describe the principal.
- **Customer**—the third party with whom the agent deals on behalf of his or her principal. The customer is owed "fair and honest dealing" by an agent transacting business on behalf of a principal, but the relationship between the agent and the customer is not a fiduciary one.

There is a distinction between the duties owed by the agent to a client and the treatment owed to a customer. The principal, or *client*, is the one to whom the agent gives *advice* and *counsel*, and whose interest must be put above the interests of all other parties to a transaction, including the interests of the agent.

The agent is entrusted with certain *confidential information* and has *fiduciary responsibilities* (discussed in greater detail later) to the principal. In contrast, the *customer* is entitled only to factual information and honest dealings as a consumer but does not receive advice and counsel or confidential information about the principal. The agent works *for* the principal and *with* the customer.

Types of Agents

Through the creation of the agency relationship, the scope of authority granted an agent will determine which of the three types of agent categories that relationship falls under. The three categories of agent relationships may be classified as follows:

1. Universal agent
2. General agent
3. Special agent

A **universal agent** has the authority to represent the principal in *all matters concerning all transactions that can be delegated*. The universal agent can enter into any contract on behalf of the principal. However, under the New York State General Obligations law, the aforementioned may not occur without a prior *written notarized power of attorney*. He or she can act for the principal in the broadest scope and range of areas. This type of agency cannot happen without this written document known as a **power of attorney**. A guardian or an individual who looks after a mentally incompetent party is an example of a universal agent. That appointed party (appointed by the courts via a written decree that replaces the written power of attorney) tends to all the needs and cares of the noncompetent party.

A **general agent** is empowered to represent the principal in *all matters concerning one transaction*. The general agent is granted authority to only transact a *specific range of matters*. As in the case of a universal agent, the general agent may bind the principal to any contract within the scope of the agent's authority. This type of authority also can be created by a power of attorney. A property manager is usually an example of a general agent. He or she performs various duties on behalf of the property owner/principal. These duties consist of rent collection, bill paying, accounting/bookkeeping functions, and maintenance of the property. As you can see, the property manager acts on numerous levels for his or her principal. However, unlike with the universal agent who bears the broadest scope of authority to transact on all matters concerning all transactions, the scope of authority granted to a general agent is limited to that assignment only.

A **special agent** is authorized to represent the principal in *one specific transaction or business activity under detailed instructions*. Under this agent category, the scope of authority granted the agent by the principal is extremely limited. For example, think of a principal and a real estate broker entering into a listing agreement (an employment agreement that engages a licensee). The role established for a real estate broker through the listing agreement is usually that of a special agent. If hired by a seller, the broker's duty is limited only to finding a ready, willing, and able buyer for the property. If hired by the buyer, the broker's duty is limited to finding a suitable property for the buyer. As a special agent, the broker is not authorized to bind the principal to any contract.

An **agency coupled with an interest** is a relationship in which the agent has some interest in the property being sold. Such an agency *cannot be revoked by the principal, nor can it be terminated on the principal's death*. For example, a broker might supply the financing for a condominium development, provided the developer agrees to give the broker the exclusive right to sell the completed condo units. Because this agent has a special interest in the transaction, the developer may not revoke the listing agreement after the broker provides the financing.

■ CREATION OF AGENCY

An agency relationship can be created by either an oral or a written agency agreement between the principal and the agent. It can also be implied from words or conduct. Of course, to ensure that all parties have a clear understanding of the agency relationship, it is in everyone's best interest to create an agency relationship with a written agreement.

There are two ways or methods by which agency relationships can be created:

1. Express agency
2. Implied agency

Express Agency

The most common way of creating an agency relationship is through an *express agreement*, an agreement that is *expressed in words, either spoken or written.*

A written agreement that creates an **express agency** relationship between a seller and a real estate broker is called a **listing agreement**. Think of the listing agreement as you would of an "employment contract." A listing agreement employs and authorizes the broker to find a buyer or a tenant for the owner's property.

An agency relationship also can be created between a buyer or a tenant. This is achieved by the use of a document called a *buyer broker agreement*, an *agreement to procure*, or a *buyer agency agreement*. This buyer agency agreement describes the activities and responsibilities the principal expects from the broker in finding the appropriate property for purchase or lease.

Implied Agency

An agency also could be created with an *implied agreement*. This occurs when *both the principal and the agent act as if an agency exists*, even though they have not expressly entered into an agreement. Providing services that are accepted by the principal can create an **implied agency** relationship. For instance, a broker advises a seller on a fair listing price, gives helpful hints on how the seller can make the house more marketable, shows the property to several buyers, and continually refers to himself or herself as the **seller's agent**. The seller sets the listing price according to the broker's advice, makes the recommended repairs to the house, and agrees to numerous showings. In this case, there may be an implied agency relationship.

The dangers of this type of relationship arise when a seller's agent offers advice to the buyer/customer. The seller's agent may unknowingly be creating what is termed as an illegal **"undisclosed dual agency."** This subject will be covered in greater detail later within this chapter.

It should be noted that it is not always the seller's agent who creates the impression of an agency relationship. In the eyes of the buyer customer, there may be occasions when he or she treats the seller's agent in a manner that gives the impression that an agency relationship has been created. In this event, it is imperative that the seller agent immediately correct the buyer customer's impression. This will avoid the risk of creating an undisclosed dual agency.

When someone claims to be an agent but there is no agreement, the principal may establish an agency by one of two implied agency subcategories: **ratification** *and* **estoppel** (defined as when a party is prevented by his or her own acts from taking a different position because it would cause detriment to another party).

Ratification can be defined as an after-the-fact acceptance of the relationship or previous agreement, while *estoppel* can be defined as accepting the benefits of the previously unauthorized act. This occurs when an individual does not stop another from performing services on his or her behalf.

As you can see, ratification and estoppel can create ostensible relationships, which are generally found to be false and misleading. The reason for this is simply that there has been no clarity or disclosure as to the relationship of the parties. A licensee must always make his or her relationships clear to all parties in a transaction (section 175.7).

Failure to disclose one's relationship at **first substantive contact** will subject the licensee to disciplinary action by the DOS. First substantive contact can be defined as follows:

- The point at which a licensee exchanges or expresses information regarding a property to an interested party
- The point at which an interested party begins to discuss or detail personal financial or other information concerning his or her interest or ability to conclude a transaction

It is upon the occurrence of these events that a licensee must disclose to a buyer, seller, landlord, or tenant (as the case may be) the nature of his or her relationship within the transaction.

The legal requirement for written agency disclosure (discussed in Chapter 3) reduces the chances for misunderstanding in a **residential transaction.** A *residential transaction* can be defined as any transaction involving the sale or rental of a building that contains four or fewer units intended for dwelling purposes. (Any transaction involving the sale or rental of a building that contains greater than four units would be considered a **commercial transaction.**)

Although the written agency disclosure forms for cooperative and condominium units in buildings that contain greater than four units are not required under state law, a licensee is still obligated to make known his or her relationship to the parties within a transaction. However, cooperative and condominium units contained in buildings of four or fewer units are required to comply with the written agency disclosure requirements.

However, members of the general public tend not to understand the complexities of the law of agency. Buyers easily can assume that when they contact a broker to show them property, the broker becomes "their agent." *Under the law, it is a person's actions, not just his or her words, that control the creation of an agency relationship.*

Compensation. It is commonly assumed that a licensee is the agent of the one who pays the compensation. However, this is not true. *The source of compensation does not determine agency;* the agent does not necessarily represent the person who pays the commission. Creation of the agency relationship by the respective parties (as detailed previously) becomes the sole determining factor as to employment and necessary duties therewith. In fact, agency can exist even if there is no fee involved (a *gratuitous agency*). Buyers, sellers, and brokers can make any agreement they choose about compensating the broker, regardless of which one is the agent's principal. For example, the seller could agree to pay a commission to a broker who is the buyer's agent. Written agency agreements should always state how the agent is to be compensated. The agent is reminded that section 175.7 also covers compensation. Under section 175.7, an agent may never receive compensation from more than one party to that transaction without the full knowledge and consent of all interested parties to the transaction.

■ AGENCY AND BROKERAGE

The business of bringing buyers and sellers or landlords and tenants together in the marketplace in order to conclude a real estate transaction is known as **brokerage.**

The principal who employs the broker may be

- a seller,
- a prospective buyer,
- an owner who wishes to lease property, or
- someone seeking property to rent.

The broker acts as the *agent* of the principal, who usually compensates the broker with a **commission** or fee for having successfully performed the service for which the broker was employed. As you already have learned, the principal is also known as the *client*.

Importance of Agency Law to Licensees

Agency law has become an increasingly vital topic for all real estate agents. While most of the legal principles of agency law have remained unchanged for decades, the practical application of those laws to real estate agents has dramatically changed the face of the real estate business in recent years. Various real estate boards and organizations promulgate a code of ethics that their members must adhere to. They offer educational seminars intended to create greater awareness of the duties and responsibilities that a licensee owes to another.

Whom does the agent represent? In the early 1980s, the Federal Trade Commission found that the public was totally confused about whom a real estate agent was working for. When buyers who bought property listed by a different firm were asked whom they thought the selling agent was working for, more than 70 percent said they believed the selling agent was working for them. The reality was that in the vast majority of these transactions, the agent was legally bound to represent and work for the best interests of the seller.

Many states began drafting legislation that would require agents to disclose whom they represented to all the parties involved. In 1991, New York enacted a disclosure law that, in the opinion of many, was a model for the nation. (Agency disclosure is discussed in Chapter 3.)

Seller as Principal

If a seller contracts with a broker to market the seller's real estate,

- the broker becomes an *agent of the seller;*
- the seller is the *principal,* or the broker's *client;*
- a buyer who contacts the broker to review properties listed with the broker's firm is the broker's customer; and
- though obligated to deal honestly with all parties to a transaction and to comply with all aspects of the license law, the broker is strictly *accountable only to the principal—in this case the seller.*

The listing contract for residential properties usually authorizes the broker to use licensees employed by the broker as well as the services of other cooperating brokers in marketing the seller's real estate. In the creation of an agency relationship, the broker is generally appointed as the sole agent transacting on the principal's behalf. Therefore, any salesperson of that broker or brokerage is considered to be an agent of his or her managing broker, and as a result, also becomes a **subagent** of any principal who is using the firm's services. In addition, it should be noted that any **cooperating agent**, the broker from another company who finds the buyer, may be acting as

- a *subagent* of the seller;
- an agent for the listing broker (broker's agent); or
- an agent for the buyer.

Buyer as Principal

The practice of buyers hiring brokers to find the desired real estate is becoming more common. In this situation, the broker and the buyer usually draw up an agreement that details the nature of the property desired, the amount of the broker's compensation, and how it is to be paid. (See the sample buyer agency agreement in Chapter 3.) The buyer becomes the *principal,* or the broker's *client.* In this case the broker, as agent, is the **buyer's broker** and is strictly accountable to the buyer. The seller becomes the *customer or* the third party to the transaction.

The same relationships apply when a prospective tenant hires a broker to locate property for rent.

Broker as Principal

A broker is licensed to act as the principal's agent and thus can collect a commission for performing his or her assigned duties. A salesperson or associate broker, on the other hand, has no authority to make contracts or receive compensation directly from a principal.

All of a salesperson's activities must be performed

1. in the name of his or her supervising broker and
2. under the direct control and supervision of his or her employing broker.

The broker is fully responsible for the real estate actions of all salespeople licensed under him or her. *The broker is the salesperson's principal.*

The salesperson functions as an *agent* of the broker and a *subagent* of the principal (the buyer or the seller). Thus, both the broker and the broker's salespersons and associate brokers have a fiduciary relationship with the principal.

Basic Agency Relationships

Before we discuss the fiduciary responsibilities owed to principals by their agents, it is important to take a quick look at the types of agency relationships that may exist in a given transaction. The first agency relationship is between the seller and the listing broker. The broker agrees to perform diligently to find a ready, willing, and able buyer. The seller is the principal; the broker is the agent.

The broker typically employs licensed salespeople to assist in the disposition of his or her duties. The licensed salesperson or associate broker helps the broker to list and market property. The salespeople are the agents of the broker and the subagents of the seller. Both the listing broker and the affiliated salespeople owe their fiduciary duties to the seller (unless otherwise agreed).

The listing broker and cooperating brokers from other firms that share listing information will begin to market the listed property. As they do so, they work with various prospective buyers. Cooperating brokers and salespeople who choose to represent the seller owe their fiduciary duties to the seller, not the buyer. They fall under the category of subagents. However, some cooperating brokers may be working under a buyer-broker agency agreement (which need not be in writing) and represent the buyer. They owe their fiduciary duties to the buyer, not the seller. Others may work not as subagents but simply as cooperating brokers.

Compensation from more than one party in a transaction. As discussed earlier, compensation has nothing to do with whom a licensee owes their allegiance to. Fact situations may arise in which a broker may encounter the need or opportunity to receive compensation from both parties in a transaction. As discussed in Chapter 1, in accordance with penalties indicated in the license law, an agent may not collect compensation from two parties within the same transaction unless the following two events have occurred:

1. The agent has provided to all the interested parties to that transaction full disclosure of the joint compensation.
2. The agent has received the informed consent to proceed from all the interested parties to the transaction.

Dual agency. Dual agency is defined as representing both parties within the same real estate transaction. The broker has two clients in the same transaction.

As is the case in any situation in which the parties demand loyalty and partiality, it is rarely possible for the broker to offer undivided loyalty to two or more principals in the same transaction. Thus, real estate license laws prohibit a broker from representing and/or collecting compensation from both parties to a transaction without their prior knowledge and written consent.

More difficult to handle is the situation in which a seller's broker, for example, emotionally adopts a buyer and unconsciously begins to work for the buyer's best interest, so that an unintended and illegal dual agency results.

A common complaint against agents is that of **undisclosed dual agency**. This relationship occurs when an agent acts in the best interests of one party to a transaction while legally representing the other party.

An example might be when a buyer's agent sells a close relative's property to a client without the **informed consent** of that client.

Another example might be when an agent and customer meet in an open house environment and warm up to each other. The customer may have no interest in the property covered by the open house, but may request that the agent show them other properties. Although it is not the intention of the agent conducting the open house to create a buyer/agent relationship, one may simply arise out of implication by the agent accepting the assignment. In an open house, it is safe to conclude that the licensee conducting the open house is always an agent of the seller and cannot offer buyer representation on the premises without the permission of the seller client. In order to avoid this occurrence, the agent is advised to make his or her relationship clear in advance of commencing any working relationship with the customer. Section 175.7 requires that a real estate broker always make it clear for which party he or she is acting on behalf of.

Self-dealing. Problems can also occur when a broker lists property, then decides to buy it and collect the agreed-on commission. This is referred to as **self-dealing**. At that point, those brokers represent themselves but continue to act as the sellers' agents as well. It is advisable for agents in this position to give up the listing, collect no commission, and just represent themselves as buyers.

Self-dealing also occurs when a licensee within the employ of a broker attempts to acquire or dispose of real property for his or her own account. Most employment contracts between licensees and their employing brokers prohibit any self-dealing unless it is accomplished in the name of the brokerage that the licensee is registered with.

For example, salesperson Ian wishes to place an advertisement in the classified section of the newspaper: "House for sale by owner. Contact Ian at 555-5555." Although license law does not restrict a licensee from selling his or her own property, it does establish procedures for how this should be done.

As it stands, the ad Ian wants to place would be considered a blind ad, which is not permitted. A blind ad is defined as any ad that does not identify the advertiser as a licensee. (See Chapter 1.)

A situation like this one would fall under the restrictions of the self-dealing section of an employment contract, and the responsibility would fall to broker-employers to exert their authority over the activities of salespersons or associate brokers in such cases.

F I G U R E   **2.1**

Agent's Responsibilities

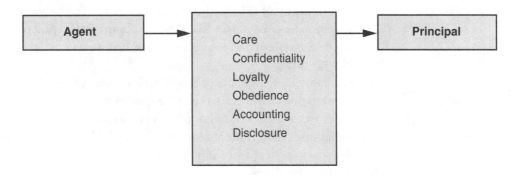

FIDUCIARY RESPONSIBILITIES

A broker has the right to reject agency contracts that in his or her judgment violate the law, ethics, or high standards of the office. After a brokerage relationship has been established, however, the broker owes the principal a host of duties, including the exercise of care, skill, and integrity in carrying out lawful instructions.

In particular, each agency relationship requires the agent provide the principal with six primary **fiduciary duties,** which can be memorized as CC-LOAD (see Figure 2.1):

1. Care
2. Confidentiality
3. Loyalty
4. Obedience
5. Accounting
6. Disclosure

An agent's **fiduciary relationship** with his or her principal is a relationship of the highest form of trust and confidence. (Other types of fiduciaries include trustees, executors, and guardians.) If the principal could not count on the agent to act in the principal's best interest, the agency relationship would be meaningless.

Care

The broker must exercise **reasonable care** while transacting business entrusted to him or her by the principal. In the eyes of the law, the individual licensee is considered an expert. Therefore, real estate brokers are expected to have special skills and expertise in the real estate field. The definition of care includes a licensee's obligation to exercise diligence on behalf of the client. They must be knowledgeable about real property laws, land-use issues, financing, transfer of title, and the like.

Brokers should be skilled in the following areas:

■ Valuing property (to determine a reasonable listing price and a reasonable purchase price)
■ Clarifying the principal's needs

- Discovering pertinent facts about the neighborhood, the property, and the parties to the transaction and disclosing this information to the principal
- Filling in and explaining in simple terms the purpose and effect of the contract forms involved (the listing agreement or buyer agency agreement and the purchase contract), while never engaging in the practice of law (unauthorized practice of which can result in license revocation as well as other civil penalties)
- Recommending that the principal seek expert advisers (such as attorneys, accountants, or inspectors) when appropriate
- Making best efforts to sell or find the property
- Explaining different financing options available from local lenders
- Negotiating offers and counteroffers
- Meeting deadlines

If a broker represents the seller, care and skill include helping the seller arrive at an appropriate and realistic listing price; discovering facts that affect the seller and disclosing them; properly presenting the contracts that the seller signs; making reasonable efforts to market the property, such as advertising and holding open houses; and helping the seller evaluate the terms and conditions of offers to purchase.

For example, suppose a broker sells a home a few days after the listing agreement is signed. While the seller is initially pleased with the quick sale, she later realizes that the broker set the listing price too low. The seller also discovers that plans for a nearby shopping center were approved a few months ago. When the shopping center is completed in eight months, her property will be worth even more. The broker, who claimed to be an expert on her neighborhood, had no idea about the new shopping center. There were also several clauses in the sales contract that the seller didn't understand. When she asked the broker about them, he shrugged off her concern. Now she realizes that the clauses were important and were not to her advantage. If she had understood their effect, she would have consulted an attorney. The broker breached his duty to exercise reasonable care and skill when fulfilling the terms of the agency contract. He should have had a basic knowledge about property values, new developments in the neighborhood, and the importance of contract terms. And he certainly should have recommended that the seller consult an attorney before signing the contract or make the contract subject to the approval of her attorney.

A broker who represents the buyer will be expected to help the buyer locate suitable property; evaluate property values, the neighborhood, and property conditions; discover financing alternatives; and handle offers and counteroffers with the buyer's interest in mind.

For example, the buyer's broker might discover that the seller is facing foreclosure if the property is not sold promptly but doesn't relay that information to the buyers. If the buyers had known, they might have bought the property for less than they offered. The broker violated fiduciary duty to the buyer.

The broker is liable to the principal for any loss resulting from the broker's negligence or carelessness.

Confidentiality

An agent may not disclose any confidential information learned from or about the principal. For example, if the agent is representing the seller, information about the principal's financial condition may not be disclosed to potential buyers, including the fact that the principal will accept a price lower than the listing price. The same rule applies to any confidential facts that might harm the principal's bargaining position, such as the fact that the seller must quickly move out of the area. Similarly, a buyer's broker would not reveal the buyer's readiness to pay more if necessary.

Confidential information never may be revealed, even if it would mean a larger commission or a quicker closing date for the agent. Even after the agency relationship has terminated—for instance, after the sale has closed—confidential information should be kept confidential.

A broker may not maintain **confidentiality**, however, if the information is something he or she is obligated to disclose because of the duty to deal honestly with a customer. For example, if the seller's broker knows about a hazardous condition on the property or that the roof leaks or the plumbing needs repairs, it must be disclosed to the buyer.

The agent should exercise extreme care to avoid violating the responsibility of confidentiality when communicating or dealing with other agents. For example, a common occurrence in the real estate industry is dealing with cooperating agents (particularly those not within the employ of the listing broker). They may inquire whether the listing price is negotiable. The listing agent should *never* imply or reply that the price is negotiable because his or her principal would then likely never achieve an amount equal to or greater than the listed price. The listing agent would be guilty of violating the fiduciary responsibility of confidentiality. This would lead to disciplinary action against the licensee.

Loyalty

The duty of **loyalty** dictates that an agent must always place the principal's interests above those of all other persons, including the agent's own interests. The seller's agent, for example, must try to obtain the highest possible price, the buyer's agent to obtain the lowest. The agent must never take advantage of a chance to profit at the principal's expense.

For example, an offer with a lower purchase price may be in the seller's best interest because of the financing terms, closing date, or other concessions. The agent must try his or her best to negotiate such an offer, even though it may mean a smaller commission for the agent.

Even when agents find themselves working for no compensation, they must have the interests of their principals in mind before they may consider themselves.

Obedience

The fiduciary relationship obligates the broker to obey the legal and reasonable instructions of the principal.

This duty of **obedience** is not absolute, however. The broker may not obey any instructions that are unlawful or unethical. For example, the broker may not follow instructions to make the property unavailable to members of a minority group or to conceal a defect in the property such as a leaking roof.

If a broker knows or has reason to suspect that the client will ask him or her to do something unlawful or unethical, the broker should either refuse to accept the listing or should terminate the listing if it already exists.

Accounting

Brokers must be able to report the status of all funds belonging to others that are entrusted to their possession. Real estate license laws require that brokers give duplicate originals of all documents to all parties affected by such documents and keep copies of them on file for *three years*. In addition, brokers must immediately deposit all funds entrusted to them in special accounts with titles that must include the words *trust* or *escrow*. It is illegal for brokers to commingle (mix) such monies with business operating funds or personal funds or to retain any interest such monies earn. This duty to account to the principal is also referred to as **accountability**.

Disclosure

It is the broker's duty to pass on to the principal all facts or information the broker obtains that could affect the principal's decisions. The duty of **disclosure** is sometimes known as the *duty of notice*. It includes not only useful information the broker knew but also relevant information or *material facts* that the agent should have known. (A material fact is any fact that affects the value of the property and is important to a person making a decision.) Under the theory of law entitled "presumption of knowledge," this applies to anything "the broker should have known."

In the course of a transaction, principals must make critical decisions. Agents must supply their clients with all the material facts, so that the principals may make informed choices.

The broker must volunteer pertinent information whether or not the client knows enough to ask for it. For example, a broker has presented an offer to her principal, the seller. The offer involves seller financing (the buyer will make a small down payment, and the seller will finance the difference between the down payment and the purchase price). The broker knows that the buyer has a history of defaulting on his obligations. Even though the seller does not ask the broker about the buyer's credit history, the broker must express a concern and perhaps recommend the seller require that the buyer obtain a preapproved mortgage. In many cases, a broker may be held liable for damages for failure to disclose material facts.

Some of the types of information it is imperative to disclose include the following:

- The relationship between an agent and other parties to the transaction. For instance, if the agent is representing the seller and the buyer is a relative of the agent, the agent must disclose that fact to the seller. Other relationships that must be disclosed include close friends and close business associates.
- Whether the agent is acting for himself or herself (self-dealing). New York forbids brokers and salespersons to buy or sell property in which they have a personal interest without informing the seller or purchaser of that interest. It is prudent to make such a disclosure in writing as part of the purchase contract before it is signed. If a buyer's broker has a similar type of relationship with the property seller, that relationship must be fully disclosed to the buyer.
- The existence of other offers. All offers should be *immediately* submitted to the principal until the sale is closed. The seller's agent must remember that it is up to the principal to reject or accept an offer; it is not the agent's job

to evaluate the offers and submit only the most favorable. Failing to submit all offers immediately is a violation of license law. This requirement applies even to properties that are in contract and waiting to close.

■ The status or form of the earnest money deposit. The seller's agent always must inform the principal if the earnest money is in the form of a promissory note or a postdated check. If the broker fails to do so and the seller cannot collect on the note or check, the broker may be liable to the seller for the amount of the deposit.

■ The buyer's financial condition. If the seller's broker knows of any negative information about the buyer, he or she must inform the seller at once. The buyer's broker, however, must keep the buyer's financial condition confidential, unless to do so would breach the agent's duty to treat the seller honestly.

■ The value of the property. One of the reasons sellers use real estate brokers to market their properties and buyers use brokers to help them purchase properties is that brokers have expertise in the area of property values. Brokers must always give their true opinions of a property's value and should never inflate that value to obtain a listing or complete a sale. The broker would be wise to disclose the sales prices of comparable properties, including those the broker should know about if he or she had studied the marketplace. The buyer's broker should suggest the lowest price the buyer should pay based on comparable values and how long a property has been listed or why the seller is selling.

■ Any commission split. The listing broker should disclose to the seller any fee-sharing arrangement with a cooperating broker. This means that the listing broker must describe to the seller the general company policy regarding cooperating with subagents, cooperating agents, and buyer's agents. This usually occurs at the time the listing agreement is entered into.

■ Contract provisions. The broker must explain to his or her client the important provisions of any contract the client is going to sign. If the client requires anything more than a simple explanation, the broker must advise the client to seek competent legal advice.

■ Property deficiencies. If a broker represents a buyer, he or she must disclose the deficiencies of a property as well as contract or financing issues that are not to the buyer's benefit.

Breach of Fiduciary Duties

If agents breach their fiduciary duties, they may be subject to a variety of penalties. Some of these penalties can be imposed regardless of whether the agent's breach of duties caused the principal any actual harm. Penalties for breaching fiduciary duties may include:

■ Loss of the commission
■ Loss of the agent's license or other disciplinary action by the state
■ Adverse judgment in a civil suit (defined as a lawsuit where violations of civil law have allegedly occurred)
■ Rescission (voiding) of the transaction by court order

Scope of Authority

While agents must fulfill their fiduciary responsibilities, they must also act within the scope of their authority. Real estate agents, who are almost always special agents, have only the authority granted to them by their listing or buyer broker agreements. For example, the listing broker is authorized to find a ready, willing, and able buyer but generally has no authority to sign contracts for the seller, initial changes to an offer, receive the purchase price on behalf of the seller, or permit early occupancy.

The authority granted to a listing broker should be stated expressly in the listing agreement. In a typical listing contract, the seller specifically authorizes the broker to place a sign on the property, advertise, show property, cooperate with other brokers, and accept earnest money deposits.

Usually, the broker is not given the right to sign contracts, although in exceptional cases, the broker may be appointed as **attorney-in-fact** under a separately granted power of attorney. (One need not be an attorney to be appointed an attorney-in-fact.)

A buyer's broker is generally given the authority to seek out appropriate property. The broker is not usually given the right to sign a purchase contract on behalf of the buyer.

Agent's Responsibilities to Other Parties in the Transaction

Even though an agent's primary responsibility is to the principal, the agent also has obligations to third parties. The duties to the third party or customer include:

- Fair and honest dealing
- Disclosure of material facts that the licensee knows or should know that affect the desirability or value of the property (or the buyer's ability to complete the transaction) and that are not easily discoverable by the customer

Opinion versus fact. Whatever the specific topic, brokers, salespeople, and other staff members must be careful about the statements they make to third parties. They must be sure that the customer understands whether the statement is an *opinion* or a *fact*. Statements of opinion are only permissible as long as they are offered as opinions and without any *intention to deceive*. When rendering an opinion, the agent should ensure that the customer does not solely rely on this opinion in the purchase of the property.

For instance, a broker is showing a house to a buyer and says, "This house has the best view in the neighborhood." This statement is obviously a statement of opinion, and because the buyer can look out the window and judge the view for himself, the statement is not made with an intent to deceive.

Statements that are an exaggeration of a property's benefits are called **puffing**. If the broker in the previous example said, "This house has the best view in the whole county—no, the whole state!" her statement would be considered puffing. It is an obvious exaggeration. Puffing is considered a sales tactic and is legal. However, real estate agents must be careful to make sure that their "puffing" is not accepted by buyers as fact. For instance, telling a prospective buyer that a home "will appreciate at least 50 percent in the next five years" may be an exaggeration, but it is also a misleading statement that a buyer could easily accept as a fact. Licensees must be sure that none of their statements can be interpreted as *fraudulent*. **Fraud** is the *intentional misrepresentation of a material fact in such a way as to harm or take advantage of another person*. Misrepresentation is discussed in more detail below.

Environmental concerns. Disclosure of environmental health hazards, which can render properties unsalable, also may be required. Frequently the buyer or the buyer's mortgage lender will request inspections or tests to determine the presence or level of risk. Licensees are urged to obtain advice from state and local authorities responsible for environmental regulation whenever toxic waste dumping, contaminated soil or water, nearby chemical or nuclear facilities, or health hazards such as radon, mold, asbestos, or lead paint may be present.

Latent defects.   Brokers and salespersons should be aware that some courts have ruled that a seller is responsible for revealing to a buyer any material (important) latent defects relating to the property. A **latent** (or hidden) **defect** is one that is not discoverable by ordinary, reasonable inspection; that is, it is simply not visible to the human eye without further inspection. Regardless of whether the agent represents the buyer or the seller, the broker likewise is responsible for disclosing known hidden defects to the buyer. Buyers have been able either to rescind the sales contract or to receive damages when latent defects are not revealed. Examples of such hidden defects include a leaking underground oil storage tank, a buried drain tile that causes water to accumulate, and a driveway built partly on adjoining property.

New York courts are continuing to rule on the duties of real estate agents toward their customers. While the traditional principle of caveat emptor (let the buyer beware) is still the law, it has been modified in certain circumstances to require that both the seller and the broker disclose known material facts. Today, with new seller property condition disclosure requirements, one can almost say "let the seller beware." To protect himself or herself from liability in this area, a broker should ask the seller for all the pertinent facts about the physical condition of the property. The broker does not have to complete a detailed physical inspection; asking the seller for all pertinent facts should be sufficient. Although a seller may be understandably reluctant to discuss such facts, the broker can assure the seller that such disclosure will protect the seller from potential liability, protect the broker from potential liability, and enable the broker to market the property in the most effective way possible.

Today, most listing agreements contain clauses intended to protect the broker against a seller's lack of property condition disclosure. A seller, in most cases, will be asked to warrant and represent to the listing broker, that the seller has disclosed all material facts that were known to him or her at the time he or she entered into the listing agreement. This clause may even include an indemnity (hold harmless) section that provides protection to the broker against any liability that arises or results from the seller's lack of disclosure to the broker.

According to the Department of State, Division of Licensing Services, it is not the broker's duty to verify all of the seller's representations, unless the broker uses such representations in marketing the property. However, if the broker knows *or has reason to know* that the seller has indeed made a misrepresentation or failed to disclose material facts, the broker is required to make a full disclosure. Remember:

■ A broker acts as an agent.
■ An agent is one who transacts on behalf of others; therefore, it is safe to deduce that an agent is a direct extension of his or her principal and, as such, may be held equally responsible for lack of making property condition or other material disclosures that would affect the price of the property.

New York State requires sellers to furnish prospective buyers with a 48-item Property Condition Disclosure Statement, which is discussed in Chapter 3.

In a New York Supreme Court Appellate Division case, *Stambovsky v. Ackley* (the haunted house case), a seller was held responsible for failing to disclose that a house was haunted. The court did rule that the broker was not at fault.

To clear up the problem of "stigmatized" properties, a 1995 amendment to the New York State Real Property Law (section 443-a) provides that an owner, occupant, or agent need *not* disclose the fact that the property is or is suspected to be the site of a homicide, suicide, other death, or any other felony.

In addition, the fact that the property was ever owned or occupied by someone who had or was suspected to have the HIV infection or AIDS or any disease highly unlikely to be transmitted through occupancy of a dwelling may not be disclosed either.

Megan's Law.   New York courts have held that brokers have no obligation to search the state records on which convicted pedophiles must register their addresses. A buyer's broker should, however, advise clients that the registry is available for public inspection.

To gain information about the possibility that crimes have been committed on the property, a prospective purchaser may submit a written inquiry; and the seller or the seller's agent may choose whether or not to respond to the inquiry.

Misrepresentations.   One of the most common complaints against real estate agents is that of **misrepresentation**. Misrepresentations violate the broker's obligation of honest dealing. Most complaints come from buyers.

To successfully sue a real estate agent for misrepresentation, the plaintiff (the one bringing the suit) must be able to prove that

- the broker made a misstatement (oral or written) to the buyer or failed to disclose a material fact to the buyer that should have been disclosed;
- the broker either knew or should have known that the statement was not accurate or that the information should have been disclosed;
- the buyer reasonably relied on such statement; and
- the buyer was damaged as a result of that reliance.

Misrepresentation can be an *affirmative* (intentional) statement, such as "A new roof was put on this house three years ago," when the broker knows that the roof is 12 years old. It can also be a failure to disclose a latent defect (discussed previously). For instance, if the broker knows the basement regularly floods but does not disclose that fact to the buyer, the broker is guilty of misrepresentation.

The misstatement does not have to be intentional to be misrepresentation. A real estate agent can be liable for misrepresentation if he or she knew or *should have known* about the falsity of the statement.

Brokers around the country have been held liable for misrepresentations in the following types of cases:

- Termite infestation. The broker, acting for the seller, plastered over termite damage.
- Free of liens and encumbrances. The broker mistakenly told the buyer that the seller owned the property free and clear of all encumbrances.
- Filled land. The broker made an unauthorized statement to the buyer that the property was not a "filled lot." (The house later sank when the fill settled.)
- Easements. When a buyer asked a broker about easements on a property, the broker said not to worry. Three months later, the city used the easement to lay water pipes.
- Zoning. The broker misrepresented the property's zoning.

If a contract to purchase real estate is obtained as a result of misstatements made by a broker or salesperson, the contract may be disaffirmed or renounced by the purchaser. In such a case, the broker will lose a commission. If either party suffers loss because of misrepresentations, the broker can be held liable for damages.

For the buyer's broker, a hidden defect requiring disclosure to the seller would be the buyer's financial inability or unwillingness to complete the purchase. Take, for example, a buyer who filed for bankruptcy two years ago. The buyer, through his or her broker, intends to submit an offer to purchase that would be contingent on the buyer obtaining financing. If the bankruptcy is known to the buyer broker, he or she is required to disclose that fact to the seller. In this unique circumstance, the buyer's broker would not be guilty of violating the fiduciary responsibility of confidentiality. Bankruptcy would generally affect any buyer's ability to obtain future financing; so it becomes a material fact concerning the buyer's ability to perform and conclude a transaction, and as such it requires disclosure. In the reverse, if no financing contingency was required for the sale to take place, no disclosure would be required on the part of the buyer or the buyer's broker.

■ THE BROKER'S COMPENSATION

The broker's compensation is specified in the listing agreement, management agreement, or other contract with the principal and is subject to negotiation between the parties. Compensation usually is computed as a percentage of the total amount of money involved, but it could be a flat fee or any other consideration.

Compensation usually is considered to be earned when the broker has accomplished the work for which he or she was hired after a seller accepts an offer from a ready, willing, and able buyer. A **ready, willing, and able buyer** is one who is *prepared to buy on the seller's terms, is financially capable, and is ready to take positive steps to complete the transaction.*

Many listing agreements contain a preclusive agreement (an "as, if, and when" clause) providing that the broker will not collect the commission unless and until the sale has actually closed. The broker, however, is usually entitled to a commission if the transaction is not completed for any of the following reasons:

- The owner changes his or her mind and refuses to sell (with no preclusive agreement as previously mentioned) when a licensee presents a full-price offer with no contingencies.

- The owner commits fraud with respect to the transaction.
- The owner is unable to deliver possession within a reasonable time.
- The owner insists on terms not in the listing (for example, the right to restrict the use of the property). The owner and the buyer agree to cancel the transaction.

In other words, *a broker generally is due a commission if a sale is not consummated because of the seller's default.* In rare situations, the commission may still be due even when it is the buyer who defaults.

There are generally three events that entitle a broker to compensation under the law:

1. He or she must be the holder of a valid license at all times during the transaction and collection.
2. He or she was either employed under a listing or other employment agreement or was authorized to perform the services in question.
3. He or she was the procuring cause.

Note: In every transaction, items 2 and 3 above go hand in hand. In other words, the one who was either authorized or employed would always end up being the procuring cause.

The broker is entitled to a fee if he or she is the **procuring cause of sale**; produces a ready, willing, and able buyer; or brings about a meeting of the minds. If several brokers disagree as to which one brought about a sale, the one with the best claim to be the procuring cause is that broker who brought the parties into agreement, as evidenced by the sales contract. A **meeting of the minds** is said to have taken place when the parties are in agreement on price, down payment, financing method, and other essential terms.

New York's Real Property Law makes it illegal for a broker to share a commission with unlicensed people. This regulation forbids any form of gift or compensation, such as giving a television to a friend for providing a valuable lead or paying finder's fees and portions of the commission.

Compensation by both parties is permissible if there is full knowledge and consent of both parties.

Salesperson's Compensation

The compensation of a salesperson is set by agreement between the broker and the salesperson. A broker may pay a salary to a salesperson or, more commonly, a share of the commissions from transactions originated by a salesperson (the commission "split"). *The salesperson may never accept compensation directly from any buyer or seller, and may not accept compensation from any broker (see paragraph directly below), except the one broker with whom he or she is associated (article 175.B).*

A salesperson may, however, accept compensation from a former broker for fees earned when he or she was associated with that broker.

■ TERMINATION OF AGENCY

Because the agency relationship involves so many responsibilities, it is important to know how agencies are created and how they are terminated. An agency relationship may be terminated at any time (except when coupled with an interest) for any of the following reasons:

An Agency May Be Terminated By:

- Death or incompetence of either party
- Destruction or condemnation of the property
- Expiration of the terms
- Mutual agreement
- Renunciation by agent
- Revocation by principal
- Bankruptcy
- Completion of the purpose

- Death or incompetence of either party (Although death will terminate an agency, it does not necessarily terminate a contract of sale that was entered into during life by the deceased party.)
- Destruction or condemnation of the property
- Expiration of the terms of the agency
- Mutual agreement to terminate the agency
- Renunciation by the agent or revocation by the principal (In New York, the principal acting in good faith always has the power to cancel a listing at any time. The principal may, however, be required to reimburse the broker for expenses if the principal cancels before the agency's expiration. Damages could be awarded to the agent if the principal acted in bad faith.)
- Bankruptcy of either party
- Completion or fulfillment of the purpose for which the agency was created

The question of when an agency relationship ends can be important. For example, suppose agent John listed and sold Margaret's property. Three weeks after closing, Margaret shows up at one of John's open houses. Is Margaret still John's client? Probably not, but John must clarify this with Margaret. Because it is often difficult to treat a former client as a customer, some firms will obtain a written dual agency consent agreement from both parties or enter into a buyer agency relationship with the former client.

The broker may not disclose to a new client information obtained in confidence from a former client during the agency relationship. Even though the agency relationship may have terminated, the duty of confidentiality has not.

■ ANTITRUST

Each brokerage is free to set its own fee schedules and to negotiate different charges with individual clients. Any agreement between two different firms to set standard rates, however, is a serious violation of antitrust laws. Additionally, any agreement between two or more companies to boycott some other company is a violation. The subject of boycotting has taken on greater importance recently with the emergence of discount brokerages. Discount brokerage firms offer "unbundled" services in return for low fees. In some cases, the only service offered may be entering the client's property into the local **multiple listing service (MLS)**.

Real estate licensees must refrain from any discussion of fees except when two firms are cooperating on the sale of a multiple-listed property. Merely remaining in the room while prohibited discussions are going on has been considered evidence of guilt in the past. Antitrust violations can have drastic consequences.

■ ANTITRUST LAWS

The real estate industry is subject to federal and state antitrust laws.

Antitrust can be defined as any business activity that would otherwise result in

- a monopoly and/or
- a restraint of trade, and
- that would be deemed a harmful act or
- that would act as an impedance against free enterprise and competition.

There are four distinct acts that violate antitrust laws:

1. Price-fixing
2. Group boycotts
3. Market allocation agreements
4. Tie-in arrangements

We will examine each of the four violations shortly, but first let's look at the history of these laws.

History of Antitrust Laws

In 1890, the Sherman Act was enacted into law. Previous to the enactment of the law, a variety of business monopolies began to develop. This required government to react to this dilemma. In 1914, the Federal Trade Commission (FTC) was created by Congress with powers that included the following:

- Overseeing business practices
- The ability to declare that certain trade practices were deemed unfair
- Enforcing compliance with the Sherman and Clayton Acts.

Similarly, in 1914, the Clayton Act was created. Its purpose was to supplement the Sherman Act (which lacked the teeth for enforcement); the act itself covered the same general purpose of the Sherman Act. The Sherman and Clayton acts prohibit the four activities detailed below.

Price-Fixing

Illegal **price-fixing** occurs when competing brokers get together to set commission rates, rather than letting competition in the open market establish those rates. This is deemed by the federal authorities to be a *conspiracy to price fix.*

A conspiracy is defined as *two or more persons or parties acting in a manner that would otherwise negatively impact the ability of others to compete within a marketplace.*

Each real estate company, of course, is free to set its own fee schedule and to negotiate various rates with individual buyers or sellers if it wishes. The violations occur *when competing firms agree to act together,* in what the U.S. Justice Department calls **restraint of trade.**

It's not that simple, though. Real estate companies—and agents—have been prosecuted under the Sherman Antitrust Act for what appeared to be innocent discussions with agents from other firms. A licensee should walk away immediately even from what might seem like the most trivial conversation about rates with someone from another brokerage. (The only exception might be concerning a particular property the two firms have cooperated in selling.)

For example, broker Max and broker Ian are owners of two competing real estate firms. As friendly competitors, they meet for dinner. Ian asks Max, "What are you guys getting these days for commission rates on sale transactions?"

The resulting conversation would be considered conspiracy to *price fix*.

Group Boycott

In the past, discussions about the negative qualities of a third company have been interpreted as a **group boycott**—a conspiracy to boycott that firm and drive it out of business. Licensees must learn which topics must be avoided when engaging in conversation with agents from other companies.

For example, broker Mark and broker Eileen are owners of two competing real estate firms. They are also friendly competitors. One night over a casual dinner, Mark brings to Eileen's attention that ABC Realty, a real estate brokerage firm, has just come to town. Mark suggests to Eileen, "Let's not do business with ABC Realty. Maybe they'll just go away."

This would be considered a conspiracy to *group boycott*.

Market Allocation

Market allocation might occur when competing firms agree to split up an area and refrain from doing business in each other's territories.

For example, as in the group boycott example above, broker Maggie and broker Isabel, owners of two friendly competing real estate firms, are meeting for coffee. Isabel suggests to Maggie, "You have always done business primarily on the east side of town, while I have always done business on the west side of town. Why don't we draw an imaginary line down the center of town, and I won't do business in your area if you don't do business in my area."

This would be a *market allocation agreement*.

Tie-in Arrangement

A **tie-in arrangement** normally occurs when a selling party conditions the sale of an item. The condition might require the buyer (as a prerequisite to the purchase of that item) to purchase another item or the seller will refuse the sale of the original item to the buyer.

For example, a buyer approaches a seller to purchase his or her property. As a condition of sale, the seller requires the buyer to obtain title insurance *only from the seller's title company* or the seller will not sell the property to the buyer.

That would be considered a *tie-in arrangement*.

Penalties for violating antitrust laws.   Penalties for violating antitrust laws exist for individuals and business entities.

Violation of the Sherman and Clayton acts for *individuals* bears the following penalties:

1. Fines of up to $350,000 and/or
2. Felony prison sentencing of up to three years

The Department of Justice may impose other fines, and the FTC, which has no penal sanctions, has powers of enforcement as they relate to the Sherman and Clayton acts.

Violation of the Sherman and Clayton acts for *business entities* bears the following penalties:

1. Fines of up to $10,000,000 and/or
2. Other fines imposed by the Department of Justice

It should be noted that the great disparity in fines between business entities and individuals is meant to compensate for the fact that a business entity cannot serve a prison sentence; therefore, heavy fines are assessed to deter a repeat offense.

■ SUMMARY

The law of agency covers the legal relationship between real estate brokers and salespersons and the sellers, buyers, landlords, and tenants who hire them to assist in real estate transactions. The person who hires an agent is known as the principal, or client. The relationship between them is known as a fiduciary one, a relationship of trust and confidence. Third parties with whom the agent deals are simply customers. The client is owed specific fiduciary duties. The customer is owed only honest dealing.

A universal agent may represent the client in all matters. A general agent such as a property manager is entrusted with a specific range of matters. Most real estate brokers act as special agents and are authorized to represent the client in one specific matter.

An agency can be created by an express agreement, oral or written, or by the action of the parties. An agent does not necessarily represent the party that pays the compensation. Dual agency, in which the broker represents both parties, is a difficult situation, but legally possible if both parties give written consent to the situation.

The agent's fiduciary duties to the principal include reasonable care, confidentiality (except when it would mean dishonesty to the customer), loyalty, and obedience to lawful instructions, accounting, and disclosure. Agents need not disclose the existence of "stigmas" on the property, but like the seller, they are responsible for disclosing "latent," or hidden, defects.

The broker's compensation may be in the form of a percentage of the sales price, a fixed fee, or an hourly wage. By law it is considered earned when the broker presents a ready, willing, and able buyer. However, the broker and principal/client can always modify this and determine that the brokerage commission shall not be deemed earned until further action, for example, a contract signing or closing has occurred.

An agency can be terminated by the death, bankruptcy, or incompetence of either party; destruction of property; expiration of the term of the agency agreement; renunciation by the agent or revocation by the principal; or completion of the purpose for which the agency was created. The duty of confidentiality, however, lasts after the agency has ended.

Antitrust laws prohibit competing brokers from discussing or publishing commission rates charged to clients. Brokers also must refrain from negative discussions about other brokers to avoid the appearance of a group boycott.

QUESTIONS

1. The relationship between broker and seller is generally a(n)
   a. special agency.
   b. general agency.
   c. ostensible agency.
   d. universal agency.

2. A broker hired by an owner to sell a parcel of real estate *MUST* comply with
   a. any instructions of the owner.
   b. the law of agency.
   c. the principle of estoppel.
   d. all instructions of the buyer.

3. A buyer's broker is told by the buyer that he had filed for bankruptcy the year before. The buyer's broker
   a. should discuss with the buyer her duty to reveal the bankruptcy to the MLS.
   b. must discuss the buyer's finances with the seller honestly.
   c. may politely refuse to provide any information to the seller that would violate her duty of confidentiality to the buyer.
   d. has no responsibility to the seller because she is the buyer's agent.

4. A listing may be terminated when either broker or principal
   a. gets married.
   b. goes bankrupt.
   c. overfinances other property.
   d. becomes terminally ill.

5. When retained by the buyer, the broker owes a prospective seller
   a. obedience to lawful instructions.
   b. confidentiality about the seller's financial situation.
   c. honest, straightforward treatment.
   d. undivided loyalty.

6. The salesperson who sincerely tries to represent both buyer and seller is practicing
   a. fraud.   c. dual agency.
   b. puffing.   d. general agency.

7. A seller who wishes to cancel a listing agreement in New York
   a. must cite a legally acceptable reason.
   b. may not cancel without the agent's consent.
   c. may be held liable for money and time expended by the broker.
   d. may not sell the property for six months afterward.

8. A broker is entitled to collect a commission from both the seller and the buyer when
   a. the broker holds a state license.
   b. the buyer and the seller are related.
   c. both parties know about and agree to such a transaction.
   d. both parties have attorneys.

9. A house was purchased in 1950 for $4,500. The seller knows properties have appreciated and asks the broker to try to sell it for $100,000. The broker knows the value could be more than $200,000. The broker should
   a. take the listing as offered and sell it quickly.
   b. purchase the house himself for the full $100,000, including in the contract that he is a licensed broker.
   c. buy the house through his aunt, who has a different last name.
   d. tell the seller that the house is worth much more.

10. An example of a latent defect would be a
    a. large crack in the dining room ceiling.
    b. roof with warped shingles.
    c. used-car lot next door.
    d. malfunctioning septic tank.

11. Commissions usually are earned when
    a. the buyer makes a purchase offer.
    b. the seller accepts the buyer's offer without conditions.
    c. a new mortgage has been promised by the lender.
    d. the title to the property is searched.

12. Even if a proposed transaction does not go through, the broker sometimes may collect a commission if the
    a. buyer turns out to be financially unable.
    b. seller refuses to do repairs required by the lender.
    c. seller simply backs out.
    d. lender does not appraise the house for the sales price.

13. A meeting of the minds occurs when the
    a. seller signs a listing agreement.
    b. buyer is introduced to the seller.
    c. buyer and seller agree on the price and terms of the sale.
    d. final closing (settlement) of the transaction takes place.

14. George signed a 120-day listing with Bay Realty. After 60 days George decided not to sell. He told Bay Realty he no longer wanted them to market his house. When is the agency of Bay Realty terminated?
    a. On the 121st day
    b. After a reasonable time
    c. On the 61st day
    d. When the listing expires

15. A seller's broker must disclose to a prospective buyer that the
    a. heating system works well.
    b. last owner was murdered there.
    c. seller has AIDS.
    d. house is haunted.

16. In the spirit of cooperation, broker Bob approached two other community brokers and recommended that they set standard fee schedules and commission rates. Bob's recommendation is
    a. legal if other community brokers are allowed to participate in the agreement.
    b. legal if the agreement is in writing..
    c. illegal if salespersons working for the brokers are not consulted.
    d. illegal under any circumstances.

17. To successfully sue a broker for misrepresentation, the buyer must be able to prove that
    a. the buyer asked the broker to verify the misstatement.
    b. the misstatement is in writing.
    c. the buyer was damaged from relying on the truth of the statement.
    d. the seller knew of the statement.

18. Seller Ed's willingness to accept buyer Betty's offer for a lot on Hill Street only if Betty will purchase homeowners' insurance from Ed's insurance brokerage is an example of
    a. a tie-in arrangement.
    b. a market allocation agreement.
    c. price-fixing.
    d. a restraint of trade.

19. Broker Bob does not think the seller will seriously consider an offer he received for 20 percent less than the listing price. Bob should
    a. discourage the potential buyer from making the offer.
    b. encourage the potential buyer to increase the offer.
    c. wait until he receives more realistic offers and present all offers together.
    d. submit the offer to the seller.

20. An acronym to help remember the fiduciary duties of a broker is
    a. CC-MOAP.
    b. CC-LOAD.
    c. CL-DOAL.
    d. PP-COLA.

CHAPTER 3

Agency and Real Estate Brokerage

■ KEY TERMS

broker's agent
commercial transaction
dual agency
exclusive-agency listing
exclusive right to
  represent

exclusive-right-to-sell
  listing
first substantive contact
listing broker
open listing
residential transaction

selling broker
subagency
undisclosed dual agency
vicarious liability

■ NEW YORK AGENCY DISCLOSURE REQUIREMENTS

New York's Real Property Law section 443 (RPL 443) requires that brokers and salespersons give prospective sellers and buyers (or landlords and tenants) upon first substantive contact a disclosure statement that describes the roles of sellers' agents, buyers' agents, listing brokers' agents, and dual agents. (See Figures 3.1 and 3.2.) The buyer or seller is asked to sign an acknowledgment certifying that he or she has read the disclosure form and understands the role of the particular agent in the transaction. The written disclosure is intended, among other things, to warn members of the public not to reveal to the other party's agent any information they would prefer to keep confidential.

RPL 443-1f applies to residential transactions involving four or fewer units intended for dwelling purposes.

A **residential transaction** is defined as *any transaction involving the sale or lease of four or fewer units intended for dwelling purposes*. However, it *does not include* unimproved real property or cooperative or condominium units in a building containing more than four dwelling units.

Any transaction involving five or more units intended for dwelling purposes would fall under the category of a **commercial transaction**, regardless of whether the property is a residential property. It is important not to confuse the definition of a residential transaction (as explained above) with the definition of residential as a category under zoning laws.

A listing agent should obtain the seller's signed acknowledgment before entering a listing agreement for a residential transaction. Likewise, a buyer's agent should obtain the buyer's signed acknowledgment before entering an agreement to represent the buyer. In 2006, the New York legislature passed a bill replacing the agency disclosure form with separate forms for sales and lease transactions and defining allowable dual agency. The law took effect January 1, 2007, and revisions went into effect on January 1, 2008.

Signed Acknowledgments

A seller's agent *must* provide the disclosure and obtain the acknowledgment from all prospective buyers or their buyer agents at the time of the **first substantive contact**. A first substantive contact with a buyer occurs when the buyer walks into the agent's office and begins discussing his or her real estate needs or financial situation, or when the buyer meets the agent at the advertised listed property with the intent to inspect the property for purchase. Disclosure should be made to the buyer *prior to* entering the property being shown.

Similarly, buyers' agents must provide the disclosure to the seller or the seller's agent at the time of first substantive contact. That might occur when the seller begins explaining his or her reasons for selling or simply greets an agent who is showing someone through the property. A copy of the required disclosure is shown in Figure 3.1. A similar form is used for landlord-tenant agency disclosures. (See Figure 3.2.)

Part 175.23a of the rules for guidance of real estate brokers and salespersons promulgated by the New York secretary of state (entitled "Records of transactions to be maintained") requires each licensed broker to keep and/or maintain transaction records obtained in the course of a broker's business—with copies of the signed agency disclosure forms—for no less than three years from conclusion of business.

RPL 443-3f states that should any buyer or seller refuse to sign the forms, the agent may make a written oath or affirmation that the disclosure form was provided to that party. This form should be notarized. (See Figure 3.3.) This statement can be kept in the broker's file in place of the signed acknowledgment. As is the case for all records of transactions held by the broker, they should be maintained for a minimum of three years following conclusion of the transaction. It should be noted that the aforementioned disclosure form does not apply to commercial transactions.

F I G U R E   **3.1**

Agency Disclosure Form for Buyer and Seller

New York State
DEPARTMENT OF STATE
Division of Licensing Services
P.O. Box 22001
Albany, NY 12201-2001

Customer Service: (518) 474-4429
Fax: (518) 473-6648
Web site: www.dos.state.ny.us

New York State Disclosure Form for Buyer and Seller

THIS IS NOT A CONTRACT

New York State law requires real estate licensees who are acting as agents of buyers and sellers of property to advise the potential buyers and sellers with whom they work of the nature of their agency relationship and the rights and obligations it creates. This disclosure will help you to make informed choices about your relationship with the real estate broker and its sales associates.

Throughout the transaction you may receive more than one disclosure form. The law requires each agent assisting in the transaction to present you with this disclosure form. A real estate agent is a person qualified to advise about real estate.

If you need legal, tax or other advice, consult with a professional in that field.

Disclosure Regarding Real Estate Agency Relationships

Seller's Agent

A seller's agent is an agent who is engaged by a seller to represent the seller's interest. The seller's agent does this by securing a buyer for the seller's home at a price and on terms acceptable to the seller. A seller's agent has, without limitation, the following fiduciary duties to the seller: reasonable care, undivided loyalty, confidentiality, full disclosure, obedience and duty to account. A seller's agent does not represent the interests of the buyer. The obligations of a seller's agent are also subject to any specific provisions set forth in an agreement between the agent and the seller. In dealings with the buyer, a seller's agent should (a) exercise reasonable skill and care in performance of the agent's duties; (b) deal honestly, fairly and in good faith; and (c) disclose all facts known to the agent materially affecting the value or desirability of property, except as otherwise provided by law.

Buyer's Agent

A buyer's agent is an agent who is engaged by a buyer to represent the buyer's interest. The buyer's agent does this

by negotiating the purchase of a home at a price and on terms acceptable to the buyer. A buyer's agent has, without limitation, the following fiduciary duties to the buyer: reasonable care, undivided loyalty, confidentiality, full disclosure, obedience and duty to account. A buyer's agent does not represent the interest of the seller. The obligations of a buyer's agent are also subject to any specific provisions set forth in an agreement between the agent and the buyer. In dealings with the seller, a buyer's agent should (a) exercise reasonable skill and care in performance of the agent's duties; (b) deal honestly, fairly and in good faith; and (c) disclose all facts known to the agent materially affecting the buyer's ability and/or willingness to perform a contract to acquire seller's property that are not inconsistent with the agent's fiduciary duties to the buyer.

Broker's Agents

A broker's agent is an agent that cooperates or is engaged by a listing agent or a buyer's agent (but does not work for the same firm as the listing agent or buyer's agent) to assist the listing agent or buyer's agent in locating a property to sell or buy, respectively, for the listing agent's seller or the buyer agent's buyer. The broker's agent does not have a direct relationship with the buyer or seller and the buyer or seller can not provide instructions or direction directly to the broker's agent. The buyer and the seller therefore do not have vicarious liability for the acts of the broker's agent. The listing agent or buyer's agent do provide direction and instruction to the broker's agent and therefore the listing agent or buyer's agent will have liability for the acts of the broker's agent.

Dual Agent

A real estate broker may represent both the buyer and seller if both the buyer and seller give their informed consent in writing. In such a dual agency situation, the agent will not be able to provide the full range of fiduciary duties to the buyer and seller. The obligations of an agent are also subject to any specific provisions set forth in an agreement between

DOS 1736 (Rev. 1/08)

Source: New York State Department of State, Division of Licensing Services.

Agency Disclosure Form for Buyer and Seller

the agent, and the buyer and seller. An agent acting as a dual agent must explain carefully to both the buyer and seller that the agent is acting for the other party as well. The agent should also explain the possible effects of dual representation, including that by consenting to the dual agency relationship the buyer and seller are giving up their right to undivided loyalty. A buyer or seller should carefully consider the possible consequences of a dual agency relationship before agreeing to such representation.

Dual Agent with Designated Sales Agents

If the buyer and seller provide their informed consent in writing, the principals and the real estate broker who represents both parties as a dual agent may designate a sales agent to represent the buyer and another sales agent to represent the seller to negotiate the purchase and sale of real estate. A sales agent works under the supervision of the real estate broker. With the informed consent of the buyer and the seller in writing, the designated sales agent for the buyer will function as the buyer's agent representing the interests of and advocating on behalf of the buyer and the designated sales agent for the seller will function as the seller's agent representing the interests of and advocating on behalf of the seller in the negotiations between the buyer and seller. A designated sales agent cannot provide the full range of fiduciary duties to the buyer or seller. The designated sales agent must explain that like the dual agent under whose supervision they function, they cannot provide undivided loyalty. A buyer or seller should carefully consider the possible consequences of a dual agency relationship with designated sales agents before agreeing to such representation.

This form was provided to me by _____ (print name of licensee) of_____ (print name of company, firm or brokerage), a licensed real estate broker acting in the interest of the:

(___) Seller as a (check relationship below)   (___) Buyer as a (check relationship below)

    (___) Seller's agent   (___) Buyer's agent

    (___) Broker's agent   (___) Broker's agent

        (___) Dual agent

        (___) Dual agent with designated sales agent

If dual agent with designated sales agents is checked: _____ is appointed to represent the buyer; and _____ is appointed to represent the seller in this transaction.

(I)(We) acknowledge receipt of a copy of this disclosure form: signature of { } Buyer(s) and/or { } Seller(s):

_____   _____

_____   _____

Date: _____   Date: _____

FIGURE 3.2

Agency Disclosure Form for Landlord and Tenant

New York State
DEPARTMENT OF STATE
Division of Licensing Services
P.O. Box 22001
Albany, NY 12201-2001

Customer Service: (518) 474-4429
Fax: (518) 473-6648
Web site: www.dos.state.ny.us

New York State Disclosure Form for Landlord and Tenant

THIS IS NOT A CONTRACT

New York State law requires real estate licensees who are acting as agents of landlords and tenants of real property to advise the potential landlords and tenants with whom they work of the nature of their agency relationship and the rights and obligations it creates. This disclosure will help you to make informed choices about your relationship with the real estate broker and its sales associates.

Throughout the transaction you may receive more than one disclosure form. The law requires each agent assisting in the transaction to present you with this disclosure form. A real estate agent is a person qualified to advise about real estate.

If you need legal, tax or other advice, consult with a professional in that field.

Disclosure Regarding Real Estate Agency Relationships

Landlord's Agent

A landlord's agent is an agent who is engaged by a landlord to represent the landlord's interest. The landlord's agent does this by securing a tenant for the landlord's apartment or house at a rent and on terms acceptable to the landlord. A landlord's agent has, without limitation, the following fiduciary duties to the landlord: reasonable care, undivided loyalty, confidentiality, full disclosure, obedience and duty to account. A landlord's agent does not represent the interests of the tenant. The obligations of a landlord's agent are also subject to any specific provisions set forth in an agreement between the agent and the landlord. In dealings with the tenant, a landlord's agent should (a) exercise reasonable skill and care in performance of the agent's duties; (b) deal honestly, fairly and in good faith; and (c) disclose all facts known to the agent materially affecting the value or desirability of property, except as otherwise provided by law.

Tenant's Agent

A tenant's agent is an agent who is engaged by a tenant to represent the tenant's interest. The tenant's agent does this by negotiating the rental or lease of an apartment or house at a rent and on terms acceptable to the tenant. A tenant's agent has, without limitation, the following fiduciary duties to the tenant: reasonable care, undivided loyalty, confidentiality, full disclosure, obedience and duty to account. A tenant's agent does not represent the interest of the landlord. The obligations of a tenant's agent are also subject to any specific provisions set forth in an agreement between the agent and the tenant. In dealings with the landlord, a tenants agent should (a) exercise reasonable skill and care in performance of the agent's duties; (b) deal honestly, fairly and in good faith; and (c) disclose all facts known to the tenants ability and/or willingness to perform a contract to rent or lease landlord's property that are not consistent with the agent's fiduciary duties to the buyer.

Broker's Agents

A broker's agent is an agent that cooperates or is engaged by a listing agent or a tenant's agent (but does not work for the same firm as the listing agent or tenant's agent) to assist the listing agent or tenant's agent in locating a property to rent or lease for the listing agent's landlord or the tenant agent's tenant. The broker's agent does not have a direct relationship with the tenant or landlord and the tenant or landlord can not provide instructions or direction directly to the broker's agent. The tenant and the landlord therefore do not have vicarious liability for the acts of the broker's agent. The listing agent or tenant's agent do provide direction and instruction to the broker's agent and therefore the listing agent or tenant's agent will have liability for the acts of the broker's agent.

Dual Agent

A real estate broker may represent both the tenant and the landlord if both the tenant and landlord give their in-

DOS 1735 (Rev. 1/08)

F I G U R E   3.2 (CONTINUED)

Agency Disclosure Form for Landlord and Tenant

formed consent in writing. In such a dual agency situation, the agent will not be able to provide the full range of fiduciary duties to the landlord and the tenant. The obligations of an agent are also subject to any specific provisions set forth in an agreement between the agent, and the tenant and landlord. An agent acting as a dual agent must explain carefully to both the landlord and tenant that the agent is acting for the other party as well. The agent should also explain the possible effects of dual representation, including that by consenting to the dual agency relationship the landlord and tenant are giving up their right to undivided loyalty. A landlord and tenant should carefully consider the possible consequences of a dual agency relationship before agreeing to such representation.

Dual Agent with Designated Sales Agents

If the tenant and the landlord provide their informed consent in writing, the principals and the real estate brok-

er who represents both parties as a dual agent may designate a sales agent to represent the tenant and another sales agent to represent the landlord. A sales agent works under the supervision of the real estate broker. With the informed consent in writing of the tenant and the landlord, the designated sales agent for the tenant will function as the tenant's agent representing the interests of and advocating on behalf of the tenant and the designated sales agent for the landlord will function as the landlord's agent representing the interests of and advocating on behalf of the landlord in the negotiations between the tenant and the landlord. A designated sales agent cannot provide the full range of fiduciary duties to the landlord or tenant. The designated sales agent must explain that like the dual agent under whose supervision they function, they cannot provide undivided loyalty. A landlord or tenant should carefully consider the possible consequences of a dual agency relationship with designated sales agents before agreeing to such representation.

This form was provided to me by _____ (print name of licensee) of _____ (print name of company, firm or brokerage), a licensed real estate broker acting in the interest of the:

    (___) Seller as a (check relationship below)   (___) Buyer as a (check relationship below)

        (___) Seller's agent   (___) Buyer's agent

        (___) Broker's agent   (___) Broker's agent

                              (___) Dual agent

                              (___) Dual agent with designated sales agent

If dual agent with designated sales agents is checked: _____ is appointed to represent the tenant; and _____ is appointed to represent the landlord in this transaction.

(I)(We) acknowledge receipt of a copy of this disclosure form: signature of { } Landlord(s) and/or { } Tenant(s):

_____   _____

_____   _____

    Date: _____   Date: _____

DOS 1735 (Rev. 1/08)

Disclosure Affirmation

DECLARATION PURSUANT TO SECTION 443 (3) (F) OF THE REAL PROPERTY LAW

_____ (name), being duly sworn, deposes and says:

1. I am the principal broker/associate broker/licensed salesperson affiliated with _____ (name of agency).

2. I make this Affidavit in compliance with Section 443 (3) (F) of the New York State Real Property Law.

3. On the _____ day of _____ _____ , 20____ , I presented to _____ (name of buyer or seller) the disclosure forms required pursuant to Section 443 of the Real Property Law. The form of the Disclosure Form as presented is attached to this statement.

4. The above named buyer/seller refused to execute an acknowledgment of the receipt of this disclosure form despite my request that it be executed.

5. A copy of this statement and additional copies of the Disclosure Form are being mailed to the person(s) named in paragraph 3, contemporaneously with the execution of this Affidavit.

_____

(Name)

RPL 443 ("Disclosure regarding real estate agency relationship; form") also provides for brokers' agents. A **broker's agent** is a cooperating broker who is an agent of the listing broker but not strictly a subagent of the seller. A broker's agent has fiduciary duties to the seller, but the seller is not liable for acts of the broker's agent unless the seller specifically authorizes those acts. This is intended to eliminate a principal's "vicarious liability" for acts of subagents within a transaction. This liability usually arises from the acts of others. (Although this concept came directly from the Department of State, it remains to be seen whether this limited liability will be upheld by the courts.)

A second disclosure requirement is found in the Department of State (DOS) Regulation 175.7, which states, "A real estate broker shall make it clear for which party he is acting and he shall not receive compensation from more than one party except with the full knowledge and consent of all parties." This requirement applies to all types of transactions, not just residential.

The requirement regarding compensation from more than one party is not strictly limited to compensation related to the sale itself; _it applies to any compensation that is in any way related to the transaction_. Thus, a selling agent who accepts compensation for arranging the buyer's loan (mortgage broker's commission) must disclose this to the parties, in addition to sharing in the commission split (if any) for the sale.

Signing an agency disclosure form (which does not apply to commercial transactions) does not in and of itself create an agency relationship, but also does not relieve the agent from other requirements under the law of agency. It is not a contract between agent and client. This form is intended to give full disclosure by a licensee to the appropriate party receiving the disclosure and to create awareness for the benefit of the general public. Merely having a prospective buyer sign the acknowledgment that a disclosure form stated the broker was acting as a buyer's agent does not make it so. The relationship should be established through a separate written buyer-agency agreement, similar to the listing agreement used by sellers' agents.

■ AGENCY ALTERNATIVES

An agent is someone who represents a principal in a transaction. The agent owes the principal the duties of *reasonable care*, *confidentiality*, *loyalty*, *obedience*, *accounting*, and *disclosure of any facts* that might affect the principal's decisions. Agency relationships between a broker and a seller are usually created through a contractual agreement, for example, a written *listing agreement*, in which a broker agrees to act as the agent of a seller. Agency relationships between a broker and a buyer are usually created through *buyer-broker agency agreements*. In either case, whether one enters into a listing agreement with a seller or a buyer-broker agreement with a buyer, both agreements will create the agency relationship. Both agreements can be thought of as "employment contracts."

Real estate brokers frequently enlist the help of other brokers to market their listed properties. In many places throughout the state of New York, a common example of this sort of collaboration is a *multiple listing service* (MLS) for residential properties. By using the MLS as a marketing vehicle, participating brokers agree to work together to achieve a sale. As a result, commissions are generally shared between the **listing broker** and the **selling broker** (the one who finds the buyer). Under certain circumstances, this arrangement may create a relationship referred to as **subagency**.

Subagency means

- the selling broker is acting as a subagent of the seller, or
- the selling broker may be acting as the *broker's agent*.

Note: When a property is listed within the MLS, it will generally (unless otherwise posted) represent an "invitation to a subagency relationship." This means that if the selling broker accepts the offer of subagency through the MLS, he or she has fiduciary responsibilities that will be owed to the seller of the property. As in any invitation that one receives in life, acceptance is not mandatory; however, declaration and disclosure of the selling broker's relationship should be made at *first substantive contact*. However, several MLS contracts offer "cooperation" to various types of agents, not just subagents. Licensees should always be familiar with the agreements they will be using when practicing their trade.

For example, selling broker Mary Anne contacts a listing agent from the MLS. Mary Anne introduces herself as the buyer's broker, or as the exclusive agent on behalf of the buyer. That introduction is a rejection of the invitation to the subagency relationship offered through the MLS; not *all* MLS postings are invitations to subagency. Mary Anne is clearly stating that she will continue acting exclusively on behalf of her principal, a buyer, and will not take on the role of seller's agent, acting on behalf of the property's seller.

■ SUBAGENCY

When a broker accepts a listing from a seller, the agency relationship is clear:

- The broker becomes the seller's agent.
- By extension, any salespersons who work for the broker become subagents of the seller, because they are agents of the broker.

The situation is less clear, however, in the case of another broker who procures a buyer for the property. Is the other broker acting as a subagent of the seller, an agent of the buyer, or an agent of the listing broker?

In the past, listed properties (particularly those offered through a multiple listing service) were offered on a "blanket unilateral offer of subagency." As a result of this arrangement, the party (someone not in the employ of the seller's listing broker) procuring the buyer would act as a subagent of the seller. As a subagent of the seller, he or she owed fiduciary responsibilities to the seller and would not act as the buyer's agent. This arrangement created vicarious liability (responsibility for the actions of another) to the seller. Today, although this form of agency relationship still exists, it is not as common as in the past. There are alternative agency relationships that eliminate a seller's vicarious liability.

Brokerage without Subagency

As a principal, the seller is liable for actions not only of the listing agent but also of subagents. This potentially enormous liability—for human rights violations, among other problems—is the reason some sellers do not want to offer any form of subagency relationship.

If a seller does not wish to offer subagency to MLS members but still wants to gain exposure through an MLS, he or she can direct that the listing agent may split the commission with another broker who produces the buyer, without the other broker acting as the seller's subagent. The seller agrees to pay the selling broker part of the commission but does not risk being held liable for any statements or actions on the part of the selling broker. With more and more buyers being represented by their own brokers these days, this simple offer of cooperation and commission sharing solves problems that used to arise about how the buyer's broker is to be paid.

Please note that although New York City does not have a formalized MLS, the attorney general's office has determined by letter ruling that if the selling agent is from a different brokerage company than the listing agent, the selling agent is a buyer's agent and not a subagent of the seller or selling agent.

Disclosure of Subagency

Buyers who use the services of a seller's broker to find a property often believe the broker is working on their behalf, when, in fact, the broker has a fiduciary duty to act in the best interest of the seller.

For example, Jameson is looking for a house. She contacts Mendez, a broker, who shows her many houses over the course of several weeks. Jameson tells Mendez the kind of house she is looking for and gives him information about her ability to buy and her time frame for buying. By the time Jameson finds a house she is interested in, she feels very comfortable with Mendez and begins to think of Mendez as her real estate agent. In fact, Mendez is a subagent of the seller. Jameson makes an offer on the house, telling Mendez that she is willing to pay up to $8,000 more than her initial offer. Mendez has a duty to relay this information to the seller, who immediately counteroffers with a higher selling price. Because she wrongly believed Mendez to be acting on her behalf, Jameson will end up paying more for the house than she otherwise might have.

The written Agency Disclosure Statement shown in Figure 3.1, which Jameson should have received at the outset, should have warned her that Mendez, however helpful, was working for the seller and could not keep her information confidential.

◼ DUAL AGENCY

In New York, within specific parameters, dual agency is a legal form of agency relationship. In a **dual agency**, the broker represents both buyer and seller in the same transaction. Because the buyer and seller have competing goals, dual agency represents an inherent conflict of interest for the broker. It is often impossible for a dual agent to fully satisfy the fiduciary requirements of confidentiality and full disclosure with respect to both parties in a transaction. Consequently, dual agency by its nature may involve something less than full representation of each client and must be undertaken with care. In a dual agency relationship, the parties give up their right to full disclosure and undivided loyalty from the dual agent.

Disclosure of any information concerning either party to the transaction becomes a violation of that party's fiduciary relationship with the agent that acts in a dual capacity. This is a very dangerous relationship for the agent, since any comment can be construed by either party to the transaction as favoritism of one party over the other.

In 1997, Florida became the first state to outlaw dual agency relationships.

Informed Consent

Dual agency is legal; however, it is legal only with

1. the full disclosure by the agent to all interested parties to the transaction, and
2. the receipt by the agent of the informed consent of all interested parties to the transaction.

The aforementioned must occur prior to the creation of the agency.

To ensure informed consent, the agent should secure a *written document* signed by all interested parties. This document should indicate that the parties consent to the dual agency and understand that

◼ the agent may not provide undivided loyalty to either party;
◼ the parties' confidential information regarding pricing strategy will be protected, as well as any other information agreed to by the parties;

- the agent may be paid fees as specified, either by one or by both parties;
- dual agency does involve potential conflicts of interest because one principal may feel compromised unfairly or one might be favored over the other;
- if either principal is uncomfortable with the dual agency process, he or she should not proceed; and
- the parties should have obtained their attorneys' advice before proceeding in a dual agency situation.

RPL 443 provides a special form of acknowledgment for consensual dual agency transactions. This acknowledgment is required by law, but the broker also may have the parties sign a more specific consent to dual agency that spells out the precise nature of the relationship of the parties in the particular transaction. (See Figure 3.4.)

There is no blanket consent to dual agency. Each agreement must apply only to specific parties.

When dual agency exists but is not fully disclosed or consented to by the parties, the broker faces serious consequences. These include loss of license or other disciplinary action, loss of commission on the sale, and liability for damages if the sale is rescinded. Because of these risks, brokers must be constantly aware of the potential for *undisclosed dual agency* situations.

Undisclosed Dual Agency

A broker does not have to embark intentionally on a dual agency situation to suffer the consequences of undisclosed dual agency. In fact, undisclosed dual agency *is often unintentional*. Although the buyer and seller may specifically request that a broker act as a dual agent, a dual agency situation may arise without the broker's realizing it. Examples of such situations include in-house sales and sales by cooperating brokers who are acting as buyers' agents.

In-house sales. Whenever a broker takes a listing, the broker is the agent, and all salespeople who work for the broker are agents of the broker and therefore subagents of the seller. This is true for all salespeople in all offices of the brokerage. Any time that a salesperson or broker acts as a buyer's agent (either explicitly or implicitly) with respect to any of the firm's own listings, dual agency exists, and appropriate steps must be taken to avoid liability.

Company policy. The possibility of dual agency should be discussed with clients at the time the agency agreement (listing or buyer's broker) is entered. Clients should be informed of the possibility of in-house sales and of the policy of the broker's office regarding such sales. Many real estate firms incorporate additional clauses relating to these situations within their agency agreements.

For example, a buyer's broker agreement may contain a provision that states, "When a buyer is brought to a listing that is handled by the same brokerage firm representing that buyer, in this event, the agent represents the seller and not the buyer." The agent is advised to exercise special care and to be clear as to his or her relationships in these types of situations. This is not intended to suggest that

F I G U R E   3.4

Dual Agency Consent Form

Form M
6/30/95

INFORMED CONSENT TO DUAL AGENCY

Property Address: _____

Seller(s): _____

Name of Brokerage Firm: _____ **("Broker")**

Listing Salesperson: _____

Buyer(s): _____

Selling Salesperson: _____

1. **Consent to Dual Agency:**

    The Seller and Buyer acknowledge and agree that Broker and the listing and selling salespersons are undertaking a Consensual Dual Agency representation in the sale of the above property. Seller and Buyer have previously been informed of the possibility of a dual agency arising if a buyer client becomes interested in a seller client's property. Seller and Buyer have consented to this dual representation and hereby confirm their consent by signing below after reading the following description of the type of representation to be provided.

2. **Description of Broker's Role: Confidentiality and Disclosure of Information:**

    Because Broker is acting as agent for both Seller and Buyer in this transaction, Broker shall make every reasonable effort to remain impartial to Seller and Buyer. Seller and Buyer acknowledge that, prior to the time this Addendum was entered into, Broker acted as (exclusive) agent of the Seller and acted as (exclusive) agent of the Buyer. In those separate roles, Broker may have obtained information which, if disclosed, could harm the bargaining position of the party providing such information to Broker. Seller and Buyer agree that Broker shall not be obligated or liable to either party for refusing or failing to disclose information which in the sole discretion of Broker would harm one party's bargaining position but would benefit the other party.

    Nothing contained herein shall prevent Broker from disclosing to Buyer any known material defects that affect the property value. Broker agrees not to disclose confidential information to the other party, such as (a) to Buyer information about what price or terms Seller will accept other than the Listing Price and terms or (b) to Seller information about what price or terms Buyer will agree to other than any written offering price. In the event that Seller and Buyer do not enter into an agreement for the purchase and sale of Seller's property to Buyer, or in the event that the purchase and sale provided for in a contract of sale between Seller and Buyer does not close in accordance with its terms, this dual agency and this Consent may be terminated by any party, by mailing written notice to the others.

3. **Description of Seller's and Buyer's Role:**

    Seller and Buyer acknowledge that they are aware of the implications and consequences of Broker's dual agency role to facilitate a transaction, rather than act as an advocate for one party over the other, and that they have determined that the benefits of entering into this transaction, with the Broker acting as a dual agent outweigh those implications and consequences.

    Seller and Buyer acknowledge that they have been advised to seek independent legal counsel in order to assist them with any matter relating to a purchase and sale contract and any other aspect of the transaction. Seller and Buyer agree to indemnify and hold Broker harmless against all claims, damages, losses, expenses or liabilities arising from Broker's role as a dual agent except those arising from Broker's intentional wrongful acts or violation of the Real Property Law of the State of New York. Seller and Buyer shall have a duty to protect their own interests and should read this Consent carefully to ensure that it accurately sets forth the terms which they want included in the transaction.

    Both BUYER and SELLER understand and agree that BROKER shall have the right to collect a commission or fee from the transaction, pursuant to existing agreements, and acknowledge that it has been disclosed that BROKER will collect a fee of $_____ or _____% of the sales price which shall be paid as a cost of this transaction from the proceeds to be paid by BUYER to SELLER. Any prior agreements to the contrary are hereby superseded.

4. **Consequences of Dual Agency:**

    Seller and Buyer are giving up their right to have Broker's undivided loyalty to act at all times solely in their individual best interests to the exclusion of all other interests. Dual Agency may thus deprive Buyer and Seller of benefits they may have otherwise received in a Single Agency relationship. For example, as a seller represented by an Agent, Seller has the right to expect that Seller's agent will attempt to obtain the full asking price for the property. As a buyer, represented by an Agent, Buyer has the right to expect the Agent to work toward bringing about a transaction at the lowest possible price. A Dual Agent will not work on behalf of either party regarding price.

Dual Agency Consent Form

5.   **Fiduciary Duties:**
  *In theory, a Dual Agent owes both the buyer and seller the same fiduciary duties as if the Agent represented each alone. These duties include loyalty, obedience, disclosure, confidentiality, reasonable care, diligence and the duty to account. By consenting to dual agency, the conflicting duties to Buyer and Seller are reconciled by mutual agreement to forego them. The duty of undivided loyalty is forfeited in a Dual Agency relationship and instead the Dual Agent is required to act with fairness to each party. In addition, most of the other fiduciary obligations are affected because of the contrasting motivations of Buyer and Seller, who have agreed that the consensual dual agent will not favor the interests of one over those of the other.

6.   **Disputes:**
  In the event a dispute arises between Buyer and Seller, Broker may elect to withdraw from the transaction.

7.   **Description of Limited Agency Services:**
  WHAT BROKER AND ITS SALESPERSONS CAN DO FOR SELLERS AND BUYERS WHEN ACTING AS A DUAL AGENT:
    We will treat the Seller and Buyer honestly and fairly.
    We will provide helpful information about the property and neighborhood to the Buyer.
    We will respond accurately to questions about the property.
    We will disclose all material facts about the property that are known to us.
    We will disclose financial qualifications of the Buyer to the Seller.
    We can explain real estate terms and procedures.
    We can help the Buyer to arrange for property inspections.
    We can help the Buyer compare financing alternatives.
    We will provide information about comparable properties so the Seller and Buyer may make an educated decision on what price to accept and/or offer.
    We will work diligently to facilitate the sale and will advise when experts should be retained (lawyer, tax accountant, architect, etc.)
    We will act as a mediator and make recommendations for compromise between Seller and Buyer.

  WHAT BROKER AND ITS SALESPERSONS CANNOT DISCLOSE TO SELLERS AND BUYERS.
    We cannot disclose confidential information that we may know about the Seller and/or Buyer (e.g., motivation, to sell/buy; price/terms; negotiating strategy), without written permission of the Seller and/or Buyer.
    We cannot disclose the price the Seller will take other than the listing price without written permission of the Seller.
    We cannot disclose the price the Buyer is willing to pay without written permission of the Buyer.
    We cannot recommend or suggest a price the Buyer should offer or pay for the property.
    We cannot recommend or suggest a price the Seller should accept or counter.

8.   **Role of Salesperson:**
  The salesperson who has executed this Informed Consent To Dual Agency as the "Listing Salesperson" agrees that she(he) will continue to represent the interests of the Seller in all negotiations, discussions and procedures relating to this transaction. The person whose signature is set forth below and is designated as "Selling Salesperson" agrees that she(he) will continue to represent the interests of the Buyer in all negotiations, discussions and procedures relating to this transaction. Broker will act as an intermediary with respect to Seller and Buyer and except for the fiduciary duty to account for any monies which come into Broker's possession and the duty to exercise reasonable care, Broker will not have fiduciary duties to either Seller or Buyer to provide "undivided loyalty or obedience." If the salesperson who acted as the Listing Salesperson is also the Selling Salesperson, then such Salesperson will act as an intermediary with respect to Seller and Buyer.

  By signing below, you approve and agree that Broker and its salespersons may act as dual agents in this transaction.

  _____   _____
  Buyer   Date   Seller   Date

  _____   _____
  Buyer   Date   Seller   Date

  Broker
                                         _____
                                         Selling Salesperson

  By:_____
                                         _____
                                         Listing Salesperson

The Selling Salesperson whose signature appears above acknowledges that Buyer has signed this Consent before signing any written offer to purchase the property. The Listing Salesperson whose signature appears above acknowledges that the Seller has signed this Consent before signing the acceptance of an offer or a counter offer.

F:\WPDOCS\WCBR3213\CDA.EIS

a dual agency is unlawful but to make clear that company policy may require the agent to work in this fashion. In either case, the agent should be cognizant of all applicable laws directing this subject.

■ SINGLE AGENCY

In a single agency, the broker represents only one of the parties in a transaction, either the buyer or the seller, but not both. The party represented by the broker is the *broker's principal or client,* and other parties or their agents are treated as customers by the broker. If the broker's client is the seller, the broker deals with buyers or their agents as customers only. If the buyer is the broker's client, sellers are treated as customers.

A single agency broker may choose to represent only sellers (seller agency) or only buyers (buyer agency), but also may choose to represent either, one at a time. This can lead to potential conflicts. A buyer-client (principal) might be interested in a property listed by a seller client (also a principal). When such situations arise, the single agency broker could formally terminate the agency relationship with the buyer. If this occurs, the broker also should inform the seller of the previous agency relationship with the buyer, although he or she may not disclose confidential information that was obtained during the time the buyer was a client. The broker may not, for example, disclose to the seller that the buyers are willing to pay *x* number of dollars for a property they really like because this is information the broker learned while representing those buyers. This situation would require careful handling.

Handling In-House Sales

A substantial part of many brokerage businesses consists of *sales of in-house listings* (listings generated by the same broker or the broker's licensees). As agents of the broker and subagents of the seller, all salespersons in the brokerage have an obligation to use their best efforts to find a buyer for properties that are listed with the brokerage. In-house sales also avoid the need to split the commission with another brokerage.

For example, Jane lists her home for sale with ABC Realty, and she also asks ABC to help her find a new home. She decides to make an offer on Fred's property, which is also listed with ABC. Because ABC is the agent of both Jane and Fred (as sellers), this situation gives rise to a dual agency. ABC cannot act as the selling broker in Jane's purchase from Fred without the informed consent of both parties. The same dilemma could arise even if Jane had no previous contact with ABC. She might have specifically hired one of its associates to act as her buyer's broker and then asked to see Fred's house. ABC would again be in the position of acting as agent for both buyer and seller.

Designated Agency

The DOS has approved a technique by which the in-house dual agency problem can be handled when a firm's buyer-client expresses interest in property that same company has listed. The Secretary of State has stated that "you (the managing broker) can designate one of your agents to represent the buyer and another to represent the seller. If designated agents are appointed, the firm continues as a dual agent representing both the buyer and seller in the same transaction. The designated agents, however, will, by virtue of the new agreement with the buyer and seller, function as single agents giving undivided loyalty to their respective clients." Informed consent (by both parties) to dual agency and then informed consent to the designated agent arrangement must be obtained.

Handling Cooperative Sales

Cooperation among brokers is common practice in the real estate industry. When a property is sold through a broker who is not the listing broker, it is important to clarify the agency relationships among all of the people involved. The cooperating or selling broker (or his or her salesperson) must inform the listing agent whether he or she is acting as a subagent of the seller, as an agent of the buyer, or simply as a broker's agent with no agency relationship with either buyer or seller. The relationship would affect the amount of information a listing agent would share about the seller's motivation or financial situation.

■ AGENCY FORMS

The majority of agency relationships of any type are created by written agreement between the agent and the principal. In the case of real estate agency, the relationship between the seller and the listing agent is defined by the *listing agreement*. The relationship between the buyer and the agent is defined by the *buyer broker agency agreement*.

In all commercial leasing transactions, it is not unusual for a broker to represent a tenant as a client. All the same requirements for disclosure, loyalty, and confidentiality apply to a tenant agency.

Listing Agreements

In New York, there are three authorized relationships that a licensee may enter into:

1. Exclusive-right-to-sell listing
2. Exclusive-agency listing
3. Open listing

These relationships are created via listing agreements. The primary difference among these types of listings relates to the conditions under which the broker will have earned a commission. Their similarities and differences are examined in Table 3.1.

Exclusive-right-to-sell listing. The **exclusive-right-to-sell listing** provides the greatest protection for the broker. The broker under this arrangement has earned a commission if the property is sold during the listing term, regardless of who procures the buyer.

Exclusive-agency listing. An **exclusive-agency listing** entitles the broker to a commission if the property is sold during the listing term, unless the seller acting alone is the one who procures the buyer. In this relationship, unlike the exclusive-right-to-sell relationship, the seller reserves the right to conduct their own sale

TABLE   3.1

Types of Listing Agreements

Exclusive-Right-to-Sell	Exclusive-Agency	Open Listing
One broker	One broker	Multiple brokers
Broker is entitled to a commission regardless of who sells the house.	Broker is paid only if he or she is procuring cause.	Only selling broker is paid.
	Seller retains the right to sell without obligation.	Seller retains the right to sell without obligation.

without compensating the exclusive agent. If the seller procures the buyer without involving any broker, no commission is due. In such cases, you may see two advertisements for the same property: one by the exclusive agent and one by the seller himself or herself.

Ultimately, the seller is acting in direct competition with the appointed agent to see who will produce the sale faster. Although this is the seller's right, it may not always be in the best interest of both agent and principal.

Three Authorized Relationships in New York:

1. Exclusive-right-to-sell
2. Exclusive-agency
3. Open listing

Open listing.   The **open listing** is the least restrictive of the three types. In an open listing, the seller may employ any number of brokers and need pay a commission only to that broker who successfully produces a ready, willing, and able buyer. In essence, the seller will only pay a fee to the party that *effects a sale* and to no other. A seller who personally sells the property without the aid of any of the brokers is not obligated to pay any of them a commission. A listing contract generally creates an open listing unless the wording specifically provides otherwise. It should be noted that the majority of open listings are not reflected in writing; however, special circumstances might call for the terms of the open listing to be memorialized.

While the open listing may seem the most favorable to the seller, it usually means that no one agent is motivated to spend a great deal of time or advertising money on the property, because no compensation will be due if someone else sells it first. Remember, brokers are businesspeople, too.

When a broker represents a landlord in procuring tenants for a property, the most common agreement is the *exclusive right to lease,* which is similar to the exclusive right to sell. The broker earns a commission if the property is leased during the term of the agreement, regardless of who procures the tenant.

Exclusive right to lease.   In this type of arrangement, a property owner engages one broker to act as his or her exclusive leasing agent. As this arrangement directly resembles the exclusive-right-to-sell listing agreement, the only difference is that the subject property is being leased and not sold. This relationship is common in large commercial and residential projects. Regardless of which party procures the tenant/lessee, the exclusive leasing agent is paid a fee. With respect to disclosures under this relationship, Part 175.7 states clearly that a broker shall always make it clear as to which party he or she represents in the transaction.

Net listing.   With a net listing, the broker is free to offer the property for sale at any price. If the property is sold, the broker pays the seller only a certain net amount previously agreed on and keeps anything above that. *This type of listing is illegal in New York.* It lends itself to fraud and is seldom in the seller's best interest. It also violates fiduciary responsibilities owed to a principal by the agent. Today, very few states in the union allow this type of relationship to exist.

Multiple listing.   Not a type of listing, a multiple listing service (MLS) is organized within a geographic area by a group of brokers who agree to distribute and share listing information.

The multiple-listing agreement, while not actually a separate form of listing, is in effect an exclusive-right-to-sell or exclusive-agency agreement with an additional authority to distribute the listing to other brokers who belong to the MLS. The obligations among member brokers of a multiple-listing organization vary widely. Most provide that on sale of the property the commission will be divided between the listing broker and the selling broker. Terms for division of the commission vary by individual arrangement among brokers.

Under most multiple-listing contracts, the broker who secures the listing is not only authorized but obligated to turn the listing over to the MLS within a definite period of time so that it can be distributed to other member brokers.

The Internet and multiple listing.   Many individual brokers showcase their listings on their own Web pages (virtual office Web sites, VOWs). Larger groups of listings are found on local, regional, and statewide multiple-listing Internet sites. Meanwhile, *Realtor.com* and other sites compete for the largest number of nationwide listings. In addition, several sites offer exposure to for-sale-by-owner (FSBO) properties.

As a result, most homebuyers today use the Internet to browse the market, particularly at the start of their searches. In the end, however, most sales are eventually made face-to-face through the services of a real estate broker. It is important to note that, for any property listed on the broker's Web site, when a sale occurs the broker should immediately remove the listing from the for-sale section of the site. Failure to do so will subject the licensee to disciplinary action by the DOS.

Termination of listings.   A listing, like any agency relationship, may be ended for any of the following reasons:

- Performance of the object (sale of the property)
- Expiration of the time period stated in the agreement
- Abandonment by a broker who spends no time on the listing
- Revocation by the owner (although the owner may be liable for the broker's expenses)
- Cancellation by the broker or by mutual consent
- Bankruptcy, death, or insanity of either party
- Destruction of the property
- A change in property use by outside forces (such as a change in zoning)

All listings should specify a definite period of time during which the broker is to be employed. *The use of automatic extensions of time in exclusive listings is illegal in New York.*

For example, a listing agreement calls for the following terms: "For 180 days, after which, the agreement shall continue on a month-to-month basis until either party cancels the agreement with one week's notice."

This would be considered an automatic extension and is unlawful. All listing agreements must have a beginning date and an ending date. This does not mean that one cannot extend an agreement with a client; however, any extension should be arranged for with the client *prior to expiration of the listing agreement's original term.*

Information needed for listing agreements.   When taking a listing, the broker must obtain as much information as possible on the parcel of real estate. This ensures that all possible contingencies can be anticipated, particularly when the listing will be shared in a multiple-listing arrangement. Some of the information accompanies the actual listing contract; some is furnished to prospective buyers on separate information sheets. The information includes the following (where appropriate):

- Names and addresses of owners
- Adequate description of the property
- Size of lot (frontage and depth; if irregular, square footage)
- Number and size of rooms and total square footage
- Construction and age of the building
- Information relative to the neighborhood (schools, transportation)
- Current taxes
- Amount of existing financing
- Utilities and average payments
- Appliances to be included in the transaction
- Date of occupancy or possession
- Possibility of seller financing
- Zoning classification (especially important for vacant land)
- Detailed list of exactly what personal property and which fixtures will or will not be included in the sales price

The agent should search the public records for information on zoning, lot size, and yearly taxes. The true tax figure must be used, disregarding any present veteran's, aged, disabled, senior apartment, "Gold Star" parent, STaR, or religious exemption, or any addition for unpaid water bills. However, when he or she is providing a customer with current property tax information, the licensee is cautioned to also provide full disclosure to the customer that the property tax in question will *only* remain at that amount within the year of sale and that the likelihood (as a result of the sale) is that the property tax will be higher in the following tax year(s). If the licensee has failed to be clear on this issue and the customer purchases the property relying solely on information regarding the lower property tax amount, this could lead to future litigation and/or a complaint filed against the licensee with the DOS.

Seller disclosures. For one- to four-family dwellings, each buyer, before any binding contract of sale is signed, is entitled to receive a Property Condition Disclosure Statement from the seller. (See Figure 3.5.) The statement starts with "1. How long have you owned the property?" and proceeds through questions about the property's environment, structure, and mechanical conditions, to "48. The property is located in the following school district_____." Any buyer who does not receive the statement is entitled to a $500 credit toward purchase. Whether or not the seller provides the disclosure form has no effect on the seller's liability for undisclosed defects. A seller's agent should inform the client about the property disclosure form and provide a blank copy, but should offer no assistance in filling it out or any legal advice about ignoring it. The requirement and a listing of the penalties associated with the failure to provide the seller disclosure are contained in Article 14 of the Real Property Law.

New York State requires that a functioning carbon monoxide detector and smoke alarm be installed in every one- or two-family house, co-op, or condo offered for sale. All sellers of housing built before 1978 must disclose the presence of known lead-based paint or lead-related hazards to prospective buyers, both at the time of listing and later before the closing. (See Figure 3.6.) The disclosure would be included with the sample listing contract shown in Figure 3.7. Sellers and landlords must also provide a HUD/EPA booklet on the subject. Failure to comply with lead-paint disclosure requirements bears a penalty of $11,000 per occurrence.

Environmental hazards. When property is listed, questions should be raised about the possible presence of environmental hazards. The real estate broker must not assume expertise in these matters. It is enough to be alert for situations that might raise a red flag and to recommend, where it seems indicated, that the seller consult a licensed engineer. In some situations, an environmental audit may be indicated. As always, troublesome questions can be taken to an attorney. Environmental hazards are of increasing importance, not only because buyers may suffer damage to their health but also because in some cases purchasers have been held responsible for cleanup costs tied to existing problems.

The New York regulatory scheme. In January 2003, the New York attorney general adopted rule changes that amended the state regulations regarding investment advisors.

Financial planners wear many different hats and include such parties as

- money managers,
- real estate agents,
- accountants,
- insurance agents, and
- financial advisors.

Investment advisors are defined as parties who engage in the business of rendering advice to a member of the general public concerning the buying selling or holding of securities.

Property Condition Disclosure Statement

NYS Department of State
Division of Licensing Services
P.O. Box 22001
Albany, NY 12201-2001
(518) 474-4429
www.dos.state.ny.us

Property Condition Disclosure Statement

Name of Seller or Sellers: _____

Property Address: _____

_____

General Instructions:

The Property Condition Disclosure Act requires the seller of residential real property to cause this disclosure statement or a copy thereof to be delivered to a buyer or buyer's agent prior to the signing by the buyer of a binding contract of sale.

Purpose of Statement:

This is a statement of certain conditions and information concerning the property known to the seller. This Disclosure Statement is not a warranty of any kind by the seller or by any agent representing the seller in this transaction. It is not a substitute for any inspections or tests and the buyer is encouraged to obtain his or her own independent professional inspections and environmental tests and also is encouraged to check public records pertaining to the property.

A knowingly false or incomplete statement by the seller on this form may subject the seller to claims by the buyer prior to or after the transfer of title. In the event a seller fails to perform the duty prescribed in this article to deliver a Disclosure Statement prior to the signing by the buyer of a binding contract of sale, the buyer shall receive upon the transfer of title a credit of $500 against the agreed upon purchase price of the residential real property.

"Residential real property" means real property improved by a one to four family dwelling used or occupied, or intended to be used or occupied, wholly or partly, as the home or residence of one or more persons, but shall not refer to (a) unimproved real property upon which such dwellings are to be constructed or (b) condominium units or cooperative apartments or (c) property on a homeowners' association that is not owned in fee simple by the seller.

Instructions to the Seller:

    a. Answer all questions based upon your actual knowledge.
    b. Attach additional pages with your signature if additional space is required.
    c. Complete this form yourself.
    d. If some items do not apply to your property, check "NA" (Non-applicable). If you do not know the answer check "Unkn" (Unknown).

Seller's Statement:

The seller makes the following representations to the buyer based upon the seller's actual knowledge at the time of signing this document. The seller authorizes his or her agent, if any, to provide a copy of this statement to a prospective buyer of the residential real property. The following are representations made by the seller and are not the representations of the seller's agent.

GENERAL INFORMATION

1. How long have you owned the property? . . . . _____

2. How long have you occupied the property? . . . . _____

3. What is the age of the structure or structures? . . . . _____
    Note to buyer – If the structure was built before 1978 you are encouraged to investigate for the presence of lead based paint..

4. Does anybody other than yourself have a lease, easement or any other right to use or occupy any part of your property other than those stated in documents available in the public record, such as rights to use a road or path or cut trees or crops? . . . . ☐ Yes ☐ No ☐ Unkn ☐ NA

5. Does anybody else claim to own any part of your property? *If Yes, explain below* . . . . ☐ Yes ☐ No ☐ Unkn ☐ NA

_____

_____

F I G U R E   3.5 (CONTINUED)

Property Condition Disclosure Statement

Property Condition Disclosure Statement

6. Has anyone denied you access to the property or made a formal legal claim challenging your title to the property? *If Yes, explain below* . . . . ❏ Yes ❏ No ❏ Unkn ❏ NA

7. Are there any features of the property shared in common with adjoining landowners or a homeowner's association, such as walls, fences or driveways? *If Yes, describe below* . . . . . ❏ Yes ❏ No ❏ Unkn ❏ NA

8. Are there any electric or gas utility surcharges for line extensions, special assessments or homeowner or other association fees that apply to the property? *If Yes, explain below* . . . . . ❏ Yes ❏ No ❏ Unkn ❏ NA

9. Are there certificates of occupancy related to the property? *If No, explain below* . . . . ❏ Yes ❏ No ❏ Unkn ❏ NA

ENVIRONMENTAL

Note to Seller:

In this section, you will be asked questions regarding petroleum products and hazardous or toxic substances that you know to have been spilled, leaked or otherwise been released on the property or from the property onto any other property. Petroleum products may include, but are not limited to, gasoline, diesel fuel, home heating fuel, and lubricants. Hazardous or toxic substances are products that could pose short or long-term danger to personal health or the environment if they are not properly disposed of, applied or stored. These include, but are not limited to, fertilizers, pesticides and insecticides, paint including paint thinner, varnish remover and wood preservatives, treated wood, construction materials such as asphalt and roofing materials, antifreeze and other automotive products, batteries, cleaning solvents including septic tank cleaners, household cleaners and pool chemicals and products containing mercury and lead.

Note to Buyer:

If contamination of this property from petroleum products and/or hazardous or toxic substances is a concern to you, you are urged to consider soil and groundwater testing of this property.

10. Is any or all of the property located in a designated floodplain? *If Yes, explain below* . . . . . . ❏ Yes ❏ No ❏ Unkn ❏ NA

11. Is any or all of the property located in a designated wetland? *If Yes, explain below* . . . . . . ❏ Yes ❏ No ❏ Unkn ❏ NA

12. Is the property located in an agricultural district? *If Yes, explain below* . . . . ❏ Yes ❏ No ❏ Unkn ❏ NA

13. Was the property ever the site of a landfill? *If Yes, explain below* . . . . ❏ Yes ❏ No ❏ Unkn ❏ NA

DOS-1614 (Rev. 8/06)

F I G U R E   3.5 (CONTINUED)

Property Condition Disclosure Statement

Property Condition Disclosure Statement

14. Are there or have there ever been fuel storage tanks above or below the ground on the property? . . . . ☐ Yes ☐ No ☐ Unkn ☐ NA
    * If Yes, are they currently in use? . . . . ☐ Yes ☐ No ☐ Unkn ☐ NA

    * Location(s) _____

    * Are they leaking or have they ever leaked? *If Yes, explain below* . . . . ☐ Yes ☐ No ☐ Unkn ☐ NA
    _____
    _____

15. Is there asbestos in the structure? *If Yes, state location or locations below* . . . . ☐ Yes ☐ No ☐ Unkn ☐ NA
    _____
    _____

16. Is lead plumbing present? *If Yes, state location or locations below* . . . . ☐ Yes ☐ No ☐ Unkn ☐ NA
    _____
    _____

17. Has a radon test been done? *If Yes, attach a copy of the report* . . . . ☐ Yes ☐ No ☐ Unkn ☐ NA

18. Has motor fuel, motor oil, home heating fuel, lubricating oil or any other petroleum product, methane gas, or any hazardous or toxic substance spilled, leaked or otherwise been released on the property or from the property onto any other property? *If Yes, describe below* . . . . . ☐ Yes ☐ No ☐ Unkn ☐ NA
    _____
    _____

19. Has the property been tested for the presence of motor fuel, motor oil, home heating fuel, lubricating oil, or any other petroleum product, methane gas, or any hazardous or toxic substance? *If Yes, attach report(s)* . . . . ☐ Yes ☐ No ☐ Unkn ☐ NA
    _____
    _____

STRUCTURAL

20. Is there any rot or water damage to the structure or structures? *If Yes, explain below* . . . . . ☐ Yes ☐ No ☐ Unkn ☐ NA
    _____
    _____

21. Is there any fire or smoke damage to the structure or structures? *If Yes, explain below* . . . . ☐ Yes ☐ No ☐ Unkn ☐ NA
    _____
    _____

22. Is there any termite, insect, rodent or pest infestation or damage? *If Yes, explain below* . . . ☐ Yes ☐ No ☐ Unkn ☐ NA
    _____
    _____

23. Has the property been tested for termite, insect, rodent or pest infestation or damage? . . . . ☐ Yes ☐ No ☐ Unkn ☐ NA
    If Yes, please attach report(s)

24. What is the type of roof/roof covering (slate, asphalt, other)? . . . . _____
    * Any known material defects? . . . . _____
    * How old is the roof? . . . . _____

Property Condition Disclosure Statement

Property Condition Disclosure Statement

- Is there a transferable warrantee on the roof in effect now? *If Yes, explain below* ..... ☐ Yes ☐ No ☐ Unkn ☐ NA

_____

_____

25. Are there any know material defects in any of the following structural systems: footings, beams, girders, lintels, columns or partitions? *If Yes, explain below* .... ☐ Yes ☐ No ☐ Unkn ☐ NA

_____

_____

MECHANICAL SYSTEMS AND SERVICES

26. What is the water source? *(Circle all that apply)* .... well,   private,   municipal, other: _____

- If municipal, is it metered? .... ☐ Yes ☐ No ☐ Unkn ☐ NA

27. Has the water quality and/or flow rate been tested? *If Yes, describe below* .... ☐ Yes ☐ No ☐ Unkn ☐ NA

_____

_____

28. What is the type of sewage system? *(Circle all that apply)* .... public sewer,   private sewer, septic,   cesspool

- If septic or cesspool, age? .... _____
- Date last pumped? .... _____
- Frequency of pumping? .... _____
- Any known material defects? *If Yes, explain below* .... ☐ Yes ☐ No ☐ Unkn ☐ NA

_____

_____

29. Who is your electrical service provider? .... _____
- What is the amperage? .... _____
- Does it have circuit breakers or fuses? .... _____
- Private or public poles? .... _____
- Any known material defects? *If yes, explain below* .... ☐ Yes ☐ No ☐ Unkn ☐ NA

_____

_____

30. Are there any flooding, drainage or grading problems that resulted in standing water on any portion of the property? *If Yes, state locations and explain below* .... ☐ Yes ☐ No ☐ Unkn ☐ NA

_____

_____

31. Does the basement have seepage that results in standing water? *If Yes, explain below* .... ☐ Yes ☐ No ☐ Unkn ☐ NA

_____

_____

Are there any known material defects in any of the following? *If Yes, explain below. Use additional sheets if necessary* ....

32. Plumbing system? .... ☐ Yes ☐ No ☐ Unkn ☐ NA

33. Security system? .... ☐ Yes ☐ No ☐ Unkn ☐ NA

34. Carbon monoxide detector? .... ☐ Yes ☐ No ☐ Unkn ☐ NA

F I G U R E 3.5 (CONTINUED)

Property Condition Disclosure Statement

Property Condition Disclosure Statement

35. Smoke detector?	☐ Yes	☐ No	☐ Unkn	☐ NA
36. Fire sprinkler system?	☐ Yes	☐ No	☐ Unkn	☐ NA
37. Sump pump?	☐ Yes	☐ No	☐ Unkn	☐ NA
38. Foundation/slab?	☐ Yes	☐ No	☐ Unkn	☐ NA
39. Interior walls/ceilings?	☐ Yes	☐ No	☐ Unkn	☐ NA
40. Exterior walls or siding?	☐ Yes	☐ No	☐ Unkn	☐ NA
41. Floors?	☐ Yes	☐ No	☐ Unkn	☐ NA
42. Chimney/fireplace or stove?	☐ Yes	☐ No	☐ Unkn	☐ NA
43. Patio/deck?	☐ Yes	☐ No	☐ Unkn	☐ NA
44. Driveway?	☐ Yes	☐ No	☐ Unkn	☐ NA
45. Air conditioner?	☐ Yes	☐ No	☐ Unkn	☐ NA
46. Heating system?	☐ Yes	☐ No	☐ Unkn	☐ NA
47. Hot water heater?	☐ Yes	☐ No	☐ Unkn	☐ NA

_____
_____
_____
_____

48. The property is located in the following school district _____ ☐ Unkn

Note: Buyer is encouraged to check public records concerning the property (e.g. tax records and wetland and floodplain maps).

The seller should use this area to further explain any item above. If necessary, attach additional pages and indicate here the number of additional pages attached.

_____
_____
_____
_____
_____
_____
_____

Property Condition Disclosure Statement

Property Condition Disclosure Statement

Seller's Certification:

Seller certifies that the information in this Property Condition Disclosure Statement is true and complete to the seller's actual knowledge as of the date signed by the seller. If a seller of residential real property acquires knowledge which renders materially inaccurate a Property Condition Disclosure Statement provided previously, the seller shall deliver a revised Property Condition Disclosure Statement to the buyer as soon as practicable. In no event, however, shall a seller be required to provide a revised Property Condition Disclosure Statement after the transfer of title from the seller to the buyer or occupancy by the buyer, whichever is earlier.

Seller's Signature

X _____   *Date* _____

Seller's Signature

X _____   *Date* _____

Buyer's Acknowledgment:

Buyer acknowledges receipt of a copy of this statement and buyer understands that this information is a statement of certain conditions and information concerning the property known to the seller. It is not a warranty of any kind by the seller or seller's agent and is not a substitute for any home, pest, radon or other inspections or testing of the property or inspection of the public records.

Buyer's Signature

X _____   *Date* _____

Buyer's Signature

X _____   *Date* _____

F I G U R E   3.6

Disclosure of Lead-Based Paint and Lead-Based Hazards

LEAD-BASED PAINT OR LEAD-BASED PAINT HAZARD ADDENDUM

It is a condition of this contract that, until midnight of _____ , Buyer shall have the right to obtain a risk assessment or inspection of the Property for the presence of lead-based paint and/or lead-based paint hazards* at Buyer's expense. This contingency will terminate at that time unless Buyer or Buyer's agent delivers to the Seller or Seller's agent a written inspection and/or risk assessment report listing the specific existing deficiencies and corrections needed, if any. If any corrections are necessary, Seller shall have the option of (i) completing them, (ii) providing for their completion, or (iii) refusing to complete them. If Seller elects not to complete or provide for completion of the corrections, then Buyer shall have the option of (iv) accepting the Property in its present condition, or (v) terminating this contract, in which case all earnest monies shall be refunded to Buyer. Buyer may waive the right to obtain a risk assessment or inspection of the Property for the presence of lead-based paint and/or lead based paint hazards at any time without cause.

*Intact lead-based paint that is in good condition is not necessarily a hazard. See EPA pamphlet "Protect Your Family From Lead in Your Home" for more information.

Disclosure of Information on Lead-Based Paint and Lead-Based Paint Hazards
Lead Warning Statement
Every Buyer of any interest in residential real property on which a residential dwelling was built prior to 1978 is notified that such property may present exposure to lead from lead-based paint that may place young children at risk of developing lead poisoning. Lead poisoning in young children may produce permanent neurological damage, including learning disabilities, reduced intelligence quotient, behavioral problems, and impaired memory. Lead poisoning also poses a particular risk to pregnant women. The Seller of any interest in residential real property is required to provide the Buyer with any information on lead-based paint hazards from risk assessments or inspections in the Seller's possession and notify the Buyer of any known lead-based paint hazards. A risk assessment or inspection for possible lead-based paint hazards is recommended prior to purchase.

Seller's Disclosure (initial)
_____ (a) Presence of lead-based paint and/or lead-based paint hazards (check one below):
❏ Known lead-based paint and/or lead-based paint hazards are present in the housing (explain).
_____
_____

❏ Seller has no knowledge of lead-based paint and/or lead-based paint hazards in the housing.
_____ (b) Records and reports available to the Seller (check one below):
❏ Seller has provided the Buyer with all available records and reports pertaining to lead-based paint and/or lead-based paint hazards in the housing (list documents below).
_____
_____

❏ Seller has no reports or records pertaining to lead-based paint and/or lead based paint hazards in the housing.

Buyer's Acknowledgment (initial)
_____ (c) Buyer has received copies of all information listed above.
_____ (d) Buyer has received the pamphlet *Protect Your Family from Lead in Your Home.*
_____ (e) Buyer has (check one below):
❏ Received a 10-day opportunity (or mutually agreed upon period) to conduct a risk assessment or inspection for the presence of lead-based paint and/or lead-based paint hazards; or
❏ Waived the opportunity to conduct a risk assessment or inspection for the presence of lead-based paint and/or lead-based paint hazards.

Agent's Acknowledgment (initial)
_____ (f) Agent has informed the Seller of the Seller's obligations under 42 U.S.C. 4582(d) and is aware of his/her responsibility to ensure compliance.

Certification of Accuracy
The following parties have reviewed the information above and certify, to the best of their knowledge, that the information provided by the signatory is true and accurate.
Buyer: _____ (SEAL) Date _____
Buyer: _____ (SEAL) Date _____
Agent: _____   Date _____
Seller: _____ (SEAL) Date _____
Seller: _____ (SEAL) Date _____
Agent: _____   Date _____

The new rules include but are not limited to the following:

- Filing requirements and registration with the state for any investment advisor with six or more clients
- Mandatory compliance by advisors and representative agents with all examination requirements, including passing the Uniform Investment Advisor Law exam (series 65) or the Uniform Combined State Law exam (series 66) and the General Securities Advisor Law exam (series 7)
- Required filing of financial information with the attorney general's office
- Requirements to make and maintain records for a period of not less than five years

Rental income-producing property.   In the sale of multifamily dwellings and other income-producing properties, the seller should be ready to present a reconstructed statement of income and expenses, preferably prepared by an accountant. A rent roll should show the name of each tenant, amount of rent, expiration date of each lease, and amount of security deposits. The listing agent should verify zoning and the legality of existing use. The seller should be informed of the necessity for a certificate of occupancy at transfer. Arranging with tenants to show the property at reasonable times also is important.

Truth-in-Heating Law.   New York's Truth-in-Heating Law requires the seller to furnish, on written request, two past years' heating and cooling bills to any prospective buyer of a one- or two-family home. Sellers also must furnish a statement of the extent and type of insulation they have installed together with any information they may have about insulation installed by previous owners.

Other government requirements.   If HUD has determined that the property is in a flood-prone area, a buyer may need to obtain flood insurance before placing certain kinds of mortgages. The listing agent can anticipate this by consulting a flood area map at the time of listing. Maps may be ordered from the Federal Emergency Management Agency, Flood Map Distribution Center, 6930 (A-F) San Tomas Road, Baltimore, MD 21227-6227, or by calling toll-free 800-333-1363. The Web site is *www.fema.gov.*

Some municipalities may have restrictive ordinances regarding aquifer protection zones, wetlands protection, or steep slopes. Listing agents should keep current with all potential restrictions on use of land.

New York State requirements.   The New York Real Property Law requires that the broker have attached to or printed on the reverse side of an exclusive agreement for a one- to three-family dwelling, a separately signed statement to the following effect:

> *An exclusive-right-to-sell listing means that if you, the property owner, find a buyer for your house or if another broker finds a buyer, you must pay the agreed-on commission to the present broker.*
>
> *An exclusive-agency listing means that if you, the property owner, find a buyer, you will not have to pay a commission to the broker. However, if another broker finds a buyer, you will owe a commission to both the selling broker and your present broker.*

F I G U R E   3.7

Listing Agreement

(1) **EXCLUSIVE RIGHT TO SELL AGREEMENT**

THIS AGREEMENT is effective (2) _____ ,19___, and confirms that _____ (3) _____ has (have) appointed _____ (4) to act as Agent for the sale of property known as _____ , New York.

(5) In return for the Agent's agreement to use Agent's best efforts to sell the above property, the Owner(s) agree(s) to grant the Agent the exclusive right to sell this property under the following terms and conditions:

PERIOD OF AGREEMENT

1.   This agreement shall be effective from the above date and shall expire at midnight on _____ (6) _____ , 19___.

PRICE AT WHICH PROPERTY WILL BE OFFERED AND AUTHORITY

2.   The property will be offered for sale at a list price of _____ (7) _____ and shall be sold, subject to negotiation, at such price and upon such terms to which Owner(s) may agree. The word Owner refers to each and ALL parties who have ownership interest in the property and the undersigned represent(s) they are the sole and exclusive owners and are fully authorized to enter into this agreement.

(8) **COMMISSION TO BE PAID TO AGENT**

3.   The Agent shall be entitled to and Owner shall pay to Agent one commission of _____ of the selling price. Both the Owner(s) and the Agent acknowledge that the above commission rate was not suggested nor influenced by anyone other than the parties to this Agreement. Owner(s) hereby authorizes Agent to make an offer of cooperation to any other licensed real estate broker with whom Agent wishes to cooperate. Any commission due for a sale brought about by a Sub-Agent (another broker who is authorized by Agent to assist in the sale of Owner(s) property) or to an authorized Buyer(s) Agent shall be paid by the Agent from the commission received by the Agent pursuant to this Paragraph.

        The commission offered by Agent to Sub-Agents shall be _____ of the gross selling price. The commission offered by Agent to Buyer(s) Agents shall be _____ of the gross selling price.

        In the event that Owner(s) authorizes Agent to compensate a Buyer('s) Agent, Owner(s) acknowledges Owner's(s') understanding that such Buyer's Agent is not representing Owner(s) as Sub-Agent and that the Buyer's Agent will be representing only the interests of the prospective purchaser.

(9) **OWNER(S) OBLIGATIONS AFTER THE EXPIRATION OF THIS AGREEMENT**

4.   Owner(s) understands and agrees to pay the commission referred to in paragraph 3, if this property is sold or transferred or is the subject of a contract of sale within _____ months after the expiration date of this agreement involving a person with whom the Agent or a Cooperating Broker or the Owner(s) negotiated or to whom the property is offered, quoted or shown during the period of this listing agreement. Owner(s) will not, however, be obligated to pay such commission if Owner(s) enters into a valid Exclusive Listing Agreement with another New York State licensed real estate broker after the expiration of this agreement.

(10) **WHO MAY NEGOTIATE FOR OWNER(S)**

5.   Owner(s) agree(s) to direct all inquiries to the Agent. Owner(s) elect(s) to have all offers submitted through Agent ___ or Cooperating Agent ___.

(11) **SUBMISSION OF LISTING TO MULTIPLE LISTING SERVICE**

6.   Both Owner(s) and Agent agree that the Agent immediately is to submit this listing agreement to the Westchester Multiple Listing Service, Inc. ("WMLS"), for dissemination to its Participants. No provision of this agreement is intended to nor shall be understood to establish or imply any contractual relationship between the Owner(s) and WMLS nor has WMLS in any way participated in any of the terms of this agreement, including the commission to be paid. Owner(s) acknowledge(s) that the Agent's ability to submit this listing to WMLS or to maintain such listing amongst those included in any compilation of listing information made available by WMLS, is subject to Agent's continued status as a member in good standing of the Westchester County Board of REALTORS, Inc., and Agent's status as a Participant in good standing of WMLS.

(12) **FAIR HOUSING**

7.   Agent and Owner agree to comply fully with local, state and federal fair housing laws against discrimination on the basis of race, color, religion, sex, national origin, handicap, age, marital status and/or familial status, children or other prohibited factors.

F I G U R E   3.7 (CONTINUED)

Listing Agreement

(13) AUTHORIZATION FOR "FOR SALE" SIGN AND OTHER SERVICES

8.   Agent __ is (__ is not) authorized to place a "For Sale" sign on the property. Owner acknowledges that Agent has fully explained to Owner(s) the services and marketing activities which Agent has agreed to provide.

(14) REQUIREMENTS FOR PUBLICATION IN WMLS COMPILATION

9.   This listing agreement is not acceptable for publication by WMLS unless and until the Owner(s) has duly signed this agreement and an acknowledgement reflecting receipt of the definitions of "Exclusive Right to Sell" and "Exclusive Agency" required by the New York State Department of State - Division of Licensing Services.

(15) RENTAL OF PROPERTY

10.   Should the Owner(s) desire to rent the property during the period of this agreement, Agent is hereby granted the sole and exclusive right to rent the property, exclusive "FOR RENT" sign privilege and the Owner(s) agrees to pay Agent a rental commission of _____. The applicable commission for the lease term is due and will be paid __ upon the execution of the lease __ upon the date of occupancy. The commission for each and any subsequent renewal thereof, is due and will be paid upon the commencement of each renewal term.

(16) TERMINATION

11.   Owner(s) understands that if Owner(s) terminates the Agent's authority prior to the expiration of its term, Agent shall retain its contract rights (including but not limited to recovery of its commission, advertising expenses and/or any other damages) incurred by reason of an early termination of this agreement.

(17) ADDITIONAL POINTS

12.   Additional Points of Agreement, if any:_____
_____

(18) IN-HOUSE SALES

13.   If the Broker has an agency relationship with the buyer ["buyer's broker"] and that buyer expresses interest in property owned by a seller who also has an agency relationship with the Broker ["seller's broker"], a conflict has arisen.

The Broker shall immediately advise both the buyer client and the seller client of the pertinent facts including the fact that a dual agency situation has arisen, and that the **following options are available:**

[a] **The Broker and buyer could dissolve their Agency relationship.** The buyer may then seek to retain another broker, and/or an attorney, or may represent (her)himself. This would release the buyer from any Broker employment contract which was entered into with the Broker. Broker may continue to act as agent for the seller.

[b] **The Broker and the seller could dissolve their Agency relationship.** The seller may then seek to retain another broker, and/or an attorney, or may represent (her)himself. This would release the seller from any listing agreement which was entered into with Broker. The Broker may continue to act as Agent for the buyer.

[c] **With fully informed consent, the buyer and seller may elect to continue with the brokerage firm serving as a consensual dual agent, which is the exception to the general rule that agents serve one principal.** As a dual agent, the firm and its licensee agents have a duty of fairness to both principals. By mutual agreement the buyer and seller may identify who will negotiate for each principal. For example: [a] the licensee who signed the buyer as a principal of the brokerage firm may negotiate on behalf of the buyer principal and [b] the licensee who signed the seller as a principal of the firm may negotiate on behalf of the seller principal.

In either case, the brokerage commission will be paid by the seller in accordance with the listing agreement with the seller, unless different arrangements have been negotiated.

As a dual agent, the firm and its agents cannot furnish undivided loyalty to either party.

As a dual agent, the firm and its licensee agents have a duty not to disclose confidential information given by one principal to the other principal, such as the price one is willing to pay or accept. Such information may already be known to the firm and its agents. If the information is of such a nature that the agent cannot fairly give advice without disclosing it, the agent cannot properly continue to act as an agent.

The buyer, seller and broker shall memorialize the option of their mutual choice by executing a statutory disclosure notice. If there is no mutual agreement, the proposed transaction between buyer and seller shall not be pursued.

F I G U R E   3.7 (CONTINUED)

Listing Agreement

(19) **ALL MODIFICATIONS TO BE MADE IN WRITING**

14.   Owner(s) and Agent agree that no change, amendment, modification or termination of this agreement shall be binding on any party unless the same shall be in writing and signed by the parties.

_____   _____   _____
(OWNER)   (DATE)   (AGENT)

                                                         By: _____
_____   _____   (Authorized Representative)   (DATE)
(OWNER)   (DATE)

Owner's Mailing Address:_____   Agent's Address: _____

_____   _____

                                                         _____
Owner's Telephone: _____   Agent's Telephone: _____

(20) **DEFINITIONS**

        In accordance with the requirements of the New York State Department of State the undersigned Owner(s) does (do) hereby acknowledge receipt of the following:

        1.   Explanation of "Exclusive Right to Sell" listing;
        2.   Explanation of "Exclusive Agency" listing;
        3.   A list of Participants of Westchester Multiple Listing Service, Inc.

EXPLANATION OF EXCLUSIVE RIGHT TO SELL: (As worded verbatim by the Department of State)

        An "exclusive right to sell" listing means that if you, the owner of the property, find a buyer for your house, or if another broker finds a buyer, you must pay the agreed commission to the present broker.

EXPLANATION OF EXCLUSIVE AGENCY: (As worded verbatim by the Department of State)

        An "exclusive agency" listing means that if you, the owner of the property, find a buyer, you will not have to pay a commission to the broker. However, if another broker finds a buyer, you will owe a commission to both the selling broker and your present broker.

(21) **"THE FAIR HOUSING ACT"**

        The Civil Rights Act of 1968 known as the Federal Fair Housing Law makes illegal any discrimination based on race, color, religion, sex or national origin in connection with the sale or rental of housing. The 1988 amendment to this Act (The Fair Housing Amendments Act of 1988) expands the coverage of this law to handicapped persons and families with children. Agent and Owner agree to comply fully with State and local statutes and Federal Fair Housing laws.

Article X of the REALTOR Code of Ethics states:

        "REALTORS shall not deny equal professional services to any person for reasons of race, color, religion, sex, handicap, familial status or national origin. REALTORS shall not be parties to any plan or agreement to discriminate against a person or persons on the basis of race, color, religion, sex, handicap, familial status or national origin."

(22) _____
                                                         Owner

        _____
                                                         Owner

If an exclusive listing of residential property is obtained by a broker who is a member of an MLS, the listing agreement must allow the seller to choose whether all negotiated offers to purchase will be submitted through the listing broker or through the selling broker. The DOS has made it clear that a buyer's broker has a right to be present. The aforementioned does not apply to cooperatives and condominiums.

Sample listing agreement.   The individual specifics of a listing may vary from area to area. Following is a section-by-section analysis of a sample agreement; the items in the list below refer to the specific provisions of the contract, identified by the circled numbers. (See Figure 3.7, used by the Westchester Putnam MLS.)

1. Exclusive right to sell. The title specifies that this document is an "exclusive right to sell" the property.
2. Date. The date of the listing contract is the date it is executed (signed); this may not always be the date the contract becomes effective.
3. Names. The names of all persons having an interest in the property should be specified.
4. Broker or firm. The name of the broker or firm entering into the listing must be clearly stated in the agreement, along with the property address.
5. Contract. This section establishes the document as a bilateral contract and states the promises by both parties that create and bind the agreement.
6. Termination of agreement. Both the exact time and the date should be stated to avoid misunderstandings.
7. Listing price. Many brokers prefer not to refer to this as the *asking price*.
8. Commission rate. This important paragraph establishes the broker's rate of commission. Each brokerage firm is free to set its own fee schedule and to negotiate commission rates if it wishes to. The paragraph also makes an offer of cooperation to other members of the MLS and states whether the seller will allow the listing agent to offer part of the commission to a buyer's broker.
9. Extension clause. This section, permitted in New York, protects the broker if, after the listing expires, the owner sells the property to someone with whom the original broker had dealt during the listing period. This extension clause does not apply if the owner has relisted the property with another agent.
10. Negotiation. The owner agrees to refer all inquiries to the agent and chooses to have any offers submitted by either the listing agent or the selling agent, who may belong to a different firm.
11. Multiple listing service. The agent will circulate information on the listing to all members of the MLS immediately. In some other areas, the listing office may have one, two, or three days of "office exclusive" before the listing is submitted to the MLS.
12. Fair housing. Both parties agree to comply with local, state, and federal fair housing laws.
13. For Sale sign. The agent may not place a sign on the property without authorization.
14. Requirements. The owner(s) must sign this agreement before it is acceptable for publication.

15. Rental. If the owner wishes to rent the property during the life of the agreement, the agent has sole and exclusive right to act as the rental agent. The owner will pay the agent a commission for this service.

16. Termination. The agent is entitled to payment for advertising expenses, damages, and commission if the owner terminates the agreement before it expires.

17. Additional points. Anything not illegal may be agreed on by seller and agent. For example, an understanding that "no commission will be due if seller's brother purchases within 30 days" would go here.

18. In-house sales. A broker must notify the seller and the buyer that a dual agency situation exists and that both the seller and buyer can dissolve their agency agreement with the broker or with informed consent continue with the broker serving as a consensual dual agent.

19. Signatures. The contract should be signed by all owners. The sales associate signs on behalf of the broker or firm; the contract is not made with the individual salesperson.

20. Definitions. The seller must receive an explanation of types of listings.

21. Civil rights legislation. This clause serves to alert the owner that both federal and state legislation protect against discrimination.

22. Owner's acknowledgment. The seller acknowledges notification of listing definitions.

■ BUYER AGENCY

In a buyer-broker agency relationship, the broker represents the buyer as a client, rather than treating the buyer as merely a customer. Buyer agency allows the broker to provide services to buyers that might otherwise be inappropriate, such as assistance in negotiating the terms of the contract to the buyer's best advantage. The buyers who specifically retain their own agents would be subject to **vicarious liability** for the acts of their agents, just as sellers are for theirs. As previously discussed, vicarious liability means being responsible for the acts of another.

Working Relationships with Buyers

Buyers as customers. Not every buyer wants to be represented by an agent. In fact, no law exists that would require a buyer or a seller to engage the services of a real estate licensee. Some buyers like working with several different brokers. Some buyers, especially experienced buyers, are happy with the services provided by a seller's agent: help in finding a suitable property, information about property values, help in preparing and presenting their offer, and aid in securing financing. All of these services can be provided to a customer by an agent representing a seller.

Buyers as clients. Other buyers, however, want more than customer services. They need and want advice, something the seller's broker cannot provide them with. These are the buyers who will benefit most from buyer agency.

Sellers' agents are cautioned not to assist buyers in any way that might be construed as creation of an agency relationship by implication. This can ultimately create an undisclosed dual agency. (See Chapter 2 for more on this subject.)

Compensating Buyer Agents

An agency relationship does not depend on the source of the agent's compensation. Buyer agents may be compensated by

1. the buyer,
2. the seller, or
3. both, but only with full disclosure to all interested parties to the transaction and with the informed consent of all interested parties to the transaction.

Naturally, the way in which fees are to be paid should be stated in writing and clearly understood well in advance to avoid potential conflict between the buyer and the broker.

Seller-paid fee.   The seller might agree to pay the buyer's broker fee, particularly during negotiations with a buyer who may be short of cash. The payment of fees does not determine whom an agent represents. As long as the agency relationship is clear and explicit, it does not matter legally whether the buyer or the seller pays the fee.

The seller may pay the buyer's broker fee through a commission split or by crediting the buyer a specific amount out of the sales proceeds at closing. The most common method is *the commission split,* where the listing broker has written authorization to split the commission with the buyer's broker. Remember, regardless of which party is charged with compensating the broker, the agent only represents the party that hired him or her and no other.

Buyer-paid fee.   Buyer's agent compensation also can be paid directly by the buyer. This arrangement has the advantage of avoiding any appearance that the buyer's agent is acting as a subagent of the seller and also gives the buyer's agent greater control over getting paid. The compensation may take the form of an hourly rate, a flat fee, or a percentage commission:

- Hourly rate. Under an hourly rate arrangement, the broker actually is acting as a consultant. The hourly fee is payable whether or not the buyer actually purchases a property.
- Percentage fee. A percentage fee is based on the sales price of the home the buyer purchases or any valuable consideration exchanged and/or received. The primary benefit of this arrangement is that real estate agents and their clients are accustomed to a percentage arrangement. The obvious disadvantage is that the broker may have a conflict of interest, because the higher the price, the higher the fee.
- Flat fee. Under this arrangement, the buyer's broker is paid a flat fee if the buyer purchases a house located through the broker. The amount of the fee is based on the broker's estimate of the work and skills involved.

Some buyer's agent agreements provide that the buyer is obligated to pay the fee but will receive a credit for any amount the seller agrees to pay. Thus, the buyer would not pay the buyer's broker fee in a typical MLS sale, where the buyer's broker will get a split of the listing broker's commission. However, the buyer would be obligated to pay the fee if the seller had not listed the property or offered any commission to a selling broker.

As always, if the agent is paid by both parties, both must understand the arrangement and give their written consent.

Buyer-Agency Agreements

Agreements between buyers and buyers' agents are sometimes referred to as *buyer listings*, *buyer representation agreements*, or *buyer-broker agency agreements*. Like a listing agreement, a buyer-agency agreement is also an employment contract. In this case, however, the broker is employed as the buyer's agent. The purpose of the agreement is to find and procure a suitable property. An agency agreement gives the buyer a degree of representation that is possible only in a fiduciary relationship.

Types of buyer-agency agreements.   Following are the three basic types of buyer-agency agreements:

1. Exclusive buyer-agency agreement. The buyer is legally bound to compensate the agent whenever he or she purchases a property of the type described in the contract. The broker is entitled to payment regardless of who located the property. Even if the buyer finds the property independently, the agent is entitled to payment. The broker has an **exclusive right to represent** the buyer. (See Figure 3.8.)
2. Exclusive-agency buyer-agency agreement. The broker is entitled to payment only if he or she locates the property that the buyer ultimately purchases. The buyer is free to find a suitable property without being obligated to pay the agent.
3. Open buyer-agency agreement. This agreement permits the buyer to enter into similar agreements with an unlimited number of brokers. The buyer is obligated to compensate only the broker who locates the property ultimately purchased by the buyer.

A broker also may wish to represent a buyer with respect to a single property only. In this arrangement, the buyer agrees to pay the broker a fee if the buyer purchases a specific property. The broker does not reveal the exact location of the property until the agreement is signed.

In any buyer-agency agreement, the buyer's broker should clarify the types of services to be offered to the buyer-client (in addition to the traditional services rendered by real estate licensees to buyers as customers). These could include such tasks as the following:

■ Structuring of the transaction
■ Investment analysis
■ Assistance in development
■ Assistance in financing
■ Negotiating the sale

Naturally, a buyer's broker must advise the buyer to seek professional legal, tax, or other experts should the need arise.

As with a listing agreement, the time and date of termination should be specified to prevent later conflicts. If the broker wants to be reimbursed for a sale that takes place on a certain property after the buyer-agency agreement terminates,

F I G U R E   3.8

Exclusive-Right-to-Represent Agreement

BUYER AGENCY AGREEMENT
Exclusive Right-to-Represent

COMMISSIONS OR FEES FOR REAL ESTATE SERVICES TO BE PROVIDED ARE NEGOTIABLE BETWEEN BROKER AND CLIENT. THIS IS A LEGALLY BINDING AGREEMENT. YOU MAY WISH TO CONSULT AN ATTORNEY BEFORE SIGNING IT. FOR THE PURPOSES OF THIS AGREEMENT, THE TERM "BUYER" SHALL BE USED TO DESCRIBE PROSPECTIVE PURCHASER(S) OR TENANT(S). THE GREATER ROCHESTER ASSOCIATION OF REALTORS® IS NOT A PARTY TO THIS AGREEMENT.

1.   APPOINTMENT OF BROKER:
The BUYER/TENANT _____ (hereinafter called the "BUYER") retains and appoints as Buyer's Broker (hereinafter called the "BROKER") _____ _____(firm) represented by _____ (agent) as buyer's exclusive agent to locate and/or negotiate for the purchase or lease of real property of the general nature shown below.

2.   PURPOSE OF AGENCY:
Buyer desires to purchase / lease real property (which may include items of personal property) described as follows:
Type: ☐ Residential   ☐ Commercial   ☐ Residential Income   ☐ Industrial   ☐ Vacant Land   ☐ Other
General Description:
_____
_____

Approximate Price Range: $ _____ to $ _____
or any other that Buyer may later agree to.

General Location: _____
_____

Preferred Terms: _____
_____

Other:
_____
_____

3.   TERM OF AGENCY: Broker's authority to act as Buyer's exclusive agent under this Agreement shall begin _____ and shall end at midnight _____ or upon closing of a property purchased under this Agreement and payment of Broker's compensation.

4.   BROKER'S REPRESENTATIONS AND SERVICES. Broker represents that Broker is duly licensed under the laws of the State of New York as a real estate broker. Broker will assist Buyer in locating property of the type described in Section 2 of this Agreement and to negotiate for Buyer any offer by Buyer to purchase or lease such property. During the term of this Agreement, Broker will give Buyer information describing and identifying properties which appear to Broker to substantially meet the terms set forth in Section 2.

5.   BUYER'S REPRESENTATIONS. By appointing Broker as Buyer's exclusive agent, Buyer agrees to conduct all negotiations for the types of property described in Section 2 of this Agreement through Broker and to refer to Broker all contact made with Buyer about such properties from other brokers, salespersons, sellers and others during the term of this Agreement. Buyer agrees to furnish Broker with all requested personal and financial information necessary to complete this transaction.

6.   COMPENSATION OF BROKER. In consideration of the services performed by Broker under the terms of this Agreement, Buyer agrees to pay Broker the following fee(s): (Initial all applicable sections.)

_____ **a. Non-Refundable Retainer:** Buyer shall pay Broker a Non-Refundable Retainer of $ _____ to be paid to Broker herewith whether or not Buyer purchases or leases any property.
_____ This Retainer shall be credited against the Hourly Fee described in subsection (b) below or the Transaction Fee described in subsection (c) below.
_____ **b. Hourly Fee:** Buyer shall pay Broker at the rate of $ _____ per hour for all services performed by Broker under the terms of this Agreement, to be billed _____ and to be paid within five (5) days after Buyer receives a bill for such services from Broker.
_____ This Hourly Fee to extent paid by Buyer shall be credited against the Transaction Fee described in subsection (c) below and shall be kept by Broker whether or not a Transaction Fee is earned.

Source: Greater Rochester Association of REALTORS® Inc.

Exclusive-Right-to-Represent Agreement

_____ **c. Transaction Fee:** Buyer shall pay Broker a Transaction Fee which is the lesser of $ _____ or _____ % of the purchase or total lease price (and renewals and/or expansions, if applicable) of any property purchased or leased by Buyer. This Transaction Fee shall be due and payable upon closing of the Purchase and Sale Contract or Lease providing, however, if such Contract or Lease fails to close due to default by the Buyer, this Transaction Fee shall become immediately due and payable to Broker. Broker is authorized to attempt TO OBTAIN PAYMENT OF THE Transaction Fee from the Seller or Lessor of the property, but Buyer shall have the obligation to pay Broker the Transaction Fee set forth in this Agreement if Broker cannot obtain payment of such fee from the Seller or Lessor of the property. However, if Buyer purchases, exchanges or leases a property within _____ days after this Agreement ends (the "Effective Period") that was shown to the Buyer by Broker, or by anyone else during the life of this Agreement, Buyer will pay Broker the same Transaction Fee agreed to above. Buyer will not owe any Transaction Fee to Broker if such purchase, exchange, or lease occurs during the life of another written Buyer Agency Agreement Buyer enters into after this Agreement ends but before the expiration of the Effective Period.

_____ **d. Other:** _____

_____.

7.   OTHER POTENTIAL BUYERS: Buyer understands that other potential buyers have entered or may enter into similar agency contracts with Broker which may involve the purchase or lease, through Broker, of the same or similar property or properties as Buyer is attempting to purchase or lease. Buyer consents to Broker's representation of such other buyers.

8.   CONFLICTING INTERESTS: If Broker has an ownership interest in or is an agent for any owner in the sale or lease of any property in which Buyer expresses an interest (e.g. a "company listing"), Broker shall immediately notify Buyer of such facts. Buyer is referred to the New York State DISCLOSURE REGARDING REAL ESTATE AGENCY RELATIONSHIPS form, a copy of which is attached.

9.   NONDISCRIMINATION: Broker and Buyer agree that all actions carried out under this Agreement shall be in full compliance with local, state and federal fair housing laws against discrimination on the basis of race, creed, color, religion, national origin, sex, familial status, marital status, age or disabilities.

10.   EARLY CONTRACT TERMINATION: In the event this Agreement is terminated by Buyer prior to the time specified in Section 3, Buyer will be liable for and will pay any compensation to Broker as specified in Section 6.

11.   RESPONSIBILITY OF BUYER(S) UNDER THIS CONTRACT: All buyers to be named on a purchase and sale contract must sign this contract. If more than one person signs this contract as Buyer, each person is fully responsible for keeping the promises made by the Buyer.

12.   RENEWAL AND MODIFICATION OF CONTRACT: Buyer may extend the life of this Agreement by signing a Renewal Agreement. All changes or modifications to the provisions of this Agreement must be made in writing and signed by Buyer(s) and Broker.

13.   PROFESSIONAL COUNSEL: Broker hereby recommends that Buyer seek legal, tax, property financing, property inspection, appraisal, environmental engineering and other professional advice (if appropriate) relating to any proposed transaction. Buyer agrees that Buyer will not rely on Broker for such professional advice nor rely on Broker for payment of such services.

14.   ATTORNEY'S FEES: In any action, proceeding or arbitration arising out of this Agreement, the prevailing party shall be entitled to reasonable attorney's fees and costs.

15.   OTHER: _____

_____

16. ENTIRE AGREEMENT AND ASSIGNABILITY: This Agreement constitutes the complete Agreement between Broker and Buyer relating to the exclusive agency of Broker for Buyer. No modification of any terms of this Agreement shall be valid or binding unless such modification is in writing and signed by Buyer and Broker. This Agreement is not assignable without written approval of Buyer and Broker.

BUYER _____   BROKER _____

BUYER _____   BY _____

DATE _____   DATE _____

the broker should insert an extension clause like that found in most listing agreements. Of course, buyer-agency agreements can be terminated by mutual consent.

Sometimes a buyer may want to purchase a property listed by the buyer's broker. In this case, unless the buyer's broker divests himself or herself of the buyer-broker relationship, the buyer's broker would be put in the position of acting as a dual agent. Another type of conflict would arise if the broker were showing more than one buyer-client the same property. The buyer-agency agreement should anticipate these types of conflicts. For instance, some agreements provide that the broker will represent the buyer in all cases except in-house listings. Many agreements include an acknowledgment by the buyer that the broker may represent more than one buyer and that if more than one buyer is interested in the same property, it will not be considered a conflict of interest.

An example of a buyer-agency agreement appears in Figure 3.9.

■ SUMMARY

New York requires brokers and salespersons to provide a written disclosure of agency at first substantive contact with prospective buyers or sellers. The disclosure is repeated when a purchase contract is signed by the parties. The licensee may state that he or she is acting as agent for the seller, landlord, buyer, tenant, or a broker.

When a broker becomes agent for a seller or buyer, the broker's salespersons become subagents of that same principal. Cooperating brokers from other firms may operate as subagents of the listing agent, as agents for their own buyers, or as subagents for the seller. The party paying the commission does not determine the principal.

In some situations, agents find themselves working for both parties. Dual agency is legally possible, though difficult. It requires written consent from both buyer and seller. The DOS allows a system of designated brokers to represent both parties for in-house sales.

Listing agreements take three forms. An exclusive-right-to-sell listing promises the broker a commission if the property is sold during the listing period. An exclusive-agency listing promises a commission if the broker sells the property; if the owner sells on his or her own, no commission is due. An open listing simply promises a commission to whatever broker produces the buyer. Net listings, which promise the broker anything above a certain sales price, are illegal in New York. Multiple listing is a form of shared marketing among broker members who can find buyers for each others' listings.

F I G U R E   3.9

Exclusive Buyer Agency Agreement

EXCLUSIVE BUYER AGENCY AGREEMENT

COMMISSIONS OR FEES FOR REAL ESTATE SERVICES TO BE PROVIDED ARE NEGOTIABLE BETWEEN REALTOR AND CLIENT. THIS IS A LEGALLY BINDING AGREEMENT. YOU MAY WISH TO CONSULT AN ATTORNEY BEFORE SIGNING IT. FOR THE PURPOSES OF THIS AGREEMENT THE TERM "BUYER" SHALL BE USED TO DESCRIBE PROSPECTIVE PURCHASER(S) OR TENANT(S).

1. APPOINTMENT OF BROKER
By this agreement,_____("Buyer") appoints

_____ ("REALTOR")
as Buyer's exclusive agent, subject to the terms and conditions stated in this Agreement.

By appointing REALTOR as Buyer's exclusive agent, Buyer agrees to conduct all negotiations for the types of property described in Section 2 below through REALTOR and to refer to REALTOR all contact made with Buyer about such properties from other brokers, salespersons, sellers and others during the term of this Agreement.

2. PURPOSE OF AGENCY
Buyer desires to purchase / lease real property (which may include items of personal property) described as follows:
Type: ( ) Residential ( ) Commercial ( ) Residential Income ( ) Industrial ( ) Vacant Land ( ) Other
General Description:

_____

_____

Approximate Price Range: $ _____ to $ _____

General Location:_____

_____

Preferred Terms:_____

_____

Other:_____

_____

3. TERM OF AGENCY: REALTOR's authority to act as Buyer's exclusive agent under this Agreement shall begin _____ and shall end at midnight _____.

4. REALTOR'S REPRESENTATIONS AND SERVICES: REALTOR represents that REALTOR is duly licensed under the laws of the State of New York as a real estate broker. REALTOR will assist Buyer in locating property of the type described in Section 2 of this Agreement and to negotiate for Buyer any offer by Buyer to purchase or lease such property. During the term of this Agreement, REALTOR will give Buyer information describing and identifying properties which appear to REALTOR to substantially meet the terms set forth in Section 2.

5. COMPENSATION OF REALTOR: In consideration of the services performed by REALTOR under the terms of this Agreement, Buyer agrees to pay REALTOR the following fee(s): (Initial all applicable sections).

_____a. **Non-Refundable Retainer:** Buyer shall pay REALTOR a Non-Refundable Retainer of $ _____ to be paid to REALTOR herewith whether or not Buyer purchases or leases any property.
_____ This Retainer shall be credited against the Hourly Fee described in subsection (b) below or the Transaction Fee described in subsection (c) below.
_____b. **Hourly Fee:** Buyer will pay REALTOR at the rate of $ _____ per hour for all services performed by REALTOR under the terms of this Agreement, to be billed _____ and to be paid within five (5) days after Buyer receives a bill for such services from REALTOR.

Exclusive Buyer Agency Agreement

_____ This Hourly Fee shall be credited against the Transaction Fee described in subsection (c) below and shall be kept by REALTOR whether or not a Transaction Fee is earned.

_____c. **Transaction Fee:** Buyer shall pay REALTOR a Transaction Fee which is the lesser of $ _____ or_____% of the purchase or total lease price (and renewals and/or expansions, if applicable) of any property purchased or leased by Buyer. This Transaction Fee shall be due and payable upon closing of the Purchase and Sale Contract or Lease providing, however, if such Contract or Lease fails to close due to default by the Buyer this Transaction Fee shall become immediately due and payable to REALTOR. REALTOR is authorized to attempt to obtain payment of the Transaction Fee from the Seller or Lessor of the property , but Buyer shall have the obligation to pay REALTOR the Transaction Fee set forth in this Agreement if REALTOR cannot obtain payment of such fee from the Seller or Lessor of the property. If within_____ days after the expiration of this Agreement, Buyer purchases or leases any property which REALTOR has submitted to Buyer during the term of this Agreement, Buyer will pay RE-ALTOR the Transaction Fee stated above.

_____d. **Other:** _____

_____

6. OTHER POTENTIAL BUYERS: Buyer understands that other potential buyers have entered or may enter into similar agency contracts with REALTOR which may involve the purchase or lease, through REALTOR, of the same or similar property or properties as Buyer is attempting to purchase or lease. Buyer consents to REALTOR'S representation of such other buyers.

7. CONFLICTING INTERESTS: If REALTOR has an ownership interest in or is an agent for any owner in the sale or lease of any property in which Buyer expressed an interest (e.g. a "company listing"), REALTOR shall immediately notify Buyer of such facts. In such event, if Buyer decides to purchase or lease such property, Buyer will acknowledge the ownership interest of REALTOR or REALTOR'S contractual relationship with that owner and will allow REALTOR to act as dual agent for Buyer and owner. While acting in a dual agency capacity, REALTOR may not, without the express permission of the respective party, disclose to the other party that owner will accept a price less than the listing price or that Buyer will pay a price greater than the price offered. Furthermore, REALTOR'S position as dual agent shall be neutral with respect to both parties, and REALTOR shall act effectively as a mediator between the parties. Buyer is encouraged to refer to New York State DISCLOSURE REGARDING REAL ESTATE AGENCY RELATIONSHIPS, a copy of which is delivered herewith.

8. NONDISCRIMINATION: REALTOR and Buyer agree that all actions carried out under this Agreement shall be in full compliance with local, state and federal fair housing laws against discrimination on the basis of race, creed, color, religion, national origin, sex, familial status, marital status, age or disabilities.

9. PROFESSIONAL COUNSEL: REALTOR hereby recommends that Buyer seek legal, tax, property financing, property inspection, appraisal, environmental engineering and other professional advice (if appropriate) relating to any proposed transaction. Buyer agrees that Buyer will not rely on REALTOR for such professional advice nor rely on REALTOR for payment for such services.

10. OTHER _____

_____

11. ENTIRE AGREEMENT AND ASSIGNABILITY: This Agreement constitutes the complete agreement between REALTOR and Buyer relating to the exclusive agency of REALTOR for Buyer. No modification of any terms of this Agreement shall be valid or binding unless such modification is in writing and signed by Buyer and REALTOR. This agreement is not assignable without written approval of Buyer and REALTOR.

Date:_____   _____BUYER

_____BUYER

REALTOR: _____   BY: _____

Agencies are created by listing agreements or buyer-agency agreements. They can be terminated in several ways, including death, bankruptcy, or insanity of either party. The seller always has the right to withdraw a listing, but may be liable for the broker's expenses.

The buyer of any one- to four-family dwelling is entitled to a written disclosure of property condition statement from the seller. The buyer who does not receive one is entitled to a $500 credit, which does not, however, relieve the seller of any liability for undisclosed defects.

QUESTIONS

1. Salesperson Sally agreed to meet buyer Bill at a home listed by Sally's broker. Sally must provide Bill with an agency disclosure
   a. in advance of the first in-person meeting.
   b. prior to entering the property.
   c. after showing the property.
   d. when Bill expresses interest in making an offer.

2. A listing contract may be ended as the result of *performance of the object*, which means the
   a. property has been destroyed.
   b. seller and broker agree to cancel.
   c. owner has decided not to sell.
   d. property has been sold.

3. The agency disclosure form must be presented, explained, and signed
   a. when the customer makes an offer.
   b. when the seller accepts an offer.
   c. at the first substantive contact.
   d. when the seller and buyer first meet.

4. When communicating the present property tax information on a listed property, the listing broker should disclose
   a. the current seller's three-year payment history.
   b. the procedure that can be followed to protest property valuation.
   c. how the assessed valuation and tax rate are determined.
   d. that the tax amount is valid only for the year of the sale.

5. In a single agency agreement in which a broker represents a seller, the
   a. buyer is the client.
   b. seller is the client.
   c. seller is the customer.
   d. buyer is a subagent.

6. The broker has the most incentive to market the property with a(n)
   a. open listing.
   b. exclusive-agency listing.
   c. net listing.
   d. exclusive-right-to-sell listing.

7. Cooperating brokers MUST inform the listing agent if they are acting as agents or subagents of other parties, because these relationships impact the listing agent's
   a. motivation in presenting the property.
   b. responsibilities to the seller.
   c. potential commission.
   d. disclosure of information.

8. Vicarious liability means being responsible for
   a. the acts of another.
   b. your previous activities.
   c. unintended consequences.
   d. undisclosed relationships.

9. When a broker takes a listing, all salespeople who work for the broker are
   a. subagents for the broker and the seller.
   b. agents for the broker and subagents for the seller.
   c. dual agents for the seller and the buyer.
   d. not designated until they enter into an agreement.

10. A seller reserves the right to conduct his or her own sale without compensating the exclusive agent in an
    a. exclusive right-to-sell listing.
    b. exclusive-agency listing.
    c. multiple listing.
    d. net listing.

11. A broker who lists a property on the broker's Web site should remove the listing from the for-sale section of the site
    a. when the listing appears on an MLS.
    b. 90 days after it appears.
    c. when an offer is made.
    d. when a sale occurs.

12. A residential transaction is defined as any transaction involving the sale or lease of four or fewer units
    a. not owned by a business.
    b. located in a residential zone.
    c. intended for dwelling.
    d. involving a sales price of $1 million or less.

13. In a dual agency relationship, the parties give up their right to
    a. undivided loyalty.
    b. obedience.
    c. care.
    d. accounting.

14. Broker Susan represents Murphy as a buyer's agent. She wants to show Murphy property a seller has listed with her. If broker Susan shows Murphy the property, she
    a. will have done nothing wrong.
    b. is violating license law.
    c. should first get the informed, written consent of both buyer and seller to act as a dual agent.
    d. must first notify the secretary of state that she intends to represent both buyer and seller.

CHAPTER

4

The Broker's Office

■ KEY TERMS

antitrust laws	employees	policy and procedures
blind ad	fair employment laws	guide
consent decree	group boycott	restraint of trade
designations	independent contractor	tie-in arrangement

■ WHO NEEDS A LICENSE

A license as a real estate broker is required for any of the services listed in Chapter 1, when they are performed *for another and for a fee*. The transactions covered include listing real estate for sale, selling, purchasing, negotiating exchanges, leasing, renting, auctioning, and negotiating the sale of a business with substantial real estate involved.

The license allows the same functions with regard to cooperatives and condominiums.

■ OTHER RELATED LICENSES

As detailed in Chapter 1, licenses are required for apartment information vendors and apartment sharing agents, who must maintain trust accounts and renew their licenses annually. Appraisers who work with federally related loans on property worth more than $250,000 require special licensing or certification (details later in this chapter). Mortgage bankers are licensed by the New York Banking Department, after proving a net worth of at least $250,000 and a line of credit of at least $1 million, at least five years' experience as lenders, and meeting other requirements. Mortgage brokers pass less stringent requirements for registration by the Banking Department. Home inspectors are licensed after study, examinations, and supervised inspection experience.

■ WHO DOES NOT NEED A LICENSE

Licensure is not required for the following:

- *Attorneys admitted to the New York bar* may act as real estate brokers without any further license, and thus could collect commissions for real estate services. The lawyer who intends to supervise associated salespersons or brokers, however, must apply for a broker's license but need not satisfy the experience, education, or examination requirements.
- Some individuals may be exempt from license requirements if they *perform services for one employer only.* The exemption might cover, for example, in-house salespersons for the developer of a real estate subdivision or the resident manager in an apartment complex. Often, though, such persons do secure licenses, just to be on the safe side.
- *Public officers in the performance of their duties* are also exempt. Negotiating the purchase of a tract of land to be used for a park, for example, would not require the town supervisor to be licensed.
- *Those acting under court order* do not need licenses. Often this is the executor of a will, who negotiates the sale of the home belonging to an estate.
- A *business broker* does not need a real estate license, unless the business being sold includes a material (significant) amount of its value in real estate.

■ OBTAINING A LICENSE

The Department of State (DOS) issues brokers' licenses to experienced real estate salespersons who have completed what is, in effect, an *apprenticeship* under supervision of a managing broker or to those with extensive other experience in real estate. In addition to the 75-hour qualifying course required of beginning salespersons, the DOS mandates an additional 45-hour course for prospective brokers. Part of this course consists of a review of license law and agency (Chapters 1, 2, and 3), to be studied in greater detail from the point of view of someone who may soon be supervising others and be responsible for their actions. The remainder of the course covers more advanced specialties within real estate brokerage. The DOS's Web page can be viewed at *www.dos.state.ny.us.*

WEB LINK

The education, experience, and examination requirements are the same for all brokers' licenses (except those issued to attorneys and brokers transferring from states with which New York has reciprocity agreements—see Table 1.3 in Chapter 1). The DOS issues licenses, however, in several different classes:

■ *Class 30* is for the applicant planning to work as an associate broker. Although fully qualified as a broker, the associate nevertheless chooses to work within another broker's firm. As with a salesperson's application, the associate broker's application is signed by a sponsoring broker. Should the associate broker ever wish to operate independently, no further study or examination would be necessary. Application would simply be made to the DOS for a license in the new class.

■ *Class 31* is issued to the officer of a corporation who conducts a brokerage business under a corporate name. (Salespersons and associate brokers may not be principals or own voting stock in a licensed brokerage corporation.) For new corporations, the application must include the filing receipt.

■ *Class 33* is for the broker who intends to do business under the name of a partnership. A copy of the county clerk's certificate of partnership must accompany the application.

■ *Class 35* is for the individual broker who will do business in his or her name only, as "John Smith" or "Jane Brown, licensed real estate broker."

■ *Class 37* signifies licensure as a trade-name broker, who will own the business as a sole proprietorship. The local county clerk, after ascertaining that no one else uses the requested trade name, will issue a D/B/A (doing business as) certificate that must accompany the license application; for example, "Juan Sanchez, d/b/a House Calls Realty."

■ *Class 49, limited liability company* or *limited liability partnership broker,* is for the member or manager of a brokerage operating under one of these relatively new types of organizations. For a new limited liability company, a copy of the articles of organization or a filing receipt must be filed with the application.

The broker who intends to use anything other than his or her own name for the firm must submit the proposed name for approval to the DOS, which will check, among other things, whether the name is identical with or misleadingly similar to one already in use for a brokerage. *It is prudent to postpone ordering stationery, yellow pages advertising, business cards, or a web page domain until the name has been cleared.*

The Broker's Application

The broker's application (see Figure 4.1) must list the street address of the proposed business. A post office box is not considered sufficient. If the address is outside the state of New York, an agreement giving irrevocable consent (to be sued within the state) must be filed. The required form is available from the DOS's Customer Services Unit (1-518-474-4429).

A check for $150 must accompany each broker's application.

It is possible to hold more than one broker's license at a time. A separate check and application are submitted for each. An associate broker may desire also to operate individually in his or her name or as a partner or member of a corporation dealing in real estate. Some other class of broker may wish to operate as an associate broker also. In either case, a letter from the sponsoring broker involved must be enclosed, indicating that he or she understands about the dual licensure.

Experience Requirement

License law requires that a broker have had at least two years' full-time experience as a licensed salesperson or three years' experience in the general real estate

F I G U R E   **4.1**

Broker's Application

FOR OFFICE USE ONLY	CLASS	KEY	UNIQUE ID NUMBER	CASH NUMBER	FEE
	|__|__|	|__|__|	|__|__|__|__|__|__|__|		**$150**

E W S \|__\|__\|__\|__\|__\| / \|__\|__\| B   \|__\|__\|__\|__\|__\| / \|__\|__\| PASSED EXAM \|__\|__\|__\|__\|__\|__\|__\|

Real Estate Broker/Associate Broker Application
PLEASE PRINT OR TYPE ALL RESPONSES IN INK

NYS Department of State
DIVISION OF LICENSING SERVICES
P.O. Box 22001
Albany, NY 12201-2001

Application as (Check one): ☐ **Individual**   ☐ **Trade Name**   ☐ **Corporation**   ☐ **Associate Broker**
☐ **Partnership**   ☐ **Limited Liability Company**   ☐ **Limited Liability Partnership**

APPLICANT'S NAME	LAST	FIRST	M.I.	SUFFIX

HOME ADDRESS	STREET ADDRESS (REQUIRED)		APT. NUMBER

CITY	STATE	ZIP+4	COUNTY

BUSINESS NAME

BUSINESS ADDRESS	STREET ADDRESS (REQUIRED)

CITY	STATE	ZIP+4	COUNTY

DAYTIME TELEPHONE NUMBER (IF PROBLEM WITH APPLICATION)	SOCIAL SECURITY NUMBER (SEE PRIVACY NOTIFICATION)	FEDERAL TAXPAYER ID (SEE PRIVACY NOTIFICATION)
( )		

E-MAIL ADDRESS (IF ANY)

1   Background Data —

1. What is your date of birth? _____

   YES   NO

2. Are you currently a member of the New York State Bar?   ____   ____

3. Have you ever held or do you currently hold a real estate license issued by the State of New York? If Yes, in what year? _____ UNIQUE ID NO. _____   ____   ____

4. Have you ever been convicted in this state or elsewhere of any criminal offense that is a misdemeanor or a felony?   ____   ____

   ➜ **IF "YES,"** you must submit with this application a written explanation giving the place, court jurisdiction, nature of the offense, sentence and/or other disposition. You must submit a copy of the accusatory instrument (e.g., indictment, criminal information or complaint) and a Certificate of Disposition. If you possess or have received a Certificate of Relief from Disabilities, Certificate of Good Conduct or Executive Pardon, you must submit a copy with this application.

5. Are there any criminal charges (misdemeanors or felonies) pending against you in any court in this state or elsewhere?   ____   ____

   ➜ **IF "YES,"** you must submit a copy of the accusatory instrument (e.g., indictment, criminal information or complaint).

6. Has any license or permit issued to you or a company in which you are or were a principal in New York State or elsewhere ever been revoked, suspended or denied?   ____   ____

   ➜ **IF "YES,"** you must provide all relevant documents, including the agency determination, if any.)

   For questions 7-10 please answer only the statement which applies to your particular licensing status. (Please enclose a copy of the required certificate)

7. I own this business and the trade name certificate has been filed in the office of the County Clerk where the business is located. (copy enclosed)   ____   ____

DOS-0036 (Rev. 7/06)   REAL ESTATE BROKER/ASSOCIATE BROKER APPLICATION PAGE 1 OF 2

F I G U R E   4.1 (CONTINUED)

Broker's Application

	YES	NO
8. I am a member of this partnership and the Certificate of Partnership has been filed in the office of the County Clerk where the business is located. (copy enclosed)	_____	_____
9. a. I am an officer of this corporation and the New York State Certification of Incorporation has been filed with the Department of State, Division of Corporations. (copy enclosed)	_____	_____
b. I am an officer of this foreign (out of state) corporation and an application for authority to do business has been filed with the Department of State, Division of Corporations. (copy enclosed)	_____	_____
c. I am currently a licensed real estate salesperson for the above corporation and will be made an officer upon approval of my application.	_____	_____
10. I am a (member) (manager) of this limited liability company, and a copy of the articles of organization have been filed with the Department of State. (copy enclosed)	_____	_____

2   Child Support Statement — *You must complete this section. If you do not complete it, your application will be returned.*

"X" A or B, below

I, the undersigned, do hereby certify that (You *must* "X" A or B, below):

A. [ ] **I am not under obligation to pay child support.** (SKIP "B" and go directly to **Applicant Affirmation**).

B. [ ] I am under obligation to pay child support. (You must "X" any of the four statements below that are true and apply to you):

    [ ] I do *not* owe four or more months of child support payments.

    [ ] I am making child support payments by income execution or court approved payment plan or by a plan agreed to by the parties.

    [ ] My child support obligation is the subject of a pending court proceeding.

    [ ] I receive public assistance or supplemental social security income.

Applicant Affirmation — I also affirm, under the penalties of perjury, that the statements made in this application are true and correct. I further affirm that I have read and understand the provisions of Article 12-A of the Real Property Law and the rules and regulations promulgated thereunder.

Applicant's Signature

X _____ *Date* _____

3   For Associate Broker Applicants Only

Association Statement — I am sponsoring this applicant.

The sponsoring broker must print and sign their name as indicated below. In addition, they must provide their UID# and the date signed.

Sponsoring Broker _____   *Sponsoring Broker* _____

               (Print name)   *(Sign your name)*

Sponsoring Broker's Unique ID Number _____   *Date* _____

business or a combination of those two requirements. A supplement detailing the claimed experience accompanies the application.

It's important that salespersons keep their own files of all transactions, so that in the case of a DOS audit or investigation they can furnish details for all points claimed on their applications.

Broker's Examination
The broker's examination is given at the test centers listed in Chapter 1. As with the salesperson's examination, expedited mail delivery of test results is available from the Albany, New York City, and Rochester sites. The applicant who wishes to begin operating as a broker as quickly as possible can bring a fully completed application and fee to the test site. A temporary Letter of Authorization will be mailed promptly to those who pass the test, pending receipt of a license.

WEB LINK

Information on dates and times is available at the Web site *www.dos.state.ny.us/ lcns/broker.html*. Online license renewals are also available. The Web site should be checked before any walk-in is attempted because regulations may change.

◼ RENEWAL OF LICENSE

The DOS sends renewal applications near the end of the two-year license period to all brokers and salespersons, which is one reason change of address notifications are important. If the application is not received, however, it is the licensee's obligation to ask for it and to complete the renewal process. The renewal application includes the signature of the sponsoring broker (for salespersons and associate brokers); the fee of $50 for a salesperson and $150 for a broker; and a statement about continuing education completed during the preceding two years. Successful completion of 22½ hours of approved courses is required for broker renewal, just as it is for salespersons, with two exceptions. Attorneys are exempt from the education requirement, and so is anyone active as an associate or active broker at the time of renewal who has been continuously licensed (as either a salesperson and/ or broker) for 15 years before July 1, 2008.

WEB LINK

Online license renewals are available at the Web site *www.dos.state.ny.us/lcns/ realestnew.html*.

◼ REVIEW OF CHAPTER ONE

The prospective broker should review Chapter 1 carefully, with special attention to the broker's responsibility for notifying the DOS whenever there is a change of address or change in a salesperson's or associate broker's status. *It must always be remembered that brokers are legally responsible for their associates' real estate activities.* When the DOS investigates violations of license law, the broker's defense that "I didn't know what that salesman was doing" probably will be countered by, "You should have known." The broker is expected to furnish close, regular supervision and guidance. This legal responsibility for the actions of others is known as *vicarious liability*.

F I G U R E   4.2

Broker's Application—Licensed Salesperson Activity

Real Estate Broker/Associate Broker Application
Licensed Salespersons Activity Only

PAGE ___ OF ___

APPLICANT NAME (ENTER NAME EXACTLY AS SHOWN ON APPLICATION PAGE 1)   **Unique ID Number**

Instructions for Completing Supplement A

You must accumulate a minimum of **1750** points* to qualify for a broker's license based on experience as a real estate salesperson. Applicants must also be licensed as a real estate salesperson for a minimum period of one year*.

1. In the Number of Transactions Performed column, enter the amount of your activity for each category.
2. Multiply the number of transactions performed by the point value indicated to arrive at the points earned for that category.
3. Add the points earned for each category to arrive at your total points.
4. Enter the total figure on the Total Qualifying Points Line. This is your final qualifying points earned.

*Except those using combined experience.

You must also complete the experience report on the other side of this page to report your qualifying experience. Points earned for that experience must be calculated below.

Category	Point Value X	Number of Transactions Performed =	Total Points Earned
Residential Sales:			
1. Single Family, condo, co-op unit, multi family (2 to 8 unit), farm (with residence, under 100 acres)	250 X	_____ =	_____
2. Exclusive listings	10 X	_____ =	_____
3. Open listings	1 X	_____ =	_____
4. Binders effected	25 X	_____ =	_____
5. Co-op unit transaction approved by seller and buyer that fails to win Board of Directors approval	100 X	_____ =	_____
Residential Rentals:			
6. Rentals or subleases effected	25 X	_____ =	_____
7. Exclusive Listings	5 X	_____ =	_____
8. Open Listings	1 X	_____ =	_____
9. Property Management - Lease renewal	2 X	_____ =	_____
- Rent collections per tenant/per year	1 X	_____ =	_____
Commercial Sales:			
10. Taxpayer/Storefront	400 X	_____ =	_____
11. Office Building	400 X	_____ =	_____
12. Apartment Building (9 units or more)	400 X	_____ =	_____
13. Shopping Center	400 X	_____ =	_____
14. Factory/Industrial warehouse	400 X	_____ =	_____
15. Hotel/Motel	400 X	_____ =	_____
16. Transient garage/parking lot	400 X	_____ =	_____
17. Multi-unit commercial condominium	400 X	_____ =	_____
18. Urban commercial development site	400 X	_____ =	_____
19. Alternative sale type transaction	400 X	_____ =	_____
20. Single-tenant commercial condo	250 X	_____ =	_____
21. Listings	10 X	_____ =	_____
Commercial Leasing:			
22. New Lease - aggregate rental $1 to $200,000	150 X	_____ =	_____
23. New Lease - aggregate rental $200,000 to $1 million	250 X	_____ =	_____
24. New Lease - aggregate rental over $1 million	400 X	_____ =	_____
25. Renewal - aggregate rental $1 to $200,000	75 X	_____ =	_____
26. Renewal - aggregate rental $200,000 to $1 million	125 X	_____ =	_____
27. Renewal - aggregate rental over $1 million	200 X	_____ =	_____
28. Listings	10 X	_____ =	_____
Commercial Financing (includes residential properties of more than four units):			
29. $1 to $500,000	200 X	_____ =	_____
30. $500,000 to $5,000,000	300 X	_____ =	_____
31. Over $5,000,000	400 X	_____ =	_____
Miscellaneous:			
32. Sale vacant lots, land (under 100 acres)	50 X	_____ =	_____
33. Sale vacant land (more than 100 acres)	150 X	_____ =	_____
34. Other, must be fully explained	___ X	_____ =	_____
Total Qualifying Points ➤			_____

DOS-036A (Rev. 07/06)

F I G U R E 4.2 (CONTINUED)

Broker's Application—Licensed Salesperson Activity

Employment History

You must indicate all employment which is commensurate with the experience claimed on the other side of this form. Please make sure that you and the sponsoring broker complete and sign the certification and indicate the total points accumulated. If you were employed with another broker(s) and are claiming experience through that association, you must also have that broker sign the certification and indicate points accumulated while working under his/her sponsorship.

Current Sponsoring Broker/Agency (please print or type)

| NAME | LAST | FIRST | M.I. | SUFFIX |

| WORK ADDRESS | STREET ADDRESS (REQUIRED) |

| CITY | STATE | ZIP+4 | COUNTY |

UNIQUE ID NUMBER

Additional Salesperson Experience (if applicable)

Salesperson Experience - I was actively engaged as a licensed real estate salesperson as indicated below:

Broker's Name and Address:	Number of Hours/Week	From: Month/Day/Year	To: Month/Day/Year

Notice to Applicant: The information given on this application is subject to verification. In order to prevent any unnecessary return of your application, we request your cooperation by providing us with information that will help us contact you by telephone if needed.

Business Phone: (   ) _____ *Home Phone:* (   ) _____ *Alternate:* (   ) _____

All claimed transactions are subject to verification. In order to claim experience points, both the broker and salesperson applicant must be able to provide documentation which clearly demonstrates the active participation of the applicant in each transaction.

Failure to provide satisfactory supporting documentation may result in denial of the application and/or disciplinary action initiated against the applicant and broker.

We, the undersigned, jointly certify that the named applicant has accumulated a total of _____ points as indicated in the preceding qualifying experience report. We further certify that the information given above is true to the best of our knowledge and belief. We understand that any material misstatement made may result in the revocation or suspension of the license, if issued, as well as any existing license of the applicant and/or the broker.

Applicant Signature/Date _____ *Broker Signature/Date* _____

Additional Affirmations if Necessary:

We, the undersigned, jointly certify that the named applicant has accumulated a total of _____ points as indicated in the preceding qualifying experience report. We further certify that the information given above is true to the best of our knowledge and belief. We understand that any material misstatement made may result in the revocation or suspension of the license, if issued, as well as any existing license of the applicant and/or the broker.

Applicant Signature/Date _____ *Broker Signature/Date* _____

DOS-036A (Rev. 07/06)

FIGURE 4.3

Broker's Application—Experience

 Real Estate Broker/Associate Broker Application
Experience

PAGE ___ OF ___

APPLICANT NAME (ENTER NAME EXACTLY AS SHOWN ON APPLICATION PAGE 1)

Unique ID Number

Combined Experience as a Licensed Real Estate Salesperson
and Equivalent Experience in General Real Estate Business
Instructions for Completing Supplement C

You must accumulate a minimum of **3500** points to qualify for a broker's license based on combined experience in General Real Estate Business and Licensed Real Estate Salesperson Experience. Applicants must also possess at least two years of experience in the real estate business equivalent to that of an active real estate salesperson.

1. You must complete both sides of Supplement A for all licensed salesperson activity of less than one year. Please disregard the minimum point requirement indicated in Supplement A.
2. You must complete both sides of Supplement B for all equivalent experience in general real estate business. Please disregard the minimum point requirement indicated in Supplement B.
3. After completing Supplements A and B, use the following table for computing your total combined experience.

Enter in the box at right your qualifying points earned from Licensed Salesperson Activity (from the Total Qualifying Points box on Supplement A). *Multiply by two.* Enter this number in the box at the far right.		X 2	
Enter in the box at right your qualifying points earned from Equivalent Experience in General Real Estate Business (from the Total Qualifying Points box on Supplement B).			
Add your qualifying points from Licensed Salesperson Activity and Equivalent Experience in General Real Estate Business and enter in the box at right. This is your total qualifying points earned.			

IMPORTANT — You must earn at least **3500** total points (from Supplement A and Supplement B) to qualify under combined experience. Please be sure that Supplement A and Supplement B are completely filled out.

Advertising Guidelines   When the new broker orders business cards or places advertisements, DOS rules will apply.

Regulation 175.25a states that all advertisements placed by a broker must make it clear that the advertiser is indeed a broker (no **blind ads**). The ad also must include the broker's telephone number. Once it does, salespersons' names also may be included.

Advertisements claiming the property is in a "vicinity" must also name the geographic area where the property is actually located ("near Fancy Heights" may really be "in Swillburg Flats").

The DOS is strict in its regulations concerning business cards. No matter how creative the broker's advertising artist, the card must contain the individual's full name, the type of license held, and name and business address of the firm. Type of license may be abbreviated ("Lic. Assoc. R. E. Broker"). Residence phone numbers may be included if they are identified as "Home," "Residence," or "Res." Additional items may include the individual's field of specialization ("Commercial Properties"); position in the firm ("Vice President"); or nickname ("Buster"). A salesperson's name may not be published in type larger than the name of the licensed broker.

The same regulations have been extended to Web sites. Any Internet advertising by a salesperson must contain a link to the firm's Web site and be supervised by the principal broker.

Regulation Z   The Truth-in-Advertising Act, known as *Regulation Z*, provides for the strict regulation of real estate advertisements that include mortgage financing terms. General statements like "liberal terms available" or "low down payment" are acceptable, but certain details, known as "triggering terms," require that additional information be included. Triggering terms are the

- amount or percentage of down payment (except for "nothing down" or "no down payment");
- number of payments or period of repayment ("five years left on mortgage");
- amount of any payment ("only $700 a month"); or
- amount of any finance charge.

If any of those items is listed, the advertisement also must contain the

- amount or percentage of down payment;
- number of payments or term of loan; and
- words *annual percentage rate*, which takes into consideration all credit costs rather than the interest rate alone.

■ ANTITRUST LAWS

Antitrust laws are designed to prevent the unreasonable restraint of trade (business) as a result of the cooperation or conspiracy of various members of the trade. One of the most important antitrust acts is the Sherman Antitrust Act of 1890. The Sherman Act prohibits any kind of contract, combination, or conspiracy in the **restraint of trade.** A *conspiracy* is defined as two or more separate business entities participating in a common scheme or plan, the effect of which is the restraint of trade. Antitrust laws prohibit practices such as

Antitrust Laws Prohibit
- price fixing;
- group boycotting;
- market allocation; and
- tie-in arrangements.

- *price-fixing:* an agreement between members of a trade to artificially maintain prices at a set level;
- *group boycott:* an agreement between members of a trade to exclude other members from fair participation in the activities of the trade;
- *market allocation:* an agreement between members of a trade to refrain from competition in specific market areas; and
- *tie-in arrangements:* arrangements by which provision of certain products or services is made contingent on the purchase of other unrelated products or services.

In 1950, in the case of *United States v. National Association of Real Estate Boards,* the Supreme Court recognized that trade, as used in the Sherman Act, included the real estate brokerage business. Therefore, the real estate business is subject to the restraints of antitrust laws. In this case, the mandatory fee schedules that were set and enforced by real estate boards were held to violate the Sherman Act.

In the 1970s several more real estate boards and associations, including some in New York State, were prosecuted under antitrust laws for unfair restraint of trade, following investigations by Assistant Attorney General Richard McLaren (whose investigations also considered firms of architects and accountants). The result of those cases is that real estate agents and professional real estate associations must exercise extreme care to avoid any appearance of price-fixing in regard to real estate commissions.

In *U.S. v. Prince Georges County Board of REALTORS®, Inc.,* the case was settled by a **consent decree,** under which the board admitted no wrongdoing but agreed to change its ways. In 1972 the Long Island Board of REALTORS® agreed, in a consent decree, never to fix the rate or amount of any commission, recommend or publish a schedule of commission rates, limit the right of REALTORS® to negotiate commissions with a client, mandate the amount of commission split between cooperating brokers, refuse to accept a listing in its MLS because of its commission rate, or establish high fees for board membership beyond what was necessary to operate the organization properly. (In some boards, unduly high membership fees and entrance requirements had the effect of blocking minority brokers from membership.)

Violation of the Sherman Act is a felony, and penalties can be as high as $350,000 for an individual and $10 million for corporations. A jail term of up to three years is also possible.

The Clayton Antitrust Act supplements the Sherman Act. Under the Clayton Act private parties are allowed to sue antitrust violators, and if successful, they can recover three times the damages incurred plus court costs and attorneys' fees.

The Federal Trade Commission (FTC) has the power to declare trade practices unfair and to enforce compliance with the Sherman Act and some sections of the Clayton Act, but it cannot impose penal sanctions. The Department of Justice also has the power to fine antitrust law violators.

Most states, including New York, also have laws against monopolies, restraints of trade, and unfair trade practices.

Commissions

Any conversation between two brokers from different brokerages regarding commission rates charged to clients is strictly off limits. The only permissible discussion of commissions between two competing brokers would be a discussion of the commission split between a listing broker and a selling broker in a cooperative sale.

Brokers may discuss client commission rates with their salespeople as a matter of office policy. Potential salespersons being interviewed certainly may inquire about the company's typical rates and how commissions are shared with the salesperson who earned them. Such conversations are perfectly proper. The danger comes when any discussion about rates takes place with brokers or salespersons from other offices.

In *United States v. Foley*, a conspiracy to fix commission rates was found when a member of a board of REALTORS® announced at a board function that he was raising his gross commission rate, and that he did not care what others did. The court viewed the announcement as an invitation to conspire, and the subsequent actions of the other board members were viewed as an acceptance of this invitation. This case is important, because it illustrates the fact that alleged conspirators do not actually have to consult with each other to be judged guilty of conspiring to fix commission rates.

The prohibition against discussion of commission rates among independent brokers extends to publication as well as conversation. Many years ago, certain real estate associations maintained mandatory commission rates for their members, but today an association would be in trouble if it attempted to publish recommended rates or even a survey of going rates. For the same reason, multiple listing services (MLSs) do not publish the commission rates that are charged by listing brokers, but only the amount of commission offered to cooperating brokers.

Group Boycotts

The object of a **group boycott** is to hurt or destroy a competitor; it takes only two brokers to form a group that can be found guilty of a group boycott. For example, if two brokers agree to refuse to cooperate with a third broker or agree to cooperate with that third broker but on less-favorable terms, that action is an *automatic violation* of the antitrust act.

Two independent brokers should never engage in negative conversation regarding the business practices of a third broker, because such a conversation could be construed as an attempt at a group boycott of the third broker. A broker who questions the ethics or practices of another broker may freely choose not to do business with such a broker but may not convey his or her feelings to other brokers in any manner that might lead them to take similar action.

Market Allocation

Agreements between brokers to divide their markets or customers and refrain from competing with each other's business violate antitrust laws. These market allocation agreements could be about geographic territories, price ranges, types of properties, sociological divisions of business, or the refusal to deal with a competitor.

Tie-in Agreements

A **tie-in arrangement,** or *tying agreement,* is defined as an agreement to sell one product only on the condition that the buyer purchase another product as well. An example of a real estate tying agreement would be a so-called list-back clause. For example, a subdivision developer may sell a lot to a builder on the condition that the builder agree to list (or list back) the improved property with the developer for resale to a homebuyer. A property management agreement that requires that the owner list the managed property with the manager should the owner decide to sell it is another example of a tying agreement. Tie-in agreements are violations of the antitrust laws.

Enforcement

The Sherman Act is enforced by the U.S. Attorney General through the Antitrust Division of the Department of Justice. Both civil and criminal actions can be brought against those who violate antitrust laws. A corporation found guilty of violating the Sherman Act can be fined up to $10 million; an individual may be fined up to $350,000 and/or be sentenced to three years in prison.

Risk Reduction

Brokers are liable both for their own actions and the actions of their licensees; therefore, it is imperative that brokers educate themselves on antitrust issues. Brokers also should train their licensees to be aware of what may constitute an antitrust law violation. Brokers never should use forms that contain preprinted commission rates, listing periods, or protection periods. Each of these provisions should include a blank that will be filled in after negotiation between the parties.

Brokers always should take care to establish their fees and other listing terms independently, without consulting any competing firms. Each business judgment and negotiated term should be documented in the form of a confidential memo. Brokers also must avoid discussing business plans with competitors.

■ MULTIPLE LISTING SERVICES

Multiple listing services play an important role in the marketing of property, especially residential property. The ability to participate in an MLS greatly enhances the exposure of a property in the market, providing advantages not only to the seller but to the participating listing broker as well. The importance of MLSs in the real estate industry has been recognized in a number of court cases that have imposed obligations on these services to provide open access on a nondiscriminatory basis.

Access to MLS

An MLS must permit access by any licensed real estate broker who can satisfy the requirements of the MLS. These requirements must be reasonable, and they may not be discriminatory in nature or effect. The charge for membership in the MLS must be equivalent to the cost involved in setting up the new member, and fees must be reasonable and nondiscriminatory.

MLS regulations may not unreasonably restrict the operations of its members. Participating brokers may not be prohibited from membership in another MLS or from cooperating with non-MLS brokers. The MLS may not regulate a broker's office hours, and it may not restrict the types of properties that can be advertised through the MLS.

A court decision from the 11th Circuit Federal Court of Appeals (which includes Florida, Georgia, and Alabama) has held that a REALTORS® MLS may not exclude non-REALTORS® from membership. The decision affected only those states, but the implications of this case may well lead to elimination of such restrictions on a nationwide basis.

■ SALESPERSON EMPLOYMENT STATUS

All licensed salespersons and associate brokers are required by law to work under the supervision of a sponsoring broker in their real estate activities. In doing so, the salesperson may be hired either as an employee or as an independent contractor. The distinction between an *employee* and an *independent contractor* is an important one, with significant tax consequences as well as important effects on the ability of a broker to control the activities of his or her salespeople.

Employee Status

The employer-employee relationship allows a broker to exercise certain controls over salespeople. The broker can require that an employee adhere to regulations affecting working hours, office routine, and dress standards.

As an employer a broker is required by the federal government to withhold Social Security tax and income tax from the compensation paid to employees. An employee is covered by unemployment insurance and workers' compensation. A broker may provide employees with fringe benefits such as health insurance, pension plans, sick leave, and paid vacations. Such benefits are variously estimated to add 25 percent to 50 percent to the cost of an employee's base salary. A broker who chooses to regard salespersons as employees must take such costs into consideration when working out commission schedules and salaries.

Independent Contractor Status

Most salespersons, however, act as independent contractors. A survey by the National Association of REALTORS® found that nine out of ten real estate firms treated their sales associates as independent contractors. Brokers traditionally have maintained this relationship to avoid the bookkeeping problems of withholding taxes, Social Security payments, unemployment insurance, and other such items that become complex when based not on a regular salary but on unpredictable commissions.

The managing broker who takes on associates to work as independent contractors should carefully avoid the words *employ, employer,* and *employee*. Merely using the words *independent contractor* is not enough, however, to establish the relationship in the eyes of the Internal Revenue Service (which is concerned with income tax withholding and employer-paid Social Security) or the State of New York (which mandates unemployment insurance and workers' compensation coverage for all employees).

Understanding the independent contractor safe-harbor guidelines is important. While safe-harbor guidelines require a contract at least every 15 months, it is wise to set an annual date, perhaps the first of each year, on which to review and re-sign the contract with each associate.

Errors and omissions insurance. A broker may carry errors and omissions insurance on all salespeople, regardless of their status as employees or independent contractors. The cost may be borne by the broker or by the salesperson.

Tests of Employment

The broker who chooses independent contractor status for associates should keep on file agreements signed by the associates, with wording that has been reviewed by the broker's attorney. Recent *safe-harbor guidelines* provide that the IRS will not challenge independent contractor status where the associate (1) is licensed as a real estate broker or salesperson; (2) has income based on sales output and subject to fluctuation; and (3) performs services pursuant to a written contract specifying independent contractor status.

In 1986, New York State adopted similar guidelines on independent contractor status for real estate licensees, whose situation had been unclear with regard to state programs such as unemployment insurance and workers' compensation insurance. The New York Department of Labor, in evaluating associates' status with regard to unemployment insurance, also stresses the importance of a current, written contract between broker and salesperson. A sample contract that meets the Department of Labor requirements, suggested by the New York State Association of REALTORS®, is shown in Figure 4.4.

The requirements for independent contractor status under New York State law are as follows:

1. Substantially all of the licensee's compensation (whether or not paid in cash) for services performed on behalf of the broker must be directly related to sales or other output, rather than to the number of hours worked.
2. There must be a written contract for services between the broker and the licensee, *executed within the past 15 months*, that indicates that the licensee is engaged as an independent contractor.
3. The written contract between the broker and licensee must not have been executed under duress (i.e., the broker may not force the licensee to sign the agreement, although the broker may choose not to maintain the licensee's license if he or she refuses to sign).
4. The written contract must contain the following provisions:
    - The licensee will be treated for all purposes by the broker as an independent contractor.
    - The licensee will be paid a commission directly related to gross sales or other output without deduction for taxes.
    - The licensee will not receive any compensation related to the number of hours worked.
    - The licensee will not be treated as an employee for federal or state tax purposes.
    - The licensee may work any hours he or she chooses.
    - The licensee may work out of his or her home as well as out of the broker's office.
    - The licensee is free to engage in outside employment.

FIGURE 4.4

Sample Independent Contractor Agreement

INDEPENDENT CONTRACTOR RELATIONSHIP AGREEMENT

AGREEMENT, this day of 200_, by and between _____ residing at _____ (hereinafter referred to as the "Sales Associate") and _____ having a principal place of business at _____ (hereinafter referred to as the "Broker").

WITNESSETH:

WHEREAS, Sales Associate and Broker are each respectively duly licensed pursuant to Article 12-A of the Real Property Law of the State of New York, and WHEREAS, the parties hereto have freely and voluntarily entered into this Agreement, without duress.

NOW, THEREFORE, in consideration of the mutual promises herein contained, it is hereby agreed as follows:

1. Sales Associate is engaged as an independent contractor associated with the Broker pursuant to Article 12-A of the Real Property Law and shall be treated as such for all purposes, including but not limited to Federal and State Income taxation, withholding tax regulations, Unemployment Insurance, and Workers' Compensation coverages.
2. Sales Associate (a) shall be paid a commission on Sales Associate's gross sales, if any, without deduction for taxes, which commission shall be directly related to sales or other output; (b) shall not be entitled to draw against commissions; (c) shall not receive any remuneration related to the number of hours worked; and (d) shall not be treated as an employee with respect to such services for Federal and State Income tax purposes.
3. Sales Associate shall be permitted to work such hours as Sales Associates may elect to work.
4. Sales Associate shall be permitted to work out of Sales Associate's residence or the offices of Broker or any other location in the sole discretion of Sales Associate.
5. Sales Associate shall be free to engage in outside employment.
6. Broker may provide office facilities and supplies for the use of Sales Associate. All other expenses, including but not limited to automobile, travel, and entertainment expenses, shall be borne by Sales Associate.
7. Broker may offer initial training and hold periodic sales meetings. The attendance by Sales Associate shall be at the option of Sales Associate.
8. Broker may offer a group insurance plan and if Sales Associate wishes to participate therein, all premiums shall be paid by Sales Associate.
9. Broker may elect, but shall be under no obligation, to assign leads to Sales Associates on a rotating basis. Sales Associate shall be responsible for procuring Sales Associate's own leads.
10. Broker and Sales Associate shall comply with the requirements of Article 12-A of the Real Property Law and the regulations pertaining thereto. Such compliance shall not affect Sales Associate's status as an independent contractor nor shall compliance be construed as an indication that Sales Associate is an employee of Broker for any purpose whatsoever.
11. This contract and the association created thereby may be terminated by either party hereto at any time upon notice give by one party to the other.
12. For purposes of this Agreement, the term "Broker" shall include individual real estate brokers, real estate brokerage companies, real estate brokerage corporations, and any other entity acting as a principal broker. The term "Sales Associate" shall include real estate sales associates and real estate brokers, who, as real estate licensees, associate with and place their real estate license with a principal broker.
13. Sales Associate hereby agrees to and hereby assigns to Broker irrevocably and without the necessity of any additional consideration, all of Sales Associate's right, title, and interest in any copyright rights or other intellectual property rights in any property listing posted by Sales Associate in the MLS system or otherwise provided to the MLS. Such right, title, and interest shall be deemed assigned as of the moment of creation without any further action of the part of either party, During and after the term of this Agreement, Sales Associate shall confirm such assignment by executing and delivering such assignments or other instruments and take any action necessary to enable Broker to secure, protect, enforce, and defend its copyrights in such data and/or content.
14. This Agreement shall be governed and construed in accordance with the laws of the State of New York.
15. No waiver of any of the provisions of this Agreement or any of the rights or remedies of the parties hereto shall be valid unless such waiver is in writing, signed by the party to be charged therewith.
16. Whenever in this Agreement any notices are required to be given, such notices shall be in writing and shall be sent by registered mail or certified mail, return receipt requested, to the party entitled to receive the same.
17. This Agreement and all of it's terms, covenants, and provisions insofar as applicable, shall be binding upon and inure to the benefit of the parties hereto, their respective heirs, executors, administrators, successors, and assigns.

IN WITNESS WHEREOF, the individual parties hereto have hereunder set their hands and seals, and any corporate party has caused this instrument to be signed by a corporate officer and caused its corporate seal to be hereunto affixed, all as of the day and the year first above written.

_____

Sales Associate

(SEAL) _____

Broker

■ The broker may provide office facilities and supplies for use by the licensee, but the licensee will otherwise bear his or her own expenses, including automobile, travel, and entertainment expenses.

■ The licensee and broker will act in accordance with the terms of the Real Property Law and Department of State real estate regulations.

■ Either the licensee or the broker may terminate the agreement at any time on notice to the other.

The existence of a written agreement is clearly an important aspect of maintaining an independent contractor relationship between the broker and the salesperson. However, the written agreement will not prevent employee status from being implied as a result of the conduct of the broker and salesperson. For example, if the broker requires that the salesperson attend staff meetings or includes the salesperson in a company pension plan, this may be seen as evidence that the relationship between them is actually that of employer and employee. The consequences of such a determination can be drastic for both the broker and the salesperson.

The contract between the broker and the salesperson or associate broker should be renewed each year. The contract should include provisions for the termination of association.

For the broker, the determination that a salesperson is actually an employee will result in liability for state and federal unemployment insurance premiums; workers' compensation and disability insurance coverages; and federal and state withholding taxes, including the employer's share of Social Security taxes. For the salesperson, the result will be the inability to claim self-employment expense deductions on IRS Form 1040 Schedule C, as well as the fact that the salesperson's commission payments will be subjected to withholding for all applicable state and federal taxes.

The dilemma for brokers who want to maintain independent contractor status for their associates is that this limits the ability of the brokers to control the activity of their salespeople. Too much control often leads to the conclusion that the salesperson is an employee. On the other hand, brokers are legally liable for the actions of their salespeople, and have an obligation under the Real Property Law and Department of State regulations to supervise their salespeople's activities. The New York State law regarding independent contractor status for real estate licensees recognizes part of this dilemma and specifically states that compliance with the Real Property Law and Department of State real estate regulations will not be construed as an indication of employee status. (See Figure 4.5.)

■ ANTITRUST LAWS

The real estate industry is subject to federal and state antitrust laws. The most common violations in the real estate industry are *price-fixing* and *allocation of customers or markets*.

F I G U R E   4.5

Unemployment Insurance Notice for Real Estate Salesperson

NEW YORK STATE,
DEPARTMENT OF LABOR,
UNEMPLOYMENT INSURANCE DIVISION
NOTICE TO EMPLOYERS

Persons Engaged in Real Estate Sales

Effective October 1, 1986, services performed by a licensed real estate broker or sales associate are excluded from coverage if it can be proven that all of the following conditions are met:

(A) substantially all of the remuneration (whether or not paid in cash) for the services performed by such broker or sales associate is directly related to sales or other output (including the performance of services) rather than to the number of hours worked;

and

(B) the services performed by the broker or sales associate are performed pursuant to a written contract executed between such broker or sales associate and the person for whom the services are performed within the past twelve to fifteen months;

and

(C) such contract was not executed under duress and contains the following provisions:

1. that the broker or sales associate is engaged as an independent contractor associated with the person for whom services are performed pursuant to Article 12-A of the Real Property Law and shall be treated as such for all purposes;

2. that they (a) shall be paid a commission directly related to their gross sales or other output without deduction for taxes; (b) shall not receive any remuneration related to the number of hours worked; and (c) shall not be treated as employees with respect to such services for federal and state tax purposes;

3. that they shall be permitted to work any hours they choose;

4. that they shall be permitted to work out of their own homes or the office of the person for whom services are performed;

5. that they shall be free to engage in outside employment;

6. that the person for whom the services are performed may provide office facilities and supplies for the use of the broker or sales associate, but that they shall otherwise bear their own expenses, including but not limited to automobile, travel, and entertainment expenses;

7. that the person for whom the services are performed and the broker or sales associate shall comply with the requirements of Article 12-A of the Real Property Law and the regulations pertaining thereto, but such compliance shall not affect their status as independent contractors nor should it be construed as an indication that they are employees of such person for any purpose whatsoever;

8. that the contract and the association may be terminated by either party at any time upon notice to the other.

Illegal **price-fixing** occurs when competing brokers get together to set commission rates, rather than let competition in the open market establish those rates.

It's not that simple, though. Real estate companies—and agents—have been prosecuted under the Sherman Antitrust Act for what appeared to be innocent discussions with agents from other firms. A licensee should walk away immediately from the slightest conversation about rates with someone from another brokerage. (The only exception might be concerning a particular property the two firms have cooperated in selling.)

In the past, discussions about the negative qualities of a third company have been interpreted as a group boycott, a conspiracy to boycott that firm and drive it out of business. Licensees must learn which topics must be avoided when engaged in conversation with agents from other companies.

Market allocation might occur when competing firms agree to split up the area and refrain from doing business in each other's territories.

Each real estate company, of course, is free to set its own fee schedule, and to negotiate various rates with individual buyers or sellers if it wishes. The violations occur when competing firms agree to act together, in what the U.S. Justice Department calls *restraint of trade*.

New York City Business Taxation

The New York City Department of Finance has issued a Statement of Audit Procedure that exempts salespersons and associate brokers from the New York City Unincorporated Business Tax if the following 11 requirements are met:

1. The individual must hold only one license as a salesperson or associate broker.
2. The individual must be affiliated with only one real estate brokerage firm at a time, and that firm must hold the individual's license and be named on such license.
3. All printed material used by the individual must display the name of the real estate brokerage firm with which the individual is affiliated.
4. The brokerage firm must provide the individual with office facilities, that is, a desk, telephone, supplies, etc., at the office of the brokerage firm at no cost to the individual.
5. All listings produced by the individual must be subject to approval by a supervising employee of the brokerage firm. The individual must not have any legal authority to bind the brokerage firm in any agreements.
6. The individual must qualify for nonemployee status under the Internal Revenue Code.
7. The individual may not have any employees. If the individual claims a deduction on Form 1040 Schedule C for commissions or other compensation paid, this requirement is not met.
8. The individual may not take a deduction on Form 1040 Schedule C for a home office. Separate deductions for telephone, automobile, entertainment, travel or postage, or contributions to a Keogh plan are permitted.
9. The individual may not engage in purchases or sales of real estate as a dealer.
10. The individual may not engage in any other regular trade or business activities related to real estate.
11. The individual may not, in his or her own name and as a salesperson or associate broker, receive checks for commissions or other payments from any person other than the brokerage firm with which he or she is affiliated, be a party to a brokerage or cobrokerage agreement, or advertise a property for sale or lease.

In addition, an individual must meet at least three of the following five requirements:

1. The individual must be subject to minimum office hours or performance goals in terms of commissions earned or listings obtained by the brokerage firm with which the individual is affiliated.
2. The individual must be subject to standards of behavior or to direction or training as to real estate sales techniques or be required to attend periodic meetings of sales staff.

3. The individual may not claim a deduction on Form 1040 Schedule C for advertising expenses.
4. The individual must be subject to periodic written performance evaluation.
5. If the brokerage firm with which the individual is affiliated carries errors and omissions insurance, the individual must be covered at no additional cost to the individual.

■ THE BROKER'S RESPONSIBILITY TO MANAGE AND SUPERVISE

A broker has many special responsibilities. A broker must be an effective real estate sales agent, a business manager, a financial analyst, a marketer, a personnel manager, and a leader. A broker should also be familiar with basic real estate law. Here we will focus on some of the basic tasks that must be accomplished before a real estate brokerage can operate effectively and within the parameters of the license law.

Organization of the Brokerage Company

Naturally, one of the first steps a broker takes when starting a brokerage business is deciding what form of ownership the company will take. The form of ownership is essentially the framework for the brokerage business. The way a business is organized will determine the broker's legal obligations for the company's debts, his or her tax obligations, and his or her decision-making powers.

Because the form of ownership has so many legal and tax implications, brokers should always consult an attorney and an accountant before making a decision.

Various forms of ownership can accommodate sole ownership or joint ownership. These include the sole proprietorship, corporation, S corporation, general partnership, limited partnership, and limited liability company.

Sole proprietorship.   The broker is the sole owner of a sole proprietorship. The broker bears all the responsibility for the company and is solely responsible for all debts and other liabilities; the broker also may claim all the earnings and profits of the company.

Many small businesses are sole proprietorships because they are relatively simple to create and the legal paperwork is minimal. However, the existence of a sole proprietorship depends largely on the broker. If the broker dies or becomes incapacitated, the company may not survive.

Corporation.   A corporation is a separate legal entity (often referred to as a *legal fiction* or an *artificial person*) created under state laws. A corporation consists of an association of one or more individuals or other corporations (shareholders) but has an existence that is separate from those shareholders. A corporation has the legal capacity to enter into contracts and own property.

There are several advantages to the corporate form of business ownership. The owners (or shareholders) of a corporation are not liable for the debts of the corporation (other than employee wages) unless they have signed a personal guarantee of the corporation's obligations. In other words, the debts, judgments, or bankruptcies of the corporation will not affect the individual shareholders. All the shareholders risk is their original investment in the corporation.

A corporation has a perpetual existence—it does not die. Therefore, if a managing broker dies or becomes incapacitated, the brokerage can continue to operate (as long as another broker is found to carry on the business). The ownership of the corporation can be easily transferred to another person simply by selling the corporate stock. In addition, a corporation may have an unlimited number of owners and may earn an unlimited amount of income.

S corporation.   An S corporation has nearly all of the advantages of a regular corporation. An added benefit is that the profits and losses of the business are passed on directly to the shareholders. There is no double taxation. The shareholders pay the taxes on the corporate profits or deduct corporate losses on their individual tax returns.

There may be no more than 75 shareholders in an S corporation, and no more than 20 percent of the income may come from passive investments (such as investment property rentals). There are also strict rules on when the corporation may declare S corporation status. If any of these rules are violated, the corporation will be deemed a regular corporation.

General partnership.   *A partnership is a business in which two or more co-owners engage in a business for profit.* All owners have an equal say in management and share equally in the profits or losses of the business. The partnership is not a taxable entity like the corporation, so the individual partners pay the taxes on the earnings. A partnership may dissolve on the death, bankruptcy, or disability of one of the partners, unless the partnership agreement provides otherwise.

Limited partnership.   In a limited partnership, one person organizes, operates, and is responsible for the entire partnership venture. This person is called the *general partner* and is responsible not only for the management of the partnership but also for its debts. The other members of the organization are known as *limited partners.* They are merely investors who have no say in the organization and direction of the operation. They share in the profits and compensate the general partner for his or her efforts. Their possible losses are limited to the amount of their investment. The general partner, on the other hand, has unlimited liability.

Limited partnerships are often used for real estate ventures because they allow investors with relatively small amounts of capital to participate in real estate projects.

Limited liability companies.   New York allows limited liability companies and limited liability partnerships to be formed. These companies enjoy the limited liability of corporate shareholders and the tax advantages of partnerships. These companies are similar in effect to S corporations, but have fewer restrictions on their formation and income sources.

Recruiting Licensees

Once a brokerage company is formed, the broker must find salespeople to recruit. Recruiting is an important part of any broker's job. Not only must the broker choose the best associates available, the broker also must be careful not to violate any antidiscrimination laws.

Before taking on associates, the owner must consider the company's overall goals, public image, and available space. Whether the firm wants part-time salespersons or only full-timers should be decided beforehand. Recruiting must be coordinated with training. The small office that offers informal one-on-one training may recruit on a continuing basis. The large firm may prefer a single recruitment campaign followed by a number of classroom training sessions. Advertising, career nights, and trial training sessions are often used for recruitment. Classified or small display ads in newspapers are common.

The broker who takes on anyone who walks in the door risks a loss in office morale, the financial drain of an unproductive associate, and legal problems arising from unethical associates. Common methods of selection include application forms, aptitude tests, and personal interviews.

Among topics explored during an interview may be the applicant's attitude toward number of hours worked, weekend and evening work, and the amount of income anticipated from commissions. Other jobs presently held should be discussed. The prospective associate's attitudes toward ethics and civil rights should be explored. The manager often cautions the applicant that no income may be forthcoming for three to six months and explains that a regular draw against future commissions is inconsistent with independent contractor status. In explaining the nature of real estate brokerage, the manager can stress the necessity for a salesperson to handle stress, face disappointments, and accept occasional rejection. The decision to take on a particular salesperson should consider not only the profit potential but also whether the individual fits the company image and will contribute to office harmony.

While going through the recruiting process, the broker must keep **fair employment laws** in mind. The broker must be sure that recruiting tools such as classified ads do not run afoul of these laws. These employment laws include Title VII of the Civil Rights Act of 1964, the Civil Rights Act of 1866, the Age Discrimination in Employment Act, and the Americans with Disabilities Act. Naturally, state laws also apply. The U.S. Department of Housing and Urban Development (HUD) has stated that *employee*, as used in the act, also refers to *independent contractor*.

Fair employment laws are designed to prevent employers from basing hiring and firing decisions on factors that are unrelated to job performance. When recruiting new licensees (as well as hiring office staff and unlicensed assistants), a broker should avoid asking questions regarding marital status, children or plans to have children, age, origin or nationality, religion, and physical and mental condition. Any applications that are used should comply with all fair employment laws. Advertisements should include such phrases as *equal opportunity employer*. All recruiting and interviewing activities should remain consistent, no matter who is applying for the job.

All managerial decisions, not just hiring decisions, should be based on job performance rather than on protected characteristics. Other types of management decisions include those regarding advancement, salary or compensation increases, fringe benefits, and firing.

Training

A good company training program aids in recruitment and builds reputation. The well-trained associate requires less attention during early transactions and is eager to try out the techniques taught. An educated salesperson is more likely to succeed and to remain with the company. The broker is legally responsible for training (and supervising) his or her affiliated salespeople.

Even a small office can usually offer excellent one-on-one, on-the-job training, with the newcomer led step by step through the first few transactions. The sales meeting technique is often used in medium-sized offices. Periodic training sessions are integrated into sales meetings. Full coverage of the material requires a number of months with this method. Organized classrooms are most often run by multiple-office companies or franchise operations. They offer efficient instruction and are one of the main inducements for franchise affiliation. Occasionally several small independent firms combine to operate an organized classroom.

It is important to include various legal issues in training sessions. Information on licensing laws, agency duties and liabilities, discrimination laws, and antitrust laws should be included.

Policy and Procedures Guide

A written **policy and procedures guide** contributes to the smooth running of the company, heads off misunderstandings, serves as a reference for settling disputes, and can be an excellent tool for recruiting and training associates. A loose-leaf format makes revisions simple. Care must be taken not to violate a salesperson's independent contractor status through inappropriate wording. *Suggested Procedures Guide* is a suitable title. Except where legal and ethical considerations are under discussion, the word *must* is inappropriate. "Sales meetings are held each Monday morning at 9:30" is better than "Associates are required to attend each Monday . . ." The guide should be as concise as possible. It should say nothing, for example, about how to secure a listing; instead, it can detail procedures to follow after the listing is obtained.

Company policy. A typical guide starts with a sketch of the company's history and goals. Background information on the owner and manager is appropriate, with names and responsibilities of personnel. A job description for the associates follows. Independent contractor status is briefly reviewed, with a list of items provided by the company and another list of those to be provided by the associate. A concise treatment of ethical and legal considerations is appropriate: civil rights guidelines to be followed both within the office and in listing and selling, a review of the fiduciary duty to clients, policy on buyers' brokers, the theory of hidden defects, nonsolicitation orders that may be in effect in the area, and local sign restrictions or regulations. Company policy regarding the termination of a salesperson is also discussed.

The associate needs to know the procedures followed in relationships with attorneys, the franchise or MLS to which the office belongs, and cooperating offices. The guide may suggest (but not dictate) appropriate goals for an associate in terms of number of listings and sales, hours of floor duty, and attendance at sales meetings, and it may discuss the desk cost per associate.

Paperwork should be described in detail: what forms are available; what reports are to be turned in with listings, contracts, or deposits, and to whom. A sample of each form and sales aid used in the office should be included. Supplies, signs, lockboxes, business cards, and use of equipment such as the copier, fax machine, or computer terminal are discussed. Housekeeping information includes rules on desk use, lights, heat, ashtrays, coffee or kitchen equipment, parking, and office hours.

Sales meetings, caravan tours, open houses, and floor duty (opportunity time, office time) should be covered in the guide. The responsibilities and opportunities of the associate on floor duty are spelled out in detail to prevent misunderstandings. Advertising policy includes a discussion of frequency and size of ads, discrimination consideration, paperwork procedures, deadlines, individual budgets, and follow-up reports to be turned in. A section on telephones describes the answering service used, specifies policy on long-distance calls and entries in a long-distance log, briefly discusses standard telephone-answering techniques, and sets standards for customer rotation and the channeling of calls.

To avoid future problems, broker and associate should have a specific agreement, at the outset, about the status of listings, unfinished transactions, and future commissions if the associate leaves. A suggested agreement is shown in Figure 4.6.

The Supervision Requirement

The New York real estate law requires that real estate brokers manage and supervise their affiliated licensees. The broker must ensure that all licensees comply with the license laws and the duties imposed by agency law. According to Regulation 175.21, a broker's supervision must consist of "regular, frequent and consistent personal guidance, instruction, oversight and superintendence by the real estate broker with respect to the general real estate brokerage business conducted by the broker, and all matters relating thereto."

By law, brokers are responsible for the actions of their salespeople. In fact, in many cases, if an affiliated licensee violates the license law, the broker may be subject to disciplinary action along with the affiliated licensee. According to Section 442-c of the Real Property Law, a violation of the license law by a real estate salesperson or employee of the broker is cause for a reprimand. It is also a cause for revocation or suspension of the broker's license if the broker (1) had actual knowledge of the violation, or (2) retained the benefits, profits, or proceeds of a transaction wrongfully negotiated by the salesperson or employee after notice of the salesperson's or employee's misconduct.

Furthermore, both the broker and any affiliated salesperson must keep written records of all the real estate listings obtained by the salesperson and of all sales and other transactions effected by the salesperson during the period of his or her affiliation with that broker.

FIGURE 4.6

Sample Termination Agreement

TERMINATION AGREEMENT

THIS AGREEMENT is made as of the _____ day of _____, 20__ by and between _____ having its principal place of business at _____ (hereinafter referred to as "Broker") and _____ and individually residing at _____ (hereinafter referred to as "Salesperson").

WITNESSETH:

WHEREAS, Salesperson is associated with Broker and is duly licensed by the New York State Department of State—Division of Licensing Services in such capacity, and;

WHEREAS, the parties desire to set forth the rights of the Salesperson in the event of the termination of his/her association with Broker;

NOW, THEREFORE, in consideration of TEN DOLLARS ($10.00) and other good and valuable consideration the parties do hereby agree as follows:

1. LISTINGS. If at the time of termination of Salesperson's affiliation with Broker, Salesperson has produced written listings for the benefit of Broker, the Salesperson shall be entitled to receive the following percentage of any commission received by the Broker:

    a. ___% if a contract of sale has been executed by all parties and all contingencies contained therein have been satisfied as of the date of Salesperson's termination.

    b. ___% if a contract of sale has been executed by all parties and any contingencies contained therein have not been satisfied as of the date of Salesperson's termination.

    c. ___% if a contract of sale has not be been executed by all parties as of the date of Salesperson's termination.

    In the event a listing was originally produced by Salesperson and therefore expires, but is subsequently renewed after the termination date of such original listing, Salesperson shall be entitled to receive ___% of the net commission received by Broker upon receipt of same by Broker.

2. SALES OF PROPERTY. Salesperson shall be entitled to receive the following percentage of the net commission received by Broker in connection with transactions in which a prospective purchaser has been produced by the Salesperson prior to the Salesperson's termination:

    a. ___% if title has closed, but the commission has not been collected as of the date of such Salesperson's termination.

    b. ___% if a contract of sale has been executed by all parties and all contingencies contained therein have been satisfied as of the date of such Salesperson's termination.

    c. ___% if a contract of sale has been executed by all parties but any contingencies contained therein have not been satisfied as of the date of such Salesperson's termination.

    d. ___% if a contract of sale has not been executed by all parties as of the date of such Salesperson's termination.

3. RENTAL TRANSACTIONS. In the event of the termination of Salesperson's association with Broker, Salesperson shall be entitled to receive the following commission in connection with rental transactions:

    a. Listings. In the event Salesperson produced prior to Salesperson's termination date, a written listing for the rental of real property, Salesperson shall be entitled to receive the following percentage of the commission received by the Broker:

        i. ___% if the tenant has taken occupancy as of such date but the commission has not yet been received.

        ii. ___% if a tenant has not taken occupancy as of such date but thereafter occupancy is taken by the tenant.

    b. Prospective Tenants. Salesperson shall be entitled to receive the following percentage of the net commission received by Broker in connection with rental transactions in which Salesperson has produced a prospective Lessee prior to the termination date of his/her association with Broker.

        i. ___% if the tenant has taken occupancy as of such date, but the commission has not yet been received.

        ii. ___% if the tenant has not taken occupancy as of such date, but thereafter occupancy is taken by the tenant.

4. For all purposes of this Agreement, the words "Received by Broker" or "Collection by Broker" shall mean "within ten (10) days after receipt by Broker of funds in cash." In the event Broker shall receive less than the full commission which is due in connection with any transaction, Broker shall be obligated to pay only the pro rata share of such funds as actually collected by Broker.

Sample Termination Agreement

5. Broker shall pay Salesperson the Salesperson's share of any commission due pursuant to the terms of this Agreement within ten (10) days after the receipt by Broker of this commission. In the event a commission is paid to Broker in which Broker is entitled to share but another real estate broker disputes or may dispute the right of Broker to receive all or any portion of such commission, Salesperson agrees that Broker may hold said commission in trust until such dispute is resolved or sufficient time has passed to indicate to Broker, in Broker's sole and absolute judgment, that no action or proceeding will be commenced by such other real estate broker regarding the subject commission.

6. In the event any transaction in which the Salesperson is involved results in dispute, litigation, or legal expense, Salesperson shall cooperate fully with Broker in the prosecution of such dispute, litigation, etc. Broker and Salesperson shall share all expenses connected therewith in the same proportion as they would normally share a commission resulting from such transaction if there were no dispute or litigation. The parties acknowledge that it is the policy of Broker to avoid litigation wherever possible and Broker may, within Broker's sole discretion, determine whether or not any litigation or dispute shall be prosecuted, defended, compromised, or settled and the terms and conditions of any compromise or settlement, or whether or not any legal expense shall be incurred shall be decided upon the sole discretion of the Broker.

7. The Agreement shall be governed and construed by and in accordance with the laws of the State of New York and shall be binding upon the heirs, executors, administrators, and assigns of the parties.

_____

Broker

_____

Salesperson

Brokers should review the list of license violations listed in Chapter 1. Violations found by the DOS include

- failure to make timely written disclosure of agency;
- commingling money with that of principals;
- failure to maintain proper escrow accounts;
- improper handling of deposits, good-faith binders, or earnest money deposits;
- inducing breach of contract of sale or lease ("get out of that deal and I'll find you a better one");
- negotiating with another exclusive agent's client;
- failure to deliver duplicate originals of documents signed by client or customer;
- writing an automatic extension clause in a listing contract; and
- soliciting listings in prohibited areas.

■ AUDITS FOR COMPLIANCE

In 1999, the Environmental Protection Agency began a series of unannounced audits of real estate offices to check whether its lead-paint disclosure requirements were being observed. The firm's files should contain signed acknowledgments from tenants and homebuyers that they had received the required information before their leases or sales contracts became final. One of the first fines, for $11,000, was levied against a broker in Oklahoma who, according to the EPA, failed to give a tenant information about the danger of lead-based paint. A fine of more than $400,000 was sought against a military housing office that did not give the disclosures to tenants of 11 housing units before finalizing leasing arrangements.

Associates in an office should be instructed to contact the managing broker whenever auditors arrive unannounced. The Department of State conducts random audits to monitor compliance with state regulations on business signs, display of brokers' licenses, and management of the escrow account. Auditors also may want to verify the amount of experience listed in a broker-license application, and will check transaction files for proof of proper agency disclosure, as mandated by Article 443 of the Real Property Law.

The U.S. Department of Housing and Urban Development works with local organizations to fund and train sets of checkers, or testers, who present themselves as would-be tenants or buyers and keep records of their treatment by real estate firms. Discrimination is not limited to differences in the choice of housing offered to members of different groups who are equally qualified financially. A Rochester firm was fined after a pair of white testers who walked into an office were greeted with a handshake, offers to hang up their coats, and cups of coffee. The African American couple who entered the office soon after received none of these welcoming gestures. In its defense, the managing broker pointed out that the two couples, whose financial situations were similar, were offered the same wide choice of listed homes in their price range. The difference in the initial greeting occurred because they just happened to encounter two different associates, whose methods were different. HUD replied, "It's your job to see that they're not."

To avoid unintentional discrimination, it's helpful to establish routine procedures for phone conversations and interviews. The goal should be to treat all clients and customers in the same fashion. To make sure the same questions are asked in the same order during a financial analysis, for example, it's helpful to use a standard written interview form. *The best protection against violation of fair housing laws is a thorough knowledge of the laws themselves.*

■ PROFESSIONAL ORGANIZATIONS

WEB LINK

Years ago real estate brokers realized the need for an organization to help improve their business abilities and to educate the public to the value of qualified ethical brokers. The National Association of REALTORS® (NAR) was organized in 1908 to meet this need. This association is the parent organization of most local real estate boards and associations that operate throughout the United States, and the professional activities of all REALTORS®—active members of local boards that are affiliated with the national association—are governed by the association's Code of Ethics. Listings and much additional information is available at its Web site, *www.realtor.com.*

The term REALTORS® is a registered trademark. A similar organization, The National Association of Real Estate Brokers (Realtists), was founded in 1947. Members subscribe to a code of ethics that sets professional standards for all Realtists. The National Organization of Hispanic Real Estate Professionals is a recent similar organization.

These are trade associations. Licensed brokers and salespersons are not required to join.

New York State Association of REALTORS®

WEB LINK

The New York State Association of REALTORS®, which represents more than 32,000 REALTORS® and REALTOR®-ASSOCIATES in New York State, is a member board of the National Association of REALTORS®. The staff consists of an executive director; an administrator; and directors of education, legislation, communications, and membership services. The New York State Society of Real Estate Appraisers is a division of the state association, as is the New York State Commercial Association of REALTORS®, Inc. NYSAR's Web site can be found at *www.nysar.com.*

Educational services. The National Association of REALTORS® and The New York REALTORS® Institute administer a structured educational program. The course of study leads to the designation Graduate, REALTORS® Institute (GRI). To earn the GRI designation, the candidate must successfully complete courses that cover business skills, law, and advanced real estate specialties. Many are approved by the state for continuing education credit. GRI courses are offered during the year at various locations around the state.

■ DESIGNATIONS

Designations, like college degrees, are awarded by various real estate organizations after study, examinations, and experience. Various real estate bodies award these designations. Some are associated with the National Association of REALTORS®, and some are independent organizations. Among the more well-known designations are

- American Society of Appraisers: ASA;
- American Society of Home Inspectors: M, Member (highest designation);
- American Society of Real Estate Counselors: CRE, Counselor of Real Estate;
- Appraisal Institute: MAI, Member of the Appraisal Institute; SRA, Senior Residential Appraiser;
- Commercial Investment Real Estate Institute: CCIM, Certified Commercial-Investment Member; Counselors of Real Estate: CRE;
- Institute of Real Estate Management: CPM, Certified Property Manager; ARM, Accredited Residential Manager; AMO, Accredited Management Organization;
- International Real Estate Federation (FIABCI): CIPS, Certified International Property Specialist;
- National Association of REALTORS®: GRI, Graduate, REALTORS® Institute;
- National Council of Exchangors: EMS, Equity Marketing Specialist;
- National Association of Exclusive Buyer's Agents: EBA, Exclusive Buyers Agent;
- Real Estate Educators Association: DREI, Distinguished Real Estate Instructor;
- Real Estate Securities and Syndication Institute: SRS, Specialist in Real Estate Securities;

- REALTORS® Land Institute: ALC, Accredited Land Consultant;
- REALTORS® National Marketing Institute: CRB, Certified Real Estate Brokerage Manager; CRS, Certified Residential Specialist;
- REALTORS® Real Estate Buyer's Agent Council: ABR, Accredited Buyer's Representative;
- Real Estate Buyers Agent Council: ACR, Accredited Buyers Representative;
- Society of Industrial and Office REALTORS®: SIOR; PRE, Professional Real Estate; and
- Women's Council of REALTORS®: LTG, Leadership Training Graduate; RRC, Referral and Relocation Certification.

■ LAW OF AGENCY

The prospective broker should undertake a careful review of Chapters 2 and 3, on law of agency, at this point.

In the situation where a buyer-client seems right for one of the firm's own listings, the managing broker and the firm can find themselves in a position of dual agency. An agent is legally bound to put the client's interests first, and of course there is only one "first." The Department of State has offered a way out of the dilemma with the following suggestion:

> *Under the following circumstances, you can designate one of your agents to represent the buyer and another to represent the seller. You must, of course, make full disclosure to both buyer and seller, and you must obtain their informed consent to the arrangement prior to appointing the designated agents.*

When a buyer [who is a client] expresses an interest in a property listed with your firm, you must obtain the consent of both the buyer and seller to proceed as a dual agent, and you use the "Agency Disclosure" form for that purpose. At the same time, you can explain the benefits of appointing a designated agent for the buyer and another for the seller. If after full disclosure, the buyer and seller agree, [one of the firm's salespersons may act as single agent for the buyer, and another for the seller].

If designated agents are appointed, the firm continues as a dual agent representing both the buyer and seller in the transaction. The designated agents, however, will, by virtue of the new agreement with the buyer and seller, function as single agents giving undivided loyalty to their respective clients.

If effected properly, an agreement for the appointment of designated agents does not violate any provision of Article 12-A or the rules of the Department of State. That is, of course, premised on (1) making full disclosure to the buyer and seller, and (2) obtaining the informed consent of both. In addition, to avoid future misunderstandings, it is good practice to reduce these agreements to writing, and to provide all of the parties with a signed copy.

A Designated Agency form suggested by the New York State Association of REALTORS® can be found in Figure 4.7.

F I G U R E   4.7

Suggested Designated Agent Agreement

Department of State

DUAL AGENT WITH DESIGNATED SALES {ASSOCIATES} AGENTS

If the tenant and the landlord provide their informed consent in writing, the principals {or} AND the real estate broker who represents both parties as a dual agent may designate a sales {associate} AGENT to represent the tenant and another sales {associate} AGENT to represent the landlord. A sales {associate} AGENT works under the supervision of the real estate broker. With the informed consent in writing of the tenant and the landlord, the designated sales {associate} AGENT for the tenant will function as the tenant's agent representing the interests of

AND ADVOCATING ON BEHALF OF the tenant and the designated sales {associate} AGENT for the landlord will function as the landlord's agent representing the interests of AND ADVOCATING ON BEHALF OF the landlord in the negotiations between the tenant and the landlord. A designated sales {associate} AGENT cannot provide the full range of fiduciary duties to the landlord or tenant. The designated sales {associate} AGENT must explain that like the dual agent under whose supervision they function, they cannot provide undivided loyalty. A landlord or tenant should carefully consider the possible consequences of a dual agency relationship with designated sales {associates} AGENTS before agreeing to such representation.

This form was provided to me by {the company named below:

Licensee or Associate of Licensee: _____ (signature) of Company: _____

The above-named company, which is licensed as a real estate broker, is (check one)

{   } the landlord's agent {   } a dual agent

{   } the tenant's agent {   } a dual agent with designated sales associates

{   } the broker's agent

(PRINT NAME OF LICENSEE) OF _____ (PRINT NAME OF COMPANY, FIRM OR BROKERAGE), A LICENSED REAL ESTATE BROKER ACTING IN THE INTEREST OF THE:

(____) LANDLORD AS A (CHECK RELATIONSHIP BELOW) _____ (____) TENANT AS A (CHECK RELATIONSHIP BELOW)

_____ (___) LANDLORD'S AGENT _____ (___) TENANT'S AGENT

_____ (___) BROKER'S AGENT _____ (___) BROKER'S AGENT

_____ (___) DUAL AGENT _____

_____ (___) DUAL AGENT WITH DESIGNATED SALES AGENTS _____

If dual agent with designated sales {associates} AGENTS is checked: _____ is appointed to represent the tenant; and _____ is appointed to represent the landlord in this transaction.

(I) (We) _____ acknowledge receipt of a copy of this disclosure form:

Signature of {   } Landlord(s) and/or {   } Tenant(s):

_____

_____

Date: _____ Date: _____

The buyer-seller form and the landlord-tenant form shall each be a one page, two-sided form, printed front and back.

This section shall not apply to a real estate licensee who works with a buyer {or a}, seller, TENANT OR LANDLORD in accordance with terms agreed to by the licensee and buyer {or}, seller, TENANT OR LANDLORD and in a capacity other than as an agent, as such term is defined in paragraph a of subdivision one of this section.

Nothing in this section shall be construed to limit or alter the application of the common law of agency with respect to residential real estate transactions.

This act shall take effect January 1, 2008.

DOS Legal Memo Regarding Dual Agency

NYS Department of State   **Counsel's Office**

Legal Memorandum LI12
BE WARY OF DUAL AGENCY

With the growing number of very large and widespread brokerages, the issue of dual agency arises more frequently than ever before. Any purchaser, seller, lessor or lessee confronted with a dual agency issue by their real estate agent should not take the issue lightly. Parties to a real estate transaction, including real estate brokers and salespersons themselves, seldom realize the inherent problems of a real estate agent acting as a dual agent.

Dual agency arises when a real estate broker or salesperson represents adverse parties (e.g., a buyer and seller) in the same transaction.

Dual agency typically arises in the following way: a real estate broker employs two salespeople, one who works for the buyer as a buyer's agent and the other who works for the seller as a seller's agent. The real estate broker and his salespeople are "one and the same" entity when analyzing whether dual agency exists. As soon as the buyer's agent introduces the buyer to property in which the seller is represented by the seller's agent, dual agency arises.

Dual agency can also arise in a more subtle way: A real estate broker who represents the seller procures a prospective purchaser who needs to sell her property before she is able to buy the seller's property. The prospective purchaser then signs a listing agreement with the real estate broker to sell her property so that she can purchase the seller's property. The real estate broker is now a dual agent representing both parties in a mutually dependent transaction.

When you employ a real estate broker or salesperson as your agent, you are the principal. "The relationship of agent and principal is fiduciary in nature, '...founded on trust or confidence reposed by one person in the integrity and fidelity of another.' (citation omitted) Included in the fundamental duties of such a fiduciary are good faith and *undivided loyalty*, and full and fair disclosure. Such duties are imposed upon real estate licensees by license law, rules and regulations, contract law, the principals of the law of agency, and tort law. (citation omitted) The object of these rigorous standards of performance is to secure fidelity from the agent to the principal and to insure the transaction of the business of the agency to the best advantage of the principal. (citations omitted)." (Emphasis added) *DOS v. Moore*, 2 DOS 99, p. 7 (1999)

"A real estate broker is strictly limited in his or her ability to act as a dual agent: As a fiduciary, a real estate broker is prohibited from serving as a dual agent representing parties with conflicting interests in the same transaction without the informed consent of the principals. (citations omitted) 'If dual interests are to be served, the disclosure to be effective must lay bare the truth, without ambiguity or reservation, in all its stark significance.' (citation omitted)

> 'Therefore, a real estate agent must prove that prior to undertaking to act either as a dual agent or for an adverse interest, the agent made full and complete disclosure to all parties as a predicate for obtaining the consent of the principals to proceed in the undertaking. Both the rule and the affirmative [defense] of full disclosure are well settled in law.' (citation omitted)" *Id*. at pp. 9-10.

In a purchaser/seller transaction in which dual agency arises, the agent must not only clearly explain the existence of the dual agency issue and its implications to the parties, the agent must also obtain a written acknowledgment from the prospective purchaser and seller to dual agency. That acknowledgment requires each principal signing the form to confirm that they understand that the dual agent will be working for both the seller and buyer, that they understand that they may engage their own agent to act solely for them, **that they understand that they are giving up their right to the agent's undivided loyalty**, and that they have carefully considered the possible consequences of a dual agency relationship.

The fiduciary duty of loyalty that your real estate agent owes to you prohibits your agent from advancing any interests adverse to yours or conducting your business to benefit the agent or others.

Significantly, by consenting to dual agency, you are giving up your right to have your agent be loyal to you, since your agent is now also representing your adversary. Once you give up that duty of loyalty, the agent can advance interests adverse to yours. For example, once you agree to dual agency, you may need to be careful about what you say to your agent because, although your agent still cannot breach any confidences, your agent may not use the information you give him or her in a way that advances **your** interests.

As a principal in a real estate transaction, you should always know that you have the right to be represented by an agent who is loyal only to you throughout the entire transaction. Your agent's fiduciary duties to you need never be compromised.

■ SUMMARY

Vicarious liability is created not because of a person's actions but because of the relationship between the liable person and other parties. Subagency can create circumstances or situations that result in vicarious liability.

Antitrust laws prohibit competing brokers from discussing commission rates charged to clients and also the publication of such rates. Brokers also must refrain from negative discussions about other brokers to avoid the appearance of a group boycott.

MLSs must operate in such a manner as not to deny reasonable access to any interested party. Membership requirements must be reasonable, and the charge for membership must be related to the costs involved. Discriminatory policies are forbidden.

An MLS may not impose restrictions on the operations of its members, such as prohibiting membership in other MLS organizations or cooperation with non-members. Attempts by an MLS to regulate the business hours of its members or to restrict the types of properties advertised through the MLS also are forbidden.

While recruiting and training licensees, brokers must pay attention to more than selecting effective, successful salespeople. Brokers must also keep fair employment laws in mind. Office policies and procedure guides should emphasize the broker's commitment to the principles of fair employment, fair housing, and full compliance with licensing regulations. In an office where salespersons and associate brokers are considered independent contractors, the state's requirement for close supervision by the broker must be observed without violating the guidelines for independent contractor treatment.

Designations are awarded after study, examinations, and experience by various organizations. The New York State Association of REALTORS® awards the GRI designation to graduates of the REALTORS® Institute.

For the agency dilemma posed by a buyer/client who wishes to see one of the firm's own listings, for which the company is already a seller's agent, the DOS has offered an acceptable solution. After full disclosure and informed consent by both parties, the managing broker, who becomes a dual agent, may designate one associate to represent the buyer and another the seller. Consent forms to the resulting dual agency and designated agencies must be properly executed, and fiduciary duties carefully observed.

QUESTIONS

1. XYZ Realty and MLN Real Estate decide that they will not cooperate with the new broker in town, Homes Bought Realty. This would be an antitrust violation called
   a. market allocation.
   b. tie-in arrangement.
   c. price-fixing.
   d. group boycotting.

2. Town House Realty offered new condominiums for sale. Buyers were told they must make their selections for appliances from Town House Realty's catalog. No other appliances would be permitted. Appliances were furnished through a distributor owned by Town House Realty. This would be an antitrust violation called
   a. market allocation.
   b. tie-in arrangement.
   c. price-fixing.
   d. group boycotting.

3. Broker Margo Marz and broker Nate National decided each could make more money if Margo took the east side of town and Nate took the west side of town. This would be an antitrust violation called
   a. market allocation.
   b. tie-in arrangement.
   c. price-fixing.
   d. group boycotting.

4. An MLS may
   a. regulate a broker's office hours.
   b. prohibit membership in another MLS.
   c. set reasonable and nondiscriminatory membership fees.
   d. restrict the types of property advertised through the MLS.

5. New salesperson Ann Apple wants to be able to claim self-employment expense deductions on IRS Form 1040 Schedule C. She should
   a. have an independent contractor agreement with her broker in writing.
   b. keep a detailed record of her expenses.
   c. pay her own state and federal taxes and Social Security.
   d. All of the above

6. In an independent contractor agreement with Ann Apple, the broker should include
   a. that she will be compensated only by commissions directly based on sales.
   b. the days and hours that she will work.
   c. that she may not work outside the office.
   d. that she will be paid both a salary and commissions.

7. A broker for North End Realty tells a broker from Valley Realty that a house has been listed "at a 7 percent commission, and we will be glad to cooperate with you and give you half, if your company sells it." There may be an antitrust violation in
   a. the offer to cooperate in marketing the property.
   b. the promise of a 50/50 split.
   c. the phrase "7 percent commission."
   d. None of the above. There is no antitrust problem here.

8. The broker candidate who has not previously been licensed as a salesperson
   a. must show twice as much real estate experience as a licensed salesperson needs.
   b. cannot become a broker at all.
   c. takes a different and more difficult state examination.
   d. must file an irrevocable consent form.

9. A blind ad is one that does not include the
   a. address of the property.
   b. name of the broker.
   c. asking price.
   d. salesperson's home phone number.

10. A licensed salesperson's business card may NOT

   a. use the licensee's nickname.
   b. list a home telephone under any circumstances.
   c. print the salesperson's name in larger type than the broker's.
   d. carry the Fair Housing logo.

11. Which person needs a license to sell someone else's real estate and collect a fee for the service?

   a. The executor of an estate
   b. An auctioneer
   c. An attorney
   d. A subdivision's in-house salesperson

12. The term *vicarious liability* refers to

   a. failure to disclose type of agency.
   b. broker's duty to supervise.
   c. independent contractor guidelines.
   d. principal's responsibility for agent's acts.

13. Which of the following phrases might violate Regulation Z advertising guidelines?

   a. "No down payment"
   b. "Assume low-interest mortgage"
   c. "Only 5% down"
   d. "Less than you're paying for rent"

14. The contract setting up an associate's independent contractor status with the broker should be

   a. either oral or written.
   b. re-signed every 15 months.
   c. specific as to number of hours to be worked.
   d. forwarded to the Department of State.

15. The partial protection from legal liability afforded by a corporation can be combined with the tax advantages of a partnership in a

   a. sole proprietorship.
   b. general partnership.
   c. limited liability company.
   d. limited partnership.

16. To preserve independent contractor status, a policy and procedures manual should probably avoid use of the word

   a. "must."
   b. "discrimination."
   c. "ethics."
   d. "termination."

17. The real estate office is sometimes visited by inspectors or auditors from the

   a. EPA.
   b. NYSAR.
   c. FTC.
   d. MLS.

18. The acronym "GRI" stands for

   a. General Real Estate Instructor.
   b. Graduate, REALTORS® Institute.
   c. General Realty Insurance.
   d. Guaranteed Realty Information.

19. In-house sales where the buyer wants individual representation after agreeing to dual agency can be handled by the use of

   a. referral sales.
   b. cooperative brokerage.
   c. designated agents.
   d. supplement A.

20. Not all brokers are

   a. REALTORS®.
   b. licensed.
   c. older than 20.
   d. experienced.

Real Estate Finance

■ KEY TERMS

bridge loans	negative amortization	sale-leasebacks
bullet loan	open-end mortgages	secondary mortgage market
construction loans	package loans	
disintermediation	participation loan	shared-equity mortgages
FHA loan	private mortgage insurance (PMI)	swing loans
home equity loan		takeout loan
index	purchase-money mortgage	underwriting
joint venture		wraparound mortgage

■ THE USE OF THE MORTGAGE

Most real estate purchases in New York state are financed through mortgage loans. The word itself comes, like so many legal terms, from Old French—*mort*, meaning *death*, and *gage*, which is still used occasionally in English for *pledge*. (When the mortgage is paid off, the real estate is no longer pledged or promised as security for the loan, and the gage will then be dead.)

A mortgage is a *voluntary lien on real estate*. The person who owns or intends to buy the property gives the lender the right to foreclose and have that property sold at public auction if the borrower fails to repay the loan. The borrower, the *mortgagor*, pledges the land to the lender, or *mortgagee*, as security for the loan. The loan itself is made in return for a *note* or *bond*, the borrower's personal promise to repay the debt.

In *title theory states*, the mortgagor actually gives title to the mortgagee or to a third party, who will hold it in trust until the loan is paid off. The document involved is called a *trust deed*, rather than a mortgage, because title is actually transferred. When the loan is paid off, a *release deed*, or *deed of reconveyance*, returns title to the original owner. If the mortgagor defaults, it is a relatively simple matter for the lender to obtain immediate possession, as opposed to the foreclosure process used in states like New York.

New York is, however, a *lien theory state*. The mortgage does not transfer title, but merely pledges the property to serve as security for the loan. Formal, and more lengthy, legal procedures are necessary to foreclose the loan.

■ HOME MORTGAGES

Brokers who specialize in residential sales will have the most experience with single-family loans and loans for one- to four-unit buildings. These loans fall into two categories. Those backed by government agencies include FHA (HUD), VA, RECDA (FmHA), and SONYMA mortgages. In recent years, all of these agencies have relaxed their guidelines to enable buyers who were formerly considered marginally qualified to buy their own homes. Municipalities, particularly larger cities, also may offer special assistance in mortgage lending, particularly for those who buy in "target" neighborhoods. New York State banking regulations allow zero-down mortgage loans.

The second source for home mortgage borrowing is the private sector. In recent years, conventional mortgage loans have often been offered with low down payments, to the point where at the turn of the century, almost half of first-time borrowers agreed to carry **private mortgage insurance (PMI)** so that they could make down payments of less than 20 percent.

■ TYPES OF MORTGAGES

The **purchase-money mortgage** is the most common (and the proper) term for any loan used in the *original purchase of property*. (In some areas, the term is reserved for seller-take-back financing, when the owner accepts a purchase-money mortgage in return for part or all of the sales price.) Contrasted with purchase-money mortgages are *refinance loans*, which borrow more money against property already owned.

With **shared-equity mortgages**, the lender receives some share of future profits on the property; **package loans,** which cover both real and personal property, such as furnishings; **open-end mortgages,** which allow for further borrowing; *blanket mortgages*, which cover more than one piece of realty; **wraparound mortgages,** which are a complex method of retaining an old mortgage while accepting a new one; and **bridge loans** (also called **swing loans** or *gap loans*), which cover a short-term need for funds when a new home is being purchased and the contracted sale of the old one has not yet closed.

Subordinate mortgages are those recorded after initial loans have already been placed against the property. They are considered junior to first mortgages, and in case of foreclosure they would wait in line to see if enough funds remained to satisfy them. Some lenders today offer them under the designation of **home equity loans,** but if the property already has a first mortgage on it, a home equity loan is really just a second mortgage. As a rule, it carries higher interest than a first mortgage, because the property usually has a substantial lien against it already.

■ BROKERS' ISSUES IN REAL ESTATE FINANCE

Brokers should become familiar with commercial mortgages, construction loans, sale-leasebacks, and how the economy affects real estate finance.

Commercial Financing

Commercial property includes property that produces income, such as apartment and office buildings, restaurants, shopping centers, hotels and motels, and gas stations. The sources of much of the financing for commercial properties are insurance companies and pension plans, which have large amounts of money to invest in long-term mortgages. Both types of lenders often work through loan correspondents such as mortgage brokers. There are other sources of commercial mortgage funds as well, including commercial banks, savings and loans, sellers, syndicates, and industrial revenue bonds.

Commercial lenders tend to have exacting **underwriting** standards and require low loan-to-value (LTV) ratios. When lenders underwrite a commercial loan, they complete a detailed analysis of the project's ability to generate adequate cash flow. The project's cash flow must be adequate to pay for principal and interest payments, property taxes, insurance, and maintenance costs. (All of these expenses must be paid before the project can reach a breakeven point.) Lenders examine existing leases and lease pledges to determine cash flow and overall financial health. Because of this, every planned and existing large commercial real estate project includes an ongoing marketing program to secure tenants.

Lenders use the property's rental income to estimate the property's value, then apply a low LTV ratio to determine the loan amount. Most commercial loans have maximum LTV ratios of between 70 percent and 75 percent, depending on the financial rating.

There are several types of common commercial real estate loans. Note that many require balloon payments.

Bullet loans (also called *intermediate financing* or *conduit financing*). A **bullet loan** has an intermediate term of three to five years; a *conduit loan* has a term of seven to ten years. It is virtually always a fixed-rate loan. It is partially amortized, so a substantial balloon payment is required at the end of the loan term. In some cases, only the interest is paid in the first years of the loan.

Miniperm loans. A *miniperm loan* is a variable-rate loan that has an interest accrual feature. This type of loan is used by borrowers who want to increase their cash flow in the early years of a project.

Floating rate loans with accrual.   These commercial loans are adjustable-rate loans, similar to those available on residential property. The interest rate is based on a standard index and then fluctuates throughout the life of the loan, depending on the movements of the index. However, unlike residential ARMs, the debt service on this loan is a fixed amount. Any deficiency in interest is added to the principal (**negative amortization**). Loan terms are quite short, usually no longer than five years.

Participation loans.   **Participation loans** give lenders the opportunity to enhance their profits by earning extra revenue from an increase in a project's net income and resale value. During periods of high interest rates and tight money, lenders will offer financing at lower-than-market rates in exchange for a percentage of net income and/or increases in value. Participation loans are often available when other types of permanent financing are not.

Land-leaseback.   In a *land-leaseback*, the investor buys the land, then leases it back to the developer under a long-term lease. The developer then constructs a building on the land. This type of transaction reduces the equity the developer needs to fund a project. Land-leasebacks are related to sale-leasebacks, discussed later.

Joint ventures.   Traditionally, when a lender or investor and borrower decide on a **joint venture,** the lender or investor puts up 100 percent of the funds and the developer does all the work. Ownership may be divided between the two 50/50, or any other split (75/25, 90/10, etc.) that equitably reflects the work and risk involved. The lender or investor generally has the first claim to any income generated from the project up to an amount that equals an agreed-on return on the original investment (a *safety-first position*). The rest of the income is divided between the partners according to a previously agreed-on formula.

Construction Loans

Construction loans (also called *interim loans*) finance the construction of improvements on real estate. A construction loan is temporary; when the construction is completed, the loan is replaced with permanent financing. One of the unique features of this loan is the fact that the building that is used as security for the loan does not exist when the loan is made. Because only the land exists at the time the loan is made, construction lenders use various methods to protect their security interest. These methods include strict underwriting procedures and unique ways of disbursing the loan funds.

Loan application.   Construction loans vary in size from one small enough to finance the construction of a home to one large enough to finance the construction of a shopping center or a multistory office building. However, the application process is essentially the same, regardless of the size of the loan. The first step the borrower takes when applying for a construction loan is to submit plans and specifications for the proposed building. Typically, the borrower already owns the lot on which the building will be constructed. Some lenders insist that the lot be owned lien-free, so that the construction lender will have the security of a first-lien position. Other lenders allow the lot to be encumbered with a mortgage loan, as long as the mortgage contains a subordination clause that gives the construction loan first priority over the previously existing mortgage.

The construction loan amount is based on the total value of the land and the future building. The LTV ratio rarely exceeds 75 percent. For instance, a borrower owns a $40,000 lot and wants to construct a $150,000 house on it. The total value of the property after the house is constructed will be $190,000. Seventy-five percent of the combined value of the lot and home is $142,500. That is the maximum loan amount the lender will agree to. Construction loans are usually large enough to cover all or most of the costs of the construction, with the owner's equity being represented by ownership of the lot.

Disbursement of funds. Construction loan funds are virtually never disbursed in one lump sum when the application process is completed. Disbursing all the funds at once would be too risky; it would be too easy for the borrower to squander the loan funds on cost overrides, on last-minute changes, or by mismanagement, leaving the lender with an incomplete building as security for the loan. Instead, the loan funds are disbursed according to a prearranged plan. One of the most common plans is that of a series of draws as construction is completed. For instance, the lender may utilize a five-stage plan, whereby 20 percent of the loan funds are distributed each time another one-fifth of the construction is completed. The last 20 percent is typically held by the lender until all labor and materials have been paid for (i.e., lien waivers have been received from contractors and subcontractors, and certificates of completion and approval for occupancy have been issued by a building inspector) and the period for filing a mechanic's lien has passed.

Another method of disbursing construction funds requires that the borrower submit the construction bills to the lender, who pays the bills as they arrive. The benefit of this method is that it gives the lender greater control over the possibility that mechanic's liens will be filed.

Note that interest is charged on the funds only after they have been disbursed. Both lenders and borrower must keep careful records showing when each disbursement was made.

Paying off construction loans. Construction loans are short-term loans. Terms may range from six months for a house to three years for a commercial project. Construction loans are set up so that the lender will be paid in full—including all accrued interest—at the end of this short loan term. Typically, the construction loan is paid off (replaced) with a permanent **takeout loan.** Often the borrower makes arrangements for permanent financing before the construction loan is even applied for. This kind of arrangement is called a *standby loan commitment*. Naturally, permanent lenders impose conditions on their standby loan commitments. For instance, when completed, the building must meet all building codes and conform to the plans and specifications that were submitted at the time of the loan application. Some lenders refuse to fund the permanent loan until the project has been leased up to its breakeven point.

Release from blanket loan. When a lender holds a blanket mortgage on a whole subdivision, the developer may not sell an individual lot or completed house until obtaining a release of that one lot from the overall blanket mortgage. As each lot is sold, the lender receives a proportional percentage of the total debt, and releases that parcel so that it can be sold to (and individually financed by) the new homebuyer.

Sale-Leasebacks

Sale-leasebacks are used to finance larger projects, nearly always commercial. The property owner sells it to an investor and then immediately leases it back. The lease is usually a full net long-term lease. The sale of the property frees up the original owner's equity in the property, and the lease is for a long enough period for the investor to recover the sale funds plus make a fair profit on the investment.

As a method of financing, sale-leasebacks offer a number of advantages. For the seller-lessee, the benefits include staying in possession of the property while receiving cash from the sale and getting a tax deduction for the full amount of the rental payments. Many seller-lessees use the cash from the sale to expand or remodel their facilities.

The primary advantage of this arrangement for the buyer-lessor is the receipt of the rental payments. The rental payments usually include a fair profit on the investment and the return of the investment capital itself.

Sometimes a sale-leaseback includes an option for the tenant to repurchase the property at the end of the lease term. This type of arrangement is called a *sale-leaseback-buyback*. At the time of the original sale, the parties will generally set the repurchase price. If the repurchase price is the same as the original sales price, the parties may run into problems with the Internal Revenue Service. Special tax and legal advice should be sought in sale-leaseback and sale-leaseback-buyback transactions.

■ GROUND LEASES

A lease of land on which the tenant intends to construct a building is usually long term, which makes it worthwhile for the tenant to construct buildings and other improvements on the property. A farmer who does not want to give up all rights to his land might give a 99-year lease to a developer, who then has enough confidence to construct a shopping mall on the property. In the usual arrangement, the farmer (or his heir) receives rent, and the developer pays property taxes and other expenses. Legal wrangles developed over expired leases on entire towns in the Southern Tier that were built on land leased from Native American tribes 99 years earlier.

■ FHA FINANCING

In the early 1900s, homeowners generally borrowed on short-term mortgages, for perhaps four or five years, and made only interest payments, often once a year. At the end of the term, the friendly local small-town banker would renew the loan for the same amount. But when the Great Depression hit in the early 1930s, the flaws in this system became evident. As factories closed down, homeowners who still owed the full value of their homes were unable to negotiate renewals and were forced into foreclosure. Banks failed, and in a vicious circle, more businesses closed down and more unemployment resulted.

The New Deal, begun by President Franklin Roosevelt in 1932, attacked the problem on many fronts. In the field of housing, a fresh idea was proposed by a secretary at the University of Rochester, whose professor went to Washington as part of the administration's Brain Trust. She conceived the idea of the long-term amortized loan. Instead of paying just interest, the homeowner would pay a bit more, in small monthly installments that would gradually whittle down the debt. The National Housing Act of 1934 set up the Federal Housing Administration (FHA), which not only adopted the idea of amortization but also set up an insurance program to protect lenders, so that the nation's growing inventory of vacant houses could be bought with low down payments. In 1968, FHA became part of the Department of Housing and Urban Development (HUD). The amortized loan quickly became a standard, both for the Veterans Administration (VA), now the Department of Veterans Affairs, when it was established after World War II and for conventional lenders as well.

On the **secondary mortgage market,** Fannie Mae (FNMA) and Ginnie Mae (GNMA) were set up to purchase packages of VA and **FHA loans,** thus returning mortgage money to the communities where it could be used to serve more borrowers. Together with Freddie Mac (FHLMC), they also tend to standardize and encourage certain types of loans, by announcing the requirements for loan packages they will buy.

Terms of FHA loans are frequently changed to meet the country's current needs: new allowances for contributions by the seller to the buyer's closing costs, relaxed qualification standards for marginal buyers, raising of maximum loan limits as median prices change. Brokers should stay abreast of current developments, and keep track of which local lenders handle these loans, which can be so useful to cash-poor homebuyers.

■ THE ECONOMY AND REAL ESTATE CYCLES

Brokers should understand the basic ways in which our economy as a whole affects the real estate market. The two are closely tied together: when interest rates and unemployment are high, real estate sales and financing activities are low, and vice versa. The general economy has some obvious impacts on real estate finance. Stock market activity, employment rates, inflation rates, and income levels all affect real estate values and the ability of potential homebuyers to purchase real estate. For example, when unemployment rates are high, interest rates are high, and income levels are low, fewer potential buyers will be able to obtain or afford the financing necessary to purchase a home. On the other hand, when the economy is healthy and interest rates and inflation are low, more people feel confident enough to apply for mortgage loans, and more applicants will qualify for those loans.

Economic Influences

Several economic factors affect real estate cycles, including supply and demand, population characteristics, social attitudes, and property value fluctuations.

The influence of supply and demand encompasses two different commodities: real property and mortgage funds. A demand for property will encourage building and cause prices to increase. For instance, in an area with a healthy economy, employment levels are high and incomes are steady. As a result of these factors, the demand for housing increases. (More people can afford to buy homes—the supply of property cannot keep pace with the demand.) This demand spurs building and causes the prices of already built homes to increase.

At the same time, the demand for mortgage funds also is increasing. As more people are able to purchase homes, more people will want to finance those homes. Thus, there needs to be a healthy supply of money to lend for a strong housing market to continue. If money is tight and interest rates are too high, fewer people will be able to qualify for mortgages and the demand for housing will decrease. Supply will outstrip demand, and housing prices will decrease.

Money may become tight because of the actions of those forces that compete for mortgage funds. The two largest competitors for mortgage funds are the federal government and industry. Both are heavy borrowers: the federal government to cover the enormous federal deficit and industry because it usually takes large sums of money to expand operations.

Economic indicators help the broker stay abreast of economic changes. Rates of *inflation* (an increase in the amount or money or credit in relation to available goods or services) and *stagflation* (persistent inflation combined with stagnant consumer demand and high unemployment rates) are important gauges of the relative health of the economy. And to judge future opportunities in real estate markets, brokers must keep aware of the possibility of *recessions* (period of low general economic activity) or, in extremely rare cases, *depressions* (periods of low general economic activity marked by rising levels of unemployment).

Influence of Individuals

The behavior of the population has a dramatic impact on real estate cycles. Demographic trends include the rate of homeownership and which kinds of homes are desired. The savings habits of individuals also affect real estate cycles. For example, when individuals invest their funds in stocks, bonds, or mutual funds instead of in savings accounts, lenders no longer have as much money to lend, and real estate loans become harder to get. This phenomenon is known as **disintermediation.**

Influence of the Federal Government

The actions of the federal government have a significant impact on real estate cycles. The federal government, through the Federal Reserve, tries to lessen the likelihood of economic downturns (recessions, depressions, and inflation) and decrease the impact of those downturns should they occur. The secondary mortgage market also helps lessen the impact of local real estate cycles by creating a national market for real estate mortgages.

Tax laws.   Tax laws also affect real estate cycles. For example, the Tax Reform Act of 1986 eliminated many tax benefits once enjoyed by real estate owners and investors. With limited exceptions, losses from property investments can no longer shelter other income. Depreciation time periods were increased significantly (making the yearly tax deduction much smaller).

On the other hand, the Taxpayer Relief Act of 1998 was a stimulus to the resale market. In previous years, homesellers who wanted to move to smaller and less expensive quarters often faced large capital gains taxes. After 1998, almost no one owed any tax on the sale of their own home, and moving around as often as every two years became a tax-free possibility.

Federal Reserve System.   The role of the Federal Reserve System (also known as the "Fed") is to maintain sound credit conditions, help counteract inflationary and deflationary trends, and create a favorable economic climate. The Federal Reserve System divides the country into 12 federal reserve districts, each served by a federal reserve bank. All nationally chartered banks must join the Federal Reserve and purchase stock in its district reserve banks.

The Federal Reserve regulates the flow of money and interest rates in the marketplace indirectly, through its member banks, by controlling their reserve requirements and discount rates.

The Federal Reserve requires that each member bank keep a certain amount of its assets on hand as reserve funds unavailable for loans or any other use. This requirement was intended primarily to protect customer deposits, but more important, it provides a means of manipulating the flow of cash in the money market.

By increasing its reserve requirements, the Federal Reserve in effect limits the amount of money that member banks can use to make loans, thus causing interest rates to rise. In this manner, the government can slow down an overactive economy by limiting the number of loans that would have been directed toward major purchases of goods and services. The opposite is also true: by decreasing the reserve requirements the Federal Reserve can allow more loans to be made, thus increasing the amount of money circulated in the marketplace and causing interest rates to drop.

Federal Reserve member banks are permitted to borrow money from the district reserve banks to expand their lending operations. The interest rate that the district banks charge for the use of this money is called the *discount rate*. This rate is the basis on which the banks determine the percentage rate of interest that they, in turn, charge their loan customers. Theoretically, when the Federal Reserve discount rate is high, bank interest rates are high; therefore, fewer loans will be made, and less money will circulate in the marketplace. Conversely, a lower discount rate results in lower interest rates, more bank loans, and more money in circulation.

Influence of Lending Policies

As mentioned earlier, the availability of mortgage money influences real estate cycles. When interest rates are high or money is tight, real estate sales decrease. Other ways lenders influence the real estate market include how stringent their lending criteria are (who can qualify for a mortgage); documentation requirements; the time frame for loan approval; and LTV ratios.

Publications

To keep up with all the elements that influence real estate cycles, real estate brokers should read various publications, including the *Wall Street Journal*, local or regional newspapers, and professional publications. All of these publications are excellent sources for various economic indicators, such as the discount rate, unemployment rate, inflation rate, interest rates, and housing starts.

Condominiums and Cooperatives

In some parts of the state, condominiums do not hold or increase their value as quickly as detached houses. The Manhattan market, however, is subject to periodic swings, closely tied to the health of the stock market. At one time condos and co-ops may be a drag on the market; six months later they may sell like hotcakes.

Loan Processing

With the growth of the Internet, systems for credit scoring, and sophisticated software programs, mortgage lending continues a trend toward streamlining. Even appraisal time may be shortened, with some loans calling for only "drive-by" appraisals. "One-stop shopping," with all the services for the transaction available from one all-purpose company, may be the real estate transaction of the future.

■ SUMMARY

New York is a lien theory state, considering mortgages as liens on the property, not as transfer of title.

Mortgage loans include conventional loans, loans insured by the FHA or an independent mortgage insurance company, those guaranteed by the VA, and loans from private lenders. Shared-equity arrangements (known as *participation loans* in commercial lending) and subordinate or junior mortgage loans are also possible.

Commercial loans include miniperm and floating interest mortgages, sometimes structured to allow lower payments at the start of the repayment term. Other commercial financing techniques include sale-leasebacks and ground leases.

Construction loans usually provide for the funds to be disbursed in installments, as the work is finished and inspected.

The federal government affects real estate financing by participating in the secondary mortgage market. The secondary market is composed of investors who purchase and hold the loans as investments. Fannie Mae (Federal National Mortgage Association), Ginnie Mae (Government National Mortgage Association), and Freddie Mac (Federal Home Loan Mortgage Corporation) take an active role in creating a secondary market by regularly purchasing mortgage loans from originators and retaining, or warehousing, them until investment purchasers are available.

Real estate brokers need to stay informed about the factors that influence the real estate market. Locally, employment levels have a major influence. Nationally, the state of the economy in general brings buyers into the market or discourages them, as the economic cycle moves from inflation to stagflation, recession, depression, and back again.

QUESTIONS

1. Farmer Macdonald wouldn't really mind a small shopping mall on the far end of his land, but he hates to see those acres go out of the family. He can solve the problem by negotiating a
   a. sale-leaseback.
   b. miniperm loan.
   c. ground lease.
   d. release deed.

2. Ginny's Minimart does a booming business, and Ginny would like to expand her store. There's plenty of room to build, but she isn't sure she could finance the construction. One remedy might be to find an investor and negotiate a
   a. sale-leaseback.
   b. ground lease.
   c. SONYMA mortgage.
   d. gap loan.

3. With the commercial loans that involve interest accrual, the borrower faces the possibility of
   a. underwriting.
   b. negative amortization.
   c. assignment.
   d. alienation.

4. Construction loans are
   a. insured by the Fed.
   b. considered subordinate.
   c. subject to disintermediation.
   d. disbursed in installments.

5. The strongest governmental influence on the country's interest rates is
   a. the Federal Reserve.
   b. SONYMA.
   c. GNMA.
   d. HUD.

6. In the future, mortgage origination is likely to become a faster process because of
   a. relaxed FNMA regulations.
   b. the Internet.
   c. Federal Reserve policies.
   d. increased use of PMI.

7. The commercial equivalent of a shared-equity home mortgage is
   a. a participation loan.
   b. a miniperm mortgage.
   c. a junior lien.
   d. cooperative financing.

8. Ginnie Mae and Fannie Mae were created to warehouse
   a. land for development by the government.
   b. assigned leases.
   c. home equity loans.
   d. FHA and VA mortgages.

9. Most home equity loans are really
   a. long-term leases.
   b. junior mortgages.
   c. purchase-money mortgages.
   d. trust deeds.

10. When a developer sells one home in a new subdivision, the blanket mortgage on that lot is
    a. secured.
    b. refinanced.
    c. accrued.
    d. released.

CHAPTER 6

Real Estate Investments

■ KEY TERMS

adjusted basis
appreciation
basis
boot
capital gain
cash flow
cost recovery
current rent roll
debt service
depreciation
discounted cash-flow
  analysis

discounting
discount rate
disposition
general partnership
holding period
installment sales
leverage
limited liability companies
  (LLCs)
limited liability partnerships
  (LLPs)
limited partnership

marginal tax rate
mortgage debt service
negative cash flow
net operating income
passive income
pro forma statements
pyramid
rate of return
real estate investment
  syndicate
real estate investment trusts
  (REITs)

real estate mortgage
  investment conduit
  (REMIC)
return
Section 1031 property
  exchange
silent partners
straight-line depreciation
tax basis
tax credit
tax-deferred exchange

■ THE NATURE OF REAL ESTATE INVESTMENT

Investing in real estate usually means buying property and holding it for the production of income. Real estate has been called the best way to build an estate.

Real estate investment, though, takes a constant investment of effort. One can buy shares of stock and then limit further effort to checking the quotations every week in the Sunday paper. Not so with a duplex three blocks from home. The owner must be ready for a 6 AM phone call about a burst water heater, have a prompt replacement delivered, and arrange for someone to meet the plumber that very day. For small properties it is very difficult to be an absentee landlord.

In addition, real estate investment is not liquid. Money can be taken out of the stock market with a simple phone call to a stockbroker. Investors in real estate, however, should not count on taking out their capital within perhaps six months. When local unemployment is high, investors may not be able to take out their money until the economic cycle changes.

■ PREPARING TO BE AN INVESTOR

An investor faces two challenges: finding and buying the right property, then managing it. The beginning investor needs

- a lawyer who specializes in real estate;
- an accountant; and
- a real estate broker familiar with investment real estate.

All three should be lined up before the first purchase so they can assist in locating and analyzing the proposed investment. Meanwhile, the new investor should get information about the market by reading the papers and visiting open houses to develop the expertise needed to recognize a bargain.

Start Small

Investors would be wise to start small for the first few transactions so they do not risk too much capital or take on too much liability while learning. A one- to six-unit building, located reasonably close to the investor's own home, is often best. Out-of-town property that cannot be monitored or controlled can be disappointing.

Avoid Vacant Land

Building lots in resort areas and vacant land held in anticipation of development are not for the beginning investor. Land would have to appreciate markedly before it would pay off, because it produces no income, ties up money, cannot be depreciated, and requires property tax payments. Judging which areas will be in demand in years to come takes skill and expertise, and even experienced investors can be burned.

Leverage

Pyramiding. Traditionally real estate investors have used **leverage** (other people's money) to **pyramid** a small amount of capital. If, for example, an investor had $100,000 and bought one property that went up in value by 5 percent in the next year, the investor would make $5,000 in **appreciation**. To use leverage, one might search for ten such parcels, putting $10,000 down on each and getting sellers to take back $90,000 mortgages. If each went up by 5 percent, the investor would have appreciation totaling $50,000 in one year and would control $1 million worth of real estate.

This technique runs into problems, however, where local conditions change, employment drops, and finding tenants who will pay enough to cover those ten mortgage payments becomes difficult. The investors who delighted in *owning* $1 million worth of real estate now find themselves *owing* on $1 million worth, which is a different matter.

Risk and Reward

The purpose of investing is to generate a **return,** or profit. An investor expects both a return *of* capital (recovery of the invested funds) and a return *on* capital (profit or reward). The **rate of return** that an investor expects is directly related to the degree of risk in the investment. Real estate investments must offer the promise of higher returns to attract capital away from other, safer investments.

One of the most important risks for a real estate investment is the possibility that the property will decline in value during the investment holding period. On the other hand, an increase in property value can be a significant component of an investment's profit. For this reason, real estate investors must give considerable attention to the trends that affect real estate values. Statistical data from government agencies and private research groups are an important source of information in this regard. Such data can help to identify economic and social trends that will affect property values over time.

■ ANALYZING PROPERTY INCOME

A key factor in any investment is the amount of income that can be expected. In the case of income-producing real estate, an investor is concerned with the amount of rent that the property can generate and also with the amount of expenses that are necessary to maintain the property. A property's income and expenses are typically recorded in the form of operating statements.

Operating Statements

An *operating statement* is basically a list of revenues and expenses associated with a property for a given time period, such as one month or one year. The different categories of revenue (rent, parking fees, etc.) are listed at the top, along with their amounts, and the amounts are totaled. Next come the various expenses associated with the property, which are also totaled. At the bottom of the statement, total expenses are subtracted from total revenues and the resulting *net operating income (NOI)* is noted. Net operating income (the "bottom line") is a critical factor in investment analysis. Figure 6.1 is an example of a completed operating statement.

Current Rent Roll

An operating statement for a property will show the total amount of rent generated for the period of the statement, but it does not go into the details. This information is found in a **current rent roll** or rent schedule, which lists the current rent for each tenant of the property. This information is important to investment analysis for several reasons. It indicates the level of vacancies in the property, and it also shows the rates at which various units are currently leased. It would be a disadvantage to the investor, for example, if units were subject to long-term leases at below-market rental rates.

Pro Forma Statements

While the owner's operating statements and rent roll are important sources of information for investment analysis, they do not predict what the property will earn in the future. And *future earnings* are precisely what investors are concerned with. Consequently, investment analysis makes use of **pro forma statements,** which are hypothetical future operating statements for a property.

Pro forma statements differ from regular operating statements in several key features. First of all, as just noted, pro forma statements list *potential* future revenues and expenses, while operating statements show actual past revenues and expenses. Second, in a pro forma statement the amount of rent is based on current market rates, as opposed to the currently scheduled rents for the property,

F I G U R E 6.1

Operating Statement

15-Nov-08	ANNUAL PROPERTY OPERATING DATA	9:27 AM
Owner: XYZ APARTMENTS	PREPARED BY:	PRICE: 3,750,000
Location: 621 DALE ROAD	R. BARRY DEICKLER, CRB, EMS	LOANS:
City: NORTH LAUDERDALE, FL 33068	DEICKLER REAL ESTATE	
Type: APARTMENT	40 WEST MAIN STREET	EQUITY: 3,750,000
Size: 100	MT. KISCO, NY	FEE:
Purpose: Owner's Statement	Financing	

Assessed/Appraised: Value %	Existing: Rate Due	Amount Int.	Mo. Pymt. Annual Pymt.
Land	1st Loan		
Improvements	2nd Loan		
Personal Property	3rd Loan		
TOTAL	**Potential:**		
Adjusted Cost Basis:	1st Loan		
Net Rentable Sq. Ft.:	2nd Loan		

	ANNUAL INCOME/EXPENSES	$SQ.FT.	GSI %	EXPENSES	INCOME		
1	GROSS SCHEDULED INCOME		100.00%		721,560	THE FIGURES AND DATA HEREIN	1
2	Less Vac. & Cr. Losses		2.99%		21,560	ARE NOT GUARANTEED, BUT	2
3	EFFECTIVE RENTAL INCOME		97.01%		700,000	ARE BELIEVED TO BE RELIABLE.	3
4	Plus: Other Income					PLEASE GET ADVICE FROM	4
5	GROSS OPERATING INCOME		97.01%		700,000	YOUR CPA and ATTORNEY.	5
6	OPERATING EXPENSES					COMMENTS/FOOTNOTES	6
7	Accounting & Legal		1.00%	7,000			7
8	Advertising		0.71%	5,000			8
9	Insurance		1.57%	11,000			9
10	Maintenance & Repair		3.57%	25,000			10
11	Management		3.57%	25,000			11
12	Payroll		4.57%	31,980			12
13	Payroll Taxes		0.36%	2,500			13
14	Postage						14
15	Real Estate Taxes		9.687%	67,808			15
16	Telephone						16
17	Other						17
18	Gas						18
19	Electric		2.87%	20,090			19
20	Water/Sewer		2.31%	16,200			20
21	Rubbish		2.48%	17,348			21
22	Reserves		2.14%	15,000			22
23	Leasing Commissions						23
24	Licenses & Permits						24
25	Supplies						25
26	Miscellaneous		0.71%	5,000			26
27	Contract Services						27
28	Lawn/Snow Removal		0.19%	1,345			28
29	Pool		0.71%	5,000			29
30	Janitorial						30
31	TOTAL EXPENSES		36.47%	255,271			31
32	NET OPERATING INCOME				444,729	CAP RATE 11.86%	32
33	Less Annual Debt Service					LTV RATIO	33
34	CASH FLOW BEFORE TAXES				444,729	CASH ON CASH 11.86%	34

unless the scheduled rents are locked in by long-term lease agreements. A pro forma statement shows the total amount of rent that the property is *capable of generating*, and then records a separate deduction for anticipated vacancies and collection losses. A regular operating statement simply shows the amount of rent that actually was collected.

Expense items also may be listed *differently* on a pro forma statement. Two critical items are *depreciation* and *mortgage debt service*. **Depreciation** is an expense item that is listed on operating statements for income tax purposes. The amount of depreciation expense is related to the owner's **tax basis** in the property and also to the relevant tax code provisions. The current owner's depreciation expense is irrelevant to investment analysis, so it is not included in a pro forma. In its place, a line item expense is shown for *replacement reserves*, the anticipated costs for replacing parts of the property (such as a roof or heating equipment) as they wear out.

Mortgage debt service refers to the *payments of principal and interest that must be made on loans that are secured by a property*. Here again, the current owner's debt service is essentially irrelevant to investment analysis, as the new investor will need to obtain new financing. In any case, *debt service is never considered to be a component of net operating income in investment analysis*. Net operating income is calculated independently, and then any debt service (current or pro forma) is deducted to determine the investment's *cash flow* (pretax cash flow). Like net operating income, *pretax cash flow* is a key figure in investment analysis.

A typical pro forma statement would first list the investment's *potential gross operating income*. Market rate rental figures may be used, unless the present rentals are locked in with long-term leases, which would survive a sale.

From potential gross rents, the following items would then be subtracted:

- An estimated allowance for vacancies and uncollected rents (normally 5 percent or so of gross rental income)
- Utilities paid by the landlord including, if applicable, electric power, fuel for heating and cooling, water, sewer, trash collection, and so forth
- Property taxes
- Hazard and liability insurance premiums
- Estimate for repairs
- Maintenance services such as janitor service, snow removal, lawn care, and the like
- Property management salaries or fees, if applicable

A reserve for future large improvements such as a new roof or furnace, with the estimated amount based on the building's present condition and perhaps running to 2 percent of the value of the property.

Projected expenses subtracted from gross rental yields annual **net operating income.** Next subtracted is **debt service** (mortgage payments). The resulting figure shows **cash flow**—actual dollars one can expect to take out of the property each year. If the figure is a minus, the investment is likely to yield **negative cash flow,** requiring a contribution from the investor's pocket each year.

■ INVESTMENT OWNERSHIP STRUCTURE

Ownership structure refers to the type of entity that will make the investment. For example, an individual may wish to purchase property through a corporation, either to limit personal liability exposure or for tax or accounting purposes. Ownership also may be structured in the form of a real estate syndicate or other specialized investment group.

A **real estate investment syndicate** is a form of business venture in which a group of people pool their resources to own and/or develop a particular piece of property. In this manner people with only modest capital can invest in large-scale, high-profit operations, such as highrise apartment buildings and shopping centers. A certain amount of profit is realized from rents collected on the investment, but the main return usually comes when the syndicate sells the property.

Syndicate participation can take many different legal forms, from tenancy in common and joint tenancy to various kinds of partnerships, corporations, and trusts.

In 1994, the New York Limited Liability Company Law was enacted, which allows the formation of **limited liability companies (LLCs)** and **limited liability partnerships (LLPs)**. Both LLCs and LLPs allow investors to take advantage of the federal tax benefits and flexibility of a partnership and the limited liability of a corporation. It is anticipated that LLCs will become a popular form of business organization.

Private syndication, which generally involves a small group of closely associated and/or widely experienced investors, is distinguished from *public syndication*, which generally involves a much larger group of investors who may or may not be knowledgeable about real estate as an investment. Any pooling of individuals' funds raises questions of registration of securities under federal securities laws and state securities laws, commonly referred to as *blue-sky laws*.

Securities laws control and regulate the offering and sale of securities to protect members of the public who are not sophisticated investors but may be solicited to participate. Real estate securities must be registered with state officials and/or with the federal Securities and Exchange Commission (SEC) *when they meet the defined conditions of a public offering*. The number of prospects solicited, the total number of investors, or participants, the financial background and sophistication of the investors, and the value or price per unit of investment are pertinent facts. Salespeople of such real estate securities may be required to obtain special licenses and register with the state's attorney general and the SEC.

Forms of Syndicates

A **general partnership** is organized so that *all members of the group share equally in the managerial decisions, profits, and losses*. A certain member (or members) of the syndicate is designated to act as trustee for the group, holding title to the property and maintaining it in the syndicate's name.

Under a **limited partnership** agreement *one party* (or parties), usually a property developer or real estate broker, organizes, operates, and is responsible for the entire syndicate. This person is called the *general partner*. The other members of the partnership are merely investors; they have no voice in the organization and direction of the operation. These passive investors are called *limited partners* (and may also be called **silent partners** or *passive partners*).

The *limited partners* share in the profits and compensate the general partner out of such profits. The limited partners stand to lose only as much as they invest, nothing more. The *general partner(s)* is (are) totally responsible for any excess losses incurred by the investment. The sale of a limited partnership interest involves the sale of an *investment security*, as defined by the SEC. Therefore, such sales are subject to state and federal laws concerning the sale of securities. Unless exempt, the securities must be registered with the SEC and the appropriate state authorities.

Real Estate Investment Trusts

By directing their funds into **real estate investment trusts (REITs)**, real estate investors can take advantage of the same tax benefits as mutual fund investors. A real estate investment trust does not have to pay corporate income tax as long as 90 percent of its income is distributed to its shareholders and certain other conditions are met. There are three types of investment trusts: *equity trusts*, *mortgage trusts*, and *combination trusts*. To qualify as a REIT, at least 75 percent of the trust's income must come from real estate.

Equity trusts.   Much like mutual fund operations, *equity REITs* pool an assortment of large-scale income properties and sell shares to investors. This is in contrast to a real estate syndicate, through which several investors pool their funds to purchase one particular property. An equity trust also differs from a syndicate in that the trust realizes and directs its main profits through the income derived from the various properties it owns rather than from the sale of those properties.

Mortgage trusts.   *Mortgage trusts* operate similarly to equity trusts, except that the mortgage trusts buy and sell real estate mortgages (usually short-term, junior instruments) rather than real property. A mortgage trust's major sources of income are mortgage interest and origination fees. Mortgage trusts also may make construction loans and finance land acquisitions.

Combination trusts.   *Combination trusts* invest shareholders' funds in both real estate assets and mortgage loans. It has been predicted that these types of trusts will be best able to withstand economic slumps because they can balance their investments and liabilities more efficiently than can the other types of trusts.

Real Estate Mortgage Investment Conduits

The **real estate mortgage investment conduit (REMIC),** which issues securities backed by a pool of mortgages, has complex qualification, transfer, and liquidation rules. Holders of regular interests receive interest or similar payments based on either a fixed rate or a variable rate. Holders of residual interests receive distributions (if any) on a pro rata basis.

■ HOLDING PERIOD AND DISPOSITION

One of the key considerations in an investment strategy is the question of when to get out of the investment, when to sell. This is especially true of real estate investments, due to the relative illiquidity of real estate. Choosing to sell at the wrong time can more than wipe out any gains that were realized during the ownership of a property. For this reason, real estate investment strategy must focus on both the *holding period* of the investment and the timing of its *disposition*.

The **holding period** is the length of time between the date the investor purchases the property and the date the investor resells the property. During this period, investment strategy is focused on the property's income and cash flow. Will the property generate enough income to cover the investor's financing costs and the expenses of maintaining the property? Does the investor have the resources to handle any periods of negative cash flow that may arise? Is the projected rate of return sufficient to compensate for the degree of investment risk posed by the property?

The strategy of **disposition** is *interrelated* with the strategy of the holding period. An anticipated gain or loss from the sale of the property will obviously affect the overall rate of return on the investment, which must be commensurate with the risk. The investor must balance the anticipated income during the holding period against the likelihood of a change in property value. A lower rate of income during the holding period may be acceptable if there is a strong probability of appreciation in value, whereas market uncertainty may demand a high rate of holding period income.

Financing considerations also come into play in the *investor's timing strategy*. Loan rates are dependent on the term of the loan, with lower rates often available for shorter term financing. An investor might be able to obtain a more favorable rate on a five-year balloon loan, for example, but then assumes the risk of needing to refinance on less desirable terms if market conditions preclude a profitable resale of the property after five years.

■ TYPES OF INVESTMENT PROPERTIES

There are several types of properties investors are interested in, including the following:

- *Retail.* Retail properties include freestanding buildings and traditional shopping centers (which range from strip centers to superregional malls).
- *Office.* Office properties can be small properties with one or two tenants, highrise complexes, or office parks. They may be situated in downtown urban areas or in suburban developments.
- *Apartment.* Multifamily housing is a popular type of investment property. Apartment buildings can range from five or six units to highrise complexes.
- *Mixed developments.* Mixed developments are increasing in popularity. These developments combine several types of property uses, such as residential (apartments), office space, and retail space.
- *Hotels/motels.* Hotels and motels are a very specialized type of property and require expert management. While the failure rate for hotels and motels is quite high, they can be a good investment if the properties are in a good location and are well managed.

■ INVESTMENT ANALYSIS TECHNIQUES

To a certain extent, investment analysis is a subjective operation, because it depends on the *goals* and the *situation* of the particular investor. One investor may have $50,000 to invest, and another may wish to invest $500,000. Some investors are naturally conservative, while others thrive on risky ventures. Often an investor has definite ideas about the type(s) of properties he or she is interested in. Although these subjective factors will affect any given investment analysis, certain techniques are widely used by a broad spectrum of real estate investors. The broker counseling a potential investor must have knowledge and expertise in the analysis of many types of investments.

Discounted Cash-Flow Analysis

Discounting is a mathematical technique for calculating the present value of a future amount. It answers the question: "Would you rather have 95 cents now or $1 one year from now?" In discounting, the value of $1 that will be received at some future date depends on two factors: the length of *time* until the money is paid and the *rate* at which the payment is discounted. In general, a shorter repayment term or a lower discount rate means a higher present value.

Selecting the *discount rate* is a critical part of **discounted cash-flow analysis.** This rate corresponds to the investor's expected rate of return on the investment. The **discount rate** must take into account *the time value of money, anticipated inflation or deflation, and the particular risks associated with the future cash flows.*

Although discounted cash-flow analysis often is used to analyze a series of regular annual cash flows, it also can be applied to *individual cash flows that vary from year to year.* Different discount rates may be used for different payments, to reflect differences in risk. Assume, for example, that a property is subject to a long-term lease with a highly reputable tenant. Because the income from lease payments is at relatively low risk in this case, it may be discounted at a lower rate than the income that will come from resale of the property at the conclusion of the investment.

■ INCOME TAX CONSIDERATIONS

Depreciation

Depreciation allows an investor to recover the cost of an income-producing asset by way of tax deductions over the period of the asset's useful life. *Land cannot be depreciated*—technically, it never wears out or becomes obsolete. If depreciation is taken in equal amounts over an asset's useful life, the method used is called **straight-line depreciation.**

In past years, tax rules allowed depreciation over as little as 15 years, allowing deduction of one-fifteenth of the cost of real property each year. For property placed in service after January 1, 1987, the Tax Reform Act of 1986 increased the **cost recovery** period for residential rental property to 27.5 years and for nonresidential property to 39 years.

Subtracting depreciation from net operating income yields the profit or loss the investor can declare on an income tax return. An accountant can determine whether any loss can be taken as a loss against other sources of income. The rules are complex. If total income is less than $100,000, the investor who actively manages the property may be able to claim up to $25,000 in losses against other types of income, such as salary or dividends. (An owner actively manages property when he or she is involved in management decisions such as setting rental rates.) With total income up to $150,000, part of a loss may be deducted. Otherwise a paper loss can be taken only against other **passive income** (the category into which all rental income now falls for tax purposes). In the 1990s real estate brokers and investors campaigned strenuously for Congress to change these passive loss tax rules. As a result, rental income is no longer considered passive for persons involved full time in real estate.

Income tax considerations are calculated at the investor's **marginal tax rate** (highest applicable tax bracket).

Capital Gains

Capital gain is defined as the difference between the adjusted basis of property and its net selling price. At various times tax law has excluded a portion of capital gains from income tax or set lower rates on long-term gains. As of 2003, the long-term holding period (minimum length of time an asset must be owned to qualify for special capital gains treatment) was 12 months. For long-term assets sold before May 6, 2003, the maximum capital gains rate was 20 percent (10 percent for any gain that fell within the lowest income tax bracket). Long-term assets sold after that date are taxed at 15 percent (5 percent for low-income taxpayers). Any part of the gain attributable to depreciation that was claimed or could have been claimed as an expense while the property was rented, however, is taxed at 25 percent.

Basis. The **basis** of property is the investor's initial cost for the real estate, plus the cost of any subsequent capital improvements. Any depreciation claimed as a tax deduction is then subtracted to arrive at the property's **adjusted basis.** Sales price also is adjusted, with commissions and legal costs of selling deducted. When the property is sold, adjusted sales price minus adjusted cost basis equals the capital gain taxable as income.

For example, an investor purchased a small one-family dwelling for use as a rental property. Purchase price was $45,000. The investor is now selling the property for $100,000. The investor made $3,000 worth of capital improvements to the house. Depreciation of $10,000 has been taken during the investor's ownership. The investor will pay a broker's commission of 7 percent of the sales price and also will pay closing costs of $600. The investor's capital gain is computed as follows:

Selling price		$100,000
Less:		
7% commission	$7,000	
closing costs	+ 600	
		− 7,600
Net sales price		$92,400
Basis:		
original cost	$45,000	
improvements	+ 3,000	
	$48,000	

Less:

depreciation	−10,000	
Adjusted basis		− 38,000
Total capital gain:		$54,400

Of the total gain, $44,000 will qualify for capital gains tax rates; the remaining $10,400, which represents past depreciation, will be taxed at 25 percent.

Exchanges

Real estate investors can postpone taxation of capital gains by arranging what is known as a **Section 1031 property exchange.** To qualify as a **tax-deferred exchange,** the properties involved must be of *like kind* and be investment property or a property used in trade or business (as defined by the IRS). For example, vacant land held as an investment may be exchanged for a shopping center, or an apartment building may be exchanged for water rights to a stream in Colorado. State law determines what qualifies as real estate. For example, a cooperative in New York and in 17 other states is considered real estate for the purpose of exchanging. Any additional capital or personal property included to even out the exchange is called **boot,** and the party receiving boot is taxed on it at the time of the exchange.

Suppose investor Brown owns an apartment building with an adjusted basis of $225,000 and a market value of $375,000. Brown exchanges the building plus $75,000 cash for another apartment building having a market value of $450,000. That building, owned by investor Grey, has an adjusted basis of $175,000. Brown's basis in the new building will be $300,000 (the $225,000 basis of the building exchanged plus the $75,000 cash boot paid), and Brown has no tax liability on the exchange. Grey must pay tax on the $75,000 boot received and has a basis of $175,000 (the same as the previous building) in the building now owned. In a 1031 exchange, the investor's basis is transferred to the new property.

Brown	Exchanges with	Grey
$375,000	Price	$450,000
225,000	Basis	175,000
75,000	Boot	

Amount necessary to exchange: $375,000 + $75,000 cash = $450,000
The $75,000 cash/boot is taxable to Grey
Brown's new basis = $300,000 ($225,000 + $75,000)
Grey's basis = $175,000

Some Section 1031 exchanges involve strict time limitations and require accurate paperwork. Property to be purchased must be identified within 45 days and the transactions completed within 180 days. In some cases proceeds must be held in escrow by a qualified intermediary third party. For these "Starker" (delayed) exchanges, the use of an attorney and/or accountant familiar with the procedure is essential.

Tax Credits

A **tax credit** is a direct reduction in tax due, rather than a deduction from income before tax is computed. A tax credit is therefore of far greater value.

Investors in older building renovations and low-income housing projects may use designated tax credits to offset tax on up to $25,000 of other income. This is a major exception to the rule requiring active participation in the project. Even passive investors can take advantage of the tax credits. The maximum income level at which the credits can be taken is also higher. Investors with adjusted gross income of up to $200,000 are entitled to the full $25,000 offset, which is reduced by $0.50 for every additional dollar of income and eliminated entirely for incomes above $250,000.

Tax credits of up to 20 percent of money spent are available for taxpayers who renovate historic property. Historic property is property so designated by the Department of the Interior and listed in the National Register of Historic Landmarks or property of historic significance located in a state or locally cer-tified *historic district*. The property may be depreciated, but the full amount of the tax credit must be subtracted from the basis derived by adding purchase cost and renovation expenses.

The work must be accomplished in accordance with federal historic property guidelines and must be certified by the Department of the Interior or other state, county, or local entity. After renovation, the property must be used as a place of business or rented; it cannot be used as the personal residence of the person taking the tax credit.

There is also a credit of 10 percent of rehabilitation costs for nonhistoric build-ings placed in service before 1936. Nonhistoric buildings must be nonresidential property.

Also available are tax credits ranging from 4 percent to 9 percent each year over a ten-year period for expenditures on new construction or renovation of certain low-income housing.

Installment Sales

A taxpayer who sells real property and receives payment on an *installment basis* may report and pay taxes on any profit on the transaction year by year as it is collected. Many complex provisions apply to **installment sales.**

■ SUMMARY

Traditionally, real estate investment has offered a high rate of return while at the same time acting as an effective inflation hedge and allowing an investor to make use of other people's money to make investments through leverage. There may also be tax advantages to owning real estate. On the other hand, real estate is not a highly liquid investment and often carries with it a high degree of risk. Also, it is difficult to invest in real estate without expert advice, and a certain amount of involvement is usually required to establish and maintain the investment.

Net operating income on an investment is calculated by subtracting expenses (including vacancies and reserve for expected improvements) from gross rental income. Subtracting debt service (mortgage payments) then yields the figure rep-resenting actual cash flow. Total return is composed of cash flow plus mortgage amortization plus appreciation and tax benefits. A property's operating statements indicate its historical performance, while future performance must be estimated through the use of pro forma statements.

An investor hoping to use maximum leverage in financing an investment will make a small down payment, pay low interest rates, and spread mortgage payments over as long a period as possible. By holding and refinancing properties, known as pyramiding, an investor may substantially increase investment holdings without contributing additional capital. The process can run into trouble if vacancy rates rise and rental income falls.

Individuals may invest in real estate through an investment syndicate; these include general and limited partnerships. Other forms of real estate investment are the real estate investment trust (REIT) and the real estate mortgage investment conduit (REMIC).

The holding period of an investment and its eventual resale are important factors in investment analysis. Discounted cash-flow analysis is commonly used to evaluate investments.

Depreciation allows an investor to recover in tax deductions the basis of an asset over the period of its useful life. Only costs of improvements to land may be recovered, not costs for the land itself.

Capital gain represents the taxable profit when property is sold, calculated by subtracting adjusted cost basis from adjusted sales price. Adjusted cost basis represents original cost plus improvements, minus depreciation claimed.

By exchanging one property for another with an equal or greater selling value, an investor can defer paying tax on the gain realized until a sale is made. Any extra cash or property received in the exchange is called *boot* and is taxed.

An investor may defer federal income taxes on gain realized from the sale of an investment property through an installment sale of property.

The real estate licensee should be familiar with the rudimentary tax implications of real property ownership, but should refer clients to competent tax advisers for answers to questions to specific matters.

QUESTIONS

1. Many experts advise that a first real estate investment be
   a. within a short drive of the investor's own home.
   b. in a popular resort area.
   c. located only where professional management is available.
   d. a handyman-special property in need of upgrading.

2. The beginning investor should first consult an accountant when
   a. preparing the present year's income tax return.
   b. establishing cost basis for depreciation.
   c. analyzing a prospective purchase.
   d. researching fair market rentals.

3. Among the disadvantages of real estate investment is
   a. leverage.
   b. the need for physical and mental effort.
   c. tax shelter.
   d. equity buildup.

4. Jim's property has a gross rental income of $12,000 a year and total expenses, including debt service, of $13,000. Jim is experiencing
   a. leverage.
   b. negative cash flow.
   c. recapture.
   d. deflation.

5. A small multifamily property generates $50,000 in rental income with expenses of $45,000 annually, including $35,000 in debt service. The property appreciates about $15,000 a year. The owner realizes another $5,000 through income tax savings. On this property, the cash flow is
   a. $5,000.   c. $20,000.
   b. $15,000.   d. $35,000.

6. In question 5, the owner's total return is
   a. $5,000.   c. $25,000.
   b. $15,000.   d. $35,000.

7. Leverage involves the extensive use of
   a. cost recovery.
   b. borrowed money.
   c. government subsidies.
   d. alternative taxes.

8. Property that has a net operating income of $28,000 with annual depreciation of $10,000 and debt service of $18,000, which includes $17,000 interest, has taxable income of
   a. $38,000.   c. $10,000.
   b. $28,000.   d. $1,000.

9. The primary source of tax shelter in real estate investments comes from the accounting concept known as
   a. recapture.
   b. boot.
   c. depreciation.
   d. net operating income.

10. For tax purposes the initial cost of an investment property plus the cost of any subsequent improvements to the property, less depreciation, represents the investment's
    a. adjusted basis.   c. basis.
    b. capital gain.   d. salvage value.

11. The money left in an investor's pocket after expenses, including debt service, have been paid is known as
    a. net operating income.
    b. gross income.
    c. cash flow.
    d. internal rate of return.

12. The concept of depreciation of income property is of most value to the taxpayer in

    a. the top income bracket.
    b. a marginal income tax bracket.
    c. the lowest income tax bracket.
    d. any tax bracket.

13. Julia Kinder is exchanging her apartment building for an apartment building of greater market value and must include a $10,000 boot to even out the exchange. Which of the following may she use as boot?

    a. $10,000 cash
    b. Emeralds with a current market value of $10,000
    c. A used automobile with a current market value of $10,000
    d. Any of the above if acceptable to the exchangers

14. In question 13, which of the following is *TRUE?*

    a. Julia may owe income tax on $10,000.
    b. Each may owe tax on $10,000.
    c. The other investor *may* owe tax on $10,000.
    d. No one owes any tax at this time.

15. An investment syndicate in which all members share equally in the managerial decisions, profits, and losses involved in the venture would be an example of a

    a. real estate investment trust.
    b. limited partnership.
    c. real estate mortgage trust.
    d. general partnership.

16. The term *debt service* refers to

    a. total operating expenses.
    b. real estate and income taxes only.
    c. principal and interest on mortgage loans.
    d. interest payments only.

17. In an installment sale of real estate, taxable gain is usually received and reported as income by the seller

    a. in the year the sale is initiated.
    b. in the year the final installment payment is made.
    c. in each year that installment payments are received.
    d. at any one time during the period installment payments are received.

18. Depreciation allows the investor to charge as an expense on each year's tax return part of the

    a. purchase price minus land value.
    b. down payment.
    c. mortgage indebtedness.
    d. equity.

19. A separate license and/or registration is required for the sale of

    a. all investment property.
    b. real estate securities.
    c. installment property.
    d. boots.

20. An investor bears unlimited liability for a share of possible losses in a

    a. general partnership.
    b. limited partnership.
    c. real estate investment trust.
    d. corporation.

21. Harvey, a limited partner in a partnership that is renovating a historic waterfront property, is entitled to offset up to $25,000 in tax credits against

    a. no more than the amount he has at risk.
    b. income up to $100,000.
    c. income up to $200,000.
    d. income up to $250,000.

22. Helen has purchased a dilapidated town house that is 40 years old and of no particular historic value. Helen intends to renovate the town house and live in it. For her renovation expenditures Helen will be entitled to tax credits of

    a. $25,000.   c. $12,500.
    b. $0.   d. 25 percent.

23. Jim exchanged his office building, purchased for $475,000 and valued at $650,000, for an office building valued at $750,000. Jim also paid $100,000 cash to the owner of the other building. Jim

    a. received $100,000 "boot."
    b. must report $100,000 as income.
    c. must reduce his adjusted basis by $100,000.
    d. now has a property basis of $575,000.

24. A new tax entity that issues securities backed by a pool of mortgages is a

    a. REIT.
    b. REMIC.
    c. TRA.
    d. general partnership.

25. The Agostinos are being transferred out of town. They decide to keep their current home as an investment property. They ask a real estate broker to manage the property for them. In the first year, they end up losing $1,500 on the investment property, due to a combination of depreciation and a three-month vacancy. For income tax purposes, they can deduct this loss

    a. against any passive income.
    b. against salary, as long as they make less than $200,000.
    c. against a 1031 exchange.
    d. under no circumstances.

CHAPTER 7

General Business Law

administrative law
administrator
arbitration
bankruptcy
case law
certificate of incorporation
civil law
commercial law
commercial paper
common law
constitutional law
contract law

corporation law
criminal law
due process
endorsement
executor
financing statement
injunction
law of agency
litigation
mediation
negotiable instruments
partnership law

personal property law
real property law
security agreement
small claims courts
statute of limitations
statutory law
torts
trustee
trusts and wills
Uniform Commercial
    Code (UCC)

■ SOURCES OF LAW

The principal sources of law in the United States, all of which affect the ownership and transfer of real estate, are *the Constitution of the United States; laws passed by Congress; state constitutions; laws passed by state legislatures; ordinances passed by cities, towns, and other local governments; regulations adopted by agencies created by Congress, state legislatures, and local governments; and court decisions.*

The U.S. Constitution and the individual state constitutions establish the rights of citizens and set forth the limits of governmental authority. **Due process refers to** our constitutional protection against the unfair taking of life, liberty, or property, and guarantees of the right to a fair hearing, notice, and the opportunity to be heard before a judge.

Laws passed by Congress and by state and local legislative bodies—statutory law— may establish specific provisions on any issue, from procedures for recording deeds and mortgages to taxation, or they may simply set broad standards of conduct and establish agencies to administer and enforce the laws.

Government agencies that enact rules and regulations range from the EPA through state real estate commissions to local zoning boards. These regulations implement and enforce legislative acts; they provide detailed information on legal and illegal actions and designate penalties for violations. These regulations have the effect of law.

Court decisions of federal, state, and municipal courts clarify and interpret laws, regulations, and constitutional provisions. By applying the laws to a specific event, a court decision expands the meaning of the law. For example, an attorney draws up what is considered a valid contract under the provisions of state law. If the court finds the contract is not valid, it will render an opinion as to why the contract does not fulfill the legal requirements for such a document. Future contracts in the state then will be based on the precedent of the court decision—**case law**—as well as on the statutes governing contracts.

The courts are not always bound by established precedent. Courts in one jurisdiction (area of authority) may not be bound by the decisions of courts in other jurisdictions. In addition, a court with superior authority in its jurisdiction may at its discretion reverse the ruling of a lower court.

Common law.   In addition to these sources of law, real estate ownership and transfer are affected indirectly by what is known as the common law, that body of rules and principles founded on custom and usage, as well as the precedents of court decisions.

■ UNIFORM COMMERCIAL CODE

The **Uniform Commercial Code (UCC)** represents commercial law that has been adopted, wholly or in part, in all states. While this code generally does not apply directly to real estate, it has replaced state laws relating to chattel mortgages; conditional sales agreements; and liens on chattels, crops, or items that are to become fixtures. Shares in an apartment cooperative are personal property, and lenders to whom they are pledged as security for a loan generally use UCC filings.

To pledge a chattel as security, including chattels that will become fixtures, the code requires the use of a **security agreement,** which must contain a complete description of the items against which the lien applies. A short notice of this agreement, called a **financing statement** or UCC-1, which includes the identification of any real estate involved, must be filed *for fixtures* with the clerk of the county where the debtor resides and *for other personal property* with the Secretary of State in Albany. The recording of the financing statement constitutes notice to subsequent purchasers and mortgagees of the security interest in chattels and fixtures on the real estate.

Many mortgages require the signing and recording of a financing statement when the mortgaged premises include chattels or readily removable fixtures (washers, dryers, and the like) as part of the security for the mortgage debt. If the financing statement has been properly recorded, on the borrower's default the creditor could repossess the chattels and cause them to be sold, applying the proceeds to the debt payment.

■ NEGOTIABLE INSTRUMENTS

A written promise to pay money is known as **commercial paper.** *Promissory notes, checks, drafts,* and *certificates of deposit,* all forms of commercial paper, are also known as **negotiable instruments.** *Negotiability* means that they can be freely transferred from one person to another. Commercial paper serves as a convenient substitute for actual money. The Uniform Commercial Code (UCC) divides commercial paper into four types: notes, drafts, checks, and certificates of deposit.

The simplest form of commercial paper, the *note,* is a promise by one person (the *maker*) to pay money to another (the *payee*) *with interest.* A promissory note may be made payable to a specific payee or simply to anyone who presents it for payment (the *bearer*). If it can be collected at any time, it is a *demand* note. Often, however, notes are not due until a specified time in the future. The bond or note accompanying a mortgage, for example, is a form of promissory note.

A *draft* is a form of commercial paper involving three parties. Sometimes known as a *bill of exchange,* a draft is issued by the *drawer,* who orders another party (the *drawee*) to pay money to the payee. Like a note, a draft may be payable either to a specific payee or to a bearer and may be payable on demand or on a certain date. Drafts are often used in connection with goods being shipped from seller to buyer. A *trade acceptance* is a form of time draft.

A *check* is a special type of draft that orders a bank to pay money to the payee on demand. A check may name a specific payee or be payable to the bearer (often, in that case, made out to "cash"). A *cashier's check,* issued by the bank, is a type of draft in which the bank orders itself to make the payment.

A *certificate of deposit* is a bank's receipt for a sum of money with a promise to repay it with interest. Certificates of deposit (CDs) are devices for investing large amounts of cash. They run for a specific length of time.

The Uniform Commercial Code sets standards for a negotiable instrument that is freely transferable. It must be in writing, be signed by the maker or drawer, contain an unconditional promise or order to pay a specific sum of money either on demand or at a definite time, and be payable either *to order* or *to a bearer.* If a third-party instrument, it must identify the drawee.

Writing.   The instrument must be written on material relatively permanent and portable. It may be written in ink or pencil, typed or printed. Standard printed forms are used most often.

Signed.   A simple X made by a person unable to write can constitute a legal signature. Initials or a thumbprint are also acceptable. A trade name or a rubber stamp, when used by someone authorized to do so, is also permitted.

Promise.   The promise or order to pay must be *unconditional*. Because it may pass from one person to another and be used in place of money, the instrument cannot be dependent on other happenings. The promise or order to pay must be clear. A simple IOU acknowledging that "I owe you $1,000" is not a promise to pay and not a negotiable instrument. A promise to pay "to Mary Doe" implies no promise to pay to anyone else. To enable Mary to sell the instrument or otherwise turn it over to someone else, it should contain a promise to pay "*to the order* of Mary Doe." Mary could then order the sum paid to another party.

Specific sum.   Negotiable paper must be payable *only in money*. It cannot promise payment in goods or services. If interest is involved, it must be stated so clearly that a computation of the sum promised is possible.

Demand or time.   A negotiable instrument must be payable "*on demand*" or at a *definite time*. Most checks are payable immediately (*on sight*, or *on presentation*). A note also may be payable *after sight*—for example, one month after it is presented for payment. It may state that it will be paid "on or before" a specific date. If it is payable in installments, it may contain an acceleration clause, allowing the full amount to fall due immediately if some event occurs, like default on payment.

Endorsement.   Instruments payable to the bearer may be transferred by *delivery*. Instruments payable to order must be transferred by **endorsement**. A note may be transferred from one party to another by one of four types of endorsements:

1. *Blank endorsement,* in which the payee signs the back of the note without further explanation. It is the riskiest form of endorsement because the note remains negotiable for any purpose, even if the holder acquired it illegally. It is almost equivalent to cash.
2. *Restrictive endorsement,* in which the negotiability of the instrument is restricted to a specific purpose, stated in the endorsement: "For deposit only."
3. *Special endorsement,* in which the payee specifically names the next holder in due course: "Pay to the order of John Smith."
4. *Qualified endorsement,* in which the phrase *without recourse* is written as part of the endorsement to relieve the person making the endorsement from any liability if the check or note is not honored. A qualified endorsement specifies that the person who originated the check remains liable for the note.

If an instrument is payable to John *or* Mary Doe, one endorsement is sufficient to transfer it. If it is payable to John *and* Mary Doe, both must endorse it.

Defenses.   Legal defense against paying on an instrument might include claims that the maker was under duress, that the instrument was intended for some illegal purpose (payment of a gambling debt or for the purchase of illegal drugs), that the instrument was obtained by fraud, or that the instrument was altered after it was signed.

The most common method of discharging commercial paper is by *payment*. It also may be *canceled* by the holder, either by marking it *paid* or by destroying it. The destruction must be deliberate, not accidental, for the instrument to be discharged. The instrument also may be *renounced* by the holder, or, in the case of a check, the maker may issue a *stop-payment* order.

■ BUSINESS ORGANIZATIONS

Partnerships

The nature of a *partnership*, defined by partnership law as an *association of two or more persons to carry on a business for profit as co-owners*, has been discussed in earlier chapters. Many brokerage firms are set up as general partnerships; limited partnerships are generally formed for commercial investment.

A *partnership agreement* sets up the powers and duties of the partners. Unless the agreement specifies otherwise, new members usually must be approved by all existing partners. When the question arises as to whether two persons are in fact partners, the chief test is whether each receives a share of profits. If one partner assigns his or her share of profits to a third person, that person may be entitled to profits but does not become a partner and has no right to share in management or examine the firm's books. Partners have a fiduciary duty to each other; notice given to one is considered given to all.

Partnership property.   Property contributed to the partnership when it is formed is considered to be *partnership property*. Creditors of the individual partners may not attach the assets of the partnership for a partner's personal debts but may attach the partner's interest in the partnership.

Dissolution.   The partnership is dissolved at a specific time originally agreed on, when requested by any partner or on the death or bankruptcy of a partner. A court order can dissolve the partnership if it is shown that one partner is insane or incapacitated, that the business cannot be operated at a profit, or that one partner is involved in impropriety affecting the partnership.

On dissolution the partnership may no longer transact new business, but the partnership continues through the process of *winding up*. Assets are distributed first to creditors who are not partners, next to partners who have lent money to the partnership, then in a refund of capital contributed by each partner. Anything remaining is distributed among the partners according to their respective interests.

Partners often buy special life insurance designed to ensure that the surviving partner can buy out the deceased partner's estate and continue the business.

Corporations

A *corporation* is an organization that is recognized by the law as a legal person. It may buy, sell, lease, mortgage, make contracts, and perform most other acts allowed to persons. It is entitled to most of the same protection guaranteed other persons by the Bill of Rights.

In most cases the persons who own shares in it bear no individual liability for the corporation's actions or debts. The corporation, in turn, cannot be held liable for the shareholders' debts.

Creation of a corporation. A corporation is created by the filing of a **certificate of incorporation** with the Secretary of State. The incorporator(s) must sign the certificate, giving their names and addresses; the name of the intended corporation and its purposes; intended duration (usually perpetual); address; and number of shares of stock authorized to be issued. On payment of a fee and approval of the Secretary of State, the corporation becomes a legal entity. Bylaws, the rules and regulations under which the corporation will operate, are usually adopted at the first organizational meeting after the certificate of incorporation has been secured.

Management. A corporation is managed by a *board of directors* elected by shareholders. Shareholders who cannot attend meetings, which are usually held annually, may vote by proxy. Once elected, the board of directors selects officers who administer the business of the corporation. Directors and officers have a fiduciary duty to the corporation and may not profit personally at its expense. Each shareholder has the right to examine the company's books.

A *closely held corporation* is one owned by a single individual or a small number of shareholders, perhaps members of the same family. The shareholders usually manage the business themselves.

Corporations are subject to the New York State franchise tax (also called *corporate income tax*) and if they do business in New York City, the city's general corporation tax.

One of the major advantages of corporate organizations, however, is the ability to shelter some income through pension and profit-sharing plans and to consider as business expense fringe benefits such as health or life insurance. Nevertheless, in recent years, liberalized tax-deferment possibilities for individuals through various retirement plans have lessened the appeal of this aspect of incorporation.

S corporations. With an *S corporation*, profits are passed directly to shareholders so that profits are taxed only once. Losses also may be passed to shareholders (although only to the limit of their investments) and used to offset ordinary income.

Limited liability companies and partnerships. *Limited liability companies* (LLCs) allow investors to take advantage of the limited liability of a corporation and also the tax advantages of a partnership, with earnings and profits taxed only to the individual members. A *limited liability partnership* is available to professionals, who have all the advantages of a limited liability company, except that their professional work is still subject to liability, as, for example, in cases of malpractice.

Termination.　*Dissolution* is the legal death of the corporation. *Liquidation* is the winding-up process. A corporation may be dissolved by an act of the legislature, expiration of the time originally planned for the business, approval of the shareholders and board of directors, unanimous action of all the shareholders, failure to pay franchise taxes, or court order. A *certificate of dissolution* is filed with the Secretary of State, and assets are distributed first to creditors, next to holders of preferred stock, and last to holders of common stock.

Security Offerings

Like other securities, shares in real estate investment trusts (described in Chapter 6) may be issued as either private or public offerings.

Public offerings.　After the stock market crash of 1929, the federal government began requiring certain disclosures by companies and others who wish to issue securities (stock, bonds, debentures, or warrants) in an effort to prevent fraud and insider trading. The Securities and Exchange Commission (SEC) administers the law.

The process includes the filing of a written registration statement and a prospectus with the SEC. They describe, among other factors, the securities being offered; the registrant's business; management, including compensation; competition in the industry; and any special risk factors. No advertisements or offers to sell the securities may be made during the prefiling period. Certain advertising is allowed during the waiting period between filing and SEC approval. The SEC does not pass on the merits of the securities offered but merely states that the issuer has met the disclosure requirements.

A simpler process, *Regulation A,* is available for issues of up to $5 million to be raised during a 12-month period. Any offering for more than $100,000 requires that an offering statement be filed with the SEC. It requires less information than a registration statement and is less costly to prepare.

Private offerings.　It is also possible to offer securities without SEC registration, if the investors are *accredited*. In general, they must be insiders of the issuer (partners, officers of the company, etc.) or "sophisticated" investors who are considered financially capable of judging for themselves: anyone with net worth of at least $1 million; anyone with annual income of at least $200,000 for the past two years; or corporations, partnerships, or business trusts with total assets in excess of $5 million.

Up to 35 *nonaccredited investors* also may buy part of a private offering, but only if they have a certain amount of financial sophistication. For private offerings, no general selling efforts or advertising to the public are allowed. Private placement securities may not be resold for a year after they are issued and in only limited amounts for the second year. After that period, there are usually no restrictions on resale.

■ THE FEDERAL COURT SYSTEM

The federal court system includes specialized courts, district courts, courts of review (appellate courts), and the Supreme Court. Federal judges receive lifetime appointments, subject to confirmation by the Senate.

District courts cover specific geographic areas, with at least one in each state. New York has four districts, referred to as the *northern, eastern, southern,* and *western districts*. District courts are the point of origin for civil cases arising from federal law and for federal crimes. They also serve as appellate courts for the U.S. bankruptcy court.

Specialized courts are established by Congress. Among them are tax court, court of claims, and bankruptcy court. The U.S. court of appeals provides review for district courts, tax courts, the court of claims, and decisions made by federal agencies such as HUD. The United States is divided into 13 judicial circuits. Appeals from district courts located in New York are heard by the second circuit court of appeals, which also covers Vermont and part of Connecticut. Decisions of this court are generally final, with further appeal to the Supreme Court the only possibility.

The Supreme Court of the United States consists of nine justices. It serves mainly as a court of appeals for cases involving federal law or constitutionality, but it also has original, or trial, jurisdiction in a few situations.

■ NEW YORK COURT SYSTEM

In New York State the supreme court is paradoxically one of the lowest courts in the system; it is so named because of its wide civil jurisdiction and because it originates most lawsuits. It is the lowest court of unlimited dollar amount of claims. It has branches in every county. Supreme court justices are also assigned to criminal cases when the caseload requires it.

County courts (outside New York City and the criminal court in New York City) have criminal jurisdiction. County courts also handle some civil cases and appeals from lower courts. The *surrogate court* handles decedents' estates, will contests, probates, adoptions (with family court), and incompetency proceedings. *Family court* handles family complaints, delinquencies, child abuse, and adoptions. Divorces, however, are heard in the supreme court. The *court of claims* has jurisdiction over claims against the state.

Small claims courts are set up for prompt and informal treatment of disputes and complaints involving less than $3,000. Fees and paperwork are nominal, and the parties generally appear for themselves, with no lawyers involved except in the case of corporations. Small claims courts may issue monetary awards and judgments but may not compel specific performance. They are part of *city, town,* or *village justice courts*. Corporations, partnerships, and associations may initiate up to five claims a month in commercial claims court. An inexpensive small claims procedure is also available for homeowners protesting their tax assessments.

The *appellate divisions* of the supreme court handle appeals by parties dissatisfied with lower court findings. The state is divided into four departments; the first and second departments cover New York City, Long Island, and the surrounding counties. The third is based in Albany and the fourth in Rochester. Five judges serve, taking no testimony but basing their decisions on the record and arguments by the parties' attorneys. Appeals are usually based on questions of law and procedure and not on disputes about the facts in the case. Occasionally the appellate division will rule, however, that the original verdict was against the weight of evidence. Those dissatisfied may, in some instances, take the case further, to the court of appeals.

The *court of appeals* is the highest court in the state. Seven judges sit. There is generally no further appeal from this court, although U.S. constitutional questions may be taken to the Supreme Court of the United States.

■ SUBSTANTIVE AND PROCEDURAL LAW

Law can be defined as either *substantive*, that portion of the law that defines our rights and responsibilities, and *procedural*, which deals with the methods for enforcing our rights.

Real estate licensees already will be familiar with at least three branches of substantive law: the law of **agency**, **contract law**, and **real property law**. Other branches include **administrative law**, through which government agencies regulate business practices; **commercial law**; **constitutional law**; **corporation law**; **personal property law**; **partnership law**; **trusts and wills**; and **criminal law**.

■ CIVIL LAW

The state prosecutes criminals who commit acts that injure the state or society as a whole under the provisions of criminal law. **Civil law,** on the other hand, deals with the injuries one person does another. These injuries can result from wrongful actions against persons or property (the legal term for which is **torts**) or from failure to perform contractual obligations. In a lawsuit for breach of contract, a court may award money damages to the plaintiff (the person bringing the complaint) or issue an *injunction*, ordering the defendant to perform his or her obligations.

While criminal law concentrates on punishing the culprit, the law of torts is intended to compensate the injured party. A single act may result in both civil and criminal court action as well as administrative procedure. The commission of a fraud, for example, may result in criminal prosecution, a civil suit by the defrauded person, and administrative action such as the revocation of a real estate license.

For a tort to be committed, three factors must exist: the plaintiff must have suffered a loss or injury; the damage must have been caused by the defendant; and depending on the type of tort, the defendant must usually have failed to exercise reasonable care or intended to do the act that caused the harm. Torts are generally classified into three groups: *intentional torts, negligence*, and *strict liability*.

Wrongs against the person include *assault* (threatening behavior); *battery* (physical contact, even without actual injury); *false imprisonment* (sometimes charged, for example, in the detention of a suspected shoplifter); and the *infliction of mental distress. Defamation* covers *slander* (oral) and *libel* (written), actions that tend to hold a person up falsely to contempt, ridicule, or hatred. Slander or libel arises when third parties can read or overhear the oral or written material. Among the grounds for libel that may concern real estate brokers are statements that a person has committed improprieties while engaging in a profession or trade. In a lawsuit the truth of the statement is almost always a complete defense. False statements about products, businesses, or title to property also can result in tort liability if actual damages occur. Torts against the person also include *misrepresentation, fraud*, and *invasion of the right to privacy*.

Wrongs against property include *trespass*, unauthorized intrusion on another's land. No actual damage need be shown; the landowner's right to exclusive possession is violated by the trespass. *Trespass to personalty* occurs when personal property is injured or the owner's right to enjoyment of it is interfered with. When property is stolen, the tort of *conversion* (to someone else's use) has occurred. *Nuisances* are acts that interfere with another's enjoyment or health. Barking dogs, searchlights that shine onto another's property, and business activities that cause unpleasant odors are typical nuisances. In addition to seeking money damages, the plaintiff may ask the court for an **injunction,** an order forbidding the offending activity.

Negligence covers actions that tend to wrong another through carelessness without any intent to cause damage. Such torts are often committed in accidents, and the court may apportion negligence between the parties. *Business torts* include infringement of copyrights, patents, and trademarks, as well as unfair competition. A business venture that is entered into for the single purpose of harming another established business becomes the tort known as *malicious injury to business. Strict liability* (usually in product liability cases) covers damages caused by unusual and abnormally dangerous activities in the course of business, such as improper manufacturing procedures that create dangerous products. Failure to warn the user of the dangers in using such an item is also covered by strict liability.

Civil Procedure

The term **litigation** refers to the process of a civil lawsuit. To start the process, the plaintiff serves or files a complaint with the proper court. A summons also is issued, directing the defendant to appear in court and answer the complaint. The defendant serves a written answer to the complaint or faces the possibility of a default judgment in the plaintiff's favor. A defendant who believes he or she has been injured by the plaintiff may file a counter-complaint or cross-complaint, which the original plaintiff must answer with a written reply.

The process of litigation continues with a procedure known as *discovery*, during which either party and witnesses give oral testimony known as *depositions*. Either party may submit *interrogatories*, written questions that must be answered in writing within a specified time. Either party may request that the other produce documents relevant to the case.

Still prior to the trial, parties may make pretrial motions in an attempt to dispose of all or part of the lawsuit immediately. One of the most common is a *motion for summary judgment*, which asks the judge to rule on the matter there and then when there is no dispute about the facts of the case. A pretrial hearing, also known as a *settlement conference*, brings the attorneys or parties together in an attempt to reach agreement before the trial begins.

The average layperson is more familiar with the trial itself, so often dramatized in movies and on TV. It begins with jury selection and opening statements by each side. The plaintiff then presents his or her case, calling witnesses and introducing evidence to support the complaint. The defendant's case follows, and then each side has a further chance to present a rebuttal and rejoinder. Closing arguments are made by each party's attorney, following which the judge instructs the jury on the law to be applied to the case. The jury then retires to deliberate and returns a verdict, after which the judge enters a judgment to the successful party.

Dispute Resolution

Disputes also can be resolved by **arbitration** or **mediation,** without using the courts. These procedures are less formal than lawsuits, much quicker, and less expensive for the parties. In most cases of arbitration, the disputing parties agree in advance that they will abide by the ruling of a disinterested third party. The arbitrator need not be a lawyer; often he or she is an expert in the matter being contested. The American Arbitration Association has a set of rules for the proceedings. (REALTORS® agree to submit disputes with fellow REALTORS® to binding arbitration rather than litigate.) The decision imposed by the arbitrator is seldom subject to appeal.

The process of mediation, often used today in cases of divorce, is growing in popularity as a less expensive, less time-consuming alternative to arbitration. It differs in that the mediator has no authority to issue a decision on the matter being disputed. Instead, a skilled attempt is made to facilitate an agreement between the parties.

Bankruptcy

Bankruptcy is a federal proceeding that allows someone whose debts have become unmanageable to be protected from creditors, gives the debtor a chance to start over, and distributes the debtor's available assets fairly to the creditors.

Bankruptcy is handled through a special federal court. Three general types of bankruptcy are known by chapter numbers. *Chapter 7* provides for the total liquidation of the debtor's assets (less certain exempt items available to individuals). *Chapter 11* and *Chapter 13* provide for the debtor's retention of assets and a corresponding adjustment in the payment of the outstanding debts.

If family income is above the median income for the state, Chapter 7 may not be an option. The debtor may be required to enter a five-year Chapter 13 plan that involves gradual repayment of some or all of the debts.

Chapter 7, often known as *straight bankruptcy,* requires that the debtor (either an individual, partnership, limited liability company, or corporation) disclose all debts and surrender all assets to a trustee. The process starts with the filing of a petition in bankruptcy court, either by the debtor (*voluntary bankruptcy*) or by creditors (*involuntary bankruptcy*). Filing of the petition automatically freezes actions against the debtor, *including any pending foreclosure suit (automatic stay).* Lawsuits in progress against the debtor are halted, and no new actions may be commenced. However, if a creditor is *secured* (the debt is backed by a lien on the debtor's real property or personal property), the secured creditor may request the court to permit the creditor to pursue foreclosure or repossession remedies. The bankruptcy judge may or may not grant this request or may require that the debtor make some payments to the secured creditor to forestall foreclosure.

An interim **trustee** is appointed. A meeting of the creditors provides an opportunity for questioning of the debtor and confirmation of the amounts owed. The creditors also may vote for the election of a permanent trustee. The trustee takes over the debtor's assets and distributes the net proceeds proportionately to creditors. With certain exceptions, the remaining debts are canceled or *discharged.* The law provides guidelines for the priority or payment of the claims.

In New York an individual debtor is allowed by law to retain up to $5,000 worth of household furnishings, equity in an automobile up to $2,400, and up to $50,000 equity in a homestead. A husband and wife filing for bankruptcy together may protect up to $100,000 in homestead equity.

Property acquired after the bankruptcy petition is filed is not administered by the trustee and belongs to the debtor (with the exception of an inheritance within six months after the petition was filed).

A *corporation, partnership, limited liability company,* or *individual* may file for Chapter 11 relief and receive the same automatic stay or freeze on creditors' actions as provided by Chapter 7. The goal of Chapter 11, however, is not immediate liquidation of the debtor's business or total distribution of assets. Instead, the debtor and a creditors' committee formulate a plan for paying a portion of the debts while the debtor continues in business under the scrutiny of the bankruptcy court and the creditors' committee. Chapter 11 plans may provide for a gradual, orderly winding up of the business or may aim at total recovery.

Persons holding mortgages on real property may be delayed in foreclosing those mortgages by order of the bankruptcy judge until a plan is proposed by the bankrupt party and either accepted or rejected by the creditors and the court. A mortgagee may have to wait a considerable time, sometimes years, before the mortgage can be foreclosed. *Bankruptcy does not, however, free the debtor or the property of a mortgage.*

After the Chapter 11 petition is filed, the debtor continues to operate the business, free of claims and judgments. *Debtor-in-possession* (DIP) is the term for this situation. The court may allow the debtor to continue in the operation of the business or may appoint a trustee. In either event, if a creditors' committee is appointed by the United States Trustee (part of the Department of Justice), that committee will oversee the management. After a plan is proposed (by the debtor or by the creditors' committee), a vote of the creditors is taken. If they favor the plan and the court approves, it is put into effect. If no plan is presented or one is turned down, the proceeding is generally converted into a straight Chapter 7 bankruptcy.

Chapter 13 is available only to *individuals* with regular income (including those with welfare, Social Security, and retirement income) or those who operate a small business. It offers a chance to work out financial problems over a period of up to five years. Creditors may be paid in part or in full as in Chapter 11, but under Chapter 13 the proposed plan is not voted on by creditors. The court makes the decisions. Chapter 13 can be initiated only by a voluntary petition and tends to avoid the stigma of bankruptcy. The automatic stay halting all pending actions and prohibiting new actions exists, just as under Chapter 7 and Chapter 11.

Certain claims may not be discharged in bankruptcy:

- Income taxes accruing within three years of the bankruptcy filing
- Sales taxes and withholding taxes collected from customers and employees but not paid over to the taxing authorities
- Claims not listed on the bankruptcy schedule
- Claims based on fraud (misrepresentation or false pretenses)
- Alimony and child support
- Claims based on willful injury (except under Chapter 13)
- Some fines or penalties due the government
- Some student loans (except where the court determines there is undue hardship or under Chapter 13)

Occasionally, debtors do not receive their discharge. Discharges may be withheld where proof is offered that the debtor has concealed assets, obtained credit under false financial statements, or failed to cooperate with the trustee.

Estates

A decedent's estate is administered and *settled by a personal representative* appointed by the surrogate court. A will may name an **executor** to serve as personal representative. If no will can be found or no executor is named, the court will appoint an **administrator**, who serves as a personal representative and performs the same duties as an executor. The executor first inventories the estate to determine its extent and value. The will, insurance policies, deeds, car registrations, and birth and marriage certificates are located. Safe deposit boxes are inventoried, and the executor takes possession of bank accounts, real estate, and personal property. Names, addresses, and Social Security numbers of all heirs are obtained. The executor files claims for Social Security, pension, and veteran's benefits.

The personal representative administers the estate as the decedent would have done, collecting debts, managing real estate, collecting insurance proceeds, continuing a family business, and arranging for the support of survivors pending final distribution of the estate. The executor also pays rightful claims against the estate, negotiates the most favorable treatment for taxes, and sells selected assets to pay taxes in time to avoid any penalties.

Final winding up of the estate involves proper division of assets, selling some to pay cash bequests and transferring title to real and personal property. Final estate costs are paid, and an accounting is prepared.

Estate and gift taxes.   Any amount may be transferred between spouses during a lifetime or at death with no federal or New York State gift or estate tax due. Transfer to a spouse is known as the *marital deduction*.

The remainder of an estate may pass to anyone tax-free up to $2 million in 2006 and $3.5 million in 2009. An estate of any amount can pass untaxed in 2010.

In 2011 the law establishing those amounts is scheduled to expire, and estate taxes would be due on any amount greater than $1 million (not counting anything left to a spouse). It is expected that Congress will make changes in the estate tax law before that date.

The figures cited above are known as *unified credits*, and may be used to cover gifts made during the donor's lifetime as well as the estate at death. In addition, any number of gifts may be made to individuals, free of federal tax, to a limit of $12,000 each in 2008 (scheduled to rise yearly with inflation).

New York has no gift tax, and currently has a limit of $1 million before estate tax is due, not counting anything left to a spouse.

If estate or gift tax is due and not paid, the government may impose a lien on property. With certain exceptions, after a tax lien attaches to property, it continues even though the property is transferred to another. Thus until taxes are paid, a cloud on the title may render property subject to the lien unmarketable.

Divorce in New York

Divorce in New York State is not granted on the grounds of incompatibility or irreconcilable differences. No-fault divorce is possible after one year of living apart under a separation agreement or a court-ordered separation decree. Four grounds for divorce in New York hold one party at fault: cruel and inhuman treatment, abandonment for one or more years, imprisonment for three years or more, and adultery.

Equitable distribution.   In New York, the courts may order division of marital property (all property acquired during the marriage except inheritance, gifts from third parties, and compensation for personal injuries). Court-ordered division can take place, no matter who holds title to the property, and need not be made on a 50/50 basis. Maintenance may be ordered for one spouse on a limited or permanent basis.

When real property is to be divided, thought must be given to the income tax liability of the person who will eventually sell the property. Cost basis for income property should be considered as carefully as the present value of the real estate.

No gift tax consequences apply when property is transferred between spouses incident to a divorce.

The ex-spouse who has moved out of a home may still be able to use the homesellers' capital gains exclusion on his or her share of a sale, if the one remaining in the home qualifies to use it.

■ STATUTE OF LIMITATIONS

Lawsuits must be commenced within a given period after damages have occurred, or the plaintiff's right to sue may be lost through *laches*. In some cases it is necessary only to file notice within the period that a suit may be instituted (a *lis pendens*). The **statute of limitations** (time within which a suit must be commenced) varies for different matters in New York State:

- To sue a governmental agency: notice of claim within 90 days
- To recover real property: 10 years
- Contracts, foreclosures, fraud: 6 years
- Personal or property injury, malpractice (other than dental and medical): 3 years
- Medical or dental malpractice: 2½ years (1 year after discovery of a foreign object in the body)
- Assault, battery, false imprisonment, right of privacy, libel and slander: 1 year

A mechanic's lien must be filed within four months of completion of work on a single dwelling, eight months on other buildings.

■ SUMMARY

The seven sources of law in the United States are the U.S. Constitution, laws passed by Congress, federal regulations, state constitutions, laws passed by state legislatures, local ordinances, and court decisions.

Common law in the United States evolved predominantly from custom and usage in England. Gradually the basis of common law expanded to include prior court decisions as well as custom. Much of real property law is founded in common law.

Under the Uniform Commercial Code, security interests in chattels must be recorded using a security agreement and financing statement.

Commercial paper, or negotiable instruments, refers to written promises or orders to pay money that may be transferred from one person to another. The Uniform Commercial Code divides commercial paper into notes, drafts, checks, and certificates of deposit. Commercial paper must be in writing, signed by the maker or drawer, payable either to bearer or a specific payee, for a specific sum of money, at a definite time or on demand. It may be transferred by four types of endorsement: blank, restrictive, special, or qualified.

A partnership is an association of two or more persons to carry on a business for profit as co-owners. Profit and loss are passed directly through to individual partners for taxation. Partners have unlimited individual liability for the partnership's debts.

A corporation is a legal person owned by any number of shareholders who have limited individual liability for the corporation's debts. It is formed through the approval of a certificate of incorporation by the secretary of state. A board of directors, elected by the shareholders, selects officers to manage the business.

Organization as an S corporation, limited liability company, or limited liability partnership offers the liability protection of a corporation without the burden of double taxation.

The federal court system includes district courts, specialized courts, courts of review, and the Supreme Court. New York State has four federal judicial district courts, which originate federal cases. Appeals from this state are heard by the second circuit court of appeals.

New York's lowest court of general jurisdiction is the supreme court. Small claims courts are courts of local jurisdiction for the prompt and informal treatment of disputes. Appeals from lower courts are handled by the appellate divisions of the supreme court. The highest court in the state is the court of appeals.

Criminal law covers acts that injure society or the state; civil law is concerned with torts, the injuries one person does another. Torts may be against a person or against property. Civil lawsuits are intended to recompense the injured party.

The process of civil litigation begins with the filing of a complaint by the plaintiff and a summons to the defendant, who files an answer. Pretrial procedures involve discovery through depositions, interrogatories, and the production of documents. Last-minute requests may include a motion for judgment on the pleadings or summary judgment. A pretrial hearing or settlement conference may bring the parties to agreement before trial.

The trial itself involves jury selection, opening statements, the plaintiff's case followed by the defendant's case, rebuttal and rejoinder, closing arguments, and the judge's instructions to the jury. Jury deliberation is followed by the verdict and judgment.

Less costly, time-consuming, and expensive than litigation are arbitration, in which the arbitrator's decision is usually binding on both parties, and mediation, which involves a skilled attempt to bring the parties into agreement.

Bankruptcy is a federal proceeding through which a debtor seeks relief from overwhelming financial problems. Chapter 7 provides for immediate liquidation of debts, Chapter 11 for reorganization or the orderly winding up of businesses, and Chapter 13 for gradual payment over a period of time, either in part or in full, by individual debtors.

A decedent's estate is settled by a personal representative, either an executor named in a will or an administrator appointed by the court. The executor inventories the estate, administers it, collects debts and pays claims, divides the assets, and distributes them to heirs. Federal and state governments levy estate taxes.

No-fault divorce is available in New York State after a year's living apart under a separation agreement or court decree. The court uses its judgment in ordering equitable distribution of marital property.

Under the statute of limitations, various time limits apply for bringing suit for different types of damage.

QUESTIONS

1. The parties are not legally bound when a dispute is settled by
   a. litigation.
   b. arbitration.
   c. laches.
   d. mediation.

2. Clifford Buntsen had a real estate brokerage in partnership with his brother Clint, who died leaving everything to Clint's wife, Brenda. Clifford is concerned because his sister-in-law is licensed only as a salesperson. In this situation
   a. Brenda must take over Clint's broker's license.
   b. Clint's death immediately dissolves the partnership.
   c. Brenda has lost her license.
   d. Clifford becomes full owner automatically on his brother's death.

3. To be negotiable, an instrument must
   a. mention a consideration.
   b. conform with Chapter 11 rules.
   c. mention a specific sum of money.
   d. qualify for dissolution.

4. The debtor who has filed for bankruptcy is still required to pay
   a. credit card debt.
   b. child support.
   c. car loans.
   d. past utility bills.

5. The Uniform Commercial Code covers
   a. bequests.
   b. realty.
   c. chattels.
   d. services.

6. A REIT is a form of
   a. litigation.
   b. debt consolidation.
   c. equitable distribution.
   d. investment.

7. Co-owners have no individual liability for the debt of a
   a. corporation.
   b. partnership.
   c. private offering.
   d. marital deduction.

8. The general partner has unlimited liability in a
   a. corporation.
   b. real estate investment trust.
   c. limited partnership.
   d. closely held corporation.

9. Most federal lawsuits and prosecution for federal crimes originate in the
   a. supreme court.
   b. court of claims.
   c. district court.
   d. court of appeals.

10. New York State's highest court is the
    a. supreme court.
    b. court of claims.
    c. district court.
    d. court of appeals.

11. Disputes of limited dollar value may be settled at nominal cost and without the use of lawyers in the
    a. small claims court.
    b. court of claims.
    c. civil court.
    d. justice court.

12. When a property owner facing foreclosure files for bankruptcy, the foreclosure
    a. is automatically stopped.
    b. proceeds against the trustee.
    c. requires permission from the creditors' committee to continue.
    d. may never be pursued.

13. Slander, libel, assault, and battery are types of torts known as
    a. negligence.
    b. wrongs against property.
    c. wrongs against the person.
    d. strict liability.

14. A court order forbidding a certain activity is known as
    a. specific performance.
    b. an injunction.
    c. conversion.
    d. a rejoinder.

15. Legal relief through the immediate canceling of most debts can be sought through which form of bankruptcy?
    a. Chapter 26
    b. Chapter 7
    c. Chapter 11
    d. Chapter 13

16. The debtor who files bankruptcy is allowed to keep
    a. household furnishings.
    b. income-producing real estate.
    c. a vacation home worth up to $100,000.
    d. income tax refunds.

17. Bankruptcy proceedings are heard in
    a. federal court.
    b. small claims court.
    c. surrogate court.
    d. family court.

18. The personal representative who handles a decedent's estate may be a(n)
    a. referee.
    b. administrator.
    c. plaintiff.
    d. proxy.

19. Federal tax law provides that one spouse may give another
    a. any amount without gift taxes due.
    b. up to $250,000 without gift taxes due.
    c. no more than $250,000 tax-free during a lifetime.
    d. up to $20,000 tax-free in any year.

20. New York's estate tax has always allowed a spouse to inherit without any estate tax due
    a. any amount.
    b. one-half the estate.
    c. $675,000.
    d. up to $250,000.

Construction and Development

■ KEY TERMS

board of directors	developer	planning boards
board of managers	disclosure statement	plat of subdivision
bylaws	environmental impact studies	preliminary prospectus
common elements		proprietary lease
completion bond	eviction plan	public offering
conversions	gridiron pattern	red herring
covenants, conditions, and restrictions (CC&Rs)	HVAC	reserves
	impact fees	sponsor
curvilinear system	Interstate Land Sales Full Disclosure Act	subdivider
declaration		subdivision
density zoning	noneviction plan	time-sharing
Department of Environmental Conservation (DEC)	planned unit development (PUD)	town house
		wetland survey

■ CONSTRUCTION STANDARDS

All real estate agents should be aware of the various sources of construction standards. These standards are established at many levels of government and by a variety of agencies.

Federal Agencies

Federal regulatory agencies include the Department of Housing and Urban Development (HUD), the Army Corps of Engineers, and the Environmental Protection Agency.

The Department of Housing and Urban Development (HUD) establishes construction standards for homes that in some way are funded through HUD programs; for instance, homes that are financed with FHA funds.

The Army Corps of Engineers regulates certain waterways and drainage into them. These regulations affect building sites and the manner in which homes may be constructed.

The Environmental Protection Agency has established standards for the protection of the environment. One of the major effects of these standards has been a general increase in the time and money required to plan and secure the necessary approvals for new developments.

State Agencies

New York State regulates minimum building standards and requires that various codes and regulations be followed, including building codes, fire codes, sanitary regulations, and environmental requirements. The state also has different code requirements for special types of construction, such as schools (for example, a state inspector must inspect schools for compliance each year).

The various state codes and other regulations are *minimum standards*. Local counties and municipalities may require stricter standards. For instance, a particular county code may require sprinkler systems in all new residential construction, even though the state code does not. The enforcement of the state codes is largely carried out on a local basis (by county or municipal inspectors), but the state agency also may become involved in enforcement.

The New York State Board of Fire Underwriters sets standards for electrical service systems in all buildings. District inspectors enforce the Board's electrical code.

The New York State Department of Transportation regulates traffic and must authorize any curb cuts onto a state highway. Naturally, transportation, ingress onto, and egress from state highways are important considerations for any type of development, especially commercial and large residential developments.

The New York State Department of State (DOS) is responsible for the Coastal Zone Management Program. Any project on the coast, navigable rivers, lakes, or islands, such as projects in Long Island Sound, must have DOS approval.

DOS is also responsible for the Local Waterfront Revitalization Program (LWRP). The DOS Office for Local Government Services oversees this program and is a resource for local officials.

Regional Agencies

The counties of Nassau, Putnam, Suffolk, Rockland, and Westchester, plus the city of New York, are under some regulation from the Metropolitan Transportation Authority (MTA). The MTA has taxing powers and controls air rights as well as land rights to all properties within these counties.

■ **EXAMPLE** The owner of an office building wanted to build a pedestrian bridge over the adjacent railroad tracks to provide more convenient access to his building from the parking lot for his tenants. To do so, he had to acquire air rights over the tracks and install a prefabricated pedestrian bridge to MTA specifications and with the supervision of MTA personnel. He also had to get approvals from Penn Central (the landowner), from the local Planning Board, and from the Zoning Board of Appeals.

New York City.   The New York City Department of Environmental Protection (DEP) has regulatory powers over New York City's water supply system, from upstate down through the aqueducts and reservoirs and the extensive drainage basins. Land in several counties is included in New York City's watershed. The New York City DEP actually stopped the construction of a modest subdivision in Somers, New York, based on its effect on the water supply system, though it had already received all final approvals from the county board of health and the local planning board.

Counties.   County boards of health have jurisdiction over sanitary systems and facilities; local water supplies (water potability); food purveyors or suppliers, and so forth.

County planning boards are largely advisory but can establish certain reporting requirements and intermunicipal standards. In more rural counties, they exercise more authority.

Local municipalities.   Most municipalities have a building department that is responsible for ensuring that minimum standards of construction are met. The building department issues a *certificate of occupancy* (C of O) when the construction is completed to its satisfaction. Lenders sometimes require a C of O on resale properties as well as on new construction. In some jurisdictions a *certificate of compliance* (C of C) is issued to indicate that the structure meets certain standards, particularly those regarding safety.

Before a building inspector may issue a C of O on a newly constructed building, the inspector must have proof that all other required permits have been issued, such as permits from the Board of Health; from the Board of Fire Underwriters; and for highway curb cuts, blasting, excavation, tree cutting, and so on. Wetlands review boards, conservation review boards, environmental review boards, architectural review boards, or historical district commissions or fire marshals also may need to inspect and approve a project.

Minimum construction standards offer a consumer some assurance of safety and quality. However, building inspectors are not expert on all matters, and their inspections only assure the consumer that *minimum* standards have been met, not that *higher* standards of quality or the parties' contractual standards have been met.

All the various permit processes, including any required inspections, could directly increase the cost of construction. In some areas the preconstruction permit process for even a small subdivision can take up to ten years and may include exorbitant costs for all kinds of specialists, such as engineers and architects, who must review and alter the plans to meet the demands of local and state agencies. The permit process poses a financial drain on the developer, who must continue to pay the property taxes as well as the other expenses of the permit process while receiving no return on his or her investment. In turn, these expenses drive up the final purchase cost to the homebuyer.

THE ROLE OF THE REAL ESTATE AGENT

Real estate agents must be knowledgeable about their products; that is, the property and its surrounding area, including any geographic and topographic peculiarities. When listing a property, agents must exercise *due diligence* when inspecting the premises. In addition to calculating the square footage and describing the style, acreage, and location of the property, the agent should take note of its general condition, including the condition of the roof; interior and exterior siding; cracks in any masonry (chimney, foundation, porches); broken windows; the type and condition of heating and cooling systems; septic or sewer systems; and the water supply (whether well, municipal, or private). Some of this information is readily obtained by a visible inspection; some must be obtained from the owner.

An agent should avoid making any judgment or statement that could cause trouble later or even result in a lawsuit.

An astute agent will use a checklist or a seller's disclosure form in addition to the listing form. The more information available to the agent, the smoother the sales transaction. Recommending that the buyer use a qualified inspector is a prudent precaution.

BUILDING INSPECTIONS

Various building inspections are required for new construction, including inspections of the

- footing forms;
- foundation;
- framing;
- roof;
- insulation;
- sheetrock;
- electrical system;
- plumbing system and **HVAC** (heating, ventilation, and air-conditioning systems); and
- all hook-ups including water and sewer.

Table 8.1 is a sample schedule of procedures to be followed when construction of a new house is undertaken.

Professional home inspections performed for potential buyers or for sellers generally include

- systems: heating, air-conditioning, septic or sewer, electric, and plumbing;
- water: potability and occasionally other (radon, lead);
- storm windows and screens;

TABLE 8.1

New Home Construction Schedule

Preliminary work: Site engineering, evaluation, preliminary plan, environmental review, etc., county and local agency reviews, signatures, and filing of plan. Obtain financing. Site development.

Construction schedule:

Building and other permits
Surveyor stakes out lot and house
Excavator digs basement
Plumber installs sanitary sewer/water service
Building inspector inspects sewer or County Board of Health inspects septic system
Excavator backfills sewer/water trench and digs trench for footings
Mason forms the footings and pours concrete footings; lays up concrete block walls or pours concrete foundation
Framer sets steel beams and columns
Framer frames house
Roofing
Rough HVAC
Rough plumbing and heating
Rough electric, security, cable TV, phone
Backfill basement walls after framing
Building inspector reviews framing, plumbing, and heating
Electric inspection, rough wiring

Simultaneous with other work:

Concrete block wall dampproofing
Box out driveway and spread gravel
Mason builds fireplace
Mason lays up exterior brick or stone
Set windows, do exterior siding
Exterior painting/staining
Gutters, leaders, garage doors
Insulation
Drywall, hanging and finishing
Mason pours concrete floors
Interior trim
Interior painting
Kitchen cabinets and vanities
Ceramic tile walls and floors
Finish flooring—hardwood, vinyl
Finish plumbing, set fixtures
Finish heating
Finish electrical, fixtures, switches
Electrical inspection—final
Mirror/shower doors
Storms and screens
Blacktop
Landscaping
Appliances
Cleanup
Certificate of Occupancy inspection
Surveyor prepares instrument survey "as built"
Building department issues Certificate of Occupancy
Buyer reviews and does a final inspection prior to closing and prepares a punch list if necessary
Close on title

■ general condition;
■ radon, lead, asbestos;
■ insulation;
■ termites, dry rot; and
■ roof, grading, and decks/porches.

A seller would be wise to have a professional inspection performed before marketing the property. Any defects that might kill the sale or cause a last-minute problem for closing can be corrected in advance. The sale price and marketability of the property are directly affected by its condition.

A buyer always should have a professional inspection done before committing to a purchase, even for new construction. Serious defects affect the marketability and value of the property.

■ SUBDIVISION

Subdivision refers to the process of dividing a single tract of land into smaller parcels. Land in large tracts must receive special attention before it can be converted into sites for homes, stores, or other uses. A **subdivider** buys undeveloped acreage and divides it into smaller lots for sale to individuals or developers or for the subdivider's own use. A **developer** (who also may be a subdivider) builds homes or other buildings on the lots and sells them. Developing is generally a much more extensive activity than subdividing. A developer may have a sales staff or may use the services of local real estate brokerage firms.

Restrictions on Land Use

No uniform city planning and land development legislation affects the entire country. Most laws governing subdividing and land planning are controlled by state and local government bodies. New York State sets standards for villages, cities, and towns. Local governments may adopt more restrictive policies. Article 9-A of New York's Real Property Law governs subdivision.

A subdivision development plan must comply with any overall local master plan adopted by the county, city, village, or town. The developer must consider zoning laws and land-use restrictions adopted for health and safety purposes. Basic city plan and zoning requirements are not inflexible, but long, expensive, and frequently complicated hearings are usually required before alterations can be authorized.

Most villages, cities, and other areas incorporated under state laws have **planning boards** and/or *planning commissioners*. Communities establish strict criteria before approving new subdivisions. Frequently required are *dedication* of land for streets, schools, and parks; assurance by *bonding* that sewer and street costs will be paid; and *compliance* with zoning ordinances governing use and lot size and with fire and safety ordinances.

Zoning ordinances that systematically exclude certain groups or classes of people from certain areas are *exclusionary* and can be considered discriminatory as well as a violation of a person's right to travel interstate, as provided by the U.S. Constitution.

Local authorities usually require that land planners submit information on how they intend to satisfy sewage disposal and water supply requirements. Developments with septic tank installation may first require a *percolation test* of the soil's absorption and drainage capacities. A planner usually will have to submit an *environmental impact report*.

Regulatory taking occurs when rules, regulations, or ordinances essentially deprive a property owner of the use or the fair return on the value of the owner's property. In these circumstances, the rules, regulations, or ordinances can be considered confiscatory and therefore unlawful or unreasonable.

Environmental Regulations

The Environmental Protection Agency (EPA) has identified 403 chemicals as highly toxic, and innocent future purchasers of land can be held liable. Previous use of land being considered for development should be carefully investigated at the outset. Chemical companies, dry cleaners, old farms with trash dumps or underground gas tanks, airports, warehouses, gas stations, and factories of all sorts may have produced potentially dangerous chemical wastes.

Problems faced by unaware future owners could include liability for cleanup, liability for health problems, unfavorable publicity, and restrictions on future use of the land. More and more, developers are turning to specialists trained in environmental compliance and documentation.

In the early 1990s New York directed each county clerk or recording officer to compile an index of past and present owners and operators of sites listed on the Inactive Hazardous Waste Registry.

The New York State Environmental Quality Act is commonly referred to as SEQRA. Every application to a planning board or a zoning board of appeals must be viewed in light of its environmental impact. Classifications of proposed actions are

- *Type I*—An *environmental impact statement (EIS)* is required unless the applicant demonstrates conclusively that one is not needed. The next step is to fill out a Preliminary Environmental Review Form (PERF).
- *Type II* or *Exempt Action*—No environmental impact statement is needed.
- *Unlisted Action*—Pending analysis of further information, an environmental impact statement may be required. An environmental assessment form must be prepared.

Most applications to a zoning board of appeals are considered Type II or exempt. Most applicants for subdivision or development before a planning board are required to prepare at least a short form. Larger projects require an EIS and could include hydrologic studies, traffic impact, population density, and even light pollution.

In some instances construction requires a permit from the New York **Department of Environmental Conservation (DEC).** Permits are necessary for work in a protected wetland or the 100-foot buffer zone around a wetland. Depending on the circumstances, permits may be needed for work that disturbs the banks of streams, for using some water supplies, for sewage discharges, and for sewer extensions. The sale of more than 1,000 tons of fill dirt or gravel per year requires a DEC mining permit. **Environmental impact studies** of varying complexity may be required when the parcel is ruled environmentally sensitive—large projects or those located on floodplains, wetlands, steep slopes, or other environmentally fragile areas.

A **wetland survey** is based on the EPA and DEC statutes and is coordinated by the U.S. Army Corps of Engineers. A wetland survey examines everything from types of plant and animal life to soil composition. Based on the findings, a parcel of land may or may not be classified as wetlands, with severe restrictions on development.

Value of Land for Subdivision

The value of a given tract of land for subdivision purposes depends on many factors. Government land-use restrictions such as minimum lot size requirements, use restrictions, and building standards limit the type of development that is possible for a given tract of land. The nature of the land itself is also a factor, particularly if significant portions of the tract are unbuildable owing to soil conditions, wetlands, slopes, or other considerations.

Location is always a prime consideration in determining real estate value as well. Land will be more valuable for subdivision purposes if it is in a desirable location in an area with strong economic growth and an increasing population.

The availability of utility services and access roads is another factor that has a major impact on the cost and practicality of development.

Value for subdivision depends on land-use restrictions, nature and location of the land, availability of services, and access.

THE PROCESS OF SUBDIVISION

The process of subdivision involves three distinct stages of development: *initial planning, final planning,* and *disposition* or *start-up*.

During the *initial planning stage* the subdivider seeks raw land in a suitable area. The property is analyzed for *highest and best use*, and preliminary subdivision plans are drawn up. Close contact starts with local planning officials. If the project requires zoning variances, negotiation begins along these lines. The subdivider also locates financial backers and initiates marketing strategies.

In the *final planning stage*, plans are prepared, approval of the **plat of subdivision** is sought from local (and, if necessary, state and federal) officials, financing is actually obtained, the land is purchased, final budgets are prepared, and marketing programs are designed.

Once final approvals are granted by all the various government agencies, the subdivider may then become the developer (or contractor), sell to a developer, or enter into a joint venture with a contractor.

The *disposition*, or *start-up*, carries the subdividing process to a conclusion. Subdivision plans are recorded with local officials, and streets, sewers, and utilities are installed. Buildings, open parks, and recreational areas are constructed and landscaped if they are part of the subdivision plan. Marketing programs then are initiated, and title to the individual parcels of subdivided land is transferred as the lots or buildings are sold or leased.

COSTS AND FINANCING

Subdivision development involves a range of different costs. In addition to the direct costs of acquiring the land and making improvements such as **clearing, grading, roads, and utilities,** there are indirect costs for subdivision and development permit fees and professional fees for engineers, attorneys, and marketing specialists. A large development also may be charged **impact fees,** intended to help a community cope with increased demand for schools, roads, and other services. If approval of the subdivision is contingent on the subdivider's making public improvements such as roads or sewers, there is usually a requirement to obtain a **completion bond** guaranteeing completion of these improvements.

With all of the costs involved, it is common for subdivision developers to rely on borrowed funds to help finance a project. Development financing is secured by a mortgage lien against the entire project. When a new lot or unit is first sold, the buyer needs to be sure that it is no longer covered by any blanket mortgage lien that applied to the overall project. Blanket mortgage liens commonly have lot release provisions that allow clear title to be passed to a buyer in these situations.

■ RESTRICTIVE COVENANTS

Often a subdivider creates and records deed restrictions as a means of *controlling and maintaining the desirable quality and character of the subdivision*. Deed restrictions can be set forth in a separate document, which is recorded later, or they can be included in the subdivision plat. When a separate document is used, that document is generally called a *declaration of restrictions*.

Sometimes a deed restriction and a zoning provision cover the same subject. When this happens, the more limiting restriction prevails. For example, if deed restrictions require that subdivision lots be used only for single-family residences but local zoning ordinances allow duplexes, the single-family restriction found in the declaration of restrictions will govern the situation and can be enforced by subdivision residents.

To be valid, a deed restriction must be both reasonable and for the benefit of neighboring owners. Deed restrictions are binding on all future property owners in that subdivision. Common types of deed restrictions include the use to which the land may be put, the type of construction, height, setbacks, square footage and cost, and parking limitations. "No off-road or recreational vehicle may be parked on the subdivision streets" is an example. Some restrictions have a time limitation; for example, "effective for a period of 25 years from this date."

Enforcement of Deed Restrictions

Neighboring lot owners may apply to a court to prevent a neighbor from violating subdivision deed restrictions. In New York State, lot owners have up to two years from the completion of the alteration or construction in which to object. After that time they lose their right through *laches*, the failure to assert a right in time.

Types of Subdivisions and Subdivision Density

Zoning ordinances often include population density requirements as well as minimum lot sizes. A zoning restriction, for example, may set the minimum lot area on which a subdivider can build a single-family housing unit at 10,000 square feet. The developer would be able to build four houses per acre. Many zoning authorities now establish special density zoning standards for certain subdivisions. **Density zoning** ordinances restrict the average maximum number of houses per acre that may be built within a particular subdivision. If the area is density-zoned at an average maximum of four houses per acre, for example, by clustering building lots the developer is free to achieve an open effect.

FIGURE 8.1

Street Patterns

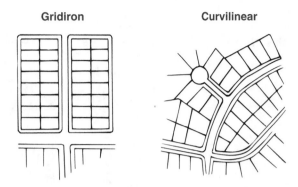

Gridiron

Curvilinear

Street patterns.   By varying street patterns and clustering housing units, a sub-divider can dramatically increase the amount of open and recreational space in a development. Some of these patterns are illustrated in Figure 8.1.

The **gridiron pattern** evolved out of the government rectangular survey system. Featuring large lots, wide streets, and limited-use service alleys, the system works reasonably well. It can result in busy streets and monotonous neighborhoods, however, and sometimes provides little or no open, park, or recreational space. The **curvilinear system** integrates major arteries of travel with smaller secondary and cul-de-sac streets carrying minor traffic. In addition, small open parks are often provided at intersections. The *loop* features serpentine streets that wind through the development, and the *radius pattern* is built on a series of cul-de-sacs that radiate from the main street.

Clustering for open space.   By slightly reducing lot sizes and clustering them around varying street patterns, a developer can house as many people in the same area as could be done using traditional subdividing plans, but with substantially increased tracts of open space.

For example, the first illustration in Figure 8.2 is a plan for a conventionally designed subdivision containing 368 housing units. It leaves only 1.6 acres open for park areas. Contrast this with the second subdivision pictured. Both subdivisions are equal in size and terrain. But when lots are minimally reduced in size and clustered around limited-access, cul-de-sac streets, the number of housing units remains nearly the same (366), with less street area and drastically increased open space (23.5 acres). In addition, with modern building designs this clustered plan could be modified to accommodate 550 patio homes or 1,100 town houses. Cluster housing may take the form of a **planned unit development (PUD)**, with some or all of an entire community's land use established by the developer's original plan.

■ LAND-USE REGULATIONS

Local governments pass zoning ordinances to control the use of land and building within designated districts. Zoning regulates such things as use of the land; lot sizes; types of structures permitted; building heights; setbacks (the minimum distance from streets or sidewalks that structures may be built); and density (the

FIGURE 8.2

Clustered Subdivision Plan

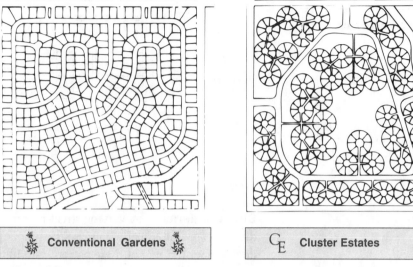

🌿 Conventional Gardens 🌿	C_E Cluster Estates
12,500-square-foot lots	7,500-square-foot lots
368 housing units	366 housing units
1.6 acres of parkland	23.5 acres of parkland
23,200 linear feet of street	17,700 linear feet of street

number of units that can be built in an area). An important purpose of zoning is to implement a local master plan.

Zoning ordinances generally divide land use into residential, commercial, industrial, vacant, agricultural, open space, institutional, and recreational classifications. Now many communities include cluster zoning and multiple-use zoning, which permit unusual planned unit developments.

Nonconforming use. When zoning laws are changed, there are usually already-existing buildings that do not conform to the new zoning laws. These buildings are referred to as *nonconforming uses* and are allowed to continue. However, if the building is destroyed or torn down, any new structure must comply with the current zoning ordinance.

Building Codes

Most cities and towns have enacted ordinances to specify construction standards that must be met during building construction or repair. These are called *building codes*, and they set requirements for kinds of materials, sanitary equipment, electrical wiring, fire prevention standards, and the like. New York has a statewide building code that applies where no local code exists or where local codes are less restrictive.

Interstate Land Sales Full Disclosure Act

The **Interstate Land Sales Full Disclosure Act** requires those engaged in the interstate sale or leasing of 25 or more lots to file a statement of record and register the details of the land with HUD.

The seller also is required to furnish prospective buyers with a property report containing all essential information about the property, such as distance over paved roads to nearby communities, number of homes currently occupied, soil conditions affecting foundations and septic systems, type of title a buyer will receive, and existence of liens. The property report must be given to a prospective purchaser at least three business days before any sales contract is signed.

If a buyer does not receive a property report, the purchaser may cancel such a contract without further liability within two years. Any buyer of land covered by this act has the right to rescind a contract within seven days after signing. If the seller misrepresents the property in any sales promotion, a buyer induced by such a promotion is entitled to sue the seller for civil damages. Failure to comply with the law also may subject a seller to imprisonment and fines.

New York State Subdivided Land Sales Law

New York considers land to be covered by subdivision regulations as soon as a fifth lot is carved from the original parcel. Land sold within New York State on the installment plan by a subdivider and out-of-state land offered for sale in New York in any manner may not be offered for sale until at least two documents have been filed with the Department of State. The first covers the identity and address of the offerer, the names of owners of the land, a statement on the subdivider's previous experience with vacant land, any criminal activity, a description of the land complete with maps, a title statement including any encumbrances or liens, and the terms on which the land will be sold, with a copy of the contract to be used.

The second document is a copy of the offering statement to be furnished to each buyer with a full financial statement of the assets and liabilities of the subdivider; a description of the subdivision and each lot; information on existing liens and encumbrances, existing or proposed utilities and area, community, and recreational facilities; and even the weather conditions of the area, as well as the terms of sale.

A copy of any advertising to be used must be filed with the Department of State. The state allows any purchaser who is not represented by an attorney to cancel a contract within ten days. (See Figure 8.3.)

In addition, New York's Public Health Laws require that any subdivider offering for sale or rent five or more residential building lots file a map of the proposed subdivision with the Department of Health, showing adequate water supply and sewerage facilities. The department must approve the plan before it can be filed. A development of 50 lots or more must have a central municipal water supply rather than individual wells. (These rules are found in the summary of Article 9-A; see Figure 8.3)

■ CONDOMINIUMS

The buyer of a condominium receives a *deed* conveying *fee simple ownership* of the unit and an undivided interest in the **common elements.** (See Figure 8.4.) The unit itself usually consists of little more than airspace bounded by the innermost layers of construction, often interior drywall.

Chief among the common elements are the land and the exteriors of the buildings. Also common property are foyers; hallways; main walls; basements; elevators; stairwells; heating, plumbing, and electrical systems; and in suburban locations, driveways, private roads, sidewalks, lawns, landscaping, and recreational facilities.

FIGURE   8.3

Subdivided Lands Property Law

SUMMARY OF ARTICLE 9-A
OF THE REAL PROPERTY LAW

Subdivided lands.   No real estate broker or real estate salesperson should be involved in any way, in the State of New York, with the sale or lease of subdivided lands located within or outside the state, unless the subdivider offering the property for sale or lease has complied with the provisions of Article 9-A of the Real Property Law.

Article 9-A of the Real Property law is designed to protect the residents of New York State in the purchase or lease of subdivided lands located within the State of New York where sold on an installment plan and located outside the State of New York, whether offered on the installment or any other plan, terms and conditions of sale or lease.

Safeguards are inserted into the law to prevent fraud or fraudulent practices that might be employed to include the purchase or lease of vacant subdivided lands. Among such safeguards is the requirement that the subdividers file with the Department of State a statement with substantiating documentation including a certified copy of a map of the subdivided lands and a search of the title to the land reciting in detail all the liens, encumbrances and clouds on the title that may or may not render the title unmarketable.

A subdivider, in addition to the statement required under the law, must file an Offering Statement with the Department of State. The Offering Statement must contain, among other facts, detailed information about the subdivision, including a description of the land, existence of utilities, area, community and recreational facilities, restriction, weather conditions, and financial statement of the subdivider. The Offering Statement must be revised yearly. It must clearly indicate that the Department of State has not passed on the merits of the offering.

No sale or lease of subdivided lands shall be made without prior delivery of an Offering Statement to the prospective customer. Any offer to sell or lease subdivided lands prior to filing both the Offering Statement and the statement constitutes a felony.

Where the land is affected by mortgages or other encumbrances, it is unlawful for the subdivider to sell such vacant lands in the subdivision unless appropriate provisions in the mortgage or lien enable the subdivider to convey valid title to each parcel free of such mortgage or encumbrance. A mortgage on an entire subdivision will usually provide for a release of individual lots from that mortgage on payment of a specified amount of money. If the land is being sold on an installment plan, the law provides that where the amount paid to the subdivider by the purchaser reaches the point where the balance owing is the amount required to release that lot from the mortgage, all monies thereafter received by the seller from the purchaser must be deemed trust funds, be kept in a separate account, and applied only toward clearance of title from the lien of the mortgage.

If, after investigation, the Secretary of State believes that the subdivider is guilty of fraud or that certain sales methods may constitute a fraud on the public, court proceedings to stop these practices may be instituted. The Secretary of State may also withdraw the acceptance previously granted and may order that all sales and advertising in New York State stop.

The law, as amended, also makes it mandatory that all advertising prior to publication be submitted to the Department for acceptance for filing. Misrepresentations in the sale or lease of subdivided lands constitute a misdemeanor.

The law now also provides that in every contract of sale or lease of subdivided lands, if the purchaser or lessee is not represented by an attorney, he or she has a ten-day cancellation privilege.

Sales may not be made based on the representation that the purchase of the property is a good investment, that the purchaser will or may make money on the transaction, or that the property can be readily sold. Nothing may be promised that is not contained in the written contract and offering Statement.

In addition, the condominium typically has an underlying loan on the land and common elements.

In most respects the law regards a residential condominium owner as it would the owner of a single detached house. The unit receives an individual tax account number and tax bill and may be mortgaged as a house would be. The owner places a separate insurance policy on the living space. Income tax advantages are identical to those for single homes. Owners are free to sell the property, lease it, give it away, or leave it to heirs. Each unit is financially independent, and if an adjoining unit is foreclosed, no obligation is incurred by the other owners.

Owners are, however, bound by the **bylaws** of an *owners' association* to which all belong. Monthly fees are levied for the maintenance, insurance, and

FIGURE 8.4

Condominium Ownership

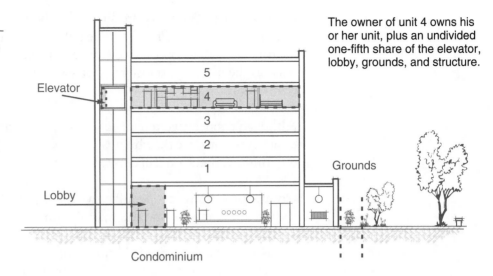

The owner of unit 4 owns his or her unit, plus an undivided one-fifth share of the elevator, lobby, grounds, and structure.

management of common elements. If unpaid, these *common charges* become a lien against the individual unit and even may be enforced by foreclosure. The bylaws also set up **covenants, conditions, and restrictions (CC&Rs),** for example, may prohibit the display of For Sale signs or painting the front door bright red. Owners even may adopt bylaws that restrict leasing of the units.

A condominium is usually managed by an elected **board of managers.** When there are more than 25 units, a board often hires professional management.

Selling Condominiums

The selling of condominiums or town houses is now among the activities covered by a broker's or a salesperson's license. The broker who deals in such properties must be concerned with some items that do not apply to the marketing of single homes. The buyer of a condominium must receive detailed statements about the property, should read the CC&Rs, and must be alerted to any unpaid common charges against the unit. Prospective buyers should also examine the **reserves,** funds set aside to accumulate for large expenses like new roofs or heating units. The sale of a condominium is arranged on a special form of contract.

Although it is most widely used for residential property, condominium ownership is growing for professional buildings, office buildings, and shopping malls.

■ COOPERATIVE OWNERSHIP

Cooperative ownership is common in the New York City metropolitan area and in some resort areas. Under the usual *cooperative arrangement,* title to land and building is held by a *corporation.* Each purchaser of an apartment in the building receives stock in the corporation and a **proprietary lease** for his or her apartment.

Real estate taxes are paid on the whole building by the corporation. A single mortgage, known as the *underlying* or *overlying mortgage,* covers the entire building. Taxes, mortgage interest and principal, and operating and maintenance expenses on the property are shared by the tenants/shareholders as monthly *maintenance charges*. Proprietary leaseholders may individually finance their apartments with a cooperative loan. Most proprietary leases provide that they may not be assigned, transferred, or sublet without the consent of the board of directors.

Although cooperative tenants/owners do not actually own an interest in real estate (they own stock, which is *personal property*), they do control the property through their *board of directors*.

One disadvantage of cooperative ownership became particularly evident during the Great Depression and still must be considered. If enough owner/occupants become unable to make prompt payment of their monthly assessments, the corporation may be forced to allow mortgage and tax payments to go unpaid. The entire property could be sold by court order in a foreclosure suit. Such a sale would destroy the interests of all occupant/shareholders, even those who paid their assessments. Accumulation of a substantial reserve fund offers some protection to the cooperative as a whole.

The tenant/owner, not owning actual real estate, may not place a regular mortgage against the unit. Instead shares are pledged against a personal loan. Boards of directors, sensitive to the financial dependence of one tenant on the others, sometimes set down payment requirements that are more stringent than those asked by lending institutions. In some cases they may even refuse prospective tenants unless the purchase is to be made for all cash.

The Internal Revenue Service, however, offers the owner of a cooperative apartment the same income tax treatment as the owner of a condominium or a single home. That portion of maintenance charges that covers property taxes and mortgage interest may be taken as a deduction as long as no more than 20 percent of the cooperative's income comes from nonshareholder sources like rental of commercial space and washing machine concessions. Interest paid on the individual's own loan is treated as mortgage interest would be.

■ CONDOMINIUM/COOPERATIVE CONSTRUCTION AND CONVERSION

Many condominium and cooperative projects, particularly in the New York City area, are **conversions** from rental properties. The sale of any form of shared housing is considered a **public offering** and falls under the jurisdiction of the New York attorney general's office. If the proposal is for a condominium, a **declaration**, together with floor plans for each unit, must be filed with the county clerk. The declaration contains a complete description of the land, building, and individual units. Common elements are described, and the percentage of ownership for each unit is stated. Bylaws also are included.

Whether for new construction or a conversion, the developer or **sponsor** must file a **disclosure statement** (or *offering plan*) with the attorney general's office. The statement includes an architect's or engineer's report of the physical condition of the building; a statement of past and projected expenses; prices for each unit and expected amount of tax deductions; management arrangements;

a description of the corporation (if a cooperative); and a sample unit deed (for a condominium). The declaration is forwarded along with the disclosure statement. If the offering is for a cooperative, the disclosure statement includes the form of the proprietary lease.

After it has been reviewed by the attorney general's office, the **preliminary prospectus** for a conversion, or **"red herring,"** is available for inspection by present tenants. At this point it is subject to modification. When a plan is accepted for filing by the attorney general's office (usually within four to six months in the case of a conversion and 30 days in the case of new construction), it is issued as a black book to potential buyers.

Conversion Restrictions

If the property is occupied, special regulations safeguarding the rights of tenants are in effect in New York City and in parts of Westchester, Nassau, and Rockland counties. Under a **noneviction plan** in Westchester, Nassau, and Rockland counties, unless at least 15 percent of present tenants agree to purchase their units, the property may not be converted to condominium or cooperative ownership. In New York City the property may be converted under a noneviction plan if purchase agreements are signed for 15 percent of the apartments (whether by tenants or outsiders). If the sponsor intends to evict present tenants—**eviction plan**—at the expiration of their leases, the requirement is that at least 51 percent of the tenants must evince their intention to purchase. Other communities across the state are eligible to adopt the regulations if they choose. Disabled persons and those older than 62 are exempt from eviction. To encourage tenant participation, the sponsor may offer discounts that frequently average one-third off the list price.

Nonpurchasers may have three-year protection from eviction under an **eviction plan** and tenants in occupancy have a 90-day exclusive right to purchase and other benefits. If the sponsor elects the noneviction (15 percent) route, all those tenants who do not wish to purchase may remain as tenants under whatever rent regulations may be in effect. The sponsor's inside sales staff, working as employees, do not require any real estate license.

■ TOWN HOUSES, PUDS, AND TIME-SHARING

The term **town house,** as it refers to shared housing, describes a type of ownership rather than an architectural style. Although the organization, similar to a *planned unit development*, often takes the form of town houses (attached row houses), it also may refer to attached ranch homes or even to small single dwellings in close proximity to each other.

A town house owner often has title to the land beneath the individual unit and owns a share in the common elements, most often in the form of shares in a corporation.

A form of ownership known as **time-sharing** or *vacation ownership* has become popular in resort and vacation areas. The buyer of a time-share receives a fraction of a year's ownership of property, which might be a condominium, town house, single-family detached home, campground, or even a motel. Although the concept is most popular in resort areas such as the Caribbean, Colorado, Vermont, and Florida, it has been used in Long Island, the Catskills, and a few other areas of New York State.

In New York, time-sharing is regulated under the blue-sky securities statute administered by the Department of Law and the Department of State. Sellers must file a public offering statement, and buyers have a ten-day rescission period in which to withdraw from a contract. Real estate licenses are required of those handling such sales.

■ SUMMARY

A subdivider buys undeveloped acreage, divides it into smaller parcels, and sells it. A land developer builds homes or other improvements on the lots and sells them, either through an in-house sales organization or through local real estate brokerage firms. City planners and land developers, working together, plan whole communities that are later incorporated into cities, towns, or villages.

Land development must generally comply with master land plans adopted by counties, cities, villages, or towns. This may entail approval of land-use plans by local planning boards or commissioners.

Environmental impact studies are generally required and for sensitive areas may involve increasingly detailed environmental audits.

The process of subdivision includes dividing the tract of land into lots and blocks and providing for utility easements, as well as laying out street patterns and widths. A subdivider generally must record a completed plat of subdivision with all necessary approvals of public officials in the county where the land is located. Subdividers usually place restrictions on the use of all lots in a subdivision as a general plan for the benefit of all lot owners.

By varying street patterns and housing density and clustering housing units, a subdivider can dramatically increase the amount of open and recreational space within a development.

Subdivided land sales are regulated on the federal level by the Interstate Land Sales Full Disclosure Act. This law requires that developers engaged in interstate land sales or the leasing of 25 or more units register the details of the land with HUD. Developers must provide prospective purchasers with a property report containing all essential information about the property at least three business days before any sales contract is signed.

Subdivided land sales also are regulated by New York laws. For the sale of subdivided land on an installment basis, and for sale of any out-of-state land offered in New York, documents must be filed in advance with the Department of State and an offering statement furnished to buyers. The sale of any subdivision of five or more lots requires approval of a water and sewerage plan by the Department of Health, and 50 or more lots requires a central municipal water system.

Condominium and cooperative arrangements for homeowning are becoming more frequent due to scarcity of land, the need for economy of construction and operation, and changing lifestyles. Both terms refer to forms of ownership and not to the type of buildings involved.

Condominiums provide fee simple ownership of real property: the living unit and an undivided interest in common elements. Owners may mortgage their units, and they receive individual tax bills and arrange homeowner's insurance. Owners bear no direct financial liability for adjoining units. Management of common elements is administered by a homeowners' association, which levies monthly fees. Bylaws provide regulations binding all owners in the form of covenants, conditions, and restrictions.

The owner of a cooperative apartment receives personal property: shares in a corporation that owns the entire building and a proprietary lease to an apartment. Financing is arranged through a single mortgage on the entire property; individual financing comes through personal loans. Each owner shares responsibility for the debts of the corporation. The corporation usually has the right to reject prospective buyers.

Plans for construction or conversion of a condominium or cooperative must be filed with the county recorder and reviewed by the attorney general's office. In the New York City area at least 15 percent of present tenants must agree to buy their apartments before conversion may take place. Regulations in some communities may differ. Certain disabled persons and senior citizens are exempt from eviction in any case.

A town house development involves fee simple ownership of the living unit and the land beneath it. All other land and common elements are owned by a homeowners' association, in which owners are members. Time-sharing involves the purchase of a resort or vacation property for a portion of the year.

Subdivision regulations are complex and require a good deal of expertise. Any property owner who wishes to subdivide and/or develop his or her land must be aware of these regulations and comply with all of them. In many cases, it is a safer course of action to sell the property to an experienced developer.

QUESTIONS

1. In New York State, building plans must be signed by a
   a. fire underwriter.
   b. licensed architect or engineer.
   c. site planner.
   d. primary contractor.

2. Joe Builder is constructing a new single-family residence. The local building inspector *MUST* inspect and certify
   a. all electrical systems.
   b. all general construction.
   c. the septic system.
   d. the financing.

3. Which of the following would *NOT* benefit from a professional house inspection?
   a. The buyer
   b. The seller
   c. The broker
   d. The Department of State

4. For new construction, New York State law requires
   a. minimum building and electrical standards.
   b. lead paint disclosures.
   c. professional property inspections.
   d. underground wiring.

5. Overall subdivision guidelines are set by
   a. the federal government.
   b. New York State.
   c. the Department of Health.
   d. the Department of Environmental Conservation.

6. Local governments often regulate subdivision through their
   a. planning boards.
   b. conservationists.
   c. site planners.
   d. building inspectors.

7. A map illustrating the sizes and locations of streets and lots in a subdivision is called a
   a. gridiron pattern.
   b. survey.
   c. plat of subdivision.
   d. property report.

8. A subdivider turns over streets to public ownership through
   a. development
   b. eminent domain.
   c. dedication.
   d. condemnation.

9. Deed restrictions are usually placed on an entire subdivision by the
   a. building inspector.
   b. state government.
   c. planning board.
   d. subdivider.

10. The Marshes received a property report and consulted a lawyer before they signed a contract to buy a lot in a retirement community in Florida covered by the Interstate Land Sales Full Disclosure Act. They may change their minds and cancel the contract within
    a. seven days.
    b. ten days.
    c. two years.
    d. zero days; they may not cancel.

11. Separate tax account numbers, insurance policies, and mortgages are available to the owners of
    a. cooperative apartments.
    b. condominiums.
    c. neither co-ops nor apartments.
    d. both co-ops and apartments.

12. Condominium common elements may include
    a. closets.
    b. kitchen equipment.
    c. personal property.
    d. elevators.

13. The owner of a cooperative apartment receives
    a. a deed.
    b. a property tax bill.
    c. a life estate.
    d. shares in a corporation.

14. The land immediately under the unit is owned individually in a
    a. condominium.
    b. cooperative.
    c. town house.
    d. time-share.

15. The changing of a rental building into shared ownership is called
    a. conversion.
    b. declaration.
    c. disclosure.
    d. offering.

CHAPTER 9

Conveyance of Real Property

■ KEY TERMS

adverse possession	executor	testate
condemnation	heirs	testator
dedications	intestate	testatrix
descent	involuntary alienation	voluntary alienation
devise	last will and testament	
escheat	probate	

■ TITLE

Title to real estate means the right to or ownership of the land; in addition it represents the *evidence* of ownership. The term *title* has two functions. It represents the "bundle of rights" the owner possesses in the real estate and denotes the facts that, if proved, would enable a person to recover or retain ownership or possession of a parcel of real estate.

Title to real estate in New York may be transferred during an owner's lifetime by *voluntary alienation* or *involuntary alienation,* and after an owner's death by *will* or *descent.*

■ VOLUNTARY ALIENATION

There are four forms of **voluntary alienation:** *sales*, *gift*, *dedication*, and *grant*. In a sale, property is transferred from a seller to a buyer in exchange for something of value, known as *consideration*. A transfer without something of value in return (without consideration) is a gift. To sell property or give it to someone, the owner uses a deed of conveyance.

Four Forms of Voluntary Alienation:

1. Sale
2. Gift
3. Dedication
4. Grant

The word *dedication* is used for a gift from a landowner to the government. A developer passes ownership of subdivision lands earmarked for streets and roads to a city, town, or village by dedicating the streets. **Dedications** are often required as a condition of subdivision approval. They benefit the subdivider by allowing development of public access and utilities for the subdivision and relieving the subdivider of responsibility for maintenance, and they benefit the local government by providing lands for these purposes at no cost to taxpayers.

In contrast to dedication, land owned by the government may be transferred to individuals through *grant*, as when public land (still available in Alaska, for example) is transferred to persons who have created homesteads on it.

■ INVOLUNTARY ALIENATION

Title to property can be transferred during the owner's lifetime by **involuntary alienation,** without the owner's consent. Land may be taken for public use (condemnation) or it may be sold at foreclosure of an unpaid lien (mortgage, judgment, property taxes). Natural processes such as *erosion* and *accretion* can result in the gain or loss of title to land, and title may also transfer involuntarily by *partition* or *adverse possession*.

Condemnation

Federal, state, and local governments; school boards; some government agencies; and certain public and quasi-public corporations and utilities (railroads and gas and electric companies) have the power of *eminent domain*. Private property may be taken for public use through a *suit for* **condemnation.** Eminent domain may be exercised only when a court determines that the use is for the benefit of the public and that equitable (just) compensation, as set by the court, will be paid to the owner. Whenever private property is taken in New York, the owner is given the opportunity to challenge in court the amount of money offered. Former property owners are entitled to a 90-day grace period when they continue to occupy the property for residential purposes after state acquisition.

Foreclosure

Land also may be transferred without an owner's consent to satisfy debts contracted by the owner. In such cases the debt is foreclosed, the property is sold, and the proceeds of the sale are applied to pay off the debt. Debts that could be foreclosed include mortgage loans, real estate taxes, mechanics' liens, or general judgments against the property owner.

Natural Processes

Involuntary alienation can occur by condemnation, foreclosure, natural processes, partition, or adverse possession.

In addition to the involuntary transfer of land by legal processes, land may be transferred by natural forces. Owners of land bordering on rivers, lakes, and other bodies of water may acquire additional land through the process of *accretion*, the slow accumulation of soil, rock, or other matter deposited by the movement of water on an owner's property. The opposite of accretion is *erosion*, the gradual wearing away of land by the action of water and wind. In addition, property may be lost through *avulsion*, the sudden tearing away of land by natural means such as earthquakes or tidal waves.

Partition

A partition is a legal proceeding used to divide a property that is jointly owned by two or more persons, such as in a joint tenancy or tenancy in common. If co-tenants cannot agree on the use or disposition of the property, one of them may start a *partition proceeding* in court. If possible, the court will attempt to physically divide the property among the co-owners, but if this is not possible, the court may order the property to be sold and the proceeds of sale to be distributed among the co-owners in proportion to their shares of ownership.

Adverse Possession

Adverse possession is another means of involuntary transfer. An owner who does not use his or her land or does not inspect it for a number of years may lose title to another person who has some claim to the land, takes possession, and, most important, uses the land. In New York a person may acquire title by adverse possession to land owned by another by the continuous, open, notorious, hostile, and exclusive occupation of the property for *ten years*. After that time the user may perfect the claim of title to land by adverse possession by bringing a court suit to quiet title.

Through a process known as *tacking*, continuous periods of adverse possession may be combined by successive users, thus enabling a person who had not been in possession for the entire ten years to establish a claim of adverse possession. The process is not automatic; legal action is necessary to *perfect* the claim. This is known as an *action to quiet title*, which is used in cases where the ownership of land is in dispute. The original owner may defend title by proving that he or she objected to the unauthorized use of the land or on the other hand specifically gave permission for the use. Adverse possession of publicly owned property is not possible.

■ TRANSFER OF A DECEASED PERSON'S PROPERTY

Even the person who dies (the decedent) transfers property in one of two ways: either voluntarily (through a will) or involuntarily (through **descent** or **escheat**). Every state has a law known as the *statute of descent and distribution*. When a person dies **intestate** (without a valid will), the decedent's real estate and personal property pass to the spouse or *natural* **heirs** according to this statute. In effect the state makes a will for such decedents. In contrast a person who dies **testate** has prepared a will indicating the way his or her property will be disposed of after death.

Legally, when a person dies, title to his or her real estate immediately passes either to the heirs by **descent** or to the persons named in the will. Before the heirs can take possession of the property, however, the estate must be probated and all claims against it satisfied.

Probate Proceedings

Probate or administration is a legal process by which a court determines who will inherit the property of a deceased person and what the assets of the estate are. Surrogate court proceedings must take place in the county where the deceased person lived. In the case of a person who has died testate, the court also rules on the validity of the will. If the will is upheld, the property is distributed according to its provisions.

If a person has died without a will, the court determines who inherits by reviewing a *proof of heirship*. This statement, usually prepared by an attorney, gives personal information regarding the decedent's spouse, children, and relatives. From this document the court decides which parties will receive what portion of the estate.

To initiate probate or administration proceedings, the custodian of the will, an heir, or another interested party must petition the court. The court then holds a hearing to determine the validity of the will and/or the order of descent, should no valid will exist. If for any reason a will is declared invalid by the court, any property owned by the decedent will pass by the laws of descent. The court will appoint an **executor,** usually named in the will, or an administrator to oversee the administration and distribution of the estate.

Transfer of Title by Will

A **last will and testament** is an instrument made by an owner to convey title to the owner's property after death. A will takes effect only after the death of the owner of the property; until that time, devisees named in the will have no claim to the property.

A party who makes a will is known as a **testator** or **testatrix** (female); the gift of real property by will is known as a **devise,** and a person who receives real property by will is known as a *devisee*. A gift of personal property is a *legacy* or *bequest*; the person receiving the personal property is a *legatee*.

In New York, children of legal age can be disinherited, but a surviving spouse is entitled to at least one-third of the estate, or $50,000 plus one-half of the remainder of the estate, whichever is greater. In a case where a will does not provide the minimum statutory inheritance, the surviving spouse may inform the court that he or she will claim the minimum rather than the lesser share provided in the will. This practice, called a *right of election*, is a right reserved only for a surviving spouse.

A will differs from a deed in that a deed conveys a present interest in real estate during the lifetime of the grantor, while a will conveys no interest in the property until after the death of the testator. To be valid, a deed must be delivered during the lifetime of the grantor. The parties named in a will have no rights or interests as long as the party who has made the will is still alive; they acquire interest or title only after the owner's death.

Legal requirements for making a will. A person must be of *legal age* and of *sound mind* when he or she executes the will. Usually the courts hold that to make a valid will the testator must have sufficient mental capacity to understand the nature and effect of his or her acts and to dispose of the property according to some plan. The courts also hold that the execution of a will must be a voluntary act, free of any undue influence by other people.

New York provides that any person of sound mind who is 18 years of age or older can make a will devising his or her real property. All wills must be in writing and signed by the testator in the presence of at least two witnesses. A holographic will is one that is written entirely in the testator's own handwriting and is not properly attested in the manner just described. Such a document will be enforced by New York courts only under limited circumstances.

A later addition or revision may be added to a will; such an addendum is known as a *codicil*.

Transfer of Title by Descent

Title to real estate and personal property of a person who dies intestate passes to what the law regards as natural heirs. Under the descent statutes the primary heirs of the deceased are his or her spouse and close blood relatives. When children have been legally adopted, New York treats them as natural children. In most states illegitimate children inherit from the mother but not from the father unless he has admitted parentage in writing or parentage has been established legally. Such a child who is legally adopted, however, will inherit.

Intestate property will be distributed according to the laws of the state in which the property is located. The New York law of descent and distribution provides that real property belonging to an individual who has died intestate is distributed in the following order. This law and the estate discussed apply only to what remains of the estate after payment of all debts. If a decedent is survived by

- a spouse and children or grandchildren, the spouse receives money or personal property not to exceed $50,000 in value and one-half of what remains of the estate, and the balance of the estate passes to the children or grandchildren;
- a spouse and parents only, the spouse receives the entire estate;
- a spouse only, the spouse receives the entire estate;
- children only, the children receive the entire estate;
- parent or parents only, the parents receive the entire estate; or
- siblings only or their children, they receive the entire estate.

If there are no heirs, the decedent's property escheats to the state of New York.

■ SUMMARY

Title to real estate is the right to and evidence of ownership of the land. It is transferred by (1) voluntary alienation, (2) involuntary alienation, (3) will, and (4) descent.

Title may be conveyed voluntarily by gift or sale during the owner's lifetime. It may be transferred without the owner's permission by a court action such as a foreclosure or judgment sale, a tax sale, condemnation under the power of eminent domain, adverse possession, or escheat. Land also may be transferred by the natural forces of water and wind, which either increase property by accretion or decrease it through erosion or avulsion.

Adverse possession allows someone to claim title to someone else's land that has been used openly for at least ten years without protest by the owner.

The real estate of an owner who makes a valid will (who dies testate) passes to the devisees. Generally, an heir or a devisee does not receive a deed, because title passes by the law or the will.

The title of an owner who dies without a will (intestate) passes according to the provisions of the laws of descent of the state in which the real estate is located.

QUESTIONS

1. Title to real estate may be transferred during a person's lifetime by
   a. devise.
   b. descent.
   c. involuntary alienation.
   d. escheat.

2. Title to an owner's real estate can be transferred at the death of the owner by which of the following documents?
   a. Warranty deed
   b. Quitclaim deed
   c. Referee's deed
   d. Last will and testament

3. Matilda Fairbanks bought acreage in a distant county, never went to see the acreage, and did not use the ground. Harold Sampson moved his mobile home onto the land, had a water well drilled, and lived there for 12 years. Sampson may become the owner of the land if he has complied with the state law regarding
   a. requirements for a valid conveyance.
   b. adverse possession.
   c. avulsion.
   d. voluntary alienation.

4. An example of voluntary alienation is transfer by
   a. eminent domain.   c. foreclosure.
   b. escheat.   d. grant.

5. A person who has died leaving a valid will is called a(n)
   a. devisee.   c. legatee.
   b. testator.   d. intestate.

6. Claude Johnson, a bachelor, died owning real estate that he devised by his will to his niece, Annette. In essence, at what point does title pass to his niece?
   a. Immediately on Johnson's death
   b. After his will has been probated
   c. After Annette has paid all inheritance taxes
   d. When Annette executes a new deed to the property

7. An owner of real estate who was adjudged legally incompetent made a will during his stay at a nursing home. He later died and was survived by a wife and three children. His real estate will pass
   a. to his wife.
   b. to the heirs mentioned in his will.
   c. according to the state laws of descent.
   d. to the state.

8. Henry inherited his father's house last year and continued the garden his father had planted on a side lot for decades. Henry recently discovered his father never owned the lot. Which is *TRUE?*
   a. Henry has no claim because he himself used the land for only one year.
   b. Henry automatically owns the land under the doctrine of adverse possession.
   c. Henry might succeed with a suit to quiet title and declare the land his.
   d. No suit will succeed unless Henry makes bona fide efforts to locate the owner and offer to pay rent.

9. The acquisition of land through deposit of soil or sand washed up by water is called
   a. accretion.   c. erosion.
   b. avulsion.   d. condemnation.

10. The person whose land is taken for public use in New York State may
    a. or may not receive compensation.
    b. refuse to give up the property.
    c. still devise it by will.
    d. challenge a money award in court.

Property Management

■ KEY TERMS

anchor stores

boiler and machinery
insurance

business interruption
insurance

capital expenses

capital reserve budget

casualty insurance

Certified Property
Manager (CPM)

contents and personal
property insurance

corrective maintenance

Division of Housing and
Community Renewal
(DHCR)

fire and hazard insurance

industrial property

liability insurance

management agreement

management proposal

market analysis

maximum base rent
(MBR)

multiperil policies

neighborhood analysis

office property

operating budget

preventive maintenance

property analysis

property maintenance

property management
reports

property manager

regional analysis

rent control

rent stabilization

replacement cost

residential property

retail property

Section 8

security deposit

surety bonds

workers' compensation
acts

■ PROPERTY MANAGEMENT

WEB LINK

In recent years, the increased size of buildings; the technical complexities of construction, maintenance, and repair; and the trend toward absentee ownership by individual investors and investment groups have led to the expanded use of professional property managers for both residential and commercial properties. The Department of Housing and Urban Development (HUD) maintains a useful Web site at *www.hud/gov/groups/landlords.cfm*.

Property management has become so important that some brokerage firms maintain separate management departments. Many corporations that own real estate have also established property management departments. Many real estate investors manage their own property, however, and must acquire the knowledge and skills of a property manager. Although the license law allows an exception for those who work for one employer alone, in other instances property managers must hold real estate licenses.

Property managers may look to corporate owners, apartment and condominium associations, homeowners' associations, investment syndicates, trusts, and absentee owners as possible sources of management business.

If you are a real estate management company, you may or may not need a real estate broker's license, depending on the services you provide. If you collect rent or place tenants in vacant spaces on behalf of your landlord client, you need a broker's license because you are acting as a fiduciary (handling other people's money). If your services are strictly maintenance, you do not need a real estate broker's license.

■ THE PROPERTY MANAGER

A **property manager** does more than just find tenants and collect rents. A property manager's job is to maximize income while maintaining the value of the property. Thus the property manager is closely involved in a variety of activities related to generating income, including budgeting, market analysis, advertising, and negotiating leases. Because it is important that the value of the property be maintained or enhanced as well, the manager is also involved in property maintenance, security supervision, and insurance evaluation.

A property manager may be an individual, a part of a property management firm, or a member of a real estate firm. He or she also may be in charge of managing corporate-owned property or work for a trust.

■ TYPES OF PROPERTY THAT ARE MANAGED

Property can be divided into four major categories for management purposes:

1. Residential property (including condominiums, cooperatives, and subsidized housing)
2. Office space
3. Retail property
4. Industrial property

Residential Property

Residential property includes any type of property that is used for dwelling space. Both single-family homes and multifamily residences can be managed by a professional property manager, although the management of multifamily properties is more common. Multifamily residences include garden apartments, walkup buildings, highrise complexes, cooperatives, and condominiums. Multifamily residences may have a live-in *resident manager*.

Office Space

Office **property** includes lowrise buildings, highrise complexes, and office or business parks. The ownership and occupancy of office property varies widely, from one owner-occupant to a multitude of individual tenants with a single, nonoccupant owner. Some office properties attract certain types of tenants, such as medical professionals, financial consultants, and so forth. Office properties can be found in both downtown urban areas and suburban areas.

Retail Property

Retail **property** comes in a wide range, from free-standing buildings to traditional shopping centers. Shopping centers come in many different sizes, including strip centers, neighborhood centers, community centers, regional shopping centers, and superregional malls. Discount and factory outlet shopping centers also are becoming increasingly common.

Industrial Property

Industrial **property** is defined as all land and facilities used for manufacturing and the storage and shipment of goods. Industrial property may be a large, individually owned and occupied property or a large industrial park with several tenants.

■ THE MANAGEMENT AGREEMENT

The first step in taking over the management of any property is to enter into a **management agreement** with the owner. This agreement creates an agency relationship between the owner and the property manager. A property manager usually is considered a *general agent*, whereas a real estate broker usually is considered a *special agent*. As agent the property manager is charged with the usual fiduciary duties.

The management agreement should be in writing and should cover the following points:

- *Identification of the parties.* The name of the owner of the property should appear in the agreement just as it does on the deed to the property. If the owner is a partnership, each partner should sign the contract. If the owner is a corporation, a duly authorized officer of the corporation must sign the contract.
- *Description of the property.* Typically, the street address of the property is sufficient, but it is always wise to use a legal description in real estate documents. It is important that the contract be clear on the extent of the property to be managed. For instance, if an office building is the subject of the management agreement but the building contains a coffee shop that is to be managed separately, that exclusion should be carefully noted.
- *Time period the agreement will be in force.* The length of the term is purely a matter of negotiation between the parties. Property owners generally want a shorter time period, to allow them to seek other management if they are not satisfied with the current arrangements. On the other hand, property managers usually insist on a contract term that is long enough to make all the extra work required during the initial start-up period worthwhile. One year is usually the minimum time period. It is also a good idea to include provisions for canceling or renewing the agreement on proper notice.

- *Definition of management's responsibilities.* All duties should be stated, and exceptions should be noted. The manager's responsibilities include preparing monthly earnings statements (itemizing income and expenses) and making the necessary disbursements to keep the property operating smoothly. It is important to detail what will happen if the property's account does not contain enough funds to cover the required disbursements.
- *Extent of manager's authority as an agent.* This provision should state what authority the manager is to have in such matters as hiring, firing, and supervising employees; fixing rental rates for space; making expenditures; and authorizing repairs within certain limits.
- *Owner's responsibilities.* The owner's responsibilities need to be as clearly defined as the manager's. For instance, is the owner responsible for maintaining proper insurance? The owner also should be responsible for providing the manager with a list of monthly payments, including debt service, taxes, and special assessments.
- *Reporting.* Frequent detailed **property management reports** allow the owner to monitor the manager's work and serve as a basis for planning policy.
- *Management fee.* The fee can be based on a percentage of gross or net income, a commission on new rentals, a fixed fee, or a combination of these. A fixed fee is often to the manager's disadvantage, because he or she has to negotiate a new fee with the owner before the fee is increased, no matter how much work the manager is completing. A percentage fee will increase if the manager is effective in generating income from the property and decrease if the property's income decreases. A minimum guaranteed fee plus a percentage guarantees the manager at least a certain amount per unit to reimburse the manager for spending time on jobs that do not necessarily increase revenues immediately.
- *Allocation of costs.* The agreement should state which of the property management expenses, such as custodial and other help, advertising, supplies, and repairs, are to be paid by the owner.

■ FUNCTIONS OF THE PROPERTY MANAGER

A property manager preserves the value of an investment property while generating income as an agent for the owners. A property manager is expected to merchandise the property and control operating expenses to maximize income. A manager should maintain and modernize the property to preserve and enhance the owner's capital investment. The manager carries out these objectives by securing suitable tenants, collecting rents, caring for the premises, budgeting and controlling expenses, hiring and supervising employees, keeping proper accounts, and making periodic reports to the owner.

■ PLANNING AND BUDGETING

One of the first things a property manager does when a property management agreement is signed (and sometimes even before a property management agreement is signed) is to develop a **management proposal.** A management proposal includes, at the minimum, a market analysis, an operating budget, financing proposals, and recommendations as to how the property should be managed.

Market Analysis

The **market analysis** includes a regional analysis, a neighborhood analysis, and a property analysis. The purpose of the market analysis is to give the manager information about the local economic conditions, the supply of and demand for similar properties in the neighborhood, and the competitiveness of other properties that are similar to the property to be managed.

Regional analysis.   A **regional analysis** includes economic and demographic information about the regional or metropolitan area in which the property is located. For example, the regional analysis may include figures on local wage levels, employment levels, major employers, population trends, and the availability of transportation and government services. All of these separate pieces of information are used to derive a clear picture of the local economy. Essentially, the property manager is seeking the answer to the question, "Is there a healthy demand for this type of property in this regional or metropolitan area?"

Neighborhood analysis.   A **neighborhood analysis** is similar to the regional analysis in its focus on economic factors, government services, demographics, and transportation. However, a neighborhood analysis focuses on the local rather than the regional level.

Generally speaking, property management activities take place on a local, or neighborhood, level, so it is important to be familiar with neighborhood trends. A neighborhood usually is defined as an area whose limits are defined by some natural or artificial boundaries, such as major arterial thoroughfares, a body of water, or a type of land use. Sometimes a neighborhood is only a few square blocks; sometimes it may be a few square miles.

A Management Plan Includes

- a market analysis;
- an operating budget;
- financing proposals; and
- recommendations for managing a property.

The health of a neighborhood's economy can be measured by several factors: the number and type of businesses in the area, growth trends, wage levels, and current rental and occupancy rates. Obviously, areas that contain well-diversified businesses, have low occupancy rates and high rents, and are experiencing growth are more economically healthy than neighborhoods that are experiencing the opposite trends. A property manager generally will have an easier time finding and keeping tenants in economically prosperous neighborhoods.

The presence of government and utility services is important. Adequate fire and police protection; well-maintained roads; and the easy availability of electricity, gas, water, and a sewage disposal system are all necessary to attract both residential and office tenants. Transportation also is important. A neighborhood that is served by good arterial roads, highways, or freeways; bus or train travel; or other means of transportation tends to be valued more highly by tenants. Good transportation makes commuting to and from work and places of entertainment easier for residential tenants, makes the transportation of goods and services easier for industrial and office tenants, and makes shopping access easier for retail tenants.

Especially for residential tenants, extra amenities that can be found in the neighborhood also are important. For example, convenient access to parks, schools, restaurants, playgrounds, theaters, and places of worship are all important to potential tenants.

Special attention should be paid to vacancy rates for similar properties in the neighborhood. Not only do vacancy (or occupancy) rates indicate the economic climate in the neighborhood, they also reflect the supply of and demand for similar properties in the neighborhood. Supply and demand has a tremendous impact on the rental levels that can be charged for the subject property. For example, an oversupply of rental space means a high vacancy rate and probably a demand for lower rates. On the other hand, an undersupply of rental space usually translates into low vacancy rates and rent increases.

Property analysis.   Examining the region and the neighborhood gives the property manager a good idea of the economic climate and the supply of and demand for similar types of properties. From the information gathered, the property manager also should be able to tell what the optimum rental rates are for competitive space in the neighborhood.

At this point, the property manager needs to turn his or her attention to the subject property itself. The property manager must determine how the subject property compares with competitive properties. Is the subject property in a stronger or a weaker position than competing properties to attract tenants?

In the **property analysis,** the property manager examines the terms of each tenant's existing lease, the quantity and quality of the rentable space, and the physical condition of the property itself.

As the property manager studies the existing leases, he or she is gauging the amount and durability of the rental income. The manager also examines the lease renewal rate for the building (tenant turnover), vacancy rate, and bad debt rate. These elements help determine whether tenant relations are managed wisely and whether the rental rate is right for the current market.

Curb appeal—the building's overall appearance—is one of the more important elements the manager studies. Curb appeal includes the building's age, design, and condition. The manager also checks the interior space, including measuring the total amount of usable space or number of units, the layout, and the hardware and fixtures (such as carpeting and plumbing). The physical condition of all aspects of the property is inspected in light of housekeeping and maintenance requirements.

Part of the property analysis includes studying the features of comparable properties in the neighborhood to determine how the subject property measures up. If the subject property has less curb appeal and higher tenant turnover than competing properties, this may mean that maintenance has been ignored in the past, that current rental rates are too high, or that tenant services are lacking.

Owner objectives.   After the property manager has analyzed the region, neighborhood, and subject property, he or she then must analyze the *goals of the owner*. Those goals may vary from maximizing income or cash flow to increasing the value of the property. It is the manager's job to put the owner's goals into concrete terms so that the management plan can reflect those goals (and the manager can more easily achieve them).

Budgeting

An important part of the planning stage includes preparing a *detailed operating budget*. A property manager should develop an **operating budget** based on anticipated revenues and expenses and reflecting the long-term goals of the owner. The manager begins by allocating money for continuous fixed expenses such as employees' salaries, real estate taxes, property taxes, and insurance premiums. Next the manager establishes a **capital reserve budget** for such variable expenses as repairs, decorating, and supplies. The amount allocated for the reserve fund can be computed from the previous yearly costs of variable expenses.

If an owner and a property manager decide that modernization or renovation of the property will enhance its value, the manager should budget money to cover the costs of remodeling, which are called **capital expenses.** The manager should be thoroughly familiar with the principle of contribution (an improvement is only worth the additional value it adds to the property, not its cost) or seek expert advice when estimating any increase in value expected from an improvement. In the case of large-scale construction, the expenses charged against the property's income should be spread over several years. Although budgets should be as accurate an estimate of cost as possible, adjustments may sometimes be necessary, especially in the case of new properties.

■ MARKETING

One of the first steps a property manager must take when beginning to manage a new property is to develop a marketing proposal. Unless a property is effectively marketed, well-qualified tenants will be difficult to find and existing tenants will fail to renew their leases.

Marketing plans will vary widely, depending on the type of property that is being managed. Obviously, a property manager will develop an entirely different marketing plan for residential property than for industrial property. However, there are some marketing principles that apply to any type of property. First, a property manager must be thoroughly acquainted with the property he or she is trying to market. The property's features, as well as the property's layout, should be known and noted. The manager must be familiar with the property's strengths as well as its weaknesses. And the manager should make sure the property is "prepared" for the marketing effort—that is, that the space is clean and in good condition.

Another marketing principle property managers should be aware of is that satisfied tenants are the best, most cost-effective way to market the property. Happy tenants give good referrals and can often supply names of other prospective tenants.

Marketing Activities

A successful marketing plan includes both advertising/promotional efforts and person-to-person selling. A property manager must be able to engage effectively in all three types of activities.

Advertising. The way in which a property manager advertises property depends a great deal on the type of property. Residential, commercial, and industrial properties draw tenants from different sectors of the public. Furthermore, new properties are often advertised in a different manner from established concerns. For example, a newly completed large apartment complex needs to find hundreds of new tenants at the same time, whereas an existing apartment complex needs to find only "replacement" tenants on an ongoing basis.

Several media can be effectively used to market rental space, including

- the Internet,
- signs,
- newspaper advertising,
- periodicals,
- radio and television, and
- direct mail.

Most advertising plans combine one or more of these media.

Signs that identify the management firm for the building and the contact person should be placed outside residential, office, and retail properties. When space is currently available, For Rent signs describing the type of space can be posted outside the building or in vacant store windows. Billboards are sometimes used for large industrial or commercial properties.

Newspaper advertising is perhaps the most commonly used medium. Classified advertisements are used for residential properties, and the larger display ads are used for large residential complexes and sometimes retail or office space. Regional periodicals and other publications are used to advertise large residential and retail properties. Many newspapers also post their classified ads on the Internet.

Radio advertising sometimes is used for large residential, commercial, and industrial properties. Its major disadvantage is that radio audiences cannot be targeted very effectively; there are likely to be few potential tenants among the listeners. The same is true for television, with the added disadvantage that television advertising is costly.

Direct mail can be used effectively for some industrial and commercial properties. Well-tailored mailing lists often can be obtained for likely prospects, so direct marketing can be targeted to an appreciative audience. Of course, the direct mail pieces must look professional. Brochures often are developed for large residential, commercial, and industrial properties and are given to prospects who actually inquire about available space.

Promotions. *Promotional efforts* include any activities that serve to improve the reputation of the building and increase its desirability to tenants. For example, the property manager may speak in front of various interest groups, offer to share professional expertise, prepare press releases and send them to various local publications, and send news releases to real estate sections of newspapers or real estate journals. Promotional activities generally translate into free advertising, which is why they can be so valuable to a property manager.

Selecting tenants.   This aspect of marketing involves the responses of the property manager or management staff to a prospective tenant. The manager or employee needs expert selling skills to deal effectively with qualifying the prospect, creating interest, dealing with objections, and negotiating and closing the agreement.

Qualifying the prospect includes determining the prospective tenant's space needs, price range, parking needs, and required improvements. In selecting commercial or industrial tenants, a manager should be sure that each tenant will "fit the space." The manager should be certain that (1) the size of the space meets the tenant's requirements; (2) the tenant will have the ability to pay for the space for which it contracts; (3) the tenant's business will be compatible with the building and the other tenants; and (4) if the tenant is likely to expand in the future, expansion space will be available. After a prospect becomes a tenant, the manager must be sure that the tenant remains satisfied.

If the tenant's needs coincide with the available space, the manager can move to the next step, creating interest and desire on the tenant's part. Note that it is a waste of time and money to try to interest a tenant in available space when it will not suit that tenant's needs. The tenant either will reject the space or will sign a lease but vacate the premises before the end of the lease term.

In selecting tenants, the property manager must comply with all federal and local fair housing laws. Tenants with handicaps must be allowed to make appropriate modifications at their own expense if they agree to return the property to its original state when they leave.

Creating interest and desire is largely a matter of describing the property's special features and benefits while showing the prospect the building. Taking a tour of both the exterior and interior of the building and of both the rentable space and the common areas is virtually always advisable. Any questions the prospect may have about the space should be answered promptly, and objections should be dealt with persuasively. Once all answers have been given and objections resolved, the manager then moves to the negotiation and closing stage of marketing. Getting the tenant to sign on the dotted line is, naturally, the prime objective of marketing.

■ MANAGING LEASES AND TENANT RELATIONS

The manager who has moved through the marketing stages and found rental prospects then must attend to managing leases and tenant relations.

Renting the Property   The role of the manager in managing a property should not be confused with that of a broker acting as a leasing agent and solely concerned with renting space. The property manager may use the services of a leasing agent, but that agent does not undertake the full responsibility of maintaining and managing the property.

For low-income or moderate-income residential rentals, managers and owners may want to consider participating in the FHA's Section 8 program. Qualified tenants pay no more than 30 percent of their income in rent, with HUD carrying the rest. The property must meet certain standards.

Setting rental rates.   A basic concern in establishing rental rates is that income from the rentable space must cover the fixed charges and operating expenses and also provide a fair return on the investment. Consideration also must be given to prevailing rates in comparable buildings and the current level of vacancy in the property to be rented—supply and demand. Following a detailed survey of the competitive space available in the neighborhood, prices should be adjusted for differences between neighboring properties and the property being managed. Annual rent adjustments are often warranted.

Rent can be calculated in at least four different ways:

1. With a *net lease*, the tenant pays not only rent but also most property charges.
2. With a *triple-net lease*, the tenant pays everything (taxes, repairs, insurance, and everything except any mortgage charges).
3. The tenant on a *percentage lease* pays a fixed rent plus a certain share of the tenant's income (for example, store sale's receipts) over a given minimum figure.
4. With residential property, most rents are on *gross leases* with the landlord bearing all property charges except, in some cases, utilities.

Office and commercial space rentals are usually quoted according to either annual or monthly rate per square foot of space.

If a high level of vacancy exists, an immediate effort should be made to determine why. *A high level of vacancy does not necessarily indicate that rents are too high.* The trouble may be inept management or defects in the property. Conversely, *a high percentage of occupancy may appear to indicate an effective rental program, but it could also mean that rental rates are too low.* With an apartment house or office building, whenever the occupancy level exceeds 95 percent, serious consideration should be given to raising rents.

Negotiating Leases

A lease is a contract and like any other contract, it must satisfy certain requirements to be valid. These requirements include competent parties, consideration, offer and acceptance, and a lawful purpose. Many leases also must be in writing, according to the provisions of the statute of frauds.

Leases also must contain a description of the property, the amount of rent and when it is due, the term of the lease, the use of the premises, and the rights and obligations of each party.

Typically, the tenant's main obligation is the prompt payment of rent. The lease usually provides for a late penalty if the rental payment is paid after a certain date and termination of the lease if the rent remains unpaid after proper notice by the landlord.

Security deposits usually are required. Security deposits protect the landlord from tenant default. They are available to the landlord should the tenant fail to pay accrued rent or should the tenant damage the property (beyond normal wear and tear). Security deposits should be in a separate account, and the tenant is entitled to all but 1 percent of the interest earned on the deposit. The 1 percent may be retained by the owner as compensation for managing the account.

Tenants usually also are required to comply with local laws and regulations (such as land-use laws and health and safety codes); seek permission before altering or improving the property; and remove personal property on vacating the premises.

Landlords generally are required to maintain the common areas and guarantee the tenant's "quiet enjoyment" of the premises. That is, the tenant has exclusive possession of the premises, and the landlord may gain entrance only for certain purposes with the proper notice or in emergency situations.

Other lease provisions may address such items as

- possession of the premises,
- rental rate adjustments,
- tax and insurance requirements,
- condemnation,
- assignment and subletting, and
- fire and casualty damage.

One of the most important elements involved with managing leases is negotiating tenant alterations and tenant concessions. The property manager must maintain a proper balance between flexibility and practicality. While the manager wants to offer the tenant the proper incentives to enter into the lease, he or she also must keep the "bottom line" in mind and not enter into a transaction that is not in the ultimate best interests of the property owner. Some concessions commonly made to tenants are rental rebates; expansion options (guaranteeing the tenant the option to lease additional space); and reimbursement of moving expenses.

Collecting Rents

Once the tenant has signed the lease and moved onto the premises, a major responsibility of the manager becomes rent collection. The best way to minimize problems with rent collection is to make a *careful selection* of tenants in the first place. A desire for a high level of occupancy should not override good judgment. A property manager should investigate financial references, local credit bureaus, and, when possible, the prospective tenant's former landlord.

The terms of rental payment should be spelled out in detail in the lease agreement. A *firm and consistent collection plan* with a sufficient system of notices and records should be established. In cases of delinquency every attempt must be made to make collections without resorting to legal action. When it is required, a property manager must be prepared to initiate and follow through with legal counsel.

Tenants' Rights

New York's Multiple Dwelling Law, in effect in New York City and Buffalo, sets the following requirements for buildings with three or more living units: automatic self-closing and self-locking doors; two-way voice buzzers (for buildings with eight or more units); mirrors in each self-service elevator; and peepholes and chain door-guards on the entrance door of each apartment. Tenants may install their own additional locks but must provide the landlord with a duplicate key on request. Heat must be provided from October 1 to May 31. Additional regulations apply in various communities.

Postal regulations require that landlords of buildings with three or more units provide secure mailboxes. *Smoke detectors* always are required. In New York City, tenants with children younger than 11 must receive *window guards* on request. Protective guards also must be installed on all public hall windows.

Throughout the state the landlord of a building with three or more apartments is specifically required to keep apartments and public areas in good repair and electrical, plumbing, sanitary, heating, and ventilation systems in good working order. Landlords also must maintain appliances that are furnished to tenants. Landlords have a legal duty to keep buildings free of vermin, dirt, and garbage. Landlords also have the duty to inform their tenants of hazards posed by lead-based paint.

A landlord may enter the tenant's apartment only with reasonable prior notice, to provide repairs or service in accordance with the lease or to show the apartment to prospective tenants or purchasers. The landlord may enter without prior permission only in an *emergency*.

A tenant who is disabled has the right to make alterations to improve accessibility at his or her own expense. The landlord may not charge this tenant more rent or a larger security deposit, but may require that the tenant post a bond to ensure that the property is restored as much as is necessary on vacating.

Mobile home park tenants must be offered at least a one-year written lease. If they do not have leases, they are entitled to 90 days' written notice before rent increases. Rules must not be changed without 30 days' written notice. Rules must be posted conspicuously or a copy given to each tenant who moves in. Late rent payment charges are limited to 5 percent after a 10-day grace period. Mobile home park tenants, whether they own or rent the home itself, are governed by the same rules as any other tenants with regard to security deposits, subleasing, sharing space, eviction, and related matters. (In New York, a mobile home is not considered real property unless it is permanently affixed to the land on a foundation.)

Owners may not discriminate against mobile home tenants with children and may not charge extra for children. Owners have the right to sell their homes within the park with the consent of the park owner, which consent may not be unreasonably withheld. Park owners may not require any fee or commission in connection with the sale of a mobile home unless they act as sales agents pursuant to a written contract. Owners may not foster park monopolies.

Owners of mobile home parks with more than two units must register with the New York **Division of Housing and Community Renewal (DHCR),** which enforces the rights of mobile home tenants in the state.

■ MAINTAINING THE PROPERTY

One of the most important functions of a property manager is the supervision of **property maintenance.** A manager must learn to balance services and costs to satisfy the tenants' needs while minimizing operating expenses. *Maintenance* covers several types of activities. First, the manager must *protect the physical integrity* of the property to ensure that the building and grounds stay in good condition over the long term. Repainting the exterior or replacing the heating system will help keep the building functional and decrease routine maintenance costs. **Preventive maintenance** is performed to head off future trouble, as contrasted with **corrective maintenance,** which repairs damage already incurred.

A property manager also must *supervise routine cleaning and repairs* of the building, including cleaning of common areas; minor carpentry and plumbing; and regularly scheduled upkeep of heating, air-conditioning, and landscaping.

In addition, especially when dealing with commercial or industrial space, a property manager will be called on to make tenant improvement alterations to the interior of the building to meet the functional demands of the tenant. These alterations can range from repainting to completely gutting the interior and redesigning the space. Tenant improvements are especially important when renting new buildings, because the interior is usually left incomplete so that it can be adapted to the needs of individual tenants ("make-ready").

Supervising the modernization or renovation of buildings that have become functionally obsolete and thus unsuited to today's building needs is also important. The renovation of a building often increases the building's marketability and thus its possible income.

Hiring Employees versus Contracting for Services

One of the major decisions a property manager faces is whether to contract for maintenance services from an outside firm or hire on-site employees to perform such tasks. This decision should be based on a number of factors, including size of the building, complexity of tenants' requirements, and availability of suitable labor.

■ OWNER RELATIONS, REPORTS, AND INSURANCE

A property manager is an agent of the property owner, and thus must act in a fiduciary capacity. The manager must act in the best interests of the owner and owes the owner the duties of loyalty and good faith.

Owner Relations

When a property manager first takes over managing a property, he or she should begin building a good foundation for effective owner/manager relations immediately. In the planning process, the manager should have learned the owner's goals and developed the management plan accordingly. The manager should have obtained all the necessary vital information about the owner, including the owner's name; address; telephone number; Social Security number; state employment number; and information on the owner's accountant, attorney, and insurance broker. Information about the owner's property financing is also vital. If the property is already operational, current tenant security deposits must be accounted for and long-term accounting procedures established. It also may be necessary for the manager to have the owner set up a working capital fund for operating expenses.

Once the relationship has been established, the manager should go about setting up a procedure for *regular owner contact*. Typically, the major form of communication between the manager and owner is a *monthly earnings report*. This report includes information on receipts, expenses, and cash flow. The report should be accompanied by a personal letter from the manager, enumerating any special concerns or other information that the manager feels the owner should know.

The property manager should quickly get to know how involved each owner wishes to be in the management of his or her property. Some owners want to be very involved, and expect frequent communication from the manager.

Insurance Coverage

One of the most important responsibilities of a property manager is to protect the property owner against all major insurable risks. In some cases a property manager or a member of the management firm may be a licensed insurance broker. To avoid charges of *self-dealing*, the owner should be made aware of the situation and consent to it.

In any case a competent, reliable insurance agent who is well versed in all areas of insurance pertaining to property should be selected to survey the property and make recommendations. Final decisions, however, must be made by the property owner. *An insurance broker must have passed a state examination to secure a special license to sell insurance.*

Many kinds of insurance coverage are available to income property owners and managers. Some of the more common types include the following:

- *Fire and hazard.* **Fire and hazard insurance** policies provide coverage against direct loss or damage to property from a fire on the premises. Standard fire coverage can be extended to cover hazards such as windstorm, hail, smoke damage, or civil insurrection. Most popular today is the all-risks or special form.
- *Business interruption.* Most hazard policies insure against the actual loss of property but do not cover loss of revenues from income property. **Business interruption insurance** covers the loss of income that occurs if the property cannot be used to produce income.
- *Contents and personal property.* Inland marine insurance, or **contents and personal property insurance,** covers building contents and personal property during periods when they are not actually located on the business premises.
- *Liability.* Public **liability insurance** covers the risks an owner assumes when the public enters the building. Medical expenses are paid for a person injured in the building as a result of landlord negligence. Another liability risk is that of medical or hospital payments for injuries sustained by building employees in the course of their employment. These claims are covered by state laws known as **workers' compensation acts.** These laws require that a

building owner who is an employer obtain a workers' compensation policy from a private insurance company.

- *Casualty*. **Casualty insurance** policies include coverage against theft, burglary, vandalism, and machinery damage as well as health and accident insurance. Casualty policies usually are written on specific risks such as theft, rather than being all-inclusive.
- *Surety bonds*. **Surety bonds** cover an owner against financial losses that result from an employee's criminal acts or negligence while carrying out his or her duties. A blanket crime policy is most often chosen.
- *Boiler and machinery coverage*. **Boiler and machinery insurance** covers repair and replacement of heating plants, central air-conditioning units, and other major equipment.

Lower premiums may be offered on property that qualifies as a *highly protected risk (HPR)*, based on the quality of water supply, sprinklers, alarms, security personnel, and loss control programs. Many insurance companies offer **multiperil policies** for apartment and business buildings. These include standard types of commercial coverage: fire, hazard, public liability, and casualty.

Claims.   When a claim is made under a policy insuring a building or other physical object, either of two methods can determine the amount of the claim. One is the depreciated, or actual, cash value of the damaged property; the other is replacement cost. If a 30-year-old building is damaged, the timbers and materials are 30 years old and therefore do not have the same value as new material. Thus in determining the amount of the loss under what is called *actual cash value*, the cost of new material would be reduced by the estimated depreciation, based on the time the item had been in the building.

The alternate method is to cover **replacement cost.** This represents the actual amount a builder would charge to replace the damaged property at the time of the loss, including materials. When purchasing insurance, a manager must assess whether the property should be insured at full replacement cost or at a depreciated cost. As with homeowners' policies, commercial policies usually carry *coinsurance* clauses that require coverage up to 80 percent of the building's replacement value.

Many property managers, faced with filing an insurance claim, call on professional *private adjusters*, who are skilled in representing owners in negotiations with insurers.

■ SKILLS REQUIRED OF A PROPERTY MANAGER

As is evident from the detailed description of a property manager's functions, a wide variety of skills are required of a property manager. During his or her career, a property manager will "wear many hats" and be called on to display expertise in a number of areas.

The property manager needs to be a *human relations expert*, because he or she handles owner–tenant relations. *Research and planning skills* are required to prepare a marketing plan and perform market analyses. The manager needs excellent *accounting skills* to prepare budgets and monthly reports and to help ensure that the owner's income goals are reached. *Marketing skills*, such as advertising, promotional activities, and person-to-person selling skills, are a must to maintain a high occupancy rate. *Negotiating skills* are required for entering into lease agreements. And of course the property must be *well maintained*, so the manager must know enough about physical operations to see to it that both the exterior and interior of a building are kept in good condition.

■ THE MANAGEMENT FIELD

Office building management requires attention to local economic conditions and planning for the specific type of tenants who are likely to suit the space best. For example, dentists and doctors are likely to remain as tenants because they hesitate to change addresses.

Managing retail space like shopping malls involves the careful selection for the right blend of tenants. Large **anchor stores,** especially with nationally known names (Sears, Macy's), will set the tone for a mall and make it easier to attract other tenants. One goal is to find the right balance: For example, too many shoe stores may make for ruinous competition, but it takes a certain number of shoe stores to attract shoebuyers to that location.

Managers of residential property handle every sort of dwelling from single houses to mobile homes. Their main concern, besides maintenance of the property, is the selection and servicing of tenants.

Professional management is usually hired by the homeowners' association of a condominium or the corporation that owns a cooperative. While management is not involved with selection of tenants, maintaining harmonious relationships while enforcing the organization's rules and regulations can be a major challenge. Security, repairs, and maintenance form a large part of the manager's duties.

WEB LINK

For those interested in pursuing a career in property management, most large cities have local associations of building and property owners and managers that are affiliates of regional and national associations. The Institute of Real Estate Management is associated with the National Association of REALTORS®. Members may earn the designation **Certified Property Manager (CPM).** Information can be found at *www.irem.com*. The Building Owners and Managers Association International (BOMA International) is a federation of local associations of owners and managers, primarily of office buildings. Participation in groups like these allows property managers to gain valuable professional knowledge and to discuss their problems with other managers facing similar issues. Management designation also is offered by the National Association of Home Builders, the New York Association of Building Owners, and the International Council of Shopping Centers.

A growing field is management of cooperatives and condominiums. The manager hired by a homeowners' organization must develop different techniques because owners and tenants are one and the same. The Community Associations Institute

(CAI) is a nonprofit organization founded in 1974 to research and distribute information on association living and offers training and designation for specialized management.

■ RENT REGULATIONS

Rent regulation in New York State is administered by the Office of Rent Administration of the New York State DHCR. It includes two programs: *rent control* and *rent stabilization*.

Rent Control

Rent control dates back to the housing shortage that followed World War II and generally covers property containing three or more units constructed before February 1947 and located in one of the 64 municipalities where the system is in effect. These include New York City, Albany, Buffalo, and parts of Albany, Erie, Nassau, Rensselaer, Schenectady, and Westchester counties. Also covered are tenants who have been in continuous residence since May 1, 1953, in one- or two-family dwellings in the participating communities.

For buildings with three or more units, the regulations apply to an apartment continuously occupied by the present tenant since July 1, 1971 (with some exceptions in Nassau County). When such an apartment is vacated, it moves to rent stabilization status or is removed from regulation, depending on the municipality.

Rents in controlled apartments initially were based on rentals in effect when rent control was first imposed in 1943. Outside New York City the DHCR determines maximum allowable rates of rent increases, which are available to landlords every two years. Within New York City a **maximum base rent (MBR)** is established for each apartment and is adjusted every two years. Tenants may challenge proposed increases if the building has been cited for violations or the owner's expenses do not warrant an increase.

Under rent control, rent may be increased (1) if the landlord increases services; (2) if the landlord installs a major capital improvement; (3) in cases of hardship; and (4) to cover high labor and fuel costs. Rents will be reduced if the landlord fails to correct violations or reduces essential services. The law prohibits harassment of rent-controlled tenants or retaliatory eviction of tenants who exercise their right to complain to a government agency about violations of health or safety laws.

Rent Stabilization

In New York City **rent stabilization** applies to apartments in buildings of six or more units constructed between February 1, 1947, and January 1, 1974. Tenants in older buildings are covered if they moved in before January 1, 1971. Buildings with three or more units that were constructed or extensively renovated since 1974 with special tax benefits are also subject to rent stabilization while the tax benefits continue.

Outside New York City rent stabilization applies in those communities that have adopted the Emergency Tenant Protection Act (**ETPA**). Each community sets a limit on the size of buildings to be covered; in no case is the program applied to property with fewer than six living units.

Where rent stabilization applies, maximum allowable rent increases are set annually by local rent stabilization boards. Tenants may choose one-year or two-year renewal leases.

The DHCR has set up a special unit to assist the owners of buildings with fewer than 50 rental units in filling out registration forms and with record keeping and bookkeeping. The department's main office is located at 25 Beaver St., New York, NY 10004. Telephone: 212-480-6700.

■ SUMMARY

Property management is a specialized service to owners of income-producing properties in which a manager, as agent of the owner, becomes administrator of the property.

A management agreement must be prepared carefully to define and authorize the manager's duties and responsibilities.

The manager draws up a budget of estimated variable and fixed expenses. The budget also should allow for any proposed expenditures for major renovations or modernizations. These projected expenses, combined with the manager's analysis of the condition of the building and the rent patterns in the neighborhood, will form the basis on which rental rates for property are determined.

The property manager is responsible for soliciting tenants whose needs are suited to the space and who are capable of meeting the proposed rents. The manager usually collects rents, maintains the building, hires employees, pays taxes for the building, and deals with tenant problems.

One of the manager's primary responsibilities is supervising maintenance, which includes safeguarding the physical integrity of the property and performing routine cleaning and repairs as well as adapting interior space and design to suit tenants' needs.

In addition the manager is expected to secure adequate insurance coverage for the premises. The basic types of coverage applicable to commercial structures include fire and hazard insurance on the property and fixtures; business interruption insurance to protect the owner against income losses; and casualty insurance to provide coverage against such losses as theft, vandalism, and destruction of machinery. The manager also should secure public liability insurance to insure the owner against claims made by people injured on the premises and workers' compensation policies to cover the claims of employees injured on the job. The Multiple Dwelling Law in New York City and Buffalo sets health and safety standards for apartment buildings. Local communities have additional regulations. The state also regulates mobile home parks.

The Institute of Real Estate Management, a branch of the National Association of REALTORS®, awards the most widely recognized designation in the field, the CPM, Certified Property Manager.

QUESTIONS

1. Must a manager allow modifications of the premises to accommodate a handicapped tenant who offers to pay for the work?
   a. Yes, and the landlord must pay for the adaptations.
   b. No, if more suitable accommodations are for rent within a reasonable distance.
   c. No, unless the apartment is located in a rent-controlled building.
   d. Yes, but the tenant must return the premises to its original condition on leaving.

2. An operating budget for income property usually is prepared on what basis?
   a. Daily
   b. Weekly
   c. Monthly
   d. Annually

3. In the absence of rent regulations the amount of rent charged is determined by the
   a. management agreement.
   b. principle of supply and demand.
   c. operating budget.
   d. local apartment owners' association.

4. Office rentals usually are figured by the
   a. front foot.
   b. amount of desk space.
   c. number of rooms.
   d. square foot.

5. From a management point of view, apartment building occupancy that reaches as high as 98 percent would tend to indicate that
   a. the building is poorly managed.
   b. the building is run-down.
   c. the building is a desirable place to live.
   d. rents should be raised.

6. Which should NOT be a consideration in selecting a tenant?
   a. The size of the space versus the tenant's requirements
   b. The tenant's ability to pay
   c. The racial and ethnic backgrounds of the tenant
   d. The compatibility of the tenant's business with other tenants' businesses

7. A property manager may be reimbursed with
   a. a percentage of rentals.
   b. rebates from suppliers.
   c. key money.
   d. a rebate from fees paid outside workers.

8. The term *make-ready* refers to
   a. cleaning a vacant apartment for the next family.
   b. obtaining clearance for Section 8 tenants.
   c. the inspection of an insurance underwriter.
   d. adaptation of space for a commercial tenant.

9. While her tenants are at work, Laura Landlady may enter their apartment
   a. to leave them a note.
   b. to check on their housekeeping.
   c. in case of fire.
   d. for any purpose.

10. Which insurance insures the property owner against the claims of employees injured on the job?
    a. Business interruption
    b. Workers' compensation
    c. Casualty
    d. Surety bond

11. A delivery person slips on a defective stair in an apartment building and is hospitalized. A claim against the building owner for medical expenses will be made under which of the following policies held by the owner?
    a. Workers' compensation
    b. Casualty
    c. Liability
    d. Fire and hazard

12. Property manager Frieda Jacobs hires Albert Weston as the full-time janitor for one of the buildings she manages. While repairing a faucet in one of the apartments, Weston steals a television set. Jacobs could protect the owner against liability for this type of loss by purchasing
    a. liability insurance.
    b. workers' compensation insurance.
    c. a surety bond.
    d. casualty insurance.

13. The initials CPM stand for
    a. chargeback percentage mortgage.
    b. contract priority maintenance.
    c. Certified Property Manager.
    d. cardiopulmonary manipulation.

14. Rent regulations in New York are administered by the
    a. New York City Housing Bureau.
    b. Department of State (DOS).
    c. Department of Housing and Urban Development (HUD).
    d. New York Department of Housing and Community Renewal (DHCR).

15. Rent control regulations are found mainly around the
    a. Adirondacks.
    b. southern tier.
    c. Finger Lakes.
    d. New York City area.

16. When the original tenant dies or moves out, a rent-controlled apartment may become eligible for
    a. rent control.
    b. rent stabilization.
    c. comparative hardship.
    d. freeze.

17. The rent stabilization program is known outside New York City as
    a. ETPA.   c. CPR.
    b. DHCR.   d. HPR.

18. The DHCR's special unit for helping owners with registration, bookkeeping, and record keeping is aimed at apartment buildings with fewer than
    a. 3 units.   c. 50 units.
    b. 8 units.   d. 100 units.

CHAPTER

11

Taxes and Assessments

■ KEY TERMS

ad valorem taxes	homestead	tax certiorari
aged exemption	in rem	tax foreclosure
appropriation	levy	tax liens
assessment roll	mill	tax sale
assessments	nonhomestead	true tax
equalization factor	statutory redemption	
full-value assessment	period	
grievance	taxable status date	

■ TAX LIENS

State and local governments impose *taxes* on real estate to support their services. Because the location of real estate is permanently fixed and ownership cannot be hidden, the government can levy taxes with a high degree of certainty that they will be collected. Liens for property taxes, which usually have priority over other previously recorded liens, may be enforced by the court-ordered sale of the real estate.

Real estate taxes can be divided into two types: *general real estate tax*, or *ad valorem tax*, and *special assessment tax*, or *improvement tax*. Both are levied against specific parcels of property and automatically become liens on those properties.

**General Tax
(Ad Valorem Tax)**

The general real estate tax is made up of taxes levied by the state, cities, towns, villages, and counties. Other taxing bodies are school districts, park districts, lighting districts, drainage districts, water districts, and sanitary districts. Municipal authorities operating recreational preserves such as forest preserves and parks also may be authorized by the legislature to levy real estate taxes.

General real estate taxes are known as **ad valorem** (to the value) **taxes** because the amount of the tax is determined by the value of the property being taxed.

**Special Assessments
(Improvement Taxes)**

Special assessments are levied only on the parcels of real estate that will benefit from improvements in a limited area. They may be levied, for example, to pay for sidewalks, curbs, or streetlights in a particular neighborhood.

Property owners may request the improvements, or the local government may propose them. Hearings are held and notices given to owners of the property affected. An *ordinance* may be adopted that sets out the nature of the improvement, its cost, and a description of the area to be assessed. The assessment is then spread over the various parcels of real estate that will benefit. The assessment often varies from parcel to parcel, because not all will benefit equally from the improvement.

■ THE TAXATION PROCESS

Assessment

Assessments in New York are made by municipal officials known as *assessors*. Assessments are made by towns, villages, cities, and, in a few cases, counties. The **assessment roll,** open to public inspection, contains assessments for all lands and buildings within the area.

In 1788 New York law mandated **full-value assessment.** The requirement was largely ignored, with most municipalities assessing at less than full value. In 1975 the court of appeals ordered the state either to enforce the law or to change it. More than 400 communities then went to full-value assessment voluntarily or under court order. In 1982 the legislature repealed the 200-year-old requirement. Under the regulations that went into force at that time, Upstate communities were simply required to assess all property at a "*uniform* percentage of value," while New York City and Long Island were allowed to divide real property into four different classes for tax purposes. The question of full-value assessment remains controversial and hotly debated, with court challenges occurring frequently.

Equalization.   Uniformity among districts that may assess at different rates is achieved through use of an **equalization factor.** The New York State Board of Equalization and Assessment receives reports on sales prices and calculates an equalization rate for each municipality. This factor is intended to equalize the assessments in every taxing jurisdiction across the state. No equalization factor applies where full-value assessment is used.

The assessed value of each property is multiplied by the equalization factor, and the tax rate then is applied to the equalized assessment. For example, the assessments in one district are determined to be 20 percent lower than average assessments throughout the rest of the state. This underassessment can be corrected by applying an equalization factor of 125 percent to each assessment in that district.

Thus a parcel of land assessed for tax purposes at $98,000 would be taxed on an equalized value of $122,500 ($98,000 × 1.25 = $122,500).

Tax rates.   The process of arriving at a real estate tax rate begins with the *adoption of a budget* by each county, city, school board, or other taxing district. The budget covers financial requirements for the coming fiscal year, which may be the January through December calendar year or some other 12-month period. The budget must include an estimate of all expenditures for the year and indicate the amount of income expected from all fees, revenue sharing, and other sources. The net amount remaining to be raised from real estate taxes is then determined from these figures.

Separate tax rates may be established for **homestead** and **nonhomestead** real estate. Homestead property in New York includes dwellings with no more than four units, mobile homes if owner-occupied and separately assessed, residential condominiums, farms, and some vacant land suitable for homestead-qualified buildings. Nonhomestead property includes industrial and commercial property and most vacant land.

Tax shares are sometimes negotiated between different taxing authorities, as when two towns support one school district or villages share the expense for a county sheriff's department.

Appropriation

The next step is **appropriation,** the action that authorizes the expenditure of funds and provides for the sources of the money. Appropriation involves the adoption of an ordinance or the passage of a law setting forth the specifics of the proposed taxation.

The amount to be raised from the general real estate tax then is imposed on property owners through a tax levy, the formal action taken to impose the tax.

The tax rate for each individual taxing body is computed separately. To arrive at a tax rate, the total monies needed for the coming fiscal year are divided by the total assessments of all real estate located within the jurisdiction of the taxing body. For example, a taxing district's budget indicates that $300,000 must be raised from real estate tax revenues, and the assessment roll (assessor's record) of all taxable real estate within this district equals $10 million. The tax rate is computed thus:

$$\$300,000 \div \$10,000,000 = 0.03 \text{ or } 3\%$$

The tax rate may be stated in a number of different ways. In many areas it is expressed in mills. A **mill** is *¹⁄₁₀ of a cent or $0.001*. The tax rate may be expressed as a mill ratio, in dollars per hundred or in dollars per thousand. The tax rate computed in the foregoing example could be expressed as follows:

$$\text{30 mills (per \$1 of assessed value) or \$3 per \$100 of assessed value}$$
$$\text{or \$30 per \$1,000 of assessed value}$$

Tax bills.   A property owner's tax bill is computed by applying the tax rate to the assessed valuation of the property. For example, on property assessed for tax purposes at $90,000, at a tax rate of 3 percent, or 30 mills, the tax will be $2,700 ($90,000 × 0.030 = $2,700). If an *equalization factor* is used, the computation on a property with an assessed value of $120,000 and a tax rate of 4 percent with an equalization factor of 120 percent would be as follows:

$$\$120,000 \times 1.20 = \$144,000$$
$$\$144,000 \times 0.04 = \$5,760 \text{ tax}$$

Penalties in the form of monthly interest charges are added to all taxes that are not paid when due. The due date also is called the *penalty date*. (Where a lending institution maintains an escrow account to meet a mortgagor's taxes, tax bills may be sent directly to the lender. After the taxes are paid, the receipted bills are forwarded to the property owner.)

New York cities, towns, villages, and school districts generally send out their own tax bills, which may include the county tax levy. Improvement district charges are usually included in the town tax bill; benefit charges are often billed separately. State, town, and county taxes run from January to December and are payable in advance. Villages may begin their tax year either in March or, more commonly, in June. School taxes are levied from July 1 through June 30, but the tax may not be payable until September or October in some areas and may be payable in installments. School taxes, therefore, are paid in arrears for several months. City taxes frequently are payable in two or four installments during the year.

Exemptions

Most property owned by cities, various municipal organizations (schools, parks, and playgrounds), the state and federal governments, religious corporations, hospitals, or educational institutions is tax-exempt. The property must be used for tax-exempt purposes; if not, it is subject to tax.

New York also allows special exemptions to reduce real estate tax bills for certain property owners or land uses. Veterans may be eligible for reductions in some property taxes. Real estate tax reductions are sometimes granted to attract industries or to encourage construction of multifamily housing. In specific agricultural districts New York may offer reductions for agricultural land to encourage the continuation of agricultural uses. Farmers may claim exemption from school taxes for some or all of their acreage. New York State allows local taxing authorities to grant partial exemptions to homeowners who construct in-law apartments, to the disabled, and to "Gold Star" parents who have lost a child in combat. Every homeowner is entitled to school tax relief (STaR), as described below.

Elderly exemption. The state allows local governments (towns, counties, and school districts) to offer partial exemption from property taxes on a primary residence to certain homeowners aged 65 or older with modest incomes, at levels that change from year to year. Exemptions can range from 10 percent to 50 percent, depending on income levels, including Social Security payments. Application is made through the local village, town, or city hall assessor's office and must be renewed each year.

Applicants who do not understand how early in the year tax rolls are closed (**taxable status date**) are often disappointed to find that they must wait up to two years before receiving any benefit. This special tax treatment is known officially by the inelegant title **aged exemption**, and is only an option that the towns, counties, and school districts may adopt. Those who receive it also will receive the STaR abatement described below. New York's tax status date, before which applications should be made, is March 1.

Veterans exemption.   Qualified veterans who served during a conflict may receive partial property tax exemption of 15 percent of the value of a primary residence (co-op apartments are not eligible). Those who served in combat are eligible for an additional 10 percent. The exemption, which may not total more than $5,000, is calculated differently for older veterans discharged before newer regulations took effect. The tax abatement is partial, applying to general municipal taxes but not to school tax. It renews automatically each year.

STaR program.   In the late 1990s, the state instituted a school tax relief program (STaR), giving every homeowner who applied a permanent reduction in school taxes on a main residence.

Elderly homeowners with income of less than $64,650 in 2006 (adjusted periodically) may apply for higher "enhanced" STaR reductions, but must reapply yearly. Any senior receiving the aged exemption described above automatically receives an enhanced STaR reduction as well.

True tax.   The real estate broker taking the listing of a parcel of real estate should be alert to the possibility of exemptions and exercise diligence in ascertaining the true tax figure, before any special exemptions held by the present owner are subtracted.

WEB LINK   A great deal of tax information is available on the Internet. New York City's Department of Finance can be accessed at *www.nyc.gov/html/dof/html/home/home.shtml.*

Protesting assessments.   Property owners who claim that errors were made in determining the assessed value of their property may present their objections and request adjustments. Those who investigate records in the assessor's office may be able to show that the description on file for their property lists more lot size, floor space, or amenities than they actually have. Also persuasive are comparisons with neighboring parcels that indicate the protester's assessment is unreasonably high. Documentation to back up the claims can be compiled from the public records.

Problems should be discussed first with the local assessor; it is not necessary to wait for an official *grievance day.* The next step is to apply for a hearing, filing a document known as a grievance with the local tax appeals board. At the next level a simple and inexpensive small claims procedure is available in New York State for owner-occupied one- to four-family dwellings if the property has an equalized value of less than $150,000 or if the reduction being sought is less than 25 percent. Protests also can be taken to the regular court system in a tax certiorari proceeding.

Enforcement of Tax Liens

To be enforceable, real estate taxes must be *valid,* which means they must be levied properly, used for a legal purpose, and applied equitably to all affected property. Real estate taxes that have remained delinquent for the period of time specified by state law can be collected through either tax foreclosure (similar to mortgage foreclosure) or tax sale. Many cities and villages enforce their own tax liens through tax sales; in most cases towns do not. Some foreclosures are **in rem,** against the property on which taxes are delinquent, without proceeding against the individual owner. When a lienholder, often a municipality, decides to go to court for an in rem foreclosure and subsequently takes title to the property, the lienholder becomes the owner, and the owner and the former owner lose any right or claim to the property. The lienholder (new owner) may then keep the property or dispose of it by sale.

Tax sales are held after a published notice and often are conducted by the tax collector as an annual public sale. The purchaser of the lien must pay at least the amount of delinquent tax and penalty owing. The delinquent taxpayer may redeem the property at any time before the tax sale by paying the delinquent taxes plus interest and charges (any court costs or attorney's fees); this is known as an *equitable right of redemption*. State laws also grant a period of redemption *after the tax sale* during which the defaulted owner or lienholders (creditors of the defaulted owner) may redeem the property by paying the amount paid at the tax sale plus interest and charges. This is known as the *statutory right of redemption*. During the **statutory redemption period** the property owner and other parties who have an interest in the property, including a mortgagee, may redeem the property by paying the back taxes together with penalties and interest.

Once property has been sold at a tax sale, the property owner is usually free of any personal liability for the unpaid taxes.

Counties, cities, and villages have different statutory redemption periods. New York City, for example, allows at least four months after taxes are foreclosed, and the period sometimes is extended.

County tax sales.   The owner of the property encumbered by the delinquent tax lien is entitled to redeem the property from the tax lien (as sold) within one year following the date of the tax sale. If the property is actually occupied (not vacant land) or if the property is mortgaged, the period for redemption is extended for an additional two years (three years total, following the date of the tax sale). This period may be shortened by a procedure involving service on the owner of a notice to redeem.

Village tax sales.   The owner of the property encumbered by the delinquent tax lien is entitled to redeem the property from the tax lien (as sold) within two years following the date of the tax sale.

In most cases the purchasers of tax titles in New York secure title insurance or bring actions to quiet any outstanding claims against the property and do not rely only on the tax deed issued by the municipality. The buyer at a tax foreclosure takes the property free of any junior liens, which is why lending institutions require escrow accounts to give them some control over tax payments.

■ SUMMARY

Real estate taxes are levied by local authorities. Tax liens generally are given priority over other liens. Payments are required before stated dates, after which penalties accrue. Special assessments are levied to spread the cost of improvements such as new sidewalks, curbs, or paving over the particular parcels of real estate that benefit from them.

Partial exemption from property taxes is granted to certain senior citizens on modest incomes (aged exemption), to some veterans, and to others for various reasons.

The appraisal process begins with assessment of the taxable value of each parcel. New York mandates either equitable or full-value assessment with variations from one jurisdiction to another adjusted through the use of equalization rates. The money to be raised through taxation is then divided by the total assessment roll to arrive at the tax rate. The tax bill for each parcel is determined by multiplying the tax rate by assessed valuation.

Various taxing authorities send tax bills at different times of the year. Unpaid taxes become a lien against property, usually taking precedence over other liens, and may be enforced through tax foreclosure or sale.

An owner may lose title to property for nonpayment of taxes if the real estate is sold at a tax sale. New York allows a time period during which a defaulted owner can redeem his or her real estate from a tax sale.

QUESTIONS

1. The broker seeking a property's true tax figure should watch for exemptions granted to
   a. veterans.
   b. senior citizens.
   c. religious organizations.
   d. any of the above.

2. Which tax is used to distribute the cost of civic services among all real estate owners?
   a. Personal property tax
   b. Inheritance tax
   c. Ad valorem tax
   d. Sales tax

3. Sidewalk repairs in one area of the town of Brighton will be paid for through a(n)
   a. mechanic's lien.
   b. special assessment.
   c. ad valorem tax.
   d. utility lien.

4. Which step is usually required before a special assessment becomes a lien against a specific parcel of real estate?
   a. The State of New York verifies the need.
   b. An ordinance is passed.
   c. The improvement is completed.
   d. A majority of affected property owners approve.

5. New York statutes require that property be assessed for taxes at which percentage of its value?
   a. 33⅓
   b. 50
   c. Any uniform percentage
   d. 100

6. When real estate is assessed for tax purposes
   a. the homeowner may appeal to a local board of review.
   b. a protest must take the form of a personal suit against the assessor.
   c. the appeal process must start in state court.
   d. no appeal is possible.

7. A specific parcel of real estate has a market value of $180,000 and is assessed for tax purposes at 25 percent of market value. The tax rate for the county in which the property is located is 30 mills. The tax will be
   a. $180.
   b. $450.
   c. $1,350.
   d. $5,400.

8. What is the annual school tax on a property that is valued at $135,000 and assessed for tax purposes at $47,250 with an equalization factor of 125 percent, when the tax rate is 25 mills?
   a. $1,417.50
   b. $1,476.56
   c. $4,050.00
   d. None of the above

9. An in rem foreclosure proceeds against
   a. the property.
   b. the owner of the property.
   c. the mortgagee of the property, if any.
   d. all of the above.

10. During the statutory period of redemption, New York property sold for delinquent taxes may
    a. be redeemed by paying back taxes, penalties, and interest.
    b. be redeemed by paying four times the delinquent taxes.
    c. be redeemed only through a court proceeding.
    d. not be redeemed.

11. The elderly homeowner who wants a large STaR property tax reduction must
    a. be qualified to receive welfare.
    b. reapply every year.
    c. have no school children living in the home.
    d. consent to a lien being placed on the property.

Broker's Practice Exam

1. An officer of a corporation who actively practices real estate for the corporation must
   a. have a salesperson's license.
   b. own 75% of the corporation stock.
   c. have a broker's license.
   d. be a director of the corporation.

2. When a broker handles funds for others, he or she must
   a. place all monies in his or her own business account.
   b. use the accrued interest to cover expenses.
   c. place all monies in a separate, special bank account.
   d. deposit the funds in the agency's vault.

3. A licensed real estate salesperson must either be a citizen of the United States or a(n)
   a. legal alien.
   b. documented immigrant.
   c. dual citizen of Canada.
   d. permanent resident.

4. An inherent conflict of interest exists when a broker holds a
   a. dual agency.   c. designated agency.
   b. single agency.   d. none of the above.

5. Dual compensation is legal if
   a. the broker has filed as a dual agent with the Department of State.
   b. the parties involved have signed an irrevocable consent form.
   c. the licensees involved are associate brokers or brokees.
   d. all parties involved have knowledge of and consent to the dual compensation.

6. A license issued to a corporation entitles a designated officer to act as a broker, but that person
   a. must be the majority shareholder.
   b. cannot be a shareholder.
   c. must be licensed personally.
   d. cannot be licensed personally.

7. A broker handling documents for a real estate transaction must
   a. immediately deliver duplicate originals to all parties who have signed.
   b. keep them in the file until closing and then destroy them.
   c. immediately deliver them only to the seller's attorney.
   d. make copies only for the buyer's attorney.

8. In New York, automatic extensions of time for listings are
   a. limited to 30 days.
   b. limited to 90 days.
   c. negotiated between seller and agent.
   d. illegal.

9. The primary differences between the exclusive right to sell listing and the open listing is the
   a. duration of the listing.
   b. seller's liability for the actions of the listing agent.
   c. condition under which the broker will have earned a commission.
   d. owner's right to terminate the listing.

10. Which type of listing is illegal in New York?
    a. Exclusive
    b. Exclusive Right to Sell
    c. Open
    d. Net

11. Broker Tanyan and Broker Stevens agree not to compete in the northeast corner of town. This is an antitrust violation called
    a. a group boycott.
    b. price fixing.
    c. market allocation.
    d. a tie-in arrangement.

12. When new Broker Brown establishes his business in town with a flat fee commission schedule, Brokers Tanyan and Stevens decide not to work with Broker Brown. This is an antitrust violation called

    a. a group boycott.
    b. price fixing.
    c. market allocation.
    d. a tie-in arrangement.

13. Tests of an independent contractor status for salespersons do *NOT* include

    a. a current written contract between broker and salesperson.
    b. guarantees of Social Security and workers' compensation.
    c. the licensure of the individual as a salesperson or broker.
    d. that the salesperson is to be treated as an independent contractor.

14. The duty of confidentiality

    a. terminates 90 days after termination of an agency relationship.
    b. terminates 120 days after termination of an agency relationship.
    c. terminates 180 days after termination of an agency relationship.
    d. lives beyond the termination of an agency relationship.

15. A salesperson must have a sponsoring broker

    a. prior to obtaining a license.
    b. within five business days of obtaining a license.
    c. within five business days of receiving their first commission.
    d. only if they received less than 70% on the licensing exam.

16. When purchasing a listing from herself, Broker Nolan may

    a. deduct the commission fee from the agreed-upon price.
    b. give up the listing and disclose herself as purchaser.
    c. insist on being paid the commission.
    d. continue to act as agent of the seller.

17. Real estate agents may routinely

    a. perform house inspections.
    b. assure buyers of the condition of a house and its systems as an expert.
    c. suggest to a buyer or seller that a professional home inspection be made.
    d. recommend his or her friend as a home inspector and receive a referral fee.

18. The New York Human Rights Law differs from federal law in that

    a. it extends protection to families with children.
    b. nondiscrimination is extended to cover commercial real estate.
    c. it covers AIDS- and HIV-infected persons.
    d. it extends protection to all public housing.

19. To a large extent, Fair Housing Laws place the burden of responsibility for effecting and maintaining fair housing on

    a. landlords.
    b. local authorities.
    c. the NAACP.
    d. real estate licensees.

20. When HUD investigates a broker for discriminatory practices, it considers failure to display the equal opportunity in housing poster to be

    a. against the law.
    b. evidence of discrimination.
    c. blockbusting.
    d. steering.

21. A landlord cannot refuse to rent to Jane, a disabled person, who insists on certain alterations to the premises if

    a. Jane promises to pay $100 more rent per month.
    b. the landlord has already provided a disabled parking area.
    c. Jane promises to alter and then restore the premises at her own expense.
    d. the laundry area is not handicapped accessible.

22. Antitrust issues are the responsibility of the

    a. sales staff.
    b. broker.
    c. broker and the agent.
    d. the client.

23. The acknowledgment of the parties to the contract on the agency disclosure form need *NOT* be completed and signed when
    a. the seller has already moved out of state.
    b. the buyer has already signed the contract of sale.
    c. both buyer and seller are represented throughout by attorneys.
    d. both buyer and seller agree that it is not necessary to sign.

24. In DOS regulation 175.7, the disclosure requirements apply to
    a. residential real estate transactions only.
    b. income property transactions only.
    c. all types of commercial real estate transactions.
    d. all types of real estate transactions.

25. When disclosing agency options to a potential client, what risk should also be discussed?
    a. Vicarious liability
    b. Loss of property
    c. Housing limitations
    d. Fair housing violations

26. Designative agency can be used
    a. in all situations.
    b. only when the broker remains as the dual agent.
    c. when the broker is the selling agent.
    d. when the broker is a principal in the transaction.

27. Dual agency requires
    a. that the broker be aware of the situation.
    b. the customer and client be with one agent.
    c. the informed consent of all parties involved.
    d. the signed consent before property is shown.

28. The first substantive contact means when the
    a. buyer or seller first contacts the agent.
    b. buyer answers an ad.
    c. seller sets an appointment to interview agents.
    d. buyer or seller begins to discuss the specifics for their potential transaction.

29. On the disclosure Form 442, what does broker agent mean?
    a. The sales staff
    b. All cooperating agents
    c. The cooperating agent has a customer and agrees to work for the broker, but not as a subagent
    d. Subagent for the seller

30. Signing the disclosure form creates
    a. an agency agreement.
    b. simply states the role of agent and consumer.
    c. a designated agent.
    d. evidence of compensation.

31. The type of mortgage a developer of a large parcel of land would get if he or she plans to sell off lots is a(n)
    a. balloon.
    b. blanket.
    c. building loan.
    d. graduated payment.

32. The amount of money borrowed as a percentage of a property value is called
    a. equity.
    b. interest.
    c. loan-to-value ratio.
    d. amortization.

33. Exempt from usury limits in New York are
    a. lending institutions.
    b. a broker lending the buyer money to help with a sale.
    c. an employer making a loan to an employee.
    d. sellers taking back purchase-money mortgages.

34. One percent of a new loan in extra prepaid interest is called
    a. points.
    b. incentive money.
    c. earnest money.
    d. imputed interest.

35. The Truth-in-Lending Act is enforced through
    a. ECOA.
    b. Regulation Z.
    c. RESPA.
    d. RHLMC.

36. The law requiring that borrowers be presented with a statement of their rights if their loan servicing is transferred is the
    a. Federal Equal Credit Opportunity Act.
    b. National Affordable Housing Act.
    c. Real Estate Settlement Procedures Act.
    d. Government National Mortgage Association.

37. When a down payment on the purchase of a house is less than 20%, a conventional loan in New York State must be accompanied by
    a. PMI.
    b. APR.
    c. ARM.
    d. MIP.

38. A type of mortgage frequently used to refinance or finance a purchase when an existing mortgage is to be retained is a
    a. reverse annuity.
    b. shared-equity.
    c. blanket.
    d. wraparound.

39. A good faith estimate of settlement costs must be provided to the borrower within
    a. 24 hours of loan application.
    b. 3 business days of loan application.
    c. 5 business days of loan application.
    d. This estimate is no longer required for residential mortgage loans.

40. RESPA regulations do not apply when a property sale is being financed
    a. by the former owner with a purchase money mortgage.
    b. with a new first mortgage loan.
    c. with a refinance loan.
    d. with a home equity loan.

41. Construction loans differ from conventional mortgages because
    a. the funds are dispersed when the construction is finished.
    b. there is no difference.
    c. the interest is always higher.
    d. the loan is usually short-term and the funds are distributed in phases.

42. If you were to seek a tax-advantaged real estate investment similar to a mutual fund, you would probably invest in a
    a. real estate investment trust.
    b. general partnership.
    c. limited partnership.
    d. corporation.

43. A method a real estate investor might use to defer capital gains tax is to
    a. sell the property for cash only.
    b. obtain the maximum amount of leverage.
    c. exchange property for like-kind property.
    d. build a reserve account for items likely to wear out.

44. The Internal Revenue Service now uses the term cost recovering instead of
    a. capitalization.
    b. depreciation.
    c. recapitalization.
    d. appreciation.

45. Predictions in what a property will earn in the future are shown on a(n)
    a. depreciation schedule.
    b. operating schedule.
    c. predictive assignment.
    d. pro forma assignment.

46. If the gross rental income from a property is $20,000, the vacancy rate is 5%, and the additional income from the laundry facilities and extra storage is $700, what is the effective gross income?
    a. $19,000
    b. $19,700
    c. $20,000
    d. $20,700

47. Purchasing a property using leverage, refinancing it after it has appreciated, and using the cash from the refinancing to purchase additional property is known as
    a. plottage.
    b. pyramiding.
    c. consolidation.
    d. contribution.

48. When discussing real estate investments, the term debt service refers to the amount paid for

    a. all of a property's operating expenses.
    b. a property's real estate and income taxes only.
    c. the principal and interest on a property's mortgage loans.
    d. a property's credit losses and vacancies.

49. Those looking to get involved with real estate investments would do well to

    a. invest in land.
    b. start with small investments such as a condominium or a two- or three-family house.
    c. begin with a large apartment complex and hire a manager.
    d. buy run-down properties and repair them to resell quickly.

50. Another word for leverage is

    a. personal financing.
    b. 401(k)s.
    c. other people's money.
    d. high, but short-term, interest.

51. The rate of return is directly related to

    a. the amount of risk.
    b. the amount of investment funds.
    c. how quickly the investment pays off.
    d. the terms of the financing package.

52. What is NOT included in calculating net operating income?

    a. Management fees
    b. Property tax
    c. Utilities
    d. Mortgage debt

53. The law governing the sale of home improvement goods and services in New York does NOT include provisions for

    a. giving out a copy of a plain-English contract before any work is begun.
    b. any work costing less than $500.
    c. a contractor waiving his or her rights to file a mechanic's lien.
    d. any work costing more than $500.

54. The "innocent landowner immunity" was created to protect owners who purchase homes that have

    a. environmental problems.
    b. mechanics' liens.
    c. zoning variances.
    d. adjustable-rate mortgages.

55. Environmental law creates little potential liability for the

    a. broker.
    b. appraiser.
    c. insurance carrier.
    d. mortgage lender.

56. The New York General Obligations Law requires a landlord to hold all security deposits in

    a. a non-interest-bearing account.
    b. his or her business account.
    c. a separate trust account.
    d. a checking account.

57. What is the Universal Commercial Code?

    a. The requirements for commercial property
    b. Commercial law adopted in all states
    c. Commercial law for international trade
    d. The regulations governing commercial property development

58. Examples of a negotiable instrument are

    a. the flexible terms in a promissory note.
    b. actual money.
    c. commercial paper that can be freely transferred from one person to another.
    d. a contract of sale.

59. A limited liability company is often chosen because

    a. it allows investors to take advantage of the limited liability of a corporation and also allows the tax advantages of a partnership.
    b. profits are passed directly to the shareholder personally.
    c. the individual shareholder is exempt from a liability.
    d. the tax liability is minimal.

60. In NYS, the Supreme Court

    a. is the highest court in the state.
    b. hears all appeals from lower courts.
    c. is the lowest court in the system.
    d. presides over all the lower criminal courts.

61. Small claims court is available for all suits less than
    a. $1,000.   c. $3,000.
    b. $2,000.   d. $5,000.

62. An example of a law that could be defined as procedural is
    a. law of agency.
    b. contract law.
    c. real property law (Article 12-A).
    d. wills and trusts.

63. The process of a civil law suit is called
    a. litigation.
    b. defense.
    c. discovery.
    d. complaint.

64. The assumption that information regarding the interest of other parties in a property is available by searching public records is known as
    a. actual notice.
    b. constructive notice.
    c. notice of fiduciary duty.
    d. unrecorded notice.

65. Which section of New York's Real Property Law governs subdivision?
    a. Article 12-A
    b. Article 9-A
    c. Article 15-A
    d. Article 4-A

66. A subdivider or developer who fails to comply with the requirements of the Interstate Land Sales Full Disclosure Act may be
    a. subject to criminal fines and penalties.
    b. ordered to cease and desist work on the project.
    c. sanctioned and blacklisted by lenders in the area.
    d. unable to secure FHA-insured and VA-guaranteed loans.

67. Minimum amperes of electrical service required on new construction in New York is
    a. 150.
    b. 75.
    c. 100.
    d. 200.

68. Which is required in new construction?
    a. Aluminum wiring
    b. A 100-volt smoke detector
    c. Lead water pipes
    d. Triple-glazed windows

69. A warranty *NOT* covered by the builder in a new home warranty would be
    a. construction work by the buyers after they move in.
    b. one year's protection against faulty workmanship and defective materials.
    c. two years' protection on plumbing, electrical, heating, cooling, and ventilation systems.
    d. six years' protection against major structural defects.

70. The state agency responsible for coastal management and local waterfront revitalization is the
    a. EPA.   c. DOT.
    b. DOS.   d. DOL.

71. Jurisdiction over local sanitary systems and water potability is the responsibility of the
    a. Environmental Protection Agency.
    b. County Boards of Health.
    c. Building Inspector.
    d. Department of Housing and Community Renewal.

72. New York state regulates minimum building standards and regulations for all *EXCEPT*
    a. sanitary requirement.
    b. environmental requirements.
    c. diversity quotas.
    d. fire codes.

73. Building inspectors are licensed by
    a. DOS.
    b. ASHI.
    c. both a and b.
    d. neither a nor b.

74. Nonconforming use refers to
    a. mortgages negotiated by a lender and borrower.
    b. renting tenants who remain in condominiums after conversion.
    c. home improvements costing less than $500.
    d. buildings that do not conform to zoning laws.

75. A special-use permit could *NOT* be legitimately issued in a residential area for a

a. chemical plant.   c. school.

b. church.   d. private club.

76. The reversion of real estate to the state because of its lack of heirs or other persons legally entitled to own the property is called

a. eminent domain.   c. attachment.

b. escheat.   d. estoppel.

77. Which statement best describes debits and credits?

a. A debit is an amount entered in someone's favor.

b. A credit is an amount that the person being credited owes.

c. A debit is an amount that the person being debited owes.

d. All of the above.

78. Which is an involuntary alienation?

a. Quitclaim   c. Eminent domain

b. Inheritance   d. Gift

79. A trespasser built a log cabin in the Adirondack State Park and occupied the structure for over 15 years. That person will never be able to claim the property under adverse possession statutes because the

a. possession was not "notorious."

b. possession was not "hostile."

c. property was not privately owned.

d. property was not properly posted and fenced.

80. According to the Interstate Land Sales Full Disclosure Act, if the property report is not given to the prospective purchaser at least three days before the contract is signed, the

a. purchaser may revoke the contract, at his or her option, up to midnight of the 14th calendar day following the signing of the contract.

b. purchaser may revoke the contract up to two years following the signing of the contract.

c. subdivider or developer must see that the purchaser receives the report within two years of the signing of the contract.

d. subdivider or developer must see that the property report is delivered to the purchaser before any construction is started on the property.

81. One of the deed restrictions covering all of the properties in a subdivision set aside the back ten feet of each parcel as a bicycle path and green belt area. Homeowner Harriet plans to covert the back half of her yard into an organic garden. Her neighbors can

a. do nothing because individual homeowners have no authority in this matter.

b. go to court to try to get injunctive relief.

c. force Homeowner Harriet to sell her property.

d. share in the profit from Homeowner Harriet's garden.

82. A person who owns one unit in a multi-unit structure together with a specified undivided interest in the common elements would own a

a. cooperative.

b. share in a real estate investment trust.

c. condominium.

d. leasehold.

83. In New York State, the transfer tax on real property equals

a. $0.55 per $500 of sales price.

b. $2 per $500 of sales price.

c. $5 per $500 of sales price.

d. The transfer tax was abolished by the NYS Legislature in 1983.

84. In the event of a sale, security deposits held in escrow by a landlord generally will be

a. returned to the tenants.

b. considered a debit to the seller.

c. transferred to the buyer and the tenants notified.

d. held in escrow by the title company.

85. A management agreement is to a property manager like a(n)

a. listing agreement is to a broker.

b. lease is to a tenant.

c. deed is to a buyer.

d. assignment is to a student.

86. In determining rental amounts, a property manager considers the economic principle of

a. marginal contribution.

b. supply and demand.

c. conformity.

d. balance.

87. The property manager's chief concern should be that the property
    a. is seldom vacant because it is consistently rented at the lowest possible rents.
    b. is managed to achieve the highest rate of return possible for the owner's investment.
    c. manager's time is maximized in his or her management of the property.
    d. exhibits the proper amount of the owner's pride of ownership.

88. New York's Multiple Dwelling Law requires that buildings with eight or more living units have
    a. three options for egress.
    b. video security in stairwells.
    c. 24-hour security guards.
    d. two-way voice buzzers.

89. Owners of mobile home parks are prohibited from
    a. charging late rent payments.
    b. changing rules without 90 days' written notice.
    c. offering one-year leases.
    d. discriminating against tenants with children.

90. Rent regulation in New York is administered by the
    a. NYS Division of Housing and Community Renewal.
    b. Department of State, Division of Licensing Services.
    c. Department of Law, Condominiums, and Cooperatives.
    d. NYS Division of Human Rights.

91. In appraisal, the "principle of contribution" refers to the
    a. underlying value of unimproved land.
    b. additional value an improvement adds to a property.
    c. relative value of a property's location.
    d. ratio of owner's equity to mortgage debt.

92. A property manager is expected to do all of the following EXCEPT
    a. merchandise the property.
    b. control expenses to maximize income.
    c. collect rents.
    d. decorate the premises.

93. A management plan includes all of the following EXCEPT
    a. market analysis.
    b. operating budget.
    c. demographic analysis.
    d. financing proposals.

94. The health of a neighborhood's economy can be measured by
    a. the number and types of businesses in the area.
    b. ethnic composition.
    c. urban renewal funds.
    d. rent control issues.

95. The property manager must exercise care in selecting commercial and industrial tenants. Which would NOT be considered when qualifying a prospective tenant?
    a. The size of the space meets the tenant's requirements
    b. The growth potential of the tenant
    c. The ability of the tenant to pay for the space
    d. The compatibility of the tenant's use with other tenants

96. The New York State Board of Equalization and Assessment calculates an equalization rate for each municipality. No equalization factor applies where
    a. the local tax appeals board sets its own rate.
    b. full-value assessment is used.
    c. the reports on sales prices are very high.
    d. the reports on sales prices are very low.

97. The amount of tax on real estate is determined by the value of the property being taxed. This is called
    a. ad valorem.
    b. equitable.
    c. assessment.
    d. exemption.

98. The current market value of a property is $255,000 and it is assessed at 35% of its current market value with an equalization factor (rate) of 1.25. What is the amount of tax due if the tax rate is $3.50 per $100 of assessed value?

    a. $2,756.25
    b. $3,445.31
    c. $3,904.69
    d. $4,880.25

99. In order for a special assessment to become a lien against a certain property, the

    a. improvements must be completed.
    b. local municipality must pass an ordinance.
    c. neighbors must approve.
    d. need must be verified by the assessor.

100. If the market value of a property is $84,500 and the assessment ratio is 35%, what are the monthly taxes if the tax rate is 30 mills?

    a. $887.25
    b. $924.50
    c. $73.94
    d. $87.72

Glossary

abstract of title   The condensed history of the title to a particular parcel of real estate.

abstract of title with lawyer's opinion   An abstract of title that a lawyer has examined and has certified to be, in his or her opinion, an accurate statement of fact.

abutting   Lying immediately next to, as with two parcels of real estate with a common lot line.

acceleration clause   The clause in a note or mortgage that can be enforced to make the entire debt due immediately if the mortgagor defaults.

accession   The acquisition of land by deposits from an adjoining stream; also the acquisition of fixtures or improvements built on one's land by another.

accessory (apartment) use   An additional apartment, usually small, sometimes allowed in an area zoned for one-family homes, which might be used for elderly grandparents; an accessory use would be something in addition to occupation of a home, possibly a small home business.

accountability   The agent's fiduciary duty to account to the principal, particularly for any money involved in the transaction.

acceptance   The grantee's taking of a deed of transfer.

accretion   The increase or addition of land by the deposit of sand or soil washed up naturally from a river, lake, or sea.

accrued items   On a closing statement, items of expense that have been incurred but are not yet payable, such as interest on a mortgage loan.

acknowledgment   A formal declaration made before a duly authorized officer, usually a notary public, by a person who has signed a document.

acre   A measure of land equal to 43,560 square feet, 4,840 square yards, 4,047 square meters, 160 square rods, or 0.4047 hectare.

active income   Any income attributable to a direct activity of employment.

act of waste   *See* waste.

actual cash value   When a claim is made under a policy insuring a building or other physical object, either of two methods can determine the amount of the claim. One is the depreciated, or actual, cash value of the damaged property. The other is replacement cost.

actual eviction   Action whereby a defaulted tenant is physically ousted from rented property pursuant to a court order. *See also* eviction.

actual notice   That which is known; actual knowledge.

adjacent   Lying near to but not necessarily in actual contact with.

adjoining   Contiguous; attaching, in actual contact with.

adjustable-rate mortgage (ARM)   A mortgage loan in which the interest rate may increase or decrease at specific intervals, following an economic indicator.

adjusted basis   The financial interest that the Internal Revenue Service attributes to an owner of an investment property for the purpose of determining annual depreciation and gain or loss on the sale of the asset.

adjustments   Divisions of financial responsibility between a buyer and seller (also called *prorations*).

administrative discipline   The Department of State's enforcement of license laws, rules, and regulations through the use of reprimands and denial, suspension, or revocation of licenses.

administrative law   Laws concerned with the conduct of government agencies.

administrator   A person appointed by the court to administer the estate of a deceased person who left no will, that is, who died intestate.

ad valorem tax   A tax levied according to value; generally used to refer to real estate tax. Also called the *general tax*.

adverse possession   The actual, visible, hostile, notorious, exclusive, and continuous possession of another's land under a claim of title. Possession for ten years may be a means of acquiring title.

affidavit   A written statement sworn to before an officer who is authorized to administer an oath or affirmation.

affidavit of entitlement to commission   A document claiming commission that may be entered in the public records but does not become a lien against the property.

affirmative marketing   Program to inform all buyers in a minority community about housing opportunities available, without discrimination.

after-tax cash flow The amount of remaining cash flow after deductions are made from the before-tax cash flow for income taxes resulting from the property's income activities.

aged exemption New York state's partial exemption of school tax for low-income elderly homeowners.

agency That relationship wherein an agent is employed by a principal to do certain acts on the principal's behalf.

agency coupled with an interest An agency relationship in which the agent has an interest in the property.

agency disclosure form Describes the roles of sellers' agents, buyers' agents, listing brokers' agents, and dual agents; New York law requires that brokers and salespersons give prospective sellers and buyers (or landlords and tenants) this disclosure statement.

agent One who undertakes to transact some business or to manage some affair for another by authority of the latter.

agreement in writing and signed New York's statute of frauds requirement for a valid sales contract, or a lease for more than one year.

agricultural real estate Farms, timberland, pasture land, and orchards.

air rights The right to use the open space above a property, generally allowing the surface to be used for another purpose.

alienation The act of transferring property to another.

alienation clause The clause in a mortgage stating that the balance of the secured debt becomes immediately due and payable at the mortgagee's option if the property is sold.

alluvion Extra soil deposited on shore by the action of water.

alteration agreement An agreement between the shareholder and the cooperative.

amenities Elements of a property or its surroundings that contribute to its attractiveness to potential buyers and to owner satisfaction.

American Bar Association The American Bar Association (ABA) is the national representative of the legal profession. Its purpose is for serving the general public as well as the legal profession through the promotion of justice, professionalism, and, most of all, respect for the law.

Americans with Disabilities Act (ADA) Federal law requiring reasonable accommodations and accessibility to goods and services for persons with disabilities.

amortized loan A loan in which the principal as well as the interest is payable in monthly or other periodic installments over the term of the loan.

amperage Amount of electrical current, measured in amperes ("amps").

anchor stores Large stores, often nationally known department stores, whose presence attracts other tenants to a shopping mall.

annual percentage rate (APR) Rate of interest charged on a loan, calculated to take into account up-front loan fees and points. Usually higher than the *contract interest rate*.

antitrust laws Laws designed to preserve the free enterprise of the open marketplace by making illegal certain private conspiracies and combinations formed to minimize competition.

apartment information vendor A person who, for a fee, brings landlords and tenants together.

apartment-sharing agent One who brings together roommates and housemates.

appeals Complaints made to a higher court requesting the correction of errors in law made by lower courts.

appellate division Courts of appeal.

apportionments Adjustment of the income, expenses, or carrying charges of real estate usually computed to the date of closing of title so that the seller pays all expenses to that date.

appraisal An estimate of a property's valuation by an appraiser who is usually presumed to be expert in this work.

Appraisal Institute Largest private organization for professional appraisers.

appraiser An independent person trained to provide an unbiased estimate of value.

appreciation An increase in the worth or value of a property due to economic or related causes; the opposite of depreciation.

appropriation The process of levying property taxes; also, the setting aside of part of a subdivision for public use. *See* dedication.

appurtenances Those rights, privileges, and improvements that belong to and pass with the transfer of real property but are not necessarily a part of the property, such as rights-of-way, easements, and property improvements.

APR *See* annual percentage rate.

arbitration A hearing before a person chosen by the parties or appointed to hear a dispute and render a determination.

architectural review board This board takes on many approval functions, primary of which involves the approval of new construction and remodeling.

ARM *See* adjustable-rate mortgage.

arm's-length transaction   A transaction between relative strangers, each trying to do the best for himself or herself.

Army Corps of Engineers   Federal body responsible for regulating waterways and drainage.

Article 9A   The section of New York State's Real Property Law relating to subdivision.

Article 12A   The section of New York State's Real Property Law relating to real estate licenses.

Article 78 procedure   Legal process for contesting the action of a governmental body.

asbestos   Commonly used insulating mineral that becomes toxic when it is exposed and fibers and dust are released into the air.

asbestosis   Lung disease caused by exposure to asbestos.

"as is"   Contract words indicating that the seller makes no guarantees or warranties about the property; not always effective if challenged in court.

assemblage   The merging of two separate parcels under one owner.

assessed value   A valuation placed on property by a public officer or a board as a basis for taxation.

assessment   The imposition of a tax, charge, or levy, usually according to established rates.

assessment review board   A local body empowered to hear protests by property-taxpayers, and to lower or raise assessments.

assessment roll   Public record listing assessed value for all real property in a village, town, city, or county.

assignment   The transfer in writing of interest in a bond, mortgage, lease, or other instrument.

associate broker   A broker who chooses to work as a salesperson under the name and supervision of another broker.

assumption of mortgage   Acquiring title to property on which there is an existing mortgage and agreeing to be personally liable for the terms and conditions of the mortgage, including payments.

attorney-in-fact   A person who has been given a power of attorney on behalf of a grantor. The power must be recorded and ends on the death of the grantor.

attorney review clause   Needed when the buyer and seller choose to have an attorney study the contract. The attorney must complete the contract review within the agreed-on time. The contract will be legally binding at the end of this period unless an attorney for the buyer or seller disapproves it.

attorney's opinion of title   Report in which a lawyer examines and evaluates an abstract of title.

avulsion   The removal of land when a stream suddenly changes its channel.

balloon payment   The final payment of a mortgage loan that is considerably larger than the required periodic payments because the loan amount was not fully amortized.

bankruptcy   A federal court procedure to relieve an overburdened debtor of certain liabilities.

bargain and sale deed   A deed that carries with it no warranties against liens or other encumbrances but that does imply that the grantor has the right to convey title.

bargain and sale deed with covenant   A deed in which the grantor warrants or guarantees the title against defects arising during the period of his or her tenure and ownership of the property but not against defects existing before that time.

basement   Space wholly or partly below grade, usually not used for living accommodations.

basis   The cost that the Internal Revenue Service attributes to an owner of an investment property for the purpose of determining annual depreciation and gain or loss on the sale of the asset.

beam   Structural member, usually horizontal, used for support.

bearing walls   Walls that serve as more than simple partitions and that support ceiling, upper stories, or roof.

benchmark   A permanent reference mark or point established for use by surveyors in measuring differences in elevation. *See* datum.

beneficiary   The person who receives or is to receive benefits resulting from certain acts.

bequeath   To give or hand down by will; to leave by will.

bequest   That which is given by the terms of a will.

bilateral contract   A contract in which both parties promise to do something; an exchange of promises.

bill of sale   A written instrument given to pass title of personal property from vendor to vendee.

binder   An agreement that may accompany an earnest money deposit for the purchase of real property as evidence of the purchaser's good faith and intent to complete the transaction.

biweekly mortgage   A loan that is paid in 26 half (biweekly) payments each year, resulting in an earlier payoff and lower interest costs over the life of the loan.

black book   Offering plan for a cooperative or condominium as accepted for filing by the attorney general and used for marketing.

blanket mortgage   A mortgage covering more than one parcel of real estate.

blanket unilateral offer of subagency Traditionally, a seller's automatic consent to subagency by submitting a listing to a MLS.

blind ad An advertisement that does not name the person placing the ad, or indicate that it was placed by a licensed real estate broker.

blockbusting The illegal practice of inducing homeowners to sell their property by making representations regarding the entry or prospective entry of minority persons into the neighborhood.

blueprint An architect's or engineer's plan for a building, including floor plan, dimensions, and specifications, to be followed by the builder.

blue-sky laws Common name for those state and federal laws that regulate the registration and sale of investment securities.

board of directors Elected managing body of a corporation, specifically of a cooperative apartment building.

Board of Fire Underwriters New York State agency responsible for oversight of electrical systems and for enforcing its electrical code.

board of managers Elected managing body of a condominium.

board package These are documents that contain personal and financial information of the prospective shareholder. The board package is submitted to the board of directors for its consideration and potential acceptance of the proposed shareholder.

boiler and machinery insurance Insurance policy covering repair and replacement of major equipment and systems such as central air conditioners and heating plants.

bond The evidence of a personal debt that is secured by a mortgage or other lien on real estate.

boot Money or property given to make up any difference in value or equity between two properties in an *exchange*.

branch office A secondary place of business apart from the principal or main office from which real estate business is conducted.

breach of contract Violation of any terms or conditions in a contract without legal excuse; for example, failure to make a payment when it is due.

bridge loan A short-term loan designed to cover a gap between the sale of one property and the purchase of another (also called a *swing loan, temporary loan,* or *interim financing*).

British thermal unit (BTU) A unit of measure of heat that is used to rate air-conditioning and heating equipment capacity. One BTU raises one pound of water one degree Fahrenheit.

broker One who buys and sells for another for a fee. *See also* real estate broker.

brokerage The business of buying and selling for another for a fee.

broker's agent A broker who assists the listing broker in marketing a property under a formal agency agreement.

building codes Regulations established by state and local governments fully stating the structural requirements for building.

building line A line fixed at a certain distance from the front and/or sides of a lot, beyond which no building can project.

building loan agreement An agreement whereby the lender advances money to an owner with partial payments at certain stages of construction.

building permit Written permission from the local government to build or alter a structure.

building-related illness (BRI) Symptoms such as hypersensitivity, asthma, and allergic reactions caused by toxic substances and pathogens in a building that remain with the affected individual even when he or she is away from the building. *See* sick building syndrome.

buildings department The municipal department entrusted with the job of ensuring the safe and lawful use of properties and buildings via enforcement of applicable municipal codes and state laws.

bullet loan A short- or intermediate-term (3 to 5 years) interest-only loan with a balloon payment at the end of the term (also called an *intermediate loan* or *conduit financing*).

bundle of legal rights The concept of land ownership that includes ownership of all legal rights to the land—for example, possession, control within the law, and enjoyment.

Bureau of Land Management A governmental agency that is part of the U.S. Department of the Interior. Its purpose is to administer public lands owned by the federal government.

business interruption insurance Insurance policy coverage against a financial loss resulting from a property's inability to generate income.

buydown A financing technique used to reduce the monthly payments for the first few years of a loan. Funds in the form of points are given to the lender by the builder or seller to buy down or lower the effective interest rate paid by the buyer, thus reducing the monthly payments for a set time.

buyer agency An agency relationship in which the broker/agent represents the interests of the buyer.

buyer's broker   A broker who has entered into an agreement to represent a buyer (the broker's principal and client) in finding a suitable property.

bylaws   Rules and regulations adopted by an association.

cap   With an adjustable-rate mortgage, a limit, usually in percentage points, on how much the interest rate or payment might be raised in each adjustment period. For *lifetime cap, see* ceiling.

capital expense   Money spent on permanent improvements that add value to property.

capital gains   Profits realized from the sale of assets such as real estate.

capitalization   A mathematical process for estimating the value of a property using a proper rate of return on the investment and the annual net income expected to be produced by the property.

capitalization rate   The rate of return a property will produce on the owner's investment.

capital reserve budget   Money set aside to meet anticipated large expenditures for major improvements.

case law   Law resulting from past court decisions.

casement window   A window that opens on hinges.

cash flow   The net spendable income from an investment.

cash-on-cash return   This is another term for equity dividend rate.

casualty insurance   Insurance policy coverage against theft, burglary, vandalism, physical damage to systems, and health and accident coverage on a specific-risk basis.

caveat emptor   A Latin phrase meaning "Let the buyer beware."

CBS   Memory aid for an appraiser's adjustments: Comparable Better, Subtract.

CC&Rs   Covenants, conditions, and restrictions of a condominium or cooperative development.

cease and desist order   A prohibition against brokers' canvassing for listings, either from certain individual homeowners or in certain areas.

ceiling   With an adjustable-rate mortgage, a limit, usually in percentage points, beyond which the interest rates or monthly payment on a loan may never rise. Sometimes known as a *lifetime cap.*

census tract   A small geographic area designated by the Bureau of the Census.

CERCLA   The federal Comprehensive Environmental, Responsibility, Compensation, and Liability Act, which established procedures for remediation of contaminated areas.

certificate of compliance (C of C)   Verification that a construction project meets certain standards, primarily safety-related.

certificate of incorporation   A document filed with the New York Secretary of State, describing the purpose of an intended corporation and details about the organization.

certificate of insurance   Whenever real estate transactions include financing (acquisition financing or refinancing of a loan), lenders require advance proof of coverage. This is usually accomplished by submitting an insurance certificate or a certificate of insurance.

certificate of occupancy (C of O)   Document issued by a municipal authority stating that a building complies with building, health, and safety codes and may be occupied.

certificate of title   A statement of opinion of title status on a parcel of real property based on an examination of specified public records.

Certified Property Manager (CPM)   A real property manager who has completed specific educational requirements, demonstration reports, and qualified for the CPM designation, which is granted by the Institute of Real Estate Management of the National Association of REALTORS®.

certiorari proceeding   A judicial proceeding seeking higher court review of a lower court's decision in a case or proceeding.

chain of title   The conveyance of real property to one owner from another, reaching back to the original grantor.

change of association/change of broker   Occurs only when a new sponsoring broker submits a change of association form to the DOS signed by the salesperson or associate broker (as the case may be) and the new sponsoring broker.

Chapter 7, Chapter 11, Chapter 13   Different forms of bankruptcy.

chattel   Personal property such as household goods or fixtures.

chattel mortgage   A mortgage on personal property.

checkers   *See* testers.

chlordane   An insecticide banned in the 1980s.

chlorofluorocarbons (CFCs)   Gases produced by propellants once used in aerosol sprays and the common coolant Freon. CFCs are linked to depletion of the earth's ozone layer.

civil law   The laws dealing with wrongs one person does another.

Civil Rights Act of 1866   Federal law that prohibits racial discrimination in the sale and rental of property.

Clean Air Act   The law prohibiting the use of Freon in refrigerators and spray cans.

client   The principal.

closing date   The date on which the buyer takes title to the property.

closing statement   A detailed cash accounting of a real estate transaction showing all cash received, all charges and credits made, and all cash paid out in the transaction.

cloud on the title   An outstanding claim or encumbrance that, if valid, would affect or impair the owner's title.

clustering   The grouping of home sites within a subdivision on smaller lots than normal with the remaining land used as common areas.

cluster zoning   Zoning that allowed the grouping of buildings on small lots to allow for extra parcels of open space.

CMA   *See* comparative market analysis.

Code for Equal Opportunity   Professional standard of conduct for fair housing compliance, promulgated by the National Association of REALTORS® (NAR).

C of C   *See* certificate of compliance.

C of O   *See* certificate of occupancy.

coinsurance clause   A clause in insurance policies covering real property that requires that the policyholder maintain fire insurance coverage generally equal to at least 80 percent of the property's actual replacement cost.

commercial law   The division of law dealing with business and industry.

commercial paper   Notes, checks, certificates of deposit, and other promises to pay money.

commercial real estate   Business property, including offices, shopping malls, theaters, hotels, and parking facilities.

commercial transaction   Any transaction involving the sale or rental of a building that contains five or more units intended for dwelling purposes or for commercial or industrial use.

commingling   The illegal act of a real estate broker who mixes other people's money with his or her own.

commission   Payment to a broker for services rendered, such as in the sale or purchase of real property; usually a percentage of the selling price.

common elements   Parts of a property normally in common use by all of the condominium residents.

common law   The body of law based on custom, usage, and court decisions.

community property   A system of property ownership not in effect in New York.

company dollar   A broker's net commission income after cooperating brokers and the firm's own salespersons have been paid.

comparable property   In appraisal, a similar nearby property, recently sold, whose price can be analyzed in relation to the property being appraised.

comparables   Properties listed in an appraisal report that are substantially equivalent to the subject property. Also called *comps*.

comparative market analysis (CMA)   A study, intended to assist an owner in establishing listing price, of recent comparable sales, properties that failed to sell, and parcels presently on the market.

competent parties   Those recognized by law as being able to contract with others; usually those of legal age and sound mind.

completion bond   Bond furnished by a subdivider, guaranteeing completion of the undertaking.

Comprehensive Environmental Response, Compensation, and Liability Act (CERCLA)   Enacted in 1980 and reauthorized by the Superfund Amendments and Reauthorization Act of 1986 (SARA), this federal law imposes liability on lenders, occupants, operators, and owners for correcting environmental problems discovered on a property.

concrete slab foundation   Foundation made of poured concrete and steel rod reinforcement, resting on a waterproof sheet directly on the ground; supported by sunken concrete beams (footings).

condemnation   A judicial or administrative proceeding to exercise the power of eminent domain through which a government agency takes private property for public use and compensates the owner.

condominium   The absolute ownership of an apartment or a unit (generally in a multiunit building) plus an undivided interest in the ownership of the common elements, which are owned jointly with the other condominium unit owners.

condop   A condop is a hybrid of condominiums and cooperatives in which the developer had solved the 80/20 issue through ownership retention in the project's income-producing sources. In a condop structure, there is condominium ownership in the land by the residential units and condominium ownership in the land by the developer for the commercial spaces. The residential portion of the property is operated as a cooperative.

confidentiality   An agent's duty to keep the principal's information confidential.

consent decree   Agreement by which an accused party promises not to do something illegal in the future, without admitting it was done in the past.

Conservation Advisory Council   Created by the local legislature to advise in the development, management, and protection of the community's natural resources and to prepare an inventory and map of open spaces.

consideration   (1) That received by the grantor in exchange for a deed. (2) Something of value that induces a person to enter into a contract. Consideration may be *valuable* (money) or *good* (love and affection).

constitutional law   That law arising from the federal and state constitutions.

construction loan   *See* interim financing.

constructive eviction   Landlord actions that so materially disturb or impair the tenant's enjoyment of the leased premises that the tenant is effectively forced to move out and terminate the lease without liability for any further rent.

constructive notice   Notice given to the world by recorded documents. Possession of property is also considered constructive notice.

contents and personal property insurance   Coverage of personal property and other building contents when they are not on the insured premises.

contingency   A provision in a contract that requires that a certain act be done or a certain event occur before the contract becomes binding.

continuing education   The Department of State's requirement that licensees complete additional study before licenses can be renewed.

contract   An agreement entered into by two or more legally competent parties by the terms of which one or more of the parties, for a consideration, undertakes to do or refrain from doing some legal act or acts.

contract for deed   A contract for the sale of real estate wherein the purchase price is paid in periodic installments by the purchaser, who is in possession of the property even though title is retained by the seller until final payment. Also called an *installment contract* or *land contract*.

contract law   That law dealing with contracts between parties.

conventional loan   A loan not insured or guaranteed by a government.

conversions   Process by which an existing residential property is changed into a cooperative or condominium.

convertibility   An adjustable-rate mortgage in which the borrower may elect to change to a fixed-rate mortgage, either whenever current rates are favorable or at specific set conversion dates.

convey   In real estate, to transfer interest or rights to another party.

conveyance   The transfer of title of land from one to another. The means or medium by which title to real estate is transferred.

cooperating broker   A broker other than the listing broker who is involved in a real estate transaction. In an MLS transaction, a subagent of the seller, unless a declared agent of the buyer.

cooperative   A residential multiunit building whose title is held by a corporation owned by and operated for the benefit of persons living within the building, who are the stockholders of the corporation, each possessing a proprietary lease.

co-op loan   An agreement entered into by a borrower and a lender to finance the borrower's acquisition of the borrower's cooperative interest.

co-ownership   Ownership by two or more persons.

corporation   An entity or organization created by operation of law whose rights of doing business are essentially the same as those of an individual.

corporation franchise tax   Tax levied on corporations as a condition of allowing them to do business in New York State.

corporation law   Those laws dealing with the creation, conduct, and dissolution of corporations.

corrective maintenance   Repairs made on damage already incurred (contrasted with *preventive maintenance*).

cost approach   The process of estimating the value of property by adding to the estimated land value the appraiser's estimate of the reproduction or replacement cost of the building, less depreciation.

cost basis   *See* basis.

cost recovery   Internal Revenue Service term for the accounting use of depreciation.

counteroffer   A new offer made as a reply to an offer received.

county boards of health   County-level boards with authority over public health issues, such as sanitary systems, water supplies, and food standards.

county planning boards   Primarily advisory county agencies that promulgate reporting requirements and standards; county planning boards have greater authority in rural counties.

covenants   Agreements written into deeds and other instruments promising performance or nonperformance of certain acts.

covenants, conditions, and restrictions (CC&Rs)   Provision in condominium bylaws restricting the owners' usage of the property.

CPA   Appraiser's memory aid in making adjustments: Comparable Poorer, Add.

CPM   Certified Property Manager, a designation awarded by the Institute of Real Estate Management.

crawlspace   Space too low for standing upright, usually in basement but occasionally in an attic.

credit   On a closing statement, an amount entered in a person's favor.

criminal law   That branch of law defining crimes and providing punishment.

cubic-foot method   A technique for estimating building costs per cubic foot.

cul-de-sac   A street that is open at one end only and usually has a circular turnaround at the other end (a blind alley).

current rent roll   List of present tenants' rent.

curtesy/dower   Legal rights each spouse has in the other's real property; no longer observed in New York State.

curvilinear system   Street pattern system that integrates major arteries with smaller winding streets and cul-de-sacs.

customer   A potential buyer of real estate; should not be confused with a property seller (i.e., listing broker's client).

damages   The indemnity recoverable by a person who has sustained an injury, either to person, property, or rights, through the act or default of another.

datum   Point from which elevations are measured. Mean sea level in New York harbor, or local datums.

DBA   "Doing business as"; an assumed business name.

dealer   An IRS classification for a person whose business is buying and selling real estate on his or her own account.

debit   On a closing statement, a charge or amount a party owes and must pay at the closing.

debtors in possession   In foreclosure, a borrower who retains possession but is still responsible for all junior liens to the property as well as liable to the IRS for tax on the debt that is forgiven. In this situation, a debtor in possession will seek a workout with a lender whenever possible.

debt service   Mortgage payments, including principal and interest on an amortized loan.

DEC   The New York Department of Environmental Conservation.

decedent   A person who has died.

declaration   A formal statement of intention to establish a condominium.

dedication   The voluntary transfer of private property by its owner to the public for some public use such as for streets or schools.

deed   A written instrument that, when executed and delivered, conveys title to or an interest in real estate.

dedication by deed   The voluntary transfer of private property by its owner to the public for some public use such as for streets or schools. A quitclaim deed is often used for the process.

deductible   As it relates to insurance policies, represents the monetary portion of the damages the property owner will bear if and when a covered loss occurs.

deed restriction   An imposed restriction in a deed for the purpose of limiting the use of the land by future owners.

default   The nonperformance of a duty, whether arising under a contract or otherwise; failure to meet an obligation when due.

deficiency judgment   A personal judgment levied against the mortgagor when a foreclosure sale does not produce sufficient funds to pay the mortgage debt in full.

delinquent taxes   Unpaid past-due taxes.

delivery and acceptance   The transfer of the possession of a thing from one person to another.

demand   The desire for economic goods people are willing and able to buy at a given price at a specific time.

demising clause   A clause in a lease whereby the landlord (lessor) leases and the tenant (lessee) takes the property.

demography   The statistical study of populations: births, deaths, ages, etc.

denial, suspension, or revocation of license   Actions by which the Department of State enforces real estate laws, rules, and regulations.

density zoning   Local ordinances that limit the number of housing units that may be built per acre within a subdivision.

Department of Environmental Conservation (DEC)   Agency that issues permits for developments in or around a protected wetland or other environmentally sensitive area.

Department of Housing and Community Renewal   The New York State department charged with administering rent regulations.

Department of Housing and Urban Development (HUD)   Federal agency that administers the Fair Housing Act of 1968.

Department of State (DOS)   The New York State agency that supervises real estate licensees, through its Division of Licensing Services.

Department of Transportation State agency with oversight of New York's highway system.

deposition Sworn testimony that may be used as evidence in a suit or trial.

depreciable basis The beginning dollar amount (representing the improvement's value) that constitutes the annual depreciation deduction allowed under the Taxpayer Relief Act.

depreciation In appraisal, a loss of value in property due to any cause, including physical deterioration, functional obsolescence, and external (locational) obsolescence.

descent Acquisition of an estate by inheritance in which an heir succeeds to the property by operation of law.

description In real estate, the portion of a document that defines the subject property in specific legal terms.

designation An indication of special training and expertise, awarded by various real estate organizations.

determinable fee estate A fee simple estate in which the property automatically reverts to the grantor on the occurrence of a specified event or condition.

developer One who improves land with buildings, usually on a large scale, and sells to homeowners and/or investors.

development rights The rights to develop and improve property, sometimes sold to another landowner to be used on a different parcel.

devise A gift of real property by will; the act of leaving real property by will.

devisee One who receives a bequest of real estate made by will.

devisor One who bequeaths real estate by will.

direct costs The expenditures necessary for the labor and materials used in the construction of a new improvement, including contractor's overhead and profit.

direct public ownership Land-use control method through which land is owned by the government for such public uses as municipal buildings, parks, schools, and roads.

direct sales comparison approach An appraisal method in which a subject property is evaluated in comparison with similar recently sold properties; most useful for single residential properties.

disclosure A broker is responsible for keeping a principal fully informed of all facts that could affect a transaction. If a broker fails to disclose such information, he or she may be liable for any damages that result.

disclosure statement Document that must be filed by the developer of a new or converted condominium or cooperative project, including an architect's or engineer's eval-

uation of the structure, an expense statement, prices per unit, and other financial and administrative information.

discounted cash-flow analysis A discounted cash flow analysis is used in a similar manner to that of a pro forma statement; however, the discounted cash flow analysis reflects an analysis of actual versus projected income activities. The discounted cash flow analysis also takes into account the time value of money.

discounting Method for mathematically calculating present value of money, based on time and the discount rate.

discount points An added loan fee charged by a lender to make the yield on a lower-than-market-value loan competitive with higher-interest loans.

discount rate Rate of return needed to compensate an investor for risk; the Federal Reserve's loan rate for eligible banks.

disintermediation A tight-money real estate lending market (in which real estate loans are more difficult to obtain) that results when investors choose to invest in stocks, bonds, and mutual funds rather than savings accounts, limiting the funds available to lenders.

disposition Investment strategy for reconciling anticipated gain or loss with the risk involved.

distance learning These are classes completed online.

Division of Housing and Community Renewal (DHCR) New York agency that administers rent control and stabilization programs.

documentary evidence *See* alienation clause.

double-hung window A sash window with two vertically sliding sashes; both single-hung and double-hung window sashes are controlled and held in place by springs or weights.

due diligence The process of investigating the circumstances regarding a financial or business transaction thoroughly enough to satisfy the care of an unrelated, objective party.

due process Legal procedures that protect the rights of the individual.

duress Unlawful constraint or action exercised on a person who is forced to perform an act against his or her will.

earnest money deposit Money deposited by a buyer under the terms of a contract, to be applied to the purchase price if the sale is closed.

easement A right to use the land of another for a specific purpose, as for a right-of-way or utilities; an incorporeal interest in land. An easement appurtenant passes with the land when conveyed.

easement appurtenant An easement involving adjacent parcels that runs with the land (is permanently attached), so that subsequent owners are bound by it, and it passes with the land when conveyed.

easement by condemnation The government's right to use private property, for example, to build a sidewalk.

easement by grant An easement given (usually by deed) by one landowner to another.

easement by implication Arises when "reasonably necessary" and created by the actions of the parties involved.

easement by necessity An easement allowed by law as necessary for the full enjoyment of a parcel of real estate; for example, a right of ingress and egress over a grantor's land.

easement by prescription An easement acquired by continuous, open, uninterrupted, exclusive, and adverse use of the property for the period of time prescribed by state law.

easement for light and air Abutting owners attempt to purchase rights to light and air over a neighbor's property. Such an easement should be granted in writing. **easement in gross** An easement that is not created for the benefit of any *land* owned by the owner of the easement but that attaches *personally to the easement owner.*

eave Overhang or roof projection beyond the outside walls of a house.

economic obsolescence A form of external obsolescence, a reduction of property value resulting from a change in the economics of the area in which the property is located.

effective gross income Effective gross income is the income attributable to a property after deductions have been made for vacancy and collection losses and after adding any other income derived from that property. Effective gross income (EGI) = Potential gross income (PGI) – Vacancy and collection loss (V&C) + Other income (OI).

electromagnetic field (EMF) Invisible energy fields created by the movement of electrical currents in high tension wires and electrical appliances. EMFs may be responsible for occurrences of cancer, hormonal changes, and behavioral disorders.

emblements Growing crops, such as grapes and corn, that are produced annually through labor and industry; also called *fructus industriales.*

eminent domain The right of a government or quasi-public body to acquire property for public use through a court action called *condemnation.*

employee One who works under the supervision and control of another, as contrasted for income tax purposes with an independent contractor.

encroachment A building or some portion of it—a wall or fence, for instance—that extends beyond the land of the owner and illegally intrudes on some land of an adjoining owner or a street or alley.

encumbrance Any claim by another—such as a mortgage, a tax or judgment lien, an easement, an encroachment, or a deed restriction on the use of the land—that may diminish the value of a property.

endorsement An act of signing one's name on the back of a check or note with or without further qualifications.

envelope The components that make up the building (also known as the *building envelope*)—roof, walls, and windows— protect occupants from intruders, noises, and the elements; they can and should be made as energy efficient as possible.

environmental impact study Report detailing the effect of a proposed development on the existing environment, including possible alternative measures to remedy or repair environmental damage.

Environmental Protection Agency (EPA) A federal agency involved with the problems of air and water pollution, noise, pesticides, radiation, and solid-waste management. EPA sets standards, enforces environmental laws, conducts research, allocates funds for sewage-treatment facilities, and provides technical, financial and managerial assistance for municipal, regional, and state pollution control agencies.

Equal Credit Opportunity Act (ECOA) The federal law that prohibits discrimination in the extension of credit because of race, color, religion, national origin, sex, age, or marital status.

equalization The raising or lowering of assessed values for tax purposes in a particular county or taxing district to make them equal to assessments in other counties or districts.

equalization factor A multiplier that adjusts for different communities' tax assessment policies.

equitable title The interest held by a vendee under a land contract or an installment contract; the equitable right to obtain absolute ownership to property when legal title is held in another's name.

equity The interest or value that an owner has in property over and above any mortgage indebtedness and other liens.

equity dividend rate This is the percentage of profit that the investor receives only on the cash he or she invested in the property (commonly referred to as cash-on-cash return).

equity of redemption A right of the owner to reclaim property before it is sold through foreclosure by the payment of the debt, interest, and costs.

erosion The gradual wearing away of land by water, wind, and general weather conditions; the diminishing of property caused by the elements.

errors and omissions insurance A form of malpractice insurance for real estate brokers.

escape clause A provision in a contract that allows one party to unilaterally void the contract without penalty; for instance, a seller may be allowed to look for a more favorable offer, while the purchaser retains the right to drop all contingencies or void the contract if another offer is received.

escheat The reversion of property to the state or county, as provided by state law, in cases where a person dies intestate without heirs capable of inheriting or when the property is abandoned.

escrow The closing of a transaction through a third party called an *escrow agent*. Also can refer to earnest money deposits or to a mortgagee's trust account for insurance and tax payments.

estate The degree, quantity, nature, and extent of interest that a person has in real property.

estate at will The occupation of lands and tenements by a tenant for an indefinite period, terminable by one or both parties at will.

estate for years An interest for a certain, exact period of time in property leased for a specified consideration.

estate in land The degree, quantity, nature, and extent of interest a person has in real property.

estate tax Federal tax levied on property transferred on death.

estoppel The situation in which a party is prevented by his or her own acts from taking a different position because it would cause detriment to another party.

estoppel certificate A document in which a borrower certifies the amount he or she owes on a mortgage loan and the rate of interest. Often used for *reduction certificate*.

evaluation An analysis of a property and its attributes in which a value estimate is not required. The study may consider any aspect of the property, including the nature, quality, and utility of an interest in the real estate.

eviction A legal process to oust a person from possession of real estate.

eviction plan Method of converting a rental property into a condominium or cooperative, in which existing tenants will be evicted when their leases expire.

evidence of title Proof of ownership of property; commonly a certificate of title, a title insurance policy, an abstract of title with lawyer's opinion, or a Torrens registration certificate.

exchange A transaction in which all or part of the consideration for the purchase of real property is the transfer of *like-kind* property (that is, real estate for real estate).

exclusive-agency listing A listing contract under which the owner appoints a real estate broker as his or her exclusive agent. The owner reserves the right to sell without paying anyone a commission.

exclusive right to represent The most common form of buyer agency agreement.

exclusive-right-to-sell listing A listing contract under which the owner appoints a real estate broker as his or her exclusive agent and agrees to pay the broker a commission when the property is sold, whether by the broker, the owner, or another broker.

executed contract A contract in which all parties have fulfilled their promises and thus performed the contract.

execution The signing and delivery of an instrument. Also, a legal order directing an official to enforce a judgment against the property of a debtor.

Executive Law New York State Human Rights Law.

executor A male person, corporate entity, or any other type of organization designated in a will to carry out its provisions.

executor's deed A document signed by the executor of an estate, transferring ownership of real property to a devisee or natural heir.

executory contract A contract under which something remains to be done by one or more of the parties.

executrix A woman appointed to perform the duties of an executor.

exemption With an exemption, a licensee is excused from a given requirement that otherwise would apply.

express agency An agency that is specifically stated, orally or in writing.

express contract An oral or written contract in which the parties state the contract's terms and express their intentions in words.

external obsolescence Reduction in a property's value caused by factors outside the subject property, such as social or environmental forces or objectionable neighboring property.

fair employment laws Laws designed to prevent employers from making their hiring and firing decisions on factors unrelated to job performance.

Fair Housing Amendment Act of 1988 Effective March 12, 1989, this amendment to the federal Fair Housing Act added two more classes protected from discrimination: those physically and mentally handicapped, and those with children under age 18.

Fair Housing Partnership Agreement Voluntary agreement between NAR and HUD to cooperate in identifying fair housing problems, issues, and solutions.

familial status A protected class under fair housing laws, which refers to the presence of children in a family.

family units For the purposes of defining single-family residence, New York State considers a family one or more persons related by blood, marriage, or adoption; or up to three persons not so related who live together.

Fannie Mae A quasi-government agency established to purchase any kind of mortgage loans in the secondary mortgage market from the primary lenders.

fascia Flat board on the outside of a soffit.

federal Fair Housing Act of 1968 The federal law that prohibits discrimination in housing based on race, color, religion, sex, handicap, familial status, or national origin. Amended in 1988 to include persons with physical and mental disabilities, and those with children under 18.

Federal Home Loan Mortgage Corporation (FHLMC) *See* Freddie Mac.

federally related transaction Any transaction in which a loan is originated by any financial institution or lender regulated by the federal government.

Federal National Mortgage Association (FNMA) *See* Fannie Mae.

fee agreement A compensation agreement that a borrower will enter into with a mortgage broker.

fee appraiser An appraiser who works as an independent contractor, performing appraisal services for various clients.

fee simple estate The maximum possible estate or right of ownership of real property, continuing forever. Sometimes called a *fee* or *fee simple absolute*.

FHA loan A loan insured by the Federal Housing Administration and made by an approved lender in accordance with the FHA's regulations.

fiduciary One in whom trust and confidence is placed; a reference to a broker employed under the terms of a listing contract or buyer agency agreement.

fiduciary duties The specific legal duties an agent owes to the principal.

fiduciary relationship A relationship of trust and confidence as between trustee and beneficiary, attorney and client, or principal and agent.

filtering down The process by which housing units formerly occupied by middle- and upper-income families decline in quality and value and become available to lower-income occupants.

financing statement *See* Uniform Commercial Code.

fire and hazard insurance Policy providing coverage for direct loss of or damage to property resulting from fire, storms, hail, smoke, or riot.

FIRREA The Financial Institutions Reform, Recovery, and Enforcement Act of 1989 regulates financial institutions and requires that either a licensed certified or general appraiser must be used to conduct any appraisal involving a federally related transaction.

first substantive contact The point at which agents must disclose and obtain signed acknowledgments of their agency relationships.

fixed expenses Expenses that do not vary as a result of a property's occupancy rate. Fixed expenses consist of only property taxes and property insurance.

fixture An item of personal property that has been converted to real property by being permanently affixed to the realty.

flashing Waterproofing material used to seal seams of roof, chimney, and walls.

flipping A transaction in which one party contracts to buy a property with the intention of quickly transferring (or flipping) the property over to the ultimate buyer.

flip tax A tax imposed by the cooperative on the sale of a unit within said building. This fee can be based on a percentage of the gross sale, net sale, gain, or the number of shares held by the shareholder or a fixed number determined by the cooperative board. The flip tax can be paid by the purchaser, seller, or shared by both parties; however, custom usually dictates that the seller pay the flip tax.

floating slab foundation Type of concrete slab foundation in which the footings and slab are poured separately.

forbearance A legally binding promise to refrain from doing some act.

foreclosure A procedure whereby property pledged as security for a debt is sold to pay the debt in the event of default in payments or terms.

franchise An organization that leases a standardized trade name, operating procedures, supplies, and referral service to member real estate brokerages.

fraud Deception that causes a person to give up property or a lawful right.

Freddie Mac A corporation established to purchase primarily conventional mortgage loans in the secondary mortgage market.

freehold estate An estate in land in which ownership is for an indeterminate length of time, in contrast to a leasehold estate.

Freon Chemical substance, formerly used in refrigerators and spray cans, now prohibited because it contributes to air pollution.

friable Crumbly, breaking off (as in some asbestos insulation).

frieze board A horizontal exterior band or molding located directly below the cornice.

front foot A standard measurement, one foot wide, of the width of land, applied at the frontage on its street line.

full covenant and warranty deed A deed that provides the greatest protection, in which the grantor makes five legal promises (covenants of seisin, quiet enjoyment, further assurances, warranty forever, against encumbrances) that the grantee's ownership will be unchallenged.

full-value assessment Practice of assessing property at its full value, rather than by a percentage of full value.

fully amortized loan A debt that is completely paid off at the end of a specific number of even payments, each containing interest and a portion toward reducing the principal.

functional obsolescence A loss of value to an improvement to real estate due to functional problems, often caused by age or poor design.

fuse box Area where electric service enters a building and is distributed to various circuits.

future interest A person's present right to an interest in real property that will not result in possession or enjoyment until some time in the future.

gains Any gains that result from a sale where the property was held for one year or less.

gap A defect in the chain of title of a particular parcel of real estate; a missing document or conveyance that raises doubt as to present ownership.

general agent One authorized to act for the principal in a specific range of matters.

general contractor A construction specialist who enters into a formal contract with a landowner or lessee to construct a building or project.

general lien The right of a creditor to have all of a debtor's property—both real and personal—sold to satisfy a debt.

general partnership *See* partnership.

general tax *See* ad valorem tax.

Ginnie Mae A government agency that plays an important role in the secondary mortgage market. It sells mortgage-backed securities that are backed by pools of FHA and VA loans.

girder The heavy beam, wood or steel, that furnishes the main support for the first floor.

Government National Mortgage Association (GNMA) *See* Ginnie Mae.

grace period Additional time allowed to perform an act or make a payment before a default occurs.

graduated lease A lease that provides for a graduated change at stated intervals in the amount of the rent to be paid; used largely in long-term leases.

graduated payment mortgage A mortgage in which the monthly payment for principal and interest graduates by a certain percentage each year for a specific number of years and then levels off for the remaining term of the mortgage.

grant A sale or gift of real property.

grantee A person who receives a conveyance of real property from the grantor.

granting clause Words in a deed of conveyance that state the grantor's intention to convey the property. This clause is generally worded as "convey and warrant," "grant," "grant, bargain and sell," or the like.

grantor The person transferring title to or an interest in real property to a grantee.

GRI (Graduate, REALTORS® Institute) A professional designation earned by any member of a state-affiliated Board of REALTORS® who completes specific courses approved by the board.

gridiron pattern Street pattern systems that evolved out of the government rectangular survey, featuring a regular grid of straight-line streets and alleys.

grievance A complaint, particularly that made by a taxpayer protesting property tax assessment figures.

gross income Total income from property before any expenses are deducted.

gross income multiplier The figure used as a multiplier of the gross annual income of a property to produce an estimate of the property's value.

gross lease A lease of property under which a landlord pays all property charges regularly incurred through ownership, such as repairs, taxes, and insurance.

gross operating income Rent actually collected on an income property.

gross rental income Total amount collected in rents, from which expenses must be paid.

gross rent multiplier (GRM) A figure used as a multiplier of the gross rental income of a property to produce an estimate of the property's value.

ground lease A lease of land only, on which the tenant usually owns a building or is required to build as specified in the lease. Such leases are usually long-term net leases; the tenant's rights and obligations continue until the lease expires or is terminated through default.

groundwater Surface runoff and underground water systems.

group boycott An agreement among members of a trade to exclude other members from fair participation in the activities of the trade.

group home A living unit housing more than three unrelated individuals.

habendum clause That part of a deed beginning with the words "to have and to hold" following the granting clause and defining the extent of ownership the grantor is conveying.

hazardous substances Materials such as chemicals, industrial and residential by-products, biological waste, and other pollutants that pose an actual or suspected threat to human health, quality of life, and the environment.

headers Horizontal supports above doors and windows.

heat pump Mechanism that uses heat from outside air to reduce heating and air-conditioning costs.

hectare Land measurement equivalent to 10,000 square meters, or approximately 2.471 acres.

heir One who might inherit or succeed to an interest in land under the state law of descent when the owner dies without leaving a valid will.

highest and best use That possible use of land that would produce the greatest net income and thereby develop the highest land value.

holder of unsold shares A holder of unsold shares is any person or legal entity designated by the original sponsor to be a holder of these shares. A holder of unsold shares receives benefits similar to those of the sponsor; these include the ability to sell the shares to anyone without the board's consent and the unlimited ability to sublease the unit to any individual without the board's consent.

holding period The time an investment or asset is possessed.

holdover tenancy A tenancy whereby a lessee retains possession of leased property after his or her lease has expired and the landlord, by continuing to accept rent, agrees to the tenant's continued occupancy.

holographic will A will that is written, dated, and signed in the testator's handwriting but is not witnessed.

home equity loan A loan (sometimes called a *line of credit*) under which a property owner uses his or her residence as collateral and can then draw funds up to a prearranged amount against the property.

home inspectors Licensed professionals who conduct a thorough visual survey of a property's structure, systems, and site conditions and prepare an analytical report that is valuable to both purchasers and homeowners.

home occupations Small business or creative activities, allowed to residents in an area otherwise zoned entirely residential.

homeowners' association A nonprofit group of homeowners in a condominium, cooperative, or planned unit development (PUD) that administers common elements and enforces covenants, conditions, and restrictions.

homeowners' insurance policy A standardized package insurance policy that covers a residential real estate owner against financial loss from fire, theft, public liability, and other commercial risks.

homestead Land that is owned and occupied as the family home. The right to protect a portion of the value of this land from unsecured judgments for debts.

household income Income earned by any lawful occupant housed within the stabilized unit.

house rules The cooperative's habitation rules that govern all shareholders are known as house rules.

HVAC Heating, ventilation, and air-conditioning systems.

hypothecation This occurs when the borrower pledges the property without giving up ownership or possession of the property.

illiquidity Refers to the difficulty in selling an asset for full value on short notice (lack of assets that can be quickly converted to cash).

impact fees Charges levied by a local government to help the community absorb the public costs involved in the development of a new subdivision.

implied agency An agency established not by words, but by the actions of the parties.

implied contract A contract under which the agreement of the parties is demonstrated by their acts and conduct.

implied creation of a subagency The unintended creation of a fiduciary relationship through an informal cooperation arrangement between brokers.

implied warranty of habitability A theory in landlord/tenant law in which the landlord renting residential property implies that the property is habitable and fit for its intended use.

improvement Any structure erected on a site to enhance the value of the property—buildings, fences, driveways, curbs, sidewalks, or sewers.

imputed interest An IRS concept that treats some concessionary low-interest loans as if they had been paid and collected at a statutory rate.

income capitalization approach The process of estimating the value of an income-producing property by capitalization of the annual net income expected to be produced by the property during its remaining useful life.

incompetent A person who is unable to manage his or her own affairs by reason of insanity, imbecility, or feeblemindedness.

independent contractor Someone retained to perform a certain act but subject to the control and direction of another only as to the end result and not as to the way in which he or she performs the act; contrasted with employee.

index With an adjustable-rate mortgage, a measure of current interest rates, used as a basis for calculating the new rate at the time of adjustment.

index lease A lease in which the rental figure is adjusted periodically according to the government's cost-of-living index.

indirect costs Construction expenses for items other than labor and materials (e.g., financing costs, taxes, administrative costs, contractor's overhead and profit, legal fees, interest payments, insurance costs during construction, and lease-up costs).

industrial real estate Warehouses, factories, land in industrial districts, and research facilites (sometimes referred to as *manufacturing property*).

inflation The gradual reduction of the purchasing power of the dollar, usually related directly to the increases in the money supply by the federal government.

informed consent Agreement to an act based on the full and fair disclosure of all the facts a reasonable person would need in order to make a rational decision.

infrastructure Basic public works such as utilities, roads, bridges, sewer and water systems, etc.

inheritance tax New York State tax levied on those who inherit property located in the state.

injunction An order issued by a court to restrain one party from doing an act deemed to be unjust to the rights of some other party.

in rem A proceeding against the realty directly as distinguished from a proceeding against a person.

installment contract *See* land contract.

installment sale A method of reporting income received from the sale of real estate when the sales price is paid in two or more installments over two or more years.

instrument A written legal document created to effect the rights of the parties.

insulation Material that protects a surface from cold or heat.

insured value Used to determine the amount of insurance carried on the property.

interest A charge made by a lender for the use of money. Also, a legal share of ownership in property, whether the entire ownership or partial.

interest-only mortgage Mortgage in which monthly payments cover only the interest due and offer no debt reduction.

interest rate The percentage of a sum of money charged for its use.

interim financing A short-term loan usually made during the construction phase of a building project (in this case often referred to as a *construction loan*).

internal rate of return (IRR) Discount rate that, when applied to both positive and negative cash flows, results in zero net present value.

Interstate Land Sales Full Disclosure Act A federal law that regulates the sale of certain real estate in interstate commerce.

intestate The condition of a property owner who dies without leaving a valid will.

involuntary alienation Transfer of real estate without the owner's initiative, as in foreclosure or condemnation.

involuntary bankruptcy A bankruptcy proceeding initiated by one or more of the debtor's creditors.

involuntary lien A lien imposed against property without consent of the owners, i.e., taxes, special assessments.

irrevocable consent An agreement filed by an out-of-state broker stating that suits and actions may be brought against the broker in the state where a license is sought.

IRV formula The relationship among Interest, Rate, and Value.

jalousie window A window that is formed by horizontal slats of glass that open or close vertically by the action of a gear.

joint tenancy Ownership of real estate between two or more parties who have been named in one conveyance as joint tenants. On the death of a joint tenant, his or her interest passes to the surviving joint tenant or tenants.

joint venture The joining of two or more people to conduct a specific business enterprise.

joist and rafter roof Roofing system that relies on sloping timbers supported by a ridge board and made rigid by interconnecting joists.

judgment The formal decision of a court regarding the respective claims of the parties to an action.

jumbo loan A loan that exceeds FNMA and FHLMC maximum loan limits.

junior lien An obligation such as a second mortgage that is subordinate in priority to an existing lien on the same realty.

kickbacks The return of part of the commission as gifts or money to buyers or sellers.

laches Loss of a legal right through undue delay in asserting it.

Lally™ columns Upright columns that support the main beams of a building.

land The earth's surface, extending downward to the center of the earth and upward infinitely into space.

land contract *See* contract for deed.

landfill A site for the burial, layering, and permanent storage of waste material, consisting of alternating layers of waste and topsoil.

landlord One who rents property to another.

land patents Document the transfer of land ownership from the federal government to individuals.

last will and testament An instrument executed by an owner to convey the owner's property to specific persons after the owner's death.

latent defects A hidden defect that is not discoverable by ordinary inspection.

law of agency The law that governs the relationships and duties of agents, clients, and customers. *See also* agent.

lead agency In an environmental survey, the one agency that coordinates the process.

lead poisoning Illness, including the impairment of physical and mental development in children and aggravated blood pressure in adults, resulting from the ingestion of lead toxins, primarily in paint or plumbing.

Leaking Underground Storage Tanks (LUST) Federal environmental protection program to protect the nation's groundwater by identifying underground tanks and preventing or correcting leakage of hazardous materials.

lease A written or oral contract between a landlord (the lessor) and a tenant (the lessee) that transfers the right to exclusive possession and use of the landlord's real property to the lesaee for a specified period of time and for a stated consideration (rent).

lease escalation clause The lease escalation clause is used to protect the commercial property owner against the increased cost in operations that arises from inflation.

leasehold estate A tenant's right to occupy real estate during the term of a lease; generally considered personal property.

legacy A disposition of money or personal property by will.

legal description A description of a specific parcel of real estate complete enough for an independent surveyor to locate and identify it.

legality of object The requirement that a valid and enforceable contract may not involve an illegal purpose or one that is against public policy.

lender's rebate A partial refund following a purchase that involves a loan.

lessee Tenant.

lessor Landlord.

letter of intent A vehicle to reserve a specific unit or units and sets forth an understanding of the terms of the transaction between the sponsor and prospective purchaser.

leverage The use of borrowed money to finance the bulk of an investment.

levy The placing of tax liens against real property.

liability insurance Standard package homeowners' insurance policy coverage for personal injuries to others resulting from the insured's acts or negligence; voluntary medical payments and funeral expenses for accidents sustained by guests or resident employees on the property and physical damage to other's property.

license (1) A privilege or right granted to a person by a state to operate as a real estate broker or salesperson. (2) The revocable permission for a temporary use of land.

lien A right given by law to certain creditors to have their debt paid out of the property of a defaulting debtor, usually by means of a court sale.

lien theory Some states interpret a mortgage as being purely a lien on real property. The mortgagee thus has no right of possession but must foreclose the lien and sell the property if the mortgagor defaults.

life estate An interest in real or personal property that is limited in duration to the lifetime of its owner or some other designated person.

life tenant A person in possession of a life estate.

like-kind exchange An exchange of property for property as opposed to property for money.

limited liability company (LLC) A hybrid business entity that combines the managerial freedom of partnerships with the limited liability for owner and avoidance of income taxes offered by corporations.

limited partnership *See* partnership.

liquidated damages An amount of money, agreed to in advance, that will serve as the total compensation due to the injured party if the other does not comply with the contract's terms.

liquidity The ability to sell an asset and convert it into cash at a price close to its true value in a short period of time.

lis pendens A recorded legal document giving constructive notice that an action affecting a particular property has been filed in court.

listing agent The broker with whom a seller enters into a valid listing agreement for the sale of his or her real estate.

listing agreement A contract between a landowner (as principal) and a licensed real estate broker (as agent) by which the broker is employed as agent to sell real estate on the owner's terms within a given time, for which service the landowner agrees to pay a commission or fee.

listing broker The agent hired by a property owner to assist in the marketing of real estate.

litigation Lawsuits.

littoral rights (1) A landowner's claim to use water in large navigable lakes and oceans adjacent to his or her property. (2) The ownership rights to land bordering these bodies of water up to the high-water mark.

LLP A limited liability partnership.

loan servicing The lender's duties in administering a loan, such as collecting payments, accounting and bookkeeping, maintaining records, and issuing loan status reports to the borrower.

loan-to-value (LTV) ratio The relationship between the amount of the mortgage loan and the market value of the real estate being pledged as collateral.

locational obsolescence A form of external obsolescence; a reduction of property value resulting from conditions outside the property.

long-term gains Any gains that result from a sale where the property was held for one year or more.

loyalty The fiduciary duty that requires an agent to put the principal's interest above all others, including the agent's.

maintenance This is defined as the general upkeep of a property.

management agreement Employment contract between property owner and manager, under which the manager assumes the responsibility for administering and maintaining the property as the owner's general agent.

management proposal A property manager's report to the owner of his or her plan for supervising the property.

margin With an adjustable-rate mortgage, the number of points over an *index* at which the interest rate is set.

marginal tax rate Percentage at which the last dollar of income is taxed; top tax bracket.

marital status A protected class under New York State law that does not allow sellers or landlords to base decisions on whether prospective occupants are married or not.

marketable title Good or clear title reasonably free from the risk of litigation over possible defects.

market allocation An agreement among members of a trade to refrain from competition in specific areas.

market analysis Study undertaken by a property manager of the local and regional market, as well as the underlying property itself, to provide information about the economic conditions, supply, demand, and similar competing properties.

market data approach *See* direct sales comparison approach.

market price The actual selling price of a property.

market value The probable price a ready, willing, able, and informed buyer would pay and a ready, willing, able, and informed seller would accept, neither being under any pressure to act.

master plan A comprehensive plan to guide the long-term physical development of a particular area.

maximum base rent (MBR) Under rent control, the maximum rent allowable for an individual unit.

mechanic's lien A statutory lien created in favor of contractors, laborers, and material suppliers who have performed work or furnished materials in the erection or repair of a building.

mediation Method for dealing with disputes; the person running the session does not make a determination, but rather brings the parties into agreement.

meeting of the minds An essential component of a valid contract, a "meeting of the minds" occurs when all parties agree to the exact terms.

memorandum of sale A nonbinding information sheet prepared by brokers in some New York localities that states the essential terms of the agreement; the final contract is later drawn up by an attorney.

metes-and-bounds description A legal description of a parcel of land that begins at a well-marked point and follows the boundaries, using direction and distances around the tract, back to the place of beginning.

Metropolitan Transport Authority (MTA) Regional agency with taxing power and jurisdiction over certain air and land rights.

mill One-tenth of one cent. A tax rate of 52 mills would be $0.052 tax for each dollar of assessed valuation of a property.

minimum building standards Degree of quality and care mandated by the state; local codes and regulations may require adherence to a higher standard.

minor A person under 18 years of age.

MIP Mortgage insurance premium.

misdemeanor A crime less than a felony but greater than a violation.

misrepresentation   A false statement or concealment of a material fact made with the intent of causing another party to act.

mold   Natural organism, a fungus, that grows in damp area; sometimes toxic.

monoline policy   This policy provides only one line or area of coverage. It bears greater relevancy to insurers than to the insured.

month-to-month tenancy   A periodic tenancy; that is, the tenant rents for one period at a time. In the absence of a rental agreement (oral or written), a tenancy is generally considered to be month to month.

monument   A fixed natural or artificial object used to establish real estate boundaries for a metes-and-bounds description.

moratorium   A period of delay; in real estate usually refers to a community's temporary halt to development.

mortgage   A conditional transfer or pledge of real estate as security for the payment of a debt. Also, the document creating a mortgage lien.

mortgage bankers   Companies that are licensed to make real estate loans that are sold to investors.

mortgage broker   An individual who acts as an intermediary between lenders and borrowers for a fee.

mortgage commitment   The process in which a lender issues a loan commitment letter to the borrower to demonstrate willingness to fund the loan.

mortgage contingency clause   A common provision that allows the buyer a certain period of time to obtain a commitment for financing at a specified interest rate for a certain amount of money. It usually lasts for 30 to 60 days, depending on the average time needed to obtain a loan commitment.

mortgage debt service   Property owner's expense for payments (usually monthly) on mortgages.

mortgagee   A lender in a mortgage loan transaction.

mortgage insurance premium (MIP)   Lump sum premium for mortgage insurance coverage, payable either in cash at closing or financed over the mortgage term.

mortgage lien   A lien or charge on the property of a mortgagor that secures the underlying debt obligations.

mortgage reduction certificate   An instrument executed by the mortgagee setting forth the present status and the balance due on the mortgage as of the date of the execution of the instrument.

mortgage value   Normally established by appraisal, it represents the amount or value that the lender is willing to commit to the loan. It is also the difference between the buyers initial equity investment (down-payment) and the purchase price or appraised value of the property, whichever is less.

mortgagor   A borrower who conveys his or her property as security for a loan.

multiperil policies   Insurance policies offering protection from a range of potential perils, such as fire, hazard, public liability, and casualty, in a single policy.

multiple listing service   A marketing organization composed of member brokers who agree to share their listings with one another in the hope of procuring ready, willing, and able buyers more quickly and efficiently.

negative amortization   Gradual building up of a large mortgage debt when payments are not sufficient to cover interest due and reduce the principal.

negative cash flow   Negative figure resulting when expenditures on an investment exceed the income it produces.

negligence   An unintentional tort caused by failure to exercise reasonable care.

negotiable instrument   A signed promise to pay a sum of money.

neighborhood analysis   A property manager's study of nearby rental availability and market rental figures.

net lease   A lease requiring that the tenant pay not only rent but also some or all costs of maintaining the property, including taxes, insurance, utilities, and repairs.

net listing   A listing based on the net price the seller will receive if the property is sold. Under a net listing the broker is free to offer the property for sale at any price to increase the commission. Outlawed in New York.

net operating income (NOI)   The income projected for an income-producing property after deducting losses for vacancy and collection and operating expenses.

net present value (NPV)   Difference between the present value of all positive and negative cash flows.

New York City Department of Environmental Protection (DEP)   Local agency with authority over the city's water supply (from its source to local reservoirs), and which ensures that construction projects do not interfere with the watershed.

New York General Obligations Law   The state's version of the Statute of Frauds, which requires, among other provisions, that any agreements relating to the sale of real estate must be in writing.

New York Human Rights Law   State law prohibiting discrimination in housing.

New York State Division of Human Rights   Agency with which a complaint of housing discrimination may file a complaint within one year of the alleged act.

New York State Lawyers' Fund   The New York State Lawyers' Fund was created in 1982. Its primary mission and purpose is the protection of legal consumers from the dishonest conduct in the practice of law.

nonconforming mortgage   Flexible loan that does not meet standard uniform underwriting requirements, usually structured for borrowers who have unique credit situations or who wish to purchase an unusual property.

nonconforming use   Use of land that is not allowed by the local zoning ordinance.

noneviction plan   Method of converting a rental property into a condominium or cooperative.

nonhomestead   Not used as the owner's primary residence: buildings with more than four dwelling units, industrial and commercial property, and most vacant land.

nonhomogeneity   A lack of uniformity; dissimilarity. Because no two parcels of land are exactly alike, real estate is said to be nonhomogeneous.

nonsolicitation order   A directive to all real estate brokers and real estate salespersons to refrain from soliciting listings for the sale of residential property within a designated geographic area. The types of solicitation that are prohibited include but are not limited to letters, postcards, telephone calls, door-to-door calls, handbills, and postings in public areas.

notary public   A public officer who is authorized to take acknowledgments to certain classes of documents such as deeds, contracts, and mortgages and before whom affidavits may be sworn.

note   An instrument of credit given to attest a debt.

notice   Information available through the public records or through inspection of property. Also, notification by landlord or tenant of intention to terminate a rental.

notice of pending legal action   *See* lis pendens.

novation   Substituting a new obligation for an old one or substituting new parties to an existing obligation.

nuisance   An act that disturbs another's peaceful enjoyment of property.

NYSAR   New York State Association of Realtors®.

obedience   The agent's fiduciary duty to obey all lawful instructions of the principal.

obsolescence   *See* external obsolescence; functional obsolescence.

offer and acceptance   Two essential components of a valid contract; a "meeting of the minds," when all parties agree to the exact terms.

offering statement/plan   A document that is created and issued by a sponsor that is either in the process of converting a building or developing a new building. Its purpose is to provide an interested party with full disclosure of all facts pertinent to the project.

office property   Any type of structure (lowrise, highrise, complex, or campus) used by nonmanufacturing, nonretail tenants such as medical, legal, and financial professionals.

open-end mortgage   A mortgage loan that is expandable to a maximum dollar amount, the loan being secured by the same original mortgage.

open listing   A listing contract under which the broker's commission is contingent on the broker's producing a ready, willing, and able buyer before the property is sold by the owner or another broker.

operating budget   A property manager's detailed plan for expenses.

OPRHP   New York State's Office of Parks, Recreation, and Historic Preservation.

option   An agreement to keep open for a set period an offer to sell or purchase property.

option to renew   Provision of a lease giving the tenant the right to extend the lease for an additional period of time on set terms.

other income (OI)   Income that is not derived from the main activity of the property.

overall capitalization rate (OAR)   A figure that estimates value by comparing capitalization rate to income.

package loan   A real estate loan used to finance the purchase of both real property and personal property, such as the purchase of a new home that includes carpeting, window coverings, and major appliances.

package mortgage   A method of financing in which the loan that finances the purchase of a home also finances the purchase of items of personal property such as appliances.

package policy   One policy that provides for a variety of different coverage types.

parcel   A specific piece of real estate.

parol evidence rule   A rule of evidence providing that a written agreement is the final expression of the agreement of the parties, not to be varied or contradicted by prior or contemporaneous oral or written negotiations.

participation financing   A mortgage in which the lender participates in the income of the mortgaged venture.

participation loan   A mortgage arrangement in which the lender receives a share of the venture's profits or the real estate's appreciation.

partition   The division of real property made between those who own it in undivided shares.

partnership   An association of two or more individuals who carry on a continuing business for profit as co-owners. A *general partnership* is a typical form of joint venture in which each general partner shares in the administration, profits, and losses of the operations. A *limited partnership* is administered by one or more general partners and funded by limited or silent partners who are by law responsible for losses only to the extent of their investments.

party wall A wall that is located on or at a boundary line between two adjoining parcels of land and is used by the owners of both properties.

passive income Income derived from an investment activity in which the investor does not take an active management or participatory role.

percentage lease A lease commonly used for commercial property whose rental is based on the tenant's gross sales at the premises.

percolation The soil's ability to process water.

percolation rate A figure establishing how quickly liquid can drain through the ground.

percolation test A test to see if a septic tank will work successfully in a specific location.

periodic estate An interest in leased property that continues from period to period—week to week, month to month, or year to year.

periodic lease A lease with has no specific ending date. Generally these leases are month-to-month. A periodic lease (also known as a periodic tenancy or period estate) is automatically renewed each time the tenant pays rent to the landlord.

personal property Items, called *chattels*, that do not fit into the definition of real property; movable objects.

personal property law That section of the law dealing with chattels.

personal representative The administrator or executor appointed to handle the estate of a decedent.

physical deterioration Loss of value due to wear and tear or action of the elements.

pier and beam foundation Foundation style in which partly submerged columns (piers) support the foundation slab, with an air pocket (crawlspace) between the slab and the ground.

pitch Slope of a roof expressed as a ratio of height to span.

PITI Principal, interest, taxes, and insurance: components of a regular mortgage payment.

planned unit development (PUD) A planned combination of diverse land uses such as housing, recreation, and shopping in one contained development or subdivision.

planning board Municipal body overseeing orderly development of real estate.

plasterboard/wallboard Prepared 4' by 8' boards often used as wall finish in place of plaster.

plat A map of a town, section, or subdivision indicating the location and boundaries of individual properties.

platform framing construction Common form of construction for one- and two-story residential buildings; one floor is built at a time, with the lower floor providing a platform on which the upper floor is built.

plat of subdivision A map of a planned subdivision, entered in the public records.

plottage The increase in value or utility resulting from the consolidation (assemblage) of two or more adjacent lots into one larger lot.

PMI Private mortgage insurance.

POB *See* point of beginning.

pocket card Copy of a real estate license, issued by the Department of State, to be carried in the licensee's wallet.

point A unit of measurement used for various loan charges; one point equals 1 percent of the amount of the loan. *See also* discount points.

point of beginning In a metes-and-bounds legal description, the starting point of the survey, situated in one corner of the parcel. Also called *place of beginning*.

police power The government's right to impose laws, statutes, and ordinances, including zoning ordinances and building codes, to protect the public health, safety, and welfare.

policy and procedures guide A broker's compilation of guidelines for the conduct of the firm's business.

pollution Artificially created environmental impurity.

polychlorinated biphenyls (PCBs) Potentially hazardous chemical used in electrical equipment, principally transformers.

portfolio income Any income derived from items such as dividends received through ownership stock, interest received from any source, and royalties received on intellectual property.

portfolio loan Mortgage loan not intended for sale on the secondary market; nonconforming loan.

possessory/nonpossessory rights Indicates and implies certain rights inherent to the occupant (possessory) or no rights to the property if person does not occupy the property. Easements fall into the category of nonpossessory rights or interests within land owned by another.

post-and-beam construction An old framing method in which ceiling planks are placed on beams (often left exposed).

potential gross income (PGI) The gross rent roll or gross receipts attributable through rental activities if a property is 100 percent leased.

potentially responsible parties (PRPs) Under Superfund, the landowners suspected of contaminating a property.

power of attorney A written instrument authorizing a person, the *attorney-in-fact*, to act as agent on behalf of another person.

preapplication Process of preapproval of the borrower.

preapproval loan A pending loan in which all of the underlying documents are in file and there is a strong probability that there are no credit or income issues stopping the loan from closing.

precedent A court decision that serves as authority for later cases.

preliminary prospectus Description of new or converted condominium or cooperative property, subject to change, available for inspection by present tenants after review by the attorney general (also referred to as a *red herring*).

premises Lands and tenements; an estate; the subject matter of a conveyance.

prepaid item A bill paid by the seller for something the buyer will benefit from: the coming year's property taxes, for example. Buyer will reimburse seller at closing for the unused portion.

prepayment clause A clause in a mortgage that gives the mortgagor the privilege of paying the mortgage indebtedness before it becomes due.

prepayment premium (penalty) A charge imposed on a borrower who pays off the loan principal early.

prequalification Refers to a pending loan in which a mortgage broker believes that, based on a preliminary interview and a credit report, the borrower will probably (subject to verification) be able to meet the loan requirements of a lender—assuming the borrower is telling the truth about his or her financial situation and income status.

present value of money Money's value changes over time. For example, the present value of $1 receivable in one year is $1 minus the lost potential interest on the dollar. If the interest rate is 7 percent, then the present value of $1 to be received in one year is 93¢ today.

preventive maintenance Maintenance done to avoid possible future damage.

price-fixing An agreement between members of a trade to artificially maintain prices at a set level.

primary mortgage market Lenders who make loans directly to real estate borrowers.

primary residence The location where a taxpayer has resided for at least two out of the previous five years prior to the sale of the property; in addition, the residence must be used as the primary place of residence (when the taxpayer files his or her income tax return).

principal (1) A sum lent or employed as a fund or an investment as distinguished from its income or profits. (2) The original amount (as in a loan) of the total due and payable at a certain date. (3) A main party of a transaction; the person for whom the agent works.

principal broker *See* supervising broker.

priority The order of position or time.

private mortgage insurance (PMI) Insurance that limits a lender's potential loss in a mortgage default, issued by a private company rather than by the FHA.

probate To establish the will of a deceased person.

procuring cause of sale The effort that brings about the desired result. Under an open listing the broker who is the procuring cause of the sale receives the commission.

professional home inspections Examination of a property's structure and systems performed by a trained professional for either prospective buyers, lenders, or home owners.

pro forma statement Financial statement showing what is expected to occur, particularly with income property.

progression Economic principle that a lower-quality property's worth will be enhanced by its proximity to higher-quality properties.

property analysis A property manager's examination of leases and rental rates.

property maintenance The care and work put into a building to keep it in operation and general repair. Contrasted with permanent improvements.

property management report A property manager's regular report to the owner.

property manager An individual who manages real estate for another person for compensation. A property manager's job is to maximize income while maintaining the value of the property. Thus, the property manager is closely involved in a variety of activities related to generating income, including budgeting, market analysis, advertising, and negotiating leases.

proprietary lease A written lease in a cooperative apartment building, held by the tenant/shareholder, giving the right to occupy a particular unit.

prorations Expenses, either prepaid or paid in arrears, that are divided or distributed between buyer and seller at the closing.

prospectus A printed statement disclosing all material aspects of a real estate project.

protected classes Groups of individuals who have been found to be in need of protection by federal, state, or local laws and regulations against discriminatory actions or conditions.

public grant A transfer of land by a government body to a private individual.

public offering A transaction falling under the jurisdiction of the New York attorney general's office, requiring certain specific transactional and financial disclosures. The sale of any form of shared housing in New York is a public offering.

public records Each company's collection of documents affecting the title to real property; filed documents affecting real estate, maintained by county officials and open to inspection by anyone who is interested.

PUD *See* planned unit development.

puffing Exaggerated or superlative comments or opinions not made as representations of fact and thus not grounds for misrepresentation.

pur autre vie For the life of another. A life estate pur autre vie is a life estate that is measured by the life of a person other than the grantee.

purchase-money mortgage (PMM) A note secured by a mortgage or deed of trust given by a buyer, as borrower, to a seller, as lender, as part of the purchase price of the real estate.

pyramid Investment strategy of refinancing existing properties and using the borrowed money.

qualified intermediary The hired entity that facilitates a like-kind exchange on behalf of the property owner/taxpayer.

quiet enjoyment The right of an owner or a person legally in possession to the use of property without interference of possession.

quiet title suit *See* suit to quiet title.

quitclaim deed A conveyance by which the grantor transfers whatever interest he or she has in the real estate, if any, without warranties or obligations.

radioactive waste Hazardous by-product of uses of radioactive materials in energy production, medicine, and scientific research.

radon gas Odorless, naturally occurring radioactive gas that becomes hazardous when trapped and accumulated in unventilated areas of buildings. Long-term exposure to radon is suspected of causing lung cancer.

rate lock A promise on the part of a lender that the mortgage loan will carry a specific interest rate, regardless of the prevailing rates when the loan is closed.

rate of return The ratio between earnings and the cost of the investment.

ratification The situation in which a party is prevented by his or her own acts from taking a different position because it would cause detriment to another party.

ready, willing, and able buyer One who is prepared to buy property on the seller's terms and is ready to take positive steps to consummate the transaction.

real estate A portion of the earth's surface extending downward to the center of the earth and upward infinitely into space, including all things permanently attached thereto, whether by nature or by a person.

real estate broker Any person, partnership, association, or corporation that sells (or offers to sell), buys (or offers to buy), or negotiates the purchase, sale, or exchange of real estate, or that leases (or offers to lease) or rents (or offers to rent) any real estate or the improvements thereon for others and for a compensation or valuable consideration.

real estate investment syndicate Business organization in which individuals combine their resources to invest in, manage, or develop a particular property.

real estate investment trust (REIT) Trust ownership of real estate by a group of individuals who purchase certificates of ownership in the trust.

real estate mortgage investment conduit (REMIC) A tax vehicle created by the Tax Reform Act of 1986 that permits certain entities that deal in pools of mortgages to pass income through to investors.

real estate sales contract A contract for the sale of real estate, in which the purchaser promises to pay the agreed purchase price and the seller agrees to deliver title to the property.

real estate salesperson A person licensed by the state to assist a licensed broker in the field of real estate.

Real Estate Settlement Procedures Act (RESPA) The federal law that requires certain disclosures to consumers about mortgage loan settlements. The law also prohibits the payment or receipt of kickbacks and certain kinds of referral fees.

real property Real estate plus all the interests, benefits, and rights inherent in ownership. Often referred to as *real estate*.

Real Property Law New York law governing the real estate profession, including prohibitions against discrimination in housing.

real property tax rates Represent the ratio of tax dollars charged in either per hundred or per thousand dollars of assessed valuation. Tax rates are also referred to as "mill rates."

REALTORS® A registered trademark term reserved for the sole use of active members of local REALTOR® boards affiliated with the National Association of REALTORS®.

reasonable care A broker's duty to perform duties properly.

receiver of taxes Party or entity that is charged with the collection of real property taxes on all properties contained within the assessment roll.

reciprocity An arrangement by which states agree to honor each other's licenses, as with real estate salespersons or brokers.

recognition agreement A document signed by the borrower, lender, and co-op board. The signature by the co-op acknowledges the lending party's lien interest in the shares covered by the unit. These agreements normally call for the cooperative to notify the lender of any default by the shareholder/borrower (such as the nonpayment of maintenance fees).

reconciliation The final step in the appraisal process, in which the appraiser weighs the estimates of value received from the direct sales comparison, cost, and income approaches to arrive at a final estimate of value for the subject property.

recording The act of entering or recording documents affecting or conveying interests in real estate in the recorder's office established in each county.

record of association A broker's report to the state about sponsorship of a salesperson or associate broker.

rectangular survey system A system established in 1785 by the federal government providing for surveying and describing land outside the 13 original colonies by reference to principal meridians and base lines.

redemption period A period of time established by state law during which a property owner has the right to redeem his or her real estate from a tax sale by paying the sales price, interest, and costs.

red herring Preliminary offering plan for a cooperative or condominium project submitted to the attorney general and to tenants and subject to modification.

redlining The illegal practice of a lending institution denying loans or restricting their number for certain areas of a community.

reduction certificate A statement from the lender detailing the amount remaining and currently due on a mortgage, usually sought when a mortgage is being assumed or prepaid (also referred to as an *estoppel certificate*).

referee's deed A deed delivered when property is conveyed pursuant to court order.

reference to a plat A form of legal description, which cites the book and page on which the subject property can be identified on a map.

regional analysis Study of the economic and demographic character of the larger regional or metropolitan area in which a property is located.

regression Economic principle that the worth of a higher-quality property will be diminished by its proximity to lower-quality properties.

Regulation Z Law requiring credit institutions and advertisers to inform borrowers of the true cost of obtaining credit; commonly called the *Truth-in-Lending Act*.

release The act or writing by which some claim or interest is surrendered to another.

release clause A mortgage clause that permits part of the mortgaged property to be released from the lien; often used with blanket mortgages.

remainder The remnant of an estate that has been conveyed to take effect and be enjoyed after the termination of a prior estate, as when an owner conveys a life estate to one party and the remainder to another.

remainder interest The remnant of an estate that has been conveyed to take effect and be enjoyed after the termination of a prior estate, such as when an owner conveys a life estate to one party and the remainder to another.

remainderman The person who is to receive the property after the death of a life tenant.

rent A fixed, periodic payment made by a tenant of a property to the owner for possession and use, usually by prior agreement of the parties.

rentable area The total area or square footage of a floor or unit of space in an office building (as determined by the property owner) to be used for the purposes of calculating the annual rent.

rent control State or local regulations restricting the amount of rent that may be charged for particular properties.

rent roll A rent roll shows the name of each tenant, amount of rent, expiration date of each lease, and amount of security deposits.

rent stabilization Local regulations that stem from the adoption of the Emergency Tenant Protection Act, and that limit maximum allowable rent increases.

replacement cost The construction cost at current prices of a property that is not necessarily an exact duplicate of the subject property but serves the same purpose or function as the original.

reproduction cost The construction cost at current prices of an exact duplicate of the subject property.

rescission The canceling of a contract.

reserves Money set aside to accumulate for future expenses.

reserves for replacements Available cash on hand to effectuate any anticipated or unanticipated major capital improvement to the property; for example, a new roof, new mechanical equipment, or façade restoration.

residential property Real estate used as a dwelling.

residential real estate All property used for housing, from acreage to small city lots, both single-family and multifamily, in urban, suburban, and rural areas.

residential transaction Any transaction involving the sale or rental of a building that contains four or fewer units intended for dwelling purposes.

resident manager A property manager who resides on the site.

restraint of trade The unreasonable restriction of business activities as the result of the cooperation or conspiracy of members of the trade.

restriction A limitation on the use of real property, generally originated by the owner or subdivider in a deed.

restrictive covenant Provisions placed in a deed by the grantor, restricting future uses for the property.

retail property Any type of property used for commercial retail purposes, including storefronts, shopping centers, and enclosed malls.

return The income from a real estate investment, calculated as a percentage of cash invested.

reverse mortgage A loan under which the homeowner receives monthly payments based on his or her accumulated equity rather than a lump sum. The loan must be repaid at a prearranged date or upon the death of the owner or the sale of the property.

reverse discrimination *(benign discrimination)* Housing discrimination, usually based on quotas, designed by a municipality to achieve a racial balance perceived as desirable.

reversion The remnant of an estate that the grantor holds after he or she has granted a life estate to another person, if the estate will return, or revert, to the grantor; also called a *reverter*.

reversionary interest The remnant of an estate that the grantor holds after he or she has granted a life estate to another person, if the estate will return, or revert, to the grantor; also called a *reverter*.

reversionary right The return of the rights of possession and quiet enjoyment to the lessor at the expiration of a lease.

revocation An act of recalling a power of authority conferred, such as the revocation of a power of attorney, a license, or an agency.

rider An amendment or attachment to a contract.

right of first refusal A provision that a condominium or cooperative association has the first right to purchase if a member wishes to sell his or her unit.

right of survivorship *See* joint tenancy.

right-of-way The right to pass over another's land more or less frequently according to the nature of the easement.

riparian rights An owner's rights in land that borders on or includes a stream, river, or lake. These rights include access to and use of the water.

risk management The evaluation and selection of appropriate property and other insurance.

R-value Numerical measurement of insulating material's resistance to heat transfer; a higher R-value indicates superior insulation.

Safe Drinking Water Act Federal law requiring local public water suppliers to periodically test the quality of drinking water.

sale-leaseback A transaction in which an owner sells his or her improved property and, as part of the same transaction, signs a long-term lease to remain in possession of the premises.

sales comparison approach The process of estimating the value of a property by examining and comparing actual sales of comparable properties.

sales contract A contract containing the complete terms of the agreement between buyer and seller for the sale of a particular parcel of real estate.

salesperson A person who performs real estate activities while employed by or associated with a licensed real estate broker.

SARA The federal Superfund Amendments and Reauthorization Act, concerned with environmental cleanups.

satisfaction of mortgage *See* satisfaction piece.

satisfaction piece A document provided by the mortgagee, stating that the debt has been paid off. A document acknowledging the payment of a debt. Also called *satisfaction of mortgage*.

S corporation A form of corporation taxed as a partnership.

secondary mortgage market A market for the purchase and sale of existing mortgages, designed to provide greater liquidity of mortgages.

section A portion of a township under the rectangular survey (government survey) system. A section is a square with mile-long sides and an area of one square mile, or 640 acres.

Section 8 Federal housing assistance program administered by the FHA, in which low- and moderate-income tenants pay a fixed portion of their income in rent, with HUD paying the remainder.

Section 1031 property exchange A tax-deferred exchange of like-kind investment or commercial property.

security agreement   A document pledging personal property as security for a debt.

security deposit   A payment by a tenant, held by the landlord during the lease term and kept (wholly or partially) on default or destruction of the premises by the tenant.

seisin   The possession of land by one who claims to own at least an estate for life therein.

self-dealing   The act of a broker who lists property and then buys it and collects the agreed-on commission.

seller agency   The practice of representing the seller in a real estate transaction.

seller's agent   Broker or agent who advises seller on a fair listing price, gives hints how the seller can enhance the marketability of the house, and shows property to several buyers.

selling broker   The broker who successfully finds a ready, willing, and able buyer for a property (may or may not be the listing broker).

sensitivity analysis   Analysis of a projected investment, to discover which variable is most significant in anticipated cash flow.

septic system   Wastewater treatment and disposal system used by individual households.

SEQRA   New York's State Environmental Quality Review Act, requiring environmental impact statements before certain development projects.

servient estate   Land on which an easement exists in favor of an adjacent property (called a *dominant estate*).

setback   The amount of space local zoning regulations require between a lot line and a building line.

severalty   Ownership of real property by one person only; also called *sole ownership*.

shared-appreciation mortgage   A mortgage loan in which the lender, in exchange for a loan with a favorable interest rate, participates in the profits (if any) when the property is eventually sold.

shared-equity mortgage   A loan in which the lender will receive part of any appreciation on the property.

share loan   An agreement entered into by a borrower and a lender to finance the borrower's acquisition of the borrower's cooperative interest.

sheathing   Material applied to framing members to form walls, often plywood, insulating material, or sheetrock.

Sherman (and Clayton) Antitrust Acts   Federal legislation prohibiting business practices that limit competition.

sick building syndrome (SBS)   Range of symptoms, such as asthma, coughing, and hoarseness, that are related to the individual's presence in the affected building, but that disappear when he or she is not exposed to the building's environment. *See* building-related illness.

siding   Exterior wall finish of a building: commonly brick, shingles, or clapboard, wood or vinyl.

silent partner   One who takes no part in managing the enterprise, and whose possible losses are usually limited to his or her investment.

sill plates   Horizontal supports on top of the foundation.

single agency   An agency relationship in which the agent represents a single party.

situs   The location of a property.

slab-on-grade construction   Concrete slab poured on prepared earth as a foundation.

small claims court   A special local court for settling disputes without the need for attorneys or expensive court costs.

Social Security tax   A tax of 15 percent required of every taxpayer; half of the tax is withheld from an employee's paycheck and half must be paid by the employer.

soffit   Horizontal finish for the underside of a roof overhang.

solar energy   Use of solar collectors to convert heat from the sun into usable heat and energy for a building.

sole proprietorship   A business owned by one individual.

Sonny Mae (SONYMA)   The State of New York Mortgage Agency.

special agent   One authorized by a principal to perform a single act or transaction.

special assessment   A tax or levy customarily imposed against only those specific parcels of real estate that will benefit from a proposed public improvement like a street or sewer.

special-purpose buildings   Real estate not residential, commercial, industrial, or agricultural. Includes schools, hospitals, churches, and government-held property.

special-purpose real estate   Religious institutions, schools, cemeteries, hospitals, and government-held land.

special-use permit   Permission granted by a local government to allow a use of property that, although in conflict with zoning regulations, is nonetheless in the public interest (a house of worship in a residential neighborhood, for instance, or a restaurant in an industrial zone).

special warranty deed   A deed in which the grantor warrants, or guarantees, the title only against defects arising during the period of his or her tenure and ownership of the property and not against defects existing before that time, generally using the language "by, through, or under the grantor but not otherwise."

specifications The architect's or engineer's detailed instructions for material used in construction.

specific lien A lien affecting or attaching only to a certain specific parcel of land or piece of property.

specific performance suit A legal action brought in a court of equity in special cases to compel a party to carry out the terms of a contract.

sponsor The developer or owner organizing and offering for sale a condominium or cooperative development.

sponsoring broker The principal broker in a real estate firm, who undertakes to train and supervise associated licensees.

spot zoning Special zoning actions that affect only a small area. Uses that are not in harmony with the surrounding uses are illegal in New York.

spread With an adjustable-rate mortgage, the percentage above an index at which the interest rate is set that represents the lender's profit when loaning to a borrower.

stabilized budget When the budgeted/allocated funds used to cover operating expenses remain constant for a period of time.

staff appraiser A professional appraiser employed in-house to perform appraisals solely for the employer.

State Environmental Quality Review Act (SEQRA) New York's State Environmental Quality Review Act, which requires environmental impact statements before certain development projects.

statute of frauds The part of state law requiring that certain instruments, such as deeds, real estate sales contracts, and certain leases, be in writing to be legally enforceable.

statute of limitations That law pertaining to the period of time within which certain actions must be brought to court; in New York, six years for contracts.

statutory law Law that is established by legislative bodies.

statutory lien A lien imposed on property by statute— a tax lien, for example—in contrast to a voluntary lien such as a mortgage lien that an owner places on his or her own real estate.

statutory redemption The right of a defaulted property owner to recover the property after its sale by paying the appropriate fees and charges.

statutory redemption period Period of time after a tax sale in which the delinquent taxpayer may regain the property by paying the back taxes, penalties, interest, and costs.

steering The illegal practice of channeling home seekers to particular areas for discriminatory ends.

straight-line depreciation An accounting "expense" against rental income, arrived at by dividing the cost of the building by the number of years allowed by the Internal Revenue Service.

straight-line method A method of calculating cost recovery for tax purposes, computed by dividing the adjusted basis of a property by the number of years chosen.

straight loan A loan in which only interest is paid during the term of the loan, with the entire principal amount due with the final interest payment.

studs Upright supports that form a part of the framing wall.

subagency An agency relationship in which the broker's sales associate, or a cooperating broker assumes a fiduciary duty to the principal who has designated the broker as an agent.

subagent A broker's sales associate in relation to the principal who has designated the broker as an agent.

subchapter S corporation *See* S corporation.

subcontractor *See* general contractor.

subdivide Partitioning a tract of land to sell it as individual lots.

subdivision A tract of land divided by the owner, known as the *subdivider*, into blocks, building lots, and streets according to a recorded subdivision plat.

subdivision regulations New York State requirements for subdivisions, which apply as soon as the fifth lot is sold off a larger parcel.

subject property The property being appraised.

subject to a mortgage When a property is taken "subject to" a mortgage, the purchaser is not personally liable to the mortgagee for satisfaction of the pre-existing debt (unless he or she agrees to be held liable).

sublease *See* subletting.

subletting The leasing of premises by a tenant to a third party for part of the tenant's remaining term. *See also* assignment.

subordination agreement These are voluntary written agreements between lienholders to change the priority of mortgage, judgment, and other liens under certain circumstances.

subrogation The substitution of one creditor for another with the substituted person succeeding to the legal rights and claims of the original claimant.

subscribing witness One who writes his or her name as witness to the execution of an instrument.

substitution An appraisal principle stating that the maximum value of a property tends to be set by the cost of purchasing an equally desirable and valuable substitute property.

subsurface rights   Ownership rights in a parcel of real estate of any water, minerals, gas, oil, and so forth that lie beneath the surface of the property.

suit for possession   A court suit initiated by a landlord to evict a tenant from leased premises after the tenant has breached one of the terms of the lease or has held possession of the property after the lease's expiration.

suit to quiet title   A court action intended to establish or settle the title to a particular property, especially when there is a cloud on the title.

Superfund Amendments and Reauthorization Act (SARA)   Federal law defining landowner responsibility for cleanup of environmental contamination resulting from past activities. Establishes innocent landowner defense against liability for contamination caused by prior owners.

supervising broker   The one broker registered with the Department of State as in charge of a real estate office, responsible for the actions of salespersons and associate brokers.

supply   The amount of goods available in the marketplace to be sold at a specific price.

surety bond   Bond covering an owner against financial losses resulting from the criminal acts or negligence of an employee in the course of performing his or her job.

surface rights   Ownership rights in a parcel of real estate that are limited to the surface of the property and do not include the air above it (air rights) or the minerals below the surface (subsurface rights).

surrender   The cancellation of a lease by mutual consent of the lessor and the lessee.

surrogate's court (probate court)   A court having jurisdiction over the proof of wills, the settling of estates, and adoptions.

survey   The process by which a parcel of land is measured and its area ascertained; also, the map showing the measurements, boundaries, and area.

suspension or revocation   The action of punishing violations of the license law by recalling a license temporarily (*suspension*) or permanently (*revocation*).

swing loan   A short-term loan similar to a bridge loan that uses the strength of the borrower's equity in the property he or she is selling to purchase a new property.

syndicate   A combination of people or firms formed to accomplish a joint venture of mutual interest.

tacking   Adding or combining successive periods of continuous occupation of real property by several different adverse possessors.

takeout loan   A loan commitment obtained prior to a lender extending a construction loan, under the terms of which the takeout lender will pay off the construction loan once the work is finished. Provides assurance for the construction lender that the initial short-term loan will be satisfied.

taking   Government restriction on use of property, to the extent that the owner must be compensated for loss of value.

taxable status date   The date, often in March, on which a community's tax assessment rolls are fixed for the coming year.

tax assessor   Municipal official who makes tax assessments for towns, villages, cities, and, in a few cases, counties.

taxation   The process by which a government or municipal quasi-public body raises monies to fund its operation.

tax basis   The original cost basis for property, reduced by depreciation and increased by the amount spent on capital improvements.

tax certiorari   Appeal in state court of a ruling by the local assessment board of review.

tax credit   A direct reduction in tax payable, as opposed to a deduciton from income.

tax deed   An instrument, similar to a certificate of sale, given to a purchaser at a tax sale.

tax-deferred exchange   A means by which one investment property can be exchanged for a similar one of equal value, with no immediate or capital gain tax consequences.

tax depreciation   *See* straight-line depreciation.

tax foreclosure   Legal proceeding (comparable to a private mortgage foreclosure) brought by a taxing body against the property itself (*in rem*); former owner loses all rights and claims.

tax lien   A charge against property created by operation of law. Tax liens and assessments take priority over all other liens.

tax rate   The rate at which real property is taxed in a tax district or county. For example, real property may be taxed at a rate of 0.056 cents per dollar of assessed valuation (56 mills).

tax sale   A court-ordered sale of real property to raise money to cover delinquent taxes.

tax shelter   Property throwing off an income-tax loss that can offset other income.

temporary certificate of occupancy (TCO)   Document issued by a municipal authority stating that a building complies with building, health, and safety codes and may be occupied; expires six months from the date of issue, or earlier if specified on the certificate itself.

tenancy at sufferance   One who comes into possession of land by lawful title and keeps it afterward without any title at all.

tenancy at will   An estate that gives the lessee the right to possession until the estate is terminated by either party; the term of this estate is indefinite.

tenancy by the entirety   The joint ownership acquired by husband and wife during marriage. On the death of one spouse, the survivor becomes the owner of the property.

tenancy for years   Refers to a less-than-freehold estate (or tenancy) in which the property is leased for a definite, fixed period of time, whether 60 days, any fraction of a year, a year, or ten years. In most states, such a tenancy can be created only by express agreement, which should be written if the tenancy is longer than one year. Most ground leases and commercial leases are tenancies for years.

tenancy in common   A form of co-ownership by which each owner holds an undivided interest in real property as if he or she were sole owner. Each individual owner has the right to partition. Tenants in common have no right of survivorship.

tenant   One who holds or possesses lands or tenements by any kind of right or title.

term   The originally scheduled period of time over which a loan is to be paid.

termination of association notice   Notice sent to the Department of State by a principal broker, stating that a particular licensee is no longer under the broker's supervision.

termites   Wood-boring insects whose presence causes structural damage.

term loan   *See* straight loan.

testate   Having made and left a valid will.

testator   The (male) maker of a valid will.

testatrix   The (female) maker of a valid will.

testers   Members of civil rights and neighborhood organizations, often volunteers, who observe real estate offices to assess compliance with fair housing laws.

tie-in arrangement   An arrangement by which provision of certain products or services is made contingent on the purchase of other, unrelated products or services.

time is of the essence   A phrase in a contract that requires the performance of a certain act within a stated period of time.

time-sharing   Undivided ownership of real estate for only a portion of the year.

time value of money   Deals with and is based on the purchasing power of the dollar when received.

title   Evidence that the owner of land is in lawful possession thereof; evidence of ownership.

title insurance policy   A policy insuring the owner or mortgagee against loss by reason of defects in the title to a parcel of real estate, other than the encumbrances, defects, and matters specifically excluded by the policy.

title search   An examination of the public records to determine the ownership and encumbrances affecting real property.

title theory   Some states interpret a mortgage to mean that the lender is the owner of mortgaged land. Upon full payment of the mortgage debt, the borrower becomes the landowner.

Torrens system   A method of evidencing title by registration with the proper public authority, generally called the *registrar*.

tort   A civil wrong done by one person against another.

town house   A hybrid form of real estate ownership in which the owner has fee simple title to the living unit and land below it, plus a fractional interest in common elements.

township   The principal unit of the rectangular survey (government survey) system, a square with six-mile sides and an area of 36 square miles.

trade fixtures   Articles installed by a tenant under the terms of a lease and removable by the tenant before the lease expires.

transfer of development rights   Method by which one developer can buy unused rights belonging to a landowner.

transfer tax   Tax stamps required to be affixed to a deed by state and/or local law.

trespass   An unlawful intrusion on another's property.

triple-net lease   A lease under which the tenant pays everything (taxes, repairs, insurance, and everything except any mortgage charges).

true tax   Actual taxes payable for a property after all exemptions and reductions for which the property or its owner is qualified.

truss roof   Particularly strong roofing system composed of chords, diagonals, and gusset plates; preassembled at a mill.

trust   A fiduciary arrangement whereby property is conveyed to a person or an institution, called a *trustee*, to be held and administered on behalf of another person, called a *beneficiary*.

trust account   Escrow account for money belonging to another.

trust deed An instrument used to create a mortgage lien by which the mortgagor conveys his or her title to a trustee, who holds it as security for the benefit of the note holder (the lender); also called a *deed of trust.*

trustee *See* trust.

trustor The individual who establishes a trust.

220-volt circuit 220-volt circuits have two hot wires and one neutral wire and may have a separate ground wire as well.

UFFI Urea-formaldehyde foam insulation, considered carcinogenic, no longer used.

umbrella policy An insurance policy that covers additional risk beyond several underlying policies.

underground storage tanks Buried containers used for storage or disposal of chemicals, fuel, and gas that pose an actual or potential environmental hazard in the event of a leak.

underlying mortgage A single mortgage, known as the underlying mortgage, covers the entire building.

underwriting The process by which a lender evaluates a prospective borrower's application through verification of employment and financial information and analysis of credit and appraisal reports.

undisclosed dual agency Representation of both principal parties in the same transaction without full written disclosure to and approval of all parties.

undivided interest *See* tenancy in common.

undivided loyalty Fiduciary duty owed by the agent to the principal or client.

unenforceable contract A contract that seems on the surface to be valid, yet neither party can sue the other to force performance of it.

Uniform Commercial Code A codification of commercial law, adopted in most states, that attempts to make uniform all laws relating to commercial transactions, including chattel mortgages and bulk transfers.

Uniform Settlement Statement (HUD Form 1) A special form designed to detail all financial particulars of a transaction.

unilateral contract A one-sided contract wherein one party makes a promise so as to induce a second party to do something. The second party is not legally bound to perform; however, if the second party does comply, the first party is obligated to keep the promise.

unities The four unities traditionally needed to create a joint tenancy: unity of title, time, interest, and possession.

universal agent One empowered by a principal to represent him or her in all matters that can be delegated.

usable area Usable area is the area obtained by subtracting the loss factor from the rentable area.

usury Charging interest at a rate higher than the maximum established by law.

valid contract A contract that complies with all the essentials of a contract and is binding and enforceable on all parties to it.

VA loan A mortgage loan on approved property made to a qualified veteran by an authorized lender and guaranteed by the Department of Veterans Affairs to limit the lender's possible loss.

valuation Estimated worth or price. The act of valuing by appraisal.

value The power of a good or service to command other goods in exchange for the present worth of future rights to its income or amenities.

value-in-use Present worth of future benefits of ownership of a parcel of real estate.

variable expense The property expenses that vary according to the occupancy level, such as supplies, water, and any management fees that are tied to the amount of rent collected.

variance Permission obtained from zoning authorities to build a structure or conduct a use that is expressly prohibited by the current zoning laws; an exception from the zoning ordinances.

vendee A buyer under a land contract or contract of sale.

vendor A seller under a land contract or contract of sale.

vicarious liability Liability that is created not because of a person's actions but because of the relationship between the liable person and other parties.

violation An infraction of the law less serious than a misdemeanor.

voidable contract A contract that seems to be valid on the surface but that may be rejected or disaffirmed by one of the parties.

void contract A contract that has no legal force or effect because it does not meet the essential elements of a contract.

voltage Force of an electric current, measured in volts.

voluntary alienation Transfer of title by gift or sale according to the owner's wishes.

voluntary lien A lien created by the owner's voluntary action, such as a mortgage.

waiver The renunciation, abandonment, or surrender of some claim, right, or privilege.

warranty deed A deed in which the grantor fully warrants good clear title to the premises.

waste An improper use or an abuse of a property by a possessor who holds less than fee ownership, such as a tenant, life tenant, mortgagor, or vendee.

wetland survey An intensive examination of property, coordinated by the U.S. Army Corps of Engineers, to determine whether it should be classified and protected as a wetland.

will A written document, properly witnessed, providing for the transfer of title to property owned by the deceased, called the *testator*.

without recourse Words used in endorsing a note or bill to denote that the future holder is not to look to the endorser in case of nonpayment.

workers' compensation acts State insurance program, paid for by employers, to compensate those hurt on the job.

wraparound loan A method of refinancing in which the lender refinances a borrower by lending an amount over the existing first mortgage amount without disturbing the priority of the first mortgage.

wraparound mortgage An additional mortgage in which another lender refinances a borrower by lending an amount including the existing first mortgage amount without disturbing the existence of the first mortgage.

year-to-year tenancy A periodic tenancy in which rent is collected from year to year.

zone An area set off by the proper authorities for specific use subject to certain restrictions or restraints.

zoning boards of appeal Official local government bodies established to hear complaints about the impact of zoning ordinances on individual properties, and to consider variances and special-use permits.

zoning ordinances An exercise of police power by a municipality to regulate and control the character and use of property.

Answer Key

CHAPTER 1
License Law

1. c.
2. d.
3. c.
4. c.
5. c.
6. d.
7. c.
8. c.
9. d.
10. c.
11. b.
12. d.
13. a.
14. b.
15. a.
16. a.
17. b.
18. c.
19. b.
20. d.
21. b.
22. a.
23. b.
24. d.
25. c.

CHAPTER 2
The Law of Agency

1. a.
2. b.
3. b.
4. b.
5. c.
6. c.
7. c.
8. c.
9. d.
10. d.
11. b.
12. c.

13. c.
14. c.
15. a.
16. d.
17. c.
18. a.
19. d.
20. b.

CHAPTER 3
Agency and Real Estate Brokerage

1. b.
2. d.
3. c.
4. d.
5. b.
6. d.
7. d.
8. a.
9. b.
10. b.
11. d.
12. c.
13. a.
14. c.

CHAPTER 4
The Broker's Office

1. d
2. b
3. a
4. c
5. d
6. a
7. d
8. a
9. b
10. c
11. b
12. d
13. c

14. b
15. c
16. a
17. a
18. b
19. c
20. a

CHAPTER 5
Real Estate Finance

1. c
2. a
3. b
4. d
5. a
6. b
7. a
8. d
9. b
10. d

CHAPTER 6
Real Estate Investment

1. a
2. c
3. b
4. b
5. a
6. c
7. b
8. d
9. c
10. a
11. c
12. a
13. d
14. c
15. d
16. c
17. c
18. a
19. b

20. a
21. c
22. b
23. d
24. b
25. a

CHAPTER 7
General Business Law

1. d
2. b
3. c
4. b
5. c
6. d
7. a
8. c
9. c
10. d
11. a
12. a
13. c
14. b
15. b
16. a
17. a
18. b
19. a
20. a

CHAPTER 8
Construction and Development

1. b
2. b
3. d
4. a
5. b
6. a
7. c
8. c
9. d
10. a
11. b
12. d
13. d
14. c
15. a

CHAPTER 9
Conveyance of Real Property

1. c
2. d
3. b
4. d
5. b
6. a
7. c
8. c
9. a
10. d

CHAPTER 10
Property Management

1. d
2. d
3. b
4. d
5. d
6. c
7. a
8. d
9. c
10. b
11. c
12. c
13. c
14. d
15. d
16. b
17. a
18. c

CHAPTER 11
Taxes and Assessment

1. d
2. c
3. b
4. b
5. c
6. a
7. c
8. b
9. a
10. a
11. b

Broker's Exam Answer Key

1. c
2. c
3. d
4. a
5. d
6. c
7. a
8. d
9. c
10. d
11. c
12. a
13. b
14. d
15. a
16. b
17. c
18. b
19. d
20. b
21. c
22. c
23. c
24. d
25. a
26. b
27. c
28. d
29. c
30. b
31. b
32. c
33. d
34. a
35. b
36. b
37. a
38. d
39. b
40. a
41. d
42. a
43. c
44. b
45. d
46. b
47. b
48. c
49. b

50.	c	68.	b	86.	b
51.	a	69.	a	87.	b
52.	d	70.	b	88.	d
53.	b	71.	b	89.	c
54.	a	72.	c	90.	a
55.	d	73.	d	91.	b
56.	c	74.	d	92.	d
57.	b	75.	a	93.	c
58.	c	76.	b	94.	a
59.	a	77.	c	95.	b
60.	c	78.	c	96.	b
61.	c	79.	c	97.	a
62.	d	80.	b	98.	c
63.	a	81.	b	99.	b
64.	b	82.	c	100.	c
65.	b	83.	b		
66.	a	84.	c		
67.	c	85.	a		

Index

A

Accountability, 42
Accretion, 200
Action to quiet title, 200
Actual cash value, 219
Address change, 13
Adjusted basis, 152
Administrative discipline, 21
Administrative law, 167
Administrator, 171
Ad valorem tax, 226
Adverse possession, 200
Advertisements
    guidelines, 107
    license law provisions, 20–21
    property management, 212
    regulations, 107
Affirmative statement, 46
Aged exemption, 228–29, 231
Agency
    alternatives, 63
    creation of, 33–35
    definition, 31
    disclosure form, 17, 58–62
    disclosure requirements, 33–34, 56–62
    forms, 70–87
    law, 35, 38–47, 126
    relationships, 36–38, 52, 63
    termination of, 49, 53
Agency coupled with an interest, 32
Agent
    authority of, 43–44
    definition, 31
    fiduciary duties, 39–44
    representation, 35
    responsibilities to others, 44–47
    role of, 181
    types of, 31–32
Agreement to procure, 33
American Society of Home Inspectors, 183
Anchor stores, 220
Antitrust
    definition, 50
    laws, 50–52, 53, 107–10
    violations, 49, 51–52
Apartment, 150
Apartment information vendor, 18, 98
Apartment-sharing agent, 18, 98
Appeal, 23
Appellate court, 167
Appraisal process, 231
Appraiser, 18, 98
Appreciation, 144
Apprenticeship, 99
Appropriation, 227–28
Arbitration, 169
Army Corps of Engineers, 179
Article 12-A, 3, 126
Article 78 procedure, 23

ASHI. *See* American Society of Home
    Inspectors
Assessment, 226, 229
Assessment roll, 226
Associate broker
    application, 9
    definition, 4
    license class, 6, 100
    qualifications, 6
Attorney, 99
Attorney-in-fact, 44
Automatic extensions, 73
Avulsion, 200

B

Bankruptcy, 169–70, 174
Basis, 152–53
Bequest, 201
Bill of exchange, 161
Blank endorsement, 162
Blanket loan, 133, 136
Blind ad, 20, 107
Blue-sky laws, 148
Board of directors, 192
Board of managers, 191
Boiler and machinery insurance, 219
Boot, 155
Boycotting, 49
Branch office, 17
Bridge loan, 133
Broker
    application, 9, 100, 101–2, 104–6
    compensation, 47–48, 52
    definition, 3
    examination, 103
    license class, 6
    license revocation, 23
    obligations of, 18
    as principal, 36–37
    qualifications, 5
    responsibilities, 117–23
    scope of authority, 43–44
    services, 3
Brokerage
    agency and, 35–38
    definition, 35
    licensed corporation, 6
    organization of, 117–18
    recruitment, 119–20, 129
    regulations, 17–18
    supervision requirements, 121, 123
    without subagency, 64
Broker's agent, 62
Building code, 188
Building inspections, 181–82
Building Owners and Managers Association
    International, 220
Bullet loan, 134

Business broker, 99
Business cards, 107
Business interruption insurance, 218
Business name, 16–17
Business organizations, 163–65
Business taxation, 116–17
Business torts, 168
Buyer
    as client, 87
    as customer, 87
    as principal, 36
    financial condition, 43
    ready, willing, and able, 47
Buyer agency
    agreement, 33, 89–92
    compensation, 88
    disclosure form, 58–59
    working relationships, 87
Buyer broker agency agreement, 33, 70
Buyer's agent, 56
Buyer's broker, 36
Bylaws, 190–92, 195

C

CAI. *See* Community Associations Institute
Capital expenses, 211
Capital gains, 152–53, 155
Capital reserve budget, 211
Care, 39–40
Case law, 160
Cash flow, 147
Cashier's check, 161
Casualty insurance, 219
CC&R. *See* Covenants, conditions, and
    restrictions
Certificate of compliance, 180
Certificate of deposit, 161
Certificate of dissolution, 165
Certificate of incorporation, 164
Certificate of occupancy, 180
Certified Property Manager, 220, 222
Change of association, 14
Change of broker, 15
Chapter 7, 169–71, 174
Chapter 11, 169–71, 174
Chapter 13, 169–71, 174
Check, 161
Civil law, 167–73, 174
Civil litigation, 174
Civil procedure, 168–69
Clayton Antitrust Act, 50–52, 108
Client, 31, 87
Closely-held corporation, 164
Clustered plan, 187, 188
Coastal Zone Management Program, 179
Codicil, 202
Combination trust, 149
Commercial financing, 134–35

Commercial law, 160, 167
Commercial loan, 141
Commercial paper, 161, 173
Commercial transaction, 34, 57
Commingle, 17
Commission
    definition, 35
    disclosures, 43
    license law and, 13–14
    sharing of, 26, 48
    split, 43, 48, 88
Common elements, 190
Common law, 160, 173
Community Associations Institute, 220–21
Company policy, 66, 69, 120–21
Compensation
    broker, 47–48, 52
    buyer agents, 87–88
    multiple parties, 37, 62
    salesperson, 48
    source of, 34–35
Complaint investigation, 22
Completion bond, 186
Compliance audit, 123–24
Condemnation, 199
Condominium
    common elements, 189
    construction, 192–93
    conversion, 193, 195
    Manhattan market, 140
    ownership, 190–91
    sales, 191
Conduit financing, 134
Confidentiality, 41
Consideration, 199
Conspiracy, 50, 108
Constitutional law, 159–60, 167
Construction loan, 135–36, 141
Construction standards, 178–81
Content and personal property insurance, 218
Continuing education, 15–16
Contract law, 167
Contract provisions, 43
Conversion, 195
Conversion restrictions, 193
Cooperating agent, 36, 37
Cooperating broker, 92
Cooperative
    construction, 192–93
    conversion, 192, 193, 195
    Manhattan market, 140
    ownership, 191–92
    sales, 70
Corporate income tax, 164
Corporation
    brokerage organization, 117–18
    creation, 164
    definition, 174
    dissolution, 165
    law, 164–65, 167
    license class, 6, 100
    license procedures, 13
    management, 164
Corrective maintenance, 217
Cost allocation, 208
Cost recovery, 151
County board of health, 180
County courts, 166

County planning boards, 180
County tax sale, 230
Court of appeals, 167
Court of claims, 166
Court decisions, 160
Court order, 99
Court system, 174
Covenants, conditions, and restrictions, 191
CPM. *See* Certified Property Manager
Criminal law, 167, 174
Curb appeal, 210
Current rent roll, 145
Curvilinear system, 187
Customer, 31, 87

D

Debt service, 147
DEC. *See* New York Department of
    Environmental Conservation
Deceased person, property transfer, 200–202
Declaration, 192
Dedication, 199
Deed of reconveyance, 133
Deed restrictions, 186
Defamation, 168
Demand note, 161
Denial/suspension/revocation of license, 2
Density zoning, 187
DEP. *See* New York City Department of
    Environmental Protection
Department of Housing and Urban
    Development, 179
Department of State, 2
    application fees, 9
    business name, 16–17
    complaint investigations, 22
    compliance audit, 123–24
    designated agency, 69–70, 126
    determinations, 25
    development under, 179
    dual agency legal memo, 128
    educational requirements, 6–7
    home inspector license, 19
    license classes, 6, 99–100
    license renewal, 103
    license status change, 13
    name/address change, 13
    penalties, 22–23
    pocket card requirements, 9, 13
    termination of association notice, 14–15
    test centers, 8
    unlicensed assistants, 23–24
Depreciation, 147, 151–52, 155
Depression, 139
Descent, 201, 202
Descent and distribution, statute of, 200
Designated agency, 69–70, 126
Designated agent agreement, 127
Designations, 125–26, 129
Developer, 183
Devise, 201
DHCR. *See* Division of Housing and
    Community Renewal
Direct mail, 212
Disclosure
    affirmation, 62
    agency, 17, 24, 34, 56–63
    agency form, 58–62

buyer's financial condition, 43
commission split, 43
contract provisions, 43
earnest money deposit, 43
environmental concerns, 44
fiduciary duty of, 42–43
of interest, 15
lead-based paint, 81
other offers, 42
property condition, 75–80, 95
property deficiencies, 43
property value, 43
relationships, 42
self-dealing, 42
seller, 73–74
statement, 192–93
of subagency, 64–65
uncapped wells, 19
Discount brokerage, 49
Discounted cash-flow analysis, 151
Discounting, 151
Discount rate, 140, 151
Disintermediation, 139
Disposition, 149–50
Dispute resolution, 169
Distance learning, 7
Division of Housing and Community Renewal,
    216
Divorce, 172–73, 175
Documentation, 17
DOS. *See* Department of State
Draft, 161
Dual agency
    consent, 52
    consent form, 67–68
    definition, 37–38
    informed consent, 65–66
    legal memo, 128
    undisclosed, 66, 69
Due diligence, 181
Due process, 159–60

E

Earnest money deposit, 43
Economy, 138–41
EIS. *See* Environmental impact statement
Emergency Tenant Protection Act, 221
Eminent domain, 199
Employee, 111, 119
Endorsement, 162
Environmental concerns, 44–45
Environmental hazards, 74
Environmental impact statement, 184
Environmental impact studies, 184, 194
Environmental Protection Agency, 123–24,
    179, 183–84
Environmental regulations, 183–85
Equal opportunity employer, 119
Equalization factor, 226
Equitable distribution, 172–73
Equitable right of redemption, 230
Equity trust, 149
Erosion, 200
Errors and omissions insurance, 112
Escheat, 200
Escrow, 17
Estate, 171–72
Estate tax, 172

Estoppel, 34
ETPA. *See* Emergency Tenant Protection Act
Eviction plan, 193
Exchanges, 153, 155
Exclusive-agency buyer-agency agreement, 89
Exclusive-agency listing, 70, 82, 92
Exclusive buyer-agency agreement, 89, 93–94
Exclusive-right-to-lease, 71
Exclusive right-to-represent agreement, 89, 90–91
Exclusive-right-to-sell listing, 70, 82, 92
Executor, 175, 201
Exempt action, 184
Exemption status, 16
Express agency, 33
Express agreement, 52

F

Fair employment laws, 119
Fair Housing Education, 24
Family court, 166
Fannie Mae, 138
Federal agencies, 179
Federal court system, 166, 174
Federal Reserve System, 140
Federal Trade Commission, 50, 108
Fee
    buyer-paid, 88
    license, 25
    management, 208
    record of association, 15
    referral, 14
    seller-paid, 88
FHA loan, 138
Fiduciary
    definition, 31
    duties, 39, 43, 52, 63
    relationship, 39
Financial planners, 74
Financing statement, 160–61
Fire and hazard insurance, 218
First substantive contact, 34, 57, 63
Flat fee arrangement, 88
Floating rate loan, 135
Flood insurance, 82
Foley, United States v., 109
Foreclosure, 199
For-sale-by-owner, 72
For Sale sign, 21
421-a Extension, 24
Franchise tax, 164
Fraud, 44
Freddie Mac, 138
FSBO. *See* For-sale-by-owner
FTC. *See* Federal Trade Commission
Full-value assessment, 226
Future earnings, 145

G

Gap loan, 133
General agent, 32, 207
General partner, 148, 149
General partnership, 118, 145
General tax, 226
Gift tax, 172
Ginnie Mae, 138

Government agencies, 160
Graduate, Realtors® Institute, 125
Grant, 199
Gratuitous agency, 35
GRI. *See* Graduate, Realtors® Institute
Gridiron pattern, 187
Grievance day, 229
Gross lease, 214
Ground lease, 137
Group boycott, 51, 108, 109, 115

H

Heirs, 200
Historic district, 154
Holding period, 149–50, 155
Home equity loan, 134
Home inspection, 181–82
Home inspector, 19, 99
Homestead, 227
Hotel/motel, 150
Hourly-rate compensation, 88
HUD. *See* Department of Housing and Urban Development
HVAC, 181

I

Impact fees, 185
Implied agency, 33–35
Improvement tax, 226
Income-producing property, 82
Incompetence, 21–22
Independent contractor, 111–14, 119
Industrial property, 206
Inflation, 139
Informed consent, 38, 65–66, 67–68
In-house sales, 66, 69
Injunction, 167
in rem, 230
Installment sales, 154
Institute of Real Estate Management, 220, 222
Interim loan, 135
Intermediate financing, 134
Internet, 72
Interstate Land Sales Full Disclosure Act, 189, 194–95
Intestate, 200, 203
Investment advisors, 74
Investment security, 149
Investor, 144–45
Involuntary alienation, 199–200
Irrevocable consent, 20

J–K

Joint venture, 135
Kickback, 14

L

Land-leaseback, 135
Landlord
    agency disclosure form, 60–61
    obligations, 216
Land use
    regulations, 187–89
    restriction, 183

Last will and testament, 201
Latent defects, 45–46
Law of agency, 126, 167
Lead-based paint disclosure, 81
Lease negotiations, 214–15
Legal defense, 163
Leverage, 144, 155
Liability insurance, 218–19
License
    apartment information vendor, 18
    apartment-sharing agent, 18
    application, 9, 10–12
    classes of, 6, 100
    educational requirements, 6–7
    examinations, 7–9
    exceptions, 4
    experience requirements, 100, 104–6
    fees, 9, 25
    home inspector, 19
    issuance of, 9, 13, 99–100
    laws, 1
    maintenance of, 13–14
    mortgage broker, 19
    nonresident, 20
    procedures, 9–13
    qualifications for, 5–7
    reciprocity, 19–20
    renewal, 15, 16, 103
    requirements, 3–6, 25, 98–99
    status change, 14, 15
    suspension/revocation of, 21–23
    violations, 123
Lien theory state, 133
Limited liability company
    benefits, 148, 164
    broker license, 6
    license class, 6, 100
    ownership, 118
Limited liability partnership
    benefits, 148, 164
    license class, 6, 100
Limited partner, 149
Limited partnership, 118, 148
Liquidation, 165
Listing agent, 57
Listing agreement
    explanation, 86–87
    information needed, 73
    listing types, 70–72
    purpose, 33
    sample, 83–85
    seller disclosures, 74
    types, 92
Listing broker, 63
Listing termination, 72–73
Litigation, 168–69
LLC. *See* Limited liability company
LLP. *See* Limited liability partnership
Loan
    application, 135–36
    processing, 141
Loan-to-value ratio, 134, 136
Local municipalities, 180–81
Lower Manhattan Tax Abatement, 24
Loyalty, 41
LTV. *See* Loan-to-value ratio

M

Management agreement, 207–8, 222
Management fee, 208
Marginal tax rate, 152
Marital deduction, 172
Market allocation, 51, 108, 109, 116
Market analysis, 209–11
Marketing, 211–13
Material facts, 42
Maximum base rent, 221
MBR. *See* Maximum base rent
Mediation, 169
Meeting of the minds, 48
Megan's Law, 46
Metropolitan Transportation Authority, 179–80
Mill, 227
Minimum construction standards, 180
Miniperm loan, 134
Misdemeanor, 3, 23
Misrepresentations, 46–47
Mixed developments, 150
MLS. *See* Multiple listing service
Mobile home park, 216
Monthly earnings report, 218
Mortgage
    banker, 18–19, 99
    broker, 19
    debt service, 147
    sources, 133
    trust, 149
    types of, 133–34
    use of, 132–33
MTA. *See* Metropolitan Transportation Authority
Multiperil policies, 219
Multiple listing service
    access to, 110–11
    commission disclosures, 109
    discount brokerage firms and, 49
    and Internet, 72
    membership requirements, 129
    subagency relationship and, 63
Mutual recognition, 20

N

Name change, 13
NAR. *See* National Association of REALTORS®
National Association of Real Estate Boards, United States v., 108
National Association of Real Estate Brokers, 124, 125
National Association of REALTORS®, 4, 121
National Housing Act, 138
National Organization of Hispanic Real Estate Professionals, 124
Negative amortization, 135
Negative cash flow, 147
Negligence, 168
Negotiable instruments, 161–63
Neighborhood analysis, 209–11
Net lease, 214
Net listing, 22, 71, 92
Net operating income, 145, 147, 154
New home construction schedule, 182
New York City business taxation, 116–17

New York City Department of Environmental Protection, 180
New York City Property Tax Rebate, 24
New York court system, 166–67, 174
New York Department of Environmental Conservation, 184
New York Limited Liability Company Law, 148
New York Multiple Dwelling Law, 215–16
New York REALTORS® Institute, 125
New York State Association of REALTORS® 125
New York State Board of Fire Underwriters, 179
New York State Department of State. *See* Department of State
New York State Department of Transportation, 179
New York State Environmental Quality Act, 184
New York State Society of Real Estate Appraisers, 125
New York State Subdivided Land Sales Law, 189
Newspaper advertising, 212
No-fault divorce, 175
NOI. *See* Net operating income
Nonconforming use, 188
Noneviction plan, 193
Nonhomestead, 227
Nonresident license, 20
Note, 161, 162
Notice, 42

O

Obedience, 41
Offer, 42
Offer to purchase, 14
Office property, 150, 206
Open buyer-agency agreement, 89
Open-end mortgage, 133
Open listing, 71, 92
Operating budget, 211
Operating statement, 145, 146
Opinion, 44
Ordinance, 226

P

Package loan, 133
Participation loan, 135, 141
Partition, 200
Partition proceeding, 200
Partnership
    agreement, 163
    definition, 174
    dissolution, 163
    law, 163, 167
    license class, 6, 100
    license procedures, 13
    property, 163
Passive income, 152
Passive partner, 149
Penalty date, 228
Percentage fee arrangement, 88
Percentage lease, 214
Percolation test, 183
PERF. *See* Preliminary Environmental Review Form
Personal property law, 167

Planned unit development, 187, 193
Planning board, 183
Plat of subdivision, 185
PMI. *See* Private mortgage insurance
Pocket card, 9, 13
Policy and procedure guide, 120–21
Power of attorney, 32
Preclusive agreement, 47
Preliminary Environmental Review Form, 184
Preliminary prospectus, 193
Pretax cash flow, 147
Preventive maintenance, 217
Price-fixing, 50–51, 108, 115
Prince Georges County Board of REALTORS®, U.S. v., 108
Principal
    broker as, 36
    buyer as, 36
    definition, 31
    seller as, 36
Private Activity Bond Allocation Act, 24
Private adjusters, 219
Private mortgage insurance, 133
Private offerings, 165
Private syndication, 148
Probate, 201
Procedural law, 167
Procuring cause of sale, 48
Professional organizations, 124–25
Pro forma statements, 145, 147
Promissory note, 161
Promotional activities, 212–13
Property
    analysis, 210–11
    condition disclosure, 95
    condition disclosure statement, 75–80
    deficiencies, 43
    income analysis, 145–47
    maintenance, 217
    rental, 213–14
Property management
    agreement, 207–8
    budget, 211, 222
    field, 220–21
    importance of, 204
    insurance coverage, 218–19
    leases, 213–15
    maintenance, 217
    owner relations, 217–18
    planning, 205–11
    property types, 206–7
    reports, 217–18
    tenant relations, 215–16
Property manager
    functions of, 208
    responsibilities, 208, 222
    role of, 204
    skills, 219–20
Proprietary lease, 191
Public liability insurance, 218–19
Public offering, 165, 192
Public officers, 99
Public syndication, 148
Public use, 199
PUD. *See* Planned unit development
Puffing, 44
Purchase-money mortgage, 133
Pyramiding, 144, 155

Q

Qualified endorsement, 162

R

Radio advertising, 212
Rate of return, 144–45
Ratification, 34
Ready, willing, and able buyer, 47
Real Estate Agency Disclosure Form
    Attachments, 24
Real estate broker. *See* Broker
Real estate cycles, 138–41
Real estate investment
    analysis techniques, 151
    disposition, 149–50
    holding period, 149–50
    income tax considerations, 151–54
    investors, 144–45
    nature of, 143–44
    ownership structure, 148–49
    property income analysis, 145–47
    property type, 150
Real estate investment syndicate, 148
Real estate investment trust, 24, 149
Real estate mortgage investment conduit, 149
Real estate salesperson. *See* Salesperson
Real Property Law, 2, 3, 167
Realtists. *See* National Association of Real
    Estate Brokers
Reasonable care, 39
Recession, 139
Reciprocity, 19, 21
Record of association, 15
Recruitment, 119–20, 129
Red herring, 193
Referral fee, 14
Refinance loan, 133
Regional agencies, 179–81
Regional analysis, 209–11
Regulation A, 165
Regulation Z, 107
Regulatory taking, 184
REIT. *See* Real estate investment trust
Release deed, 133
REMIC. *See* Real estate mortgage investment
    conduit
Rent
    collection plan, 215
    control, 221
    rate-setting, 214
    stabilization, 221–22
Replacement cost, 219
Replacement reserves, 147
Residential property, 206
Residential transaction, 34, 57
Restraint of trade, 50, 108, 116
Restrictive endorsement, 162
Retail property, 150, 206
Return, 144
Revocation, 21, 23
Right of election, 201

S

Safety-first position, 135
Sale-leaseback, 137
Sale-leaseback-buyback, 137

Salesperson
    application, 9, 10–12
    compensation, 48
    definition, 3–4
    educational requirements, 7
    employment status, 111–14
    qualifications, 5
    unemployment insurance notice, 115
S corporation, 118, 164
SEC. *See* Securities and Exchange Commission
Secondary mortgage market, 138, 141
Section 1031 property exchange, 153
Securities and Exchange Commission, 148, 165
Security agreement, 160
Security deposit, 215
Security offerings, 165
Self-dealing, 14, 38, 42, 218
Seller
    agency disclosure form, 58–59
    default, 48
    disclosures, 74
    as principal, 36
Seller's agent, 33, 57
Selling broker, 63
Shared-equity mortgage, 133
Sherman Antitrust Act
    enforcement, 110, 115
    penalties, 51–52
    price-fixing under, 50
    prohibitions, 107
    violations, 108
Signage, 16, 17, 21, 212
Signed acknowledgment, 57, 62–63
Silent partner, 149
Single agency, 69–70
Small claims courts, 166–67
Sole proprietorship, 117
Special agent, 32, 207
Special assessment, 226, 231
Special endorsement, 162
Sponsor, 193
Sponsoring broker, 4
Stagflation, 139
Stambovsky v. Ackley, 46
Standby loan commitment, 136
StaR program, 229
State agencies, 179
State Board of Real Estate, 2–3
Statement of Audit Procedures, 116
Statute of limitations, 173, 175
Statutory law, 160
Statutory redemption period, 230
Stigmatized properties, 46
Straight-line depreciation, 151–52
Street patterns, 187
Strict liability, 168
Subagency, 63, 64–65
Subagent, 36
Subdivided Lands Property Law, 190
Subdivider, 183
Subdivision
    costs/financing, 186
    environmental regulations, 183–84
    land value, 184–85
    plat of, 185
    process, 185, 194
    regulations, 195
    restrictions, 183–84

    restrictive covenants, 186–88
    types, 186–87
Subordinate mortgage, 134
Substantive law, 167
Supply and demand, 138–39
Surety bonds, 219
Surrogate court, 166
Suspension, 21
Swing loan, 133
Syndicate, 148–49

T

Tacking, 200
Takeout loan, 136
Tax
    basis, 147
    bill, 227–28, 231
    certiorari proceeding, 229
    credit, 153–54
    foreclosure, 229
    lien, 225–26, 229–30, 231
    rates, 227
    sale, 229–30, 231
    shares, 227
Taxable status date, 228
Tax-deferred exchange, 153
Taxpayer Relief Act, 139
Tax Reform Act of 1986, 139, 151
Tenant
    agency disclosure form, 60–61
    relations, 215–16
    rights, 215–16
    selection, 213
Termination agreement, 122–23
Termination of association notice, 15
Test centers, 8
Testate, 200, 203
Testator/testatrix, 201
Tie-in arrangement, 51–52, 108, 110
Time-sharing, 194
Title
    function, 198
    transfer, 198, 199–201
Title theory states, 133
Torts, 167, 168, 174
Town house, 193–94, 195
Trade acceptance, 161
Trade, restraint of, 50
Trade-name broker, 6, 100
Training, 120
Transaction records, 57, 62
Triple-net lease, 214
True tax, 229
Trust deed, 133
Trustee, 170
Trusts and wills, 167
Truth-in-Advertising Act, 107
Truth-in-Heating Law, 82

U

UCC. *See* Uniform Commercial Code
Uncapped wells, 19
Underwriting, 134
Undisclosed dual agency, 33, 38, 66
Undivided loyalty, 37
Unifed credits, 172
Uniform Commercial Code, 160–61, 173

United States v. Foley, 109
United States v. National Association of Real Estate Boards, 108
Universal agent, 32, 52
Unlicensed real estate assistants, 23–24
Unlisted action, 184
Untrusworthiness, 21–22

V

Vacation ownership, 194
Value, disclosure of, 43
Veterans exemption, 229
Vicarious liability, 103, 129
Vicarious liability, 62
Village tax sale, 230
Voluntary alienation, 199

W

Web sites, 107
Wetland survey, 185
Will, 201
Wraparound mortgage, 133

Z

Zoning ordinances, 183, 186